Praise for *The Lesbian and Gay*

"This is an extraordinary book filled ~~~~~~~~~~~~~~~~~~~~~~~~ith the experiences of gay and lesbian coup~~~~~~~~~~~~~~~~~~~~~~ted or birthed a child. Read this book if yo~~~~~~~~~~~~~~~~~~~~~~~nging a child into your home."

—Charles Silverstein, Ph.D., coauthor of *The New Joy of Gay Sex*

"*The Lesbian and Gay Parenting Handbook* will be an indispensable resource for lesbians and gay men who are either planning to have children or who are already parents. It will also provide much-needed assistance to both mental health and education professionals, helping sensitize them to the issues of lesbian and gay families."

—Ronnie C. Lesser, Ph.D., Adjunct Assistant Professor,
City College of New York

"If you are a gay or lesbian person or couple considering parenthood, you and your family will find a wealth of practical information in this clearly written, comprehensive book. In this age of redefining 'traditional family values,' Dr. Martin shows you that children who are wanted and loved by their parents have the best chance to grow up as productive members of our society."

—Paulette Goodman, former President of the Federation of
Parents and Friends of Lesbians and Gays

"This book is all about family values. It shows us that people who live together and love each other really define the word 'family.'"

—Cindy Crawford, model and MTV host

"This is a truly wonderful and remarkable book! It is an invaluable resource with all the latest, most up-to-date information on every issue imaginable. *The Lesbian and Gay Parenting Handbook* is a celebration of the love that lesbian moms and gay dads are giving to their children and society."

—Emily B. McNally, founder of the National Association of
Lesbian and Gay Alcoholism Professionals

The LESBIAN and GAY
PARENTING HANDBOOK

The LESBIAN and GAY PARENTING HANDBOOK

CREATING AND RAISING OUR FAMILIES

APRIL MARTIN, Ph.D.

HarperPerennial
A Division of HarperCollins*Publishers*

HarperCollins books may be purchased for educational, business, or sales promotional use. For information please write: Special Markets Department, HarperCollins Publishers, Inc., 10 East 53rd Street, New York, NY 10022.

Designed by Laura Hough Design

Library of Congress Cataloging-in-Publication Data

Martin, April, 1948–
    The lesbian and gay parenting handbook : creating and raising our families / April Martin.
        p.   cm.
    Includes bibliographical references and index.
    ISBN 0-06-096929-6
    1. Gay parents—United States.   2. Children of gay parents—United States.   3. Parenting—United States.   I. Title.
    HQ76.3.U5M36   1993   92-54782
    306.874—dc20

    00 01 02 HC 13 12 11

For Susan, Emily, and Jesse

CONTENTS

Part II: **Making It Work**

ACKNOWLEDGMENTS

I was truly moved by the generosity and responsiveness of an enormous number of people who contributed time and energy to this book. Their assistance not only made this book possible, it also reminded me of how wonderful people can be. I am deeply grateful to all.

Many families allowed me into their homes and lives as they contributed their stories. They shared their experiences candidly, the pain as well as the joy, in the hopes that other families would benefit from them.

I am similarly grateful to the lesbian and gay families who have consulted me over the years in my psychotherapy practice, and to those who have shared their stories with me in workshops and at conferences. I also want to thank all the lesbian and gay parenting groups who agreed to be listed in the book, many of whom sent letters and warm words of encouragement.

Several people whose opinions I greatly respect volunteered to read the manuscript in its entirety and offered valuable comments. The hard work and careful attention of Cindy Crawford, Paulette Goodman, Ronnie Lesser, Eric Marcus, Emily McNally, Dan McPherson, Cheri Pies, and Charles Silverstein have all helped make this a better book than I could have achieved alone.

Abby Ruder of Adoption Information Services spent countless hours supporting this project and offering help with the chapter on adoption. Wayne Steinman, founder of Center Kids in New York, Catherine Unsino in New York, and Dawn Smith-Pliner also contributed generously of their time and expertise on adoption issues.

Paula Ettelbrick, Judith Turkel, Nancy Polikoff, and Liz Hendrickson provided information on the legal issues. Paula also devoted time and attention to careful scrutiny of the chapter on legal issues in its manuscript stages.

Many attorneys and other professionals contributed information and expertise to the chapter on surrogate motherhood. Among them were Lori B. Andrews, Noel Keane, Steven Litz, Hilary Hanafin, Nancy Hughes, Norma Thorsen, and Kathryn Wyckoff.

Several researchers in psychology and education discussed their work with me and sent me their publications and dissertations. Among them were Virginia Caspar, Anthony D'Augelli, Tom Domenici, Sally Hand, Dawn Osterweiler, Charlotte Patterson, Claire Riley, Al Sbordone, and Elaine Wickens.

Psychologist Diane Ehrensaft contributed to the discussion of the child-development issues that arise when a gay or lesbian family with children breaks up.

Joan Nestle of the Lesbian Herstory Archives and Barbara Raboy of the Sperm Bank of California also took time out of their busy schedules to talk with me.

Many of those already mentioned provided contacts to families and other professionals around the country. In addition, other people offered wonderful ideas, contacts, and enthusiasm along the way. Kevyn Aucoin, Terry Boggis, Will Dixon-Gray, Chinazo Echezona, Tim Fisher, Phyllis Mark, Maidi Nickele, Cheryl Pearlman, Lynne Roberts, Ariel Shidlo, and my sister, Brenda Trammell, each made valuable contributions.

My agent, Irene Skolnick, helped me loosen up my original concept of this book and did a wonderful job of finding a publisher.

My editor at HarperCollins, Janet Goldstein, had a clear vision from the beginning of what this book should be. She and her gifted associate editor, Peternelle van Arsdale, encouraged me to stretch and gave me the guidance and direction I needed. It was a pleasure to work with such talented and competent professionals.

Lisa Ross's beautiful photography on the cover adds much to our pride and visibility.

My mother, Dr. Constance Martin Norbom, has always been an

impressive example of what a woman can achieve professionally and intellectually. She was confident about my ability to write this book, even when I had my doubts.

My children, Emily and Jesse, have understood what this book means to me personally and to other families like ours. They lovingly and generously tolerated my absence from family activities this past year, cheerfully asking about the book's progress and encouraging me in the most touching ways. I hope they understand how much they give me.

I can barely begin to express my gratitude to my life partner, Susan, who contributed to this book in a thousand ways. She listened endlessly to me talk about the ideas, feelings, logistics, progress, and anxieties that arose during the process. She also took over all of the household duties and child care this past year, leaving me at my computer, undisturbed by worldly distractions. She has always encouraged me to follow my heart and rise to a challenge. Her devotion has been more than I dreamed of.

INTRODUCTION

We're Here

Keisha's moms host the preschool picnic in their backyard early in the term. They introduce themselves to the other parents as Keisha's two mothers. One father can be overheard explaining to his daughter that, yes, Keisha has two mothers, and isn't that nice?

Isaac, eighteen, gets a send-off to college from his family. His biological mother, Roberta, her partner, Elizabeth, and Roberta's friend and former lover, Shirley, have all shared in the financial and emotional work of raising him. Shirley's daughter is considered by all to be Isaac's sister, and the man who is now Shirley's partner, along with his two children, are also part of Isaac's family circle.

Ryan's junior high school friends know that if it's Monday, he can be reached at the home where his mother, Liz, lives with her partner, Gina. Gina has recently given birth to a baby boy, and Ryan invites his friends to see his new brother before they go off to soccer practice. The second half of the week, Ryan lives with his other mother, Rosemary, and her partner, Ellie. In that household Ryan has a sister, the child Ellie and Rosemary adopted together.

Jorge snuggles on his Daddy's lap, listening to a story about

Babar the elephant, while his other father, Papa, is in the upstairs bath-room running his bath. His grandparents on Papa's side were there today, fussing over him and spoiling him as usual. It was a good day.

My own children, Emily and Jesse, are sitting with me on the couch while we look through old family photos. There are pictures of my lover, Susan, and me when we were pregnant with them. They love to hear the stories, over and over, of how we wanted them and came to have them.

Susan and I began planning our family fifteen years ago, when we first fell in love. I was twenty-nine at the time, and up until then I always assumed I'd marry a man and have children in the usual way. My long-term relationships with men were basically good, though for one reason or another they didn't work out. I assumed that when the right man came along, I would get on with becoming a mother.

Becoming a mother was very important to me, and always had been. As a teenager in the sixties, when everyone I knew was trying hal-lucinogens, I was adamant about not wanting to take any drug that might affect the health of my future offspring. When I was in therapy in my twenties, I felt keenly that working out issues about my own childhood and my relationships with my parents was the best way I could prepare myself to provide a healthy environment for my future children. When the time came to have a baby, I wanted to be ready.

Graduate school, writing a dissertation, and struggling to pay the bills took up my early twenties, but once I had my degree I felt ready to think about having a family. The trouble was, Mr. Right didn't seem to be there. The men who loved me didn't offer enough of what I wanted, and the ones I loved didn't feel the same way about me. It began to occur to me that I might have to adapt to life as a single woman. While it was not my first choice, I felt I could manage it. I immediately real-ized, though, that having a child was important enough to me that I wasn't prepared to forgo it. If the right man was not going to come along in the next five years or so, I was going to plan to become a single mother.

With therapy came more self-awareness and maturity, and long-suppressed feelings came to the fore. For the first time I allowed myself a consciousness of the strong desires I felt for women. It finally became possible for me to put two and two together. Before I quite knew what was happening, I found myself deeply, urgently, and passionately in love with a woman. To my amazement, she loved me back with an intensity that matched my own. Finally, the right *woman* had come along.

In general, Susan tends to be less of a planner than I am, taking things more as they come. She had never had a timetable for marriage and family the way I had. She hadn't necessarily been looking for a mate, male or female, but she wasn't one to pass up true love either. Though we found ourselves stepping into the title "lesbian," we didn't know very much about what that meant. We hadn't heard of Stonewall, and knew nothing of the history and complexities of the lesbian community. We were just joyfully and naively in love. Being lesbians was a little scary, but the fear was not all that important compared to the joy of discovering how much we had in common. Between us we had five cats, and we moved them all in together.

I don't remember our first conversation about having children, but it was within the early weeks of our marriage. I was probably the one who brought it up, but maybe not. What I do remember is singing "Tea for Two" together in one of our silly exchanges, coming to the part about how "We could raise a family, a boy for you, a girl for me," and both of us agreeing that it was a lovely idea.

That was in 1978, nine years after the first gay riot at the Stonewall Inn heralded the birth of militancy in the demand for gay rights. It was just five years after the American Psychiatric Association removed homosexuality from its manual of mental diseases. It was the decade of the feminist movement, paralleling and incorporating the Civil Rights movement. Though I don't remember thinking much about the debt we owed to those movements and the changes they effected, Susan and I were among the generation that came of age in an era which promised to celebrate differences.

It was also a time when divorce rates were skyrocketing. When I was growing up there was one divorced woman in the neighborhood. She lived with her daughter in the house across the street. Though people were nice to them to their faces, a certain tone of disparagement was always present in references to them. In a white suburban neighborhood, they just weren't considered a proper family.

By 1978 much had changed. No longer was the same stigma attached to a mother raising her children without a man. Unmarried, middle-class heterosexual women who wanted children were becoming single parents by choice. Though it wasn't common, it wasn't a rarity either. The ancient specter of illegitimacy became a dowdy old notion. There were possibilities.

If it hadn't been for these changes, Susan and I probably would never have considered having children. We have never been mavericks trying to defy the system against all odds. On the contrary, we are both homebodies whose ideas of adventure are very tame. We wanted to know that the children we brought into the world would have a reasonable expectation of having friends and community acceptance. The social climate had given us an opening.

At the time we knew of no one who had done it. We started discussing it with our friends, both straight and gay. Their reactions ranged mostly from polite to enthusiastic, but no one we spoke with had ever heard of it being done. We knew we couldn't be the first lesbian couple to start a family, and we know now that thousands of other families like ours were out there, but there was no network for finding them.

The library revealed very little. We could find nothing about lesbians or gay men choosing to raise children in a gay context. Del Martin and Phyllis Lyon's classic book *Lesbian/Woman* at least provided a start by talking about lesbian mothers who had been heterosexually married and divorced. The few things that were written about lesbian mothers seemed to presume that heterosexual marriage was the only way to start a family, but at least they offered some direction.

Then we heard about the Lesbian Herstory Archives. Founded in 1973 by Joan Nestle and Deborah Edel with a collective of about twenty women, it is a combination of a library, a museum, and a family album. It collects, preserves, catalogs, and makes available the books, both fiction and nonfiction, papers, photographs, artwork, tapes, personal memoirs, newspaper accounts, and other records of our lesbian and gay culture. I went there as a newly "out" lesbian and felt that I had come home to my people.

Though the Archives didn't have much at that time on the topic of lesbians choosing parenthood, what little I found there excited me tremendously. A tiny pink pamphlet entitled *Woman Controlled Conception,* by Sarah and Mary Anonymous, published in 1979 by Womanshare Books in Berkeley, California, gave us all the go-ahead we needed. In twenty-three pages of text and drawings, it described how two lesbians used artificial insemination to become pregnant. It discussed ovulation and showed how to chart a menstrual cycle. It talked about finding donors. There was a drawing of a woman inseminating herself with a turkey baster. Any mystery about the process was completely dispelled. It was thrilling to discover it could be done so easily.

Not only had I found the first relevant, practical information on how to do this, but I finally had some role models. Even if they were thousands of miles away and I knew nothing about them, Sarah and

Mary Anonymous showed us that we were not alone. Susan and I would have gone ahead with having children if Sarah and Mary hadn't published their pamphlet, but the impact of knowing that other lesbians were, in fact, making babies was profound. With the well-being of our future children at stake, we wanted to learn from other people's experiences. We did not want to pioneer in completely uncharted territory. Finding that little pamphlet was a major boost to my confidence about the whole undertaking.

The pamphlet concluded with a brave declaration of strength in adversity: "We would like to end with a photograph of our beautiful children and our friends with their big bellies. Although nothing we've done is illegal—yet—people in power don't want women to have this kind of control over their lives. This means we must protect our anonymity. The beauty of artificial insemination is that we can do it ourselves, no matter what laws they might pass. But we're still up against the problems of how to survive and raise healthy children. Though often we feel we are barely surviving, our goal is to find ways to fight back."

Many years later, lesbian mothers and gay fathers are no longer just barely surviving. Nor are we any longer so afraid of "going public." Lesbian moms and gay dads have appeared on national and international television, on radio talk shows, and in major magazines. There are parenting conferences which attract hundreds of lesbians and gay men at a time. They are there—pushing strollers, wearing maternity clothes, showing photos, and holding the tiny hands of a new generation taking its first wobbly steps. There are gay and lesbian parenting organizations in scores of cities throughout the United States and Canada, as well as an international coalition. These organizations provide newsletters and networking information, and they coordinate social events. Many organizations and private therapists offer workshops for lesbians and gay men who are considering parenthood. Every new family that openly chooses parenthood adds to our sense of community, and the vastness of our numbers and the richness of our diversity help to increase the options for all of us.

Of course, there have always been lesbian and gay parents, long before alternative insemination, surrogate motherhood, or adoption opportunities for unmarried people existed. Most have opted for heterosexual marriage as a way of having children, sometimes discovering or revealing their sexual orientation later. Some inner-city black lesbians and a few other independent lesbians here and there chose parenthood without heterosexual marriage long before the words "lesbian" and "mother" were ever put together. The best estimates we have today suggest that there are between 3 and 8 million gay and lesbian parents in the United States, raising between 6 and 14 million children.[1] Now, however, a new generation of families is being created. Creating a family no longer requires heterosexual sex. And raising a family no longer requires even an attempt at parenting in a mom-and-dad household. The lesbian and gay baby boom is creating a culture of its own, evolving new definitions of family relationships.

Until now, the seeming incompatibility of parenthood and a lesbian or gay orientation has caused many people to delay or forgo their hearts' desires. Fortunately, things are changing. As lesbian and gay cultures become more visible, the shame that results from secrecy and persecution is gradually fading. We have come to know that we are entitled to love and live as we want. I look forward to a time when the designations "parent" and "lesbian" or "gay man" are so completely, casually, and familiarly compatible that no one will ever have to deny a part of themselves again. We are in the process of a creating a world in which there is genuine freedom to follow our hearts. Having claimed our right to love, the next step for those of us who wanted it—claiming the right to fulfill our humanity as parents—was inevitable.

Lesbians and gay men have always broken the mold in creative ways. Though we were raised with the same prescriptions as heterosexuals for what a woman should be, what a man should be, and how a life should be lived, long ago we started inventing our own rules. Even under the most severe persecution, our spirits have prevailed. We have learned to make our differentness our strength. The creativity of our community, which has allowed us to redefine healthy sexuality, loving relationships, and the bonds of friendship, is now evolving new ways of having, loving, and relating to children.

About This Book

Over the years I have spoken with hundreds of lesbians and gay men who have become parents or are considering parenting. Some of the questions people ask have remained the same: How do you go about getting pregnant? Can you come out to your doctor? Should we consider known or anonymous donors? How expensive is it? What are the possibilities for adoption? How "out" can you be? What are the legal issues and how do we protect ourselves? As offspring grow beyond babyhood, people want to know about schools, babysitters, social communities. They want to know what to tell the children, and how to present the family to the world at large.

In addition to practical information, however, I find that what prospective parents most want to know is, "What's it like?" They want to know if it's been hard, if we're happy, what our children think of it all, how our relationships have fared, how our extended families have responded. At conferences and at workshops, as they listen to parents telling their stories, they are wondering to themselves, "Could I handle that? Would that situation work for us? Does the way we want to do it make sense? Does anyone else feel what we feel?"

It is my hope that this book can provide some of the answers to those questions. It represents the things I've learned from participants at my workshops and talks, and from lesbian and gay families who have consulted me in my psychology practice. I have also pulled together information from experts in psychology, law, adoption, and reproductive medicine as it relates to the creation of lesbian and gay families. In addition, over the past year and a half I have interviewed fifty-seven families living in different areas of the country. Many come from the New York City and San Francisco areas, but I also spoke with families from Texas, Iowa, Ohio, Vermont, Pennsylvania, Washington, and other states. I was surprised to find so many gay families living outside of large cities, in tiny towns and rural areas. (One family lives on a 300-acre farm.) Each provides a different perspective on what it's like to be a gay or lesbian family.

Most of the parents who offered their stories have formed two-mother or two-father households. Some are single parents. Some are also coparenting with people outside the household—biological fathers or mothers, ex-lovers, and committed friends. They have created their families through adoption, alternative insemination, foster parenthood, and surrogate motherhood. The majority of the families are white, but about a fourth contain at least one member of color, representing a variety of races and ethnicities. A few families have six-figure incomes, while three have been on welfare at some point; most are somewhere in between. They all responded eagerly and generously to the opportunity to share their stories with others in our community. Their candor affords us a glimpse into their homes and hearts.

Quite a few families said I was welcome to use their full names and the cities in which they lived. In fact, some really wanted the opportunity to offer that degree of openness. I made the decision, however, in the interest of uniformity and confidentiality, to use fictitious first names for everyone. (The one exception to this is the Hester-Mautner family described in Chapter Ten.) Though all of the names have been changed—and in some cases people's locations, occupations, or other identifying details have been obscured—the families are very real.

These families have offered their reflections on how it seems to be working. How do we work out parenting roles and child care? What do we tell our children about sperm donors and birthparents? How do we address issues of racial identity and racism in our children's lives? How do we nurture our adult relationships? What kind of response do we get from our families of origin? How do we present our family to the outside world? What if we have a crisis or a tragedy? Where does our support come from?

While most of the issues I focus on in this book have to do with the very special concerns of gay and lesbian families, some of what is presented here is universal to all parents and children.

Finally, this book also reflects the personal experiences Susan and I have had giving birth to three children, suffering the death of one, and raising two. I have done my best to weave our story throughout these pages in the most honest way I can. There are no perfect families, and ours is no exception. Every family is a complex, dynamic, struggling entity, changing over time, trying to coordinate the needs and temperaments of its very different members. Some days it feels as though we have it all worked out, while other days we wonder if we're all going to pull through unscathed. The point is to tell it as it is.

The focus of this book is parents who identified themselves as gay or lesbian before choosing children. I have not attempted to deal with the many issues specific to gay and lesbian parents who started their families in heterosexual marriages, because they deserve a more detailed discussion of their own.[2] However, there are enough similarities between both types of families that every lesbian or gay parent should find relevant things in these pages, regardless of how his or her family was formed.

This book is for and about both lesbian mothers and gay fathers. The lesbian and gay male communities have historically had many differences which have given rise to conflict and sometimes bitterness. For many women, separatism has helped the process of emerging from the domination of sexist culture. Parenthood, however, raises issues which require us to transcend our gender differences.

Lesbians raising boys often find they feel closer to men than they once did. And then, of course, most of our daughters grow up and want to date boys; we may spend their teen years with heterosexual adolescent males trooping through our kitchens. Many lesbian mothers have come to feel that they want men to be a part of their children's lives, whether they have sons or daughters. Men are the uncles, grandfathers, godfathers, trusted friends, and sometimes the involved biological fathers of those children. Parenthood is bringing us together.

Meanwhile, gay fathers are just coming into their own. There are fewer gay men than lesbians who have chosen to become parents in a gay context, but they are growing in number. Years ago, at a talk I gave, there was one man in the audience. When he raised his hand to speak, he introduced himself as a lesbian mother. We all did a double take, as he went on to explain that he felt lesbian mothers were his reference group. He knew no other men who were doing what he and his lover were doing, and the identity which best described what his life was about was that of lesbian mother. Since then, the growing number of gay dads by choice has hopefully begun to contribute to some sense of community for that lone, self-designated male lesbian mother. The community of lesbian mothers, however, continues to provide a major support for gay fathers.

While there is much variety among the families I interviewed, and the book also draws on my experience with scores of other parents and children, there is no way to adequately represent all possible family constellations, circumstances, ethnicities, and concerns. We are too diverse a group. The advice or guidelines that I offer in these pages will not apply to everyone, and may overlook the relevant issues of some. This book is not intended to be a complete and comprehensive presentation of our options, our lives, or our needs. My hope, however, is that it does contain enough of what lesbian and gay families are about to resonate with many of us.

Issues presented in this book which are politically controversial represent the conclusions I have arrived at, at this point in my life, through my own experience as a psychologist, a parent, and a lesbian. For example, my perspectives on such things as the identities of sperm donors, the ethics of surrogacy, the complexities of transracial adoption, or the choices about revealing one's sexual orientation, as well as other issues, do not necessarily reflect the viewpoints of lesbian and gay families in general, nor even the opinions of the families whose stories appear in this book. The limitations of the views I express reside in the limitations of my experience and vision, and I take sole responsibility for them.

Finally, the picture is changing so rapidly that some of the information in this book may be obsolete by the time you read it. Laws, courts, adoption professionals, physicians, schools, and other institutions, as well as society in general, are incorporating a new awareness of our families into their modes of operation. I certainly hope that some situations which appear problematic at this writing may be no big deal in a short time. This book is not intended to be anyone's only source of information about creating lesbian and gay families; it is merely an addition to a growing body of resources. The most important resource will always be lesbian and gay parents themselves.

A Note on Terminology

I have used the expression "alternative insemination" in most places as a less offensive and more realistically descriptive term than "artificial insemination," except where context or quotation requires the latter, more conventionally used term. On occasion I simply use "donor insemination" to mean the same thing.

The term "coparent" refers to any person sharing the work and responsibilities of raising a child with another adult. Technically it should indicate nothing about whether the adults are lovers, ex-lovers, friends of either gender, or a biological mother and father. In the section on lesbians and gay men parenting together, I use "coparents" to refer specifically to a mother and a father raising a child together; in other places, context should make clear what is meant. In general, however, I have used the term sparingly, because I am concerned that it may become a way of designating second-class parenthood, as in "she's not the mother, she's the comother." Instead, I try wherever possible to refer to both parents as "the mothers" or "the fathers," and to designate someone as "the child's other father," for example. Where their legal status is relevant, I discuss the "legal parent" and the "nonlegal parent," terms which can be used with both biological parenthood and parenthood by adoption. We do not yet have language adequate to portray all of our various roles and relationships.

I have tried as much as possible to use language which is free from gender bias, but English has its limitations. Wherever it has seemed reasonable, I have used the cumbersome "she or he" and "his or her." On occasion I have substituted one gender to represent both, attempting to give equal time to each.

Part I

CREATING
A FAMILY

1

THE BIG DECISION

As lesbian and gay prospective parents we do an extraordinarily thorough and responsible job of exploring our concerns and evaluating our suitability for parenthood. The children of lesbians and gay men are the most considered and planned-for children on earth. There is virtually no such thing as an unwanted child among us. We go to support groups and workshops on considering parenthood. We talk to our friends and lovers and family. We talk to our therapists. We read books. Many years may go into the planning process. We do an impressively careful job of weighing our needs, our resources, and our expectations.

If you are just considering whether or not to bring a child into your life, this is the time to do some serious exploration of yourself and your circumstances. Whether we are gay or straight, parenthood is a monumental step which requires lots of thought. The universal questions for potential parents of any sexual orientation are: Do you really want to raise a child? Do you have the financial, emotional, and situational resources at this point in your life to go ahead with it? If you are in a relationship, how stable, resilient, and nurturing is it? Do you have access to support systems—in the form of family, friends, and community—to help out?

In addition, there are questions which we must address because of the different nature of our families. Because we have broken the mold, we have more choices to make. We have to ask ourselves: How will we get a baby or child? Who will be the designated parents, and how will we define each parent's roles? What legal safeguards can we arrange to insure that our definition of the family is respected? How open are we willing to be about our sexual orientations to schools, neighbors, medical people, and others? How will our families of origin respond? Can our children grow up healthy and happy without a father/mother? Will our children have a hard time socially because of their lesbian or gay parents? How will we deal with people who have negative reactions?

This chapter presents an overview of the decision-making process, while subsequent chapters take a more in-depth look at the various issues to consider. By reading the stories families have shared, you may avoid some of the pitfalls they encountered. You may also find reassurance in their successes and discover possibilities you might not have considered which could help make your road smoother. One thing we have all learned from the experience of parenthood is that it cannot be done in isolation. A child is raised in a family, and a family exists in the context of extended family, friends, and community. We all need support to make these decisions and carry out these plans.

If you are already raising children, you may find it useful to go back and reexamine the decisions you made initially. The process may help validate and affirm the way you went about things. It may remind you that you deserve a lot of credit for all the hard work you put in, doing research and overcoming obstacles. It may also help identify the resources that were lacking when you started out, or clarify issues which were not fully considered. If your situation has changed over time, looking back at where you started as a parent may help you to focus your attention on current needs or to predict future difficulties.

Do I Want to Be a Parent?

We live in a society which pressures heterosexuals to raise children and pressures lesbians and gay men not to raise children. The desire to become a parent, however, recognizes no distinctions based on sexual orientation. If we could remove the effects of all that pressure, we would undoubtedly find that heterosexuals want children a good deal less of the time than they have them, and that lesbians and gay men want them more. As a community of lesbians and gay men, we are just beginning to open ourselves to those desires. A decade ago, only rarely did one of my gay or lesbian clients mention the question of children.

Today, the issue of whether or not a life's plan will include parenting comes up with a great many of the gay men and lesbians I see.

This doesn't mean that everyone wants to become a parent. On the contrary, many of us do not. And it is important that we not fall prey to the pressures of straight society, which depicts the choice not to parent as immature, self-centered, or irresponsible. There is absolutely no virtue to becoming a parent. It does not represent any greater achievement of mental health or adulthood. It is no more worthwhile than any other kind of life. It is simply the road you take if you want to take it.

Recognizing those wants, however, may take work for some of us. Now that we are asking ourselves the questions, we may have to overcome the effects of homophobia to find our answers.

Sometimes the perceived incongruity of being gay and raising children has led to painful consequences. We all know of lesbian and gay relationships which broke up because one partner wanted desperately to have children. He or she then went off to make a heterosexual marriage, the only context imaginable for becoming a parent. In the process, heartbreak was left behind, and passions were silently locked away for years.

On the flip side, many people recognizing their same-sex attractions assume that having children will not be a possibility. For them, the question of parenting may simply never be raised. One woman, who had wanted children when she was younger, said, "When I came out as a lesbian I thought that meant I couldn't have children. I put it out of my mind. I just didn't think about it. Getting close to a straight woman and her little girl filled the void for a while, but I just assumed I couldn't have my own children because I was a lesbian and I didn't know there was any other way." In order to really evaluate our feelings about parenting, to weigh our desires against our reservations, we have to be able to recognize that being a parent, as a lesbian or a gay man living in an openly lesbian or gay context, is genuinely possible.

Once that possibility is opened up, there are many different ways in which the wish to parent may make itself felt. Depending on our personalities, histories, and circumstances, we may be seized by a powerful, urgent longing of awesome proportions, or we may cautiously and ambivalently feel that parenthood is something we are willing to consider. If we are at the former end of the scale, raising a child may be the single most important thing on life's agenda. The prospect of never having a child may feel extremely painful. The concerns about doing it as a lesbian or gay man, the potential difficulties of doing it without a partner, or the sacrifices of time, money, and career goals may be of minimal concern. If we tend toward the other end of the scale, the option of not having a child may have definite attractions. The child-free life may appear genuinely satisfying in many respects, and a lot of thinking has to go into whether or not to trade all that freedom for the responsibilities of parenthood.

For me, becoming a mother was of compelling importance. I had spent a lifetime preparing for parenthood, always casually making mental notes about how I wanted to raise my children. As a late-blooming lesbian, I saw myself as unquestionably heterosexual until I was twenty-nine. I was sexually active with men, and scrupulous about using birth control. When I got pregnant it was going to be because I planned and chose it, and felt ready for it in every way.

By the time I came out as a lesbian, the vision of myself as a mother was so indelibly a part of my identity that nothing was going to disrupt it. Whatever being a lesbian was supposed to involve, there was no question that for me it would involve being a mother.

My experience paralleled that of several of the people I spoke with. There are lesbians and gay men who simply never felt there was any incompatibility between their sexual orientation and parenthood. Sharon said, "I always felt having children was the most challenging thing you could do, the most creative thing you could do as a person. It was something I was always going to do with my life." Sharon came out at seventeen and saw no reason why that should interfere with her having children. "I never thought it would be easy, but I always thought I could do it. Even when I was in law school I remember doing research on artificial insemination and surrogate parenting and alternative resources for parenting, so I always knew that it was out there and it existed. I didn't personally know any people who had done it, but I just knew that it was possible."

Harriet similarly felt that being a lesbian would not interfere with becoming a parent. For Harriet, the crucial variable was that she had lesbian mothers as role models. "Right around when I first realized I was gay, my sister became the drummer of a women's band, and she and I both came out. The band was all gay women, older, mostly in their thirties [Harriet was seventeen at the time], and at least one woman had a child with her lover. So all of a sudden lesbian motherhood was just there in my life as a reality. My whole world was gay women, and it was pretty amazing. At the same time I realized that all of my mother's friends were gay, from a whole other generation. My mother also had experiences with women that she wasn't that verbal about, but she did say that it had happened. Some of the women had had children, like my mother did. They got into marriages but still carried on their relationships with their women friends and lovers. I don't remember ever thinking that I couldn't become a mother."

Many other lesbians, and most gay men I have encountered, at some point in their lives made the decision that their sexual orientation and parenthood didn't go together. For Paula, it was the logistics of acquiring a child that stopped her. Before she came out, Paula wanted children very much. "In eighth grade I remember a friend giving me this cartoon of a woman, a harried mother with twelve kids. She put an arrow on it and wrote Paula next to it. When I came out as a lesbian, I thought that meant I couldn't have children. I was twenty at the time, and I just put having children out of my mind. I wasn't willing to sleep with a man and I didn't know there was any other way."

Dana always wanted a child but then became active in the women's movement. The political climate of academic feminism put some pressure on her to stop considering parenthood. "I came out in a real political community, in a women's studies program at college. It was not politically correct to have babies at that time, so I just didn't think about it a whole lot. The people in the program had the attitude that mothering took women's focus away from the real stuff of politics and fighting patriarchy. Though I didn't totally buy into it, I did put those thoughts [of motherhood] on a back burner. I was busy with coming out and falling in love and getting into this radical headset."

Sally came out in a small midwestern town. She had no idea that there were other lesbians on the planet. The stress of growing up gay and isolated was enough to preempt any thoughts of motherhood. It didn't seem possible to have it all. "I did a lot of babysitting and I loved kids, but I associated the family thing with men, and I couldn't see myself with a man. So I didn't really give a whole lot of thought to 'Gee, I guess this means I won't be able to have kids.' I never really thought about it at all. I just thought about growing up and getting out on my own." After she had established a life for herself as a lesbian, an intense longing for a baby began to make itself felt. Eventually it began to occur to her that she could be both a lesbian and a mother.

If the concept of lesbians being mothers has been hard for people to grasp, the concept of gay fathers has been even harder. We have all been raised to believe that only women are nurturers. In addition, since men cannot get pregnant and adoption resources may be somewhat more limited for them, some men have assumed that the difficulties of just obtaining a child are insurmountable. There are many men who would choose to have children if they knew it can be done and saw other gay men doing it. There are many more who have not even asked themselves whether they want to parent because they never imagined it was truly feasible.

Barry is forty-one. He and his partner, Tony, are the parents of four year-old Carla. Barry tells their story: "It goes back to nineteen years ago, when Tony and I first met, in 1972. From the very beginning, Tony was talking about having kids, and I told him he was totally out of his mind. It just wasn't done. I was involved in the gay community and was attentive to all that was going on, and I knew this wasn't anything that was being spoken about. There was no place for kids in the gay community. I think I bought into a lot of internalized homophobia saying gays don't have children.

"Growing up I had no desire for children. I have a sister fifteen years my junior and I'm very much a father figure to her, so I felt I had had that sort of relationship with someone. To do it as a gay man, though, was unthinkable. We don't do that. We go out at night, we don't have children. I was also young. It took me a long time, about thirteen years, to get around to saying, yeah, I want to be a parent.

"I started doing a lot of soul-searching, and you know who's fault this whole thing is? Cheri Pies.[1] I attended a workshop she gave at the National Lesbian and Gay Health Conference in Washington back in 1986 that was specifically for gay men considering parenting. It had never been done before. A group of about a dozen of us got together and validated our feelings. It was like getting permission, realizing that there is nothing wrong with gay parenting and that the obstacles that might fall in our way are easily surmountable.

"I didn't tell Tony I was doing this. I was at the conference for professional reasons, and this was the one workshop I was doing for me. When I arrived home, Tony picked me up at the train. I remember it as clear as day. I got into the car and said 'Let's do it!' He didn't have to think; he knew exactly what I was talking about. Then we started doing what was necessary to start the process."

Barry had to overcome a lot of assumptions and prejudices to arrive at his desire to parent. Not only are we brought up to believe that a child needs a mother, we are also tied into our visions of life in the gay community. For those of us whose lives revolve around active participation in gay social circles, until recently there was no place for children. When the gay community feels like our family and our lifeline, the thought of leaving it to raise children may feel like facing social isolation. Barry had no role models of men who were able to integrate life in the gay community with parenthood. The parenting desires he finally recognized might have been there all along if he had grown up seeing gay men hold and care for their sons and daughters, and had known a gay community that included family picnics and pool parties.

For some people, although being gay or lesbian doesn't feel like a barrier to parenthood, the idea of raising children just doesn't seem all that appealing until their late twenties or thirties. Then they may find themselves suddenly surprised to be bitten by the parenting bug. Sometimes life events, especially family losses, help to catalyze the change.

Willa is now a single mother by adoption. She says, "At twenty-eight, five years ago, I lost six family members and friends in two years. I was left really on my own. I went through a long depression. During that period, I spent a lot of time thinking about what I wanted in my life and where I would go from here. I knew at that time in my life that I had to go forward and create a family, and I knew that would involve children. I didn't feel that coming out or being a lesbian was something that would stop me."

Harriet's desire for motherhood was similarly jolted by her mother's death. "When my mother died I wanted to have a child immediately. With a good stroke of wisdom, I realized that it was a replacement kind of thing and that I really wasn't in a position to do it. I didn't have my life in a place where it would be the best thing. I said I would like to do it when I'm thirty-two, kind of randomly, but somehow by the time I was thirty-two I really had gotten my life into a place where it was possible to do it. I was working at home, and was really happy. So I wasn't having him in order to make my life happy. It was much better that way, I think, than filling a gap or a void."

Many lesbians and gay men who want to care for a child start by taking in foster children on a temporary basis as a way of getting accustomed to the role of parent. Linda reported, "The woman I was living with wanted to birth a child. I said to her that we needed to have experience in parenting before we decided if we really wanted to birth a child. So we got into foster care."

During Barry's soul-searching about parenthood, a foster child came into their lives. Barry and Tony were adult advisers to Gay and Lesbian Youth of New York. They had just moved into a larger apartment with a second bedroom, and Barry was grateful for finally having some extra space to work in. A week later, a member of GLYNY approached them, pleading that they had a boy who needed a home. He had been thrown out of his house for being gay and had nowhere to go. He was too old for foster care, and they were afraid he'd be eaten alive in a shelter. So would Barry and Tony mind putting him up for a few days? Reluctantly they agreed, and a few days turned into a year and a half. Barry says, "While he was living with us it felt like a permanent headache, but I got in touch with all these parenting urges I had which had been very well suppressed."

Willa also took in a foster child to help her decide. "I saw someone on the Phil Donahue show making a plea to come take a boarder baby.[2] That was in January of 1987. They said don't ask what age or what race or what sex the child is. Just come and take a baby. There seemed to be such a need."

Willa became foster mother to Shawna, a seven-week-old preemie who was placed with her for several months. Her friends and her therapist all got a chance to see her parent this baby. Their support for her parenting helped her determination to go ahead and adopt a child of her own. "They all said, 'I saw you with Shawna and I know how you are, and I think this would be absolutely wonderful.'"

For some people, considering parenthood has little to do with their own desire for children. You may never have felt any particular interest in parenting yet find yourself in love with someone who desperately wants to raise a child. You are then forced to examine your willingness to commit your life in that direction. This places tremendous demands on you and your partner to do a lot of soul-searching. It isn't likely that you can maintain a relationship and a household with a lover who is parenting and not play some kind of parenting role yourself. That role will doubtless involve some responsibility, and it will impact on your life's activities and plans. One man who is now a father said, "I never saw myself as a father. This was entirely my partner's idea, and I was very reluctant when he brought it up. But I saw how strongly he felt about it, and I knew this was something he had to do. If we were going to stay together, I would have to be willing to put myself into this. It took me four years of thinking about it because I knew it would mean a complete change in my life." In my experience, there is a relationship between how strongly a person wants to parent, and how easily he or she adapts to the stresses of it. Deciding to go ahead with parenthood when you genuinely don't want it is going to lead to painful times for all involved, so it is important that your concern for your relationship not lead you to make a decision in haste which you might later regret.

Whether we are going to have a child come hell or high water, or are not so sure and need to weigh the options, we all have concerns about what's involved. Just contemplating the awesome responsibility of being a parent is enough to take one's breath away. Children change your life profoundly and forever; though the changes may be strongly desired, none of us encounters major change without some anxiety.

Furthermore, just being sure that we want to be parents doesn't necessarily mean that we have the resources to be parents. As strong as our desire may be, we still have to evaluate the limits imposed on us by our careers, our health and physical capacities, our finances, the stability of our relationships, our living arrangements, our personal temperaments, and other factors. With a realistic sense of what the needs of a developing human are, any prospective parent should measure whether she or he can deliver the goods.

In evaluating whether or not we want a child, it can be helpful to look at our fantasies of parenthood. The more detailed and realistic those visions are, the more we can be sure that we genuinely want the job. Almost anyone can picture themselves in a greeting-card moment, holding a sweet-smelling newborn cuddled trustingly in their arms. And, yes, parenthood contains many such moments. But there are twenty-four hours in the day, and a lot of work goes into producing and supporting those blissful interludes. With an infant there may be sleep deprivation, loss of time and spontaneity for you and your partner, money stresses, unrelenting responsibility, and worry—along with the joys. In the toddler years there is the ongoing work of keeping your cool in response to sometimes maddening opposition, physically following and picking up after a mobile and reckless little being, and continued unrelenting responsibility. By the school years there is the daily chore of homework supervision, transportation to music lessons, birthday parties, and play dates, plus additional responsibilities, and, if you're like me, more worry. And then comes adolescence.

And those are just the routine stresses. Though all may go smoothly in your lives, there is no guarantee. Your child may have health problems, learning disabilities, or other special needs. And everything goes on in the context of your other life stresses, such as aging parents, perhaps, or career difficulties. Make sure that when you try on your fantasies of parenthood, they include the moments of fatigue, irritability, and anxiety. If you can picture yourself at those times, still feeling joy and satisfaction that you have committed your life to raising a child, then you will be better prepared for things to come.

An excellent way to get a realistic sense of what parenthood entails is to observe other parents and talk with them about their experiences. If you live in a city that has an active lesbian and gay parenting group, attend the meetings and workshops available. Spend time in the homes of families with children, preferably not just when they have been scrubbed up for visitors. Offer to babysit. Read parenting books that attempt to portray the experience of parenting realistically, even though they are written for heterosexual parents. Spending a long time in the planning will pay off later.

Do the exercises in the wonderful book *Considering Parenthood: A Workbook for Lesbians,* by Cheri Pies. The book is addressed to lesbians but can also be very useful to gay men. In it Pies offers probing questions prospective parents can ask themselves about what they expect from parenthood. Many of the exercises encourage you to think deeply about what you value in your life. They help to focus your attention on how you apportion your resources, and the changes that having a child would cause in your life.

How Do You Get a Baby?

Though in the long run it is by no means the biggest difficulty we will encounter in parenthood, the first concern which comes up is: How can we get a baby? Women, of course, have the option of getting pregnant (see Chapter Two: Lesbians Choosing Pregnancy) and have to decide if they want to go that route or would prefer to adopt a child. If they opt for biological parenthood, they must decide who the sperm donor or biological father will be, whether he will be known to the child, and whether he will assume a parenting role. In short, they have to define the family (see Chapter Three: Donors and Coparents).

Men may feel daunted by the obstacles to becoming a parent. If they want to have a biological connection to their child, they require greater participation and cooperation from a woman than women require from a sperm donor. They may choose to find a surrogate mother who will conceive and bear a child for them (see Chapter Four: Gay Dads Making Babies), or they may elect to conceive with a woman, usually a lesbian, who will share custody and parenting with them (see Chapter Three: Donors and Coparents). Either way involves a lot of careful planning. Again, the family unit has to be defined.

For both lesbians and gay men who want to adopt a child, there are decisions to make about which of several adoption routes to consider. Depending on the money you can spend and your personal needs and preferences, there are numerous options. Adoption is a wonderful way to make a family, though it also requires a lot of work and planning (see Chapter Five: Adoption).

There is no question that this can be done. Lesbians and gay men by the tens, and maybe hundreds of thousands have managed to create and adopt children.[3] There are more physicians and sperm banks willing to help us inseminate than there used to be. There are more adoption counselors and agencies who are supportive of lesbian and gay adoptions. There are more lawyers familiar with our families' issues. There are more lesbian and gay parenting groups to provide networks to those physicians, lawyers, and agencies. If you are prepared to put in the effort, you can become a parent. Plug into the network of lesbian and gay parents and learn what they have done, where they have found services, and how it has worked out.

Can Lesbian and Gay Parents Raise Healthy Children?

One tired lesbian mother of a very assertive child bemoaned, "I think we made her *too* secure." Barring such outcomes, however, there is a large body of research which supports the fact that our children are at least as healthy as anyone else's. (A few studies show that children raised by lesbians are *better* adjusted than children from straight families.)[4] The studies have examined the children's social functioning, self-esteem, ability to express feelings, intelligence, and tendencies toward one or another sexual orientation. Though the courts and even the mental health profession are slow to catch on, the data is there and irrefutable. What we have to offer in our lesbian and gay families is exactly what children need to grow into healthy, happy, and well-adjusted children.

Many of us found growing up as lesbians or gay men to be painful, isolating, shameful, and frightening. If we endured teasing or rejection from others because we were different, we undoubtedly suffered a lot. We may imagine that our children will have to go through a similarly hurtful social ostracism, and will grow up feeling bad about themselves. We may worry that they will be angry with us for thrusting them into such a difficult life.

The reality is not like this, however. People's worst fears—that our children will be harmed by teasing, shaming, or social ostracism for coming from a gay family—do not seem to be coming to pass. On the contrary, the pride we feel in our families gives our children the tools to deal with prejudice. As in any family that contains a member of an oppressed minority, our children learn to understand the problems of ignorance and bias. Depending on where they live and who they are, they make decisions about whom to tell and whom not to tell. In general, our children only rarely encounter any significant homophobic treatment. In instances when they do, they are prepared to handle it.

One young man, now thirteen, made a statement that echoed the sentiments of many other children I spoke with. He said, "I think growing up with lesbian parents taught me about how people can be different. And being different is just different, it isn't better or worse. I feel good about myself for understanding some things that a lot of other kids don't know. My moms have helped me a lot."

For some children, this means there aren't even any difficult feelings to contend with about coming from a different kind of family. Other children, though, do go through some sad feelings about not having a father, for example, or feel some frustration about explaining their families to schoolmates. *The fact of their having some negative feelings does not mean that they are psychologically damaged by them.* This is an important distinction. The truth is that everyone, from whatever kind of family, wishes that some things about their family were different. Our task as parents is to listen to our children's feelings with compassion, and without guilt or defensiveness in response. For children, coming to terms with the disappointments in life is part of growing up. Ultimately it is feeling loved and understood that helps all of us overcome life's imperfections. We are giving our children love of the very best quality, and they will feel it.

Paula's personal history affected her beliefs about what a child would need. "I thought my child would grow up and want a daddy or be angry with me for not providing one. My father had died when I was young and I knew the feelings I had had were painful. I was worried, even though I knew I had *lost* my father, and this child would never know a father."

Gloria was also raised without a father, and her experience led her to the opposite conclusion. "I never missed having a father. I grew up in a family of women, my mother, my aunt, and my grandmother. My father was never involved with the family. I had male cousins, and other male relatives, and that seemed just fine to me. I felt that even if I had a boy, I could do everything with him that a father would do, and he wouldn't be missing anything. And I have men friends who would be close to him."

The world consists of two genders, and our children, whether boys or girls, need to grow up having relationships with both men and women, but those relationships can be with people other than parents. No parent can give a child everything. Nor can we predict which things our children will miss most. However, your pride and confidence about your family structure will be communicated to your child. Your willingness to listen to your child's changing needs, and to whatever wishes or longings there may be, will make it possible for any family configuration, with or without a father or a mother, to be a healthy environment (see Chapter Seven: Raising Our Children).

We are all concerned about how our children will handle the world's response to their families. Will they be stigmatized for their parents' sexuality? Will they suffer the discomforts of prejudice that many of us have felt? Some of the answers have to do with how open we are able to be about our family structure in our neighborhoods, families, and communities. The degree of openness we are able to maintain, and the amount of community support we have for our openness, will have a great influence on how comfortable our children are able to be with their friends and schoolmates. The easier it is for our children to discuss their families, the less stress they will experience. Even when children feel a need to be evasive with some people about their families, they manage to find close relationships in which they can be open. Our children are doing a fine job of developing social circles, fitting in, and living quite healthy lives.

Will There Be Enough Money?

There is a tremendous range of what it can cost to become a parent as a lesbian or a gay man. The starting costs can be close to zero, as in the case of a conception arranged by a man and a woman who are friends (assuming insurance covers the prenatal care and delivery), or in adoptions of special needs children through the public child welfare system, for example. At the other end of the price range, becoming a parent can cost $30,000 or more for a high-end commercial surrogacy arrangement or the most expensive of adoption situations. In between, there are the more moderate costs of most adoption routes (see Chapter

Five) or the costs of alternative insemination (see Chapter Two).

Once the child is in your home, there are the ongoing costs of parenting that exist in any household. The experts calculate that the total costs of raising a child from birth to age eighteen are likely to run between $150,000 to $250,000.[5] That comes out to approximately $8,000 to $14,000 a year, although actual costs are not spread evenly over the eighteen years. The costs are high in the first couple of years because of baby equipment, diapers, child-care costs, and well-baby pediatric care which may not be covered by insurance. There may be time lost from work in the early weeks or months, with resultant loss of income. You may have to move to larger quarters and increase your housing costs. The next few years lighten up a little, but the older children get the more likely you are to spend money on their video games, tutors, music lessons, hockey skates, and orthodontia. By the time they get to adolescence they start spending more on clothes, they eat nonstop, and they need money for their social lives. And then, of course, there is college to think about.

Money worries are uppermost in many people's minds. Singles and young couples are often especially concerned about how they will manage financially if they have a child. The figures given above presume a middle-class lifestyle, but for the most part it is possible to raise healthy, happy children on much more limited resources. The more limited your finances are, however, the more stress you are likely to feel. The time we spend making money takes us away from our children, and we may be concerned about depriving them of contact with us as we struggle to pay the bills. Not being able to afford a babysitter, having very little privacy in your living space, being unable to take time off from work for vacation or relaxation, or having to deal with the public assistance system can make for a lot of emotional wear and tear.

Millie is a painter who earns a living in her spare time. She was very concerned about what having a child would do to her life. "I'm interested in pursuing my career as a painter, and didn't think I could find the time to be a painter and to earn a living, and then on top of that to raise kids. It seemed like more than I could handle, and that I'd be giving up too much. At the time I was earning a lot less money than I do now, and trying to balance everything—it just wouldn't fit." Millie and her partner, Sima, spent years in the talking and planning stages. A major factor in their ultimate decision to go ahead with parenting was that Millie became able to earn more money per hour at a different type of work.

Dana and her lover, Wendy, came up with a plan to deal with their financial worries that helped crystallize their decision to have a baby.

Dana said, "I spoke with a friend of mine about my money concerns, and she made a suggestion that would be an experiment and a way to save money. Wendy and I really got into it. For the first time we put our money together. We each have a little pool of our own, and we have spending money of our own that we take as an allowance each week, but we put away some money every month, keeping a pool for bills and a pool for personal, and so on. I thought it was very symbolic. It was trying out another level of commitment and sharing, to see if we could do this baby thing. It felt grown up to both of us, and it worked out really well. We managed to save quite a bit of money. We never thought we could."

Dana got paychecks from two different part-time jobs. They reasoned that if they could put away one of those checks, it would demonstrate to them that they could manage if Dana quit that one job to care for the baby. Together they put in over a year working on it.

If finances are a concern, it's a good idea to put yourself on a spending plan during the decision-making months or years. See if you can get your debts paid off, and put away enough of a cushion to pay for medical costs and baby supplies. It will help reduce stress later on.

Starting Out Healthy

Though there is no way to insure that life will keep us healthy while our children are still dependent on us, we can assess the state of our health at the outset. Especially if you are planning to make babies biologically, but also if you are just committing yourself to the role of parent, it behooves you to get a thorough medical evaluation. It is worth knowing ahead of time if you have a health condition which might interfere with your ability to parent. Barry and Tony, for example, were concerned about their HIV status before adopting Carla. Barry states, "We did not wish to leave any stone unturned. Neither one of us wanted to be a single parent. We felt it would not be fair to the child. We made a decision immediately to find out our HIV status. It was an easy decision to come to. If one or both of us was HIV positive, we would not pursue the adoption." Your decision will be your own, but it should be an informed decision, made in the best interests of the child.

It is also important that you assess your drug and alcohol consumption. If you have a tendency to use alcohol or drugs to reduce stress, there is a strong likelihood that your substance use will increase with the stresses of parenthood. The time to spot a developing problem is before a child is depending on you. If you are not sure if your drinking or drug use is a problem, have a consultation with a therapist who specializes in addictions.[6] This is a worthwhile expenditure of time and money.

If you have physical limitations or disabilities, you may wonder whether you will be able to provide the physical care a baby or a toddler needs, or to continue to work and provide for the family's financial needs. When Claire decided to become a single parent, she knew there was a great likelihood she would spend extended periods in a wheelchair. Claire has severe bouts of arthritis, which periodically goes into remission. She recalls, "After I decided I would get pregnant I had to wait for about a year or so because I needed to figure out what the heck was going on with my health and whether I really could do this. I had a lot of feelings about what a mother who was not mobile would be like. It terrified me."

Claire's inspiration came from a film she saw about a disabled mother. She explains: "It might have been on some show about unusual people, miracles of the world or something. She had no arms at all, and it showed her being a mother, doing everything with her feet. She had a stool in her kitchen with wheels and she'd scoot herself around from counter to counter. She would cut tomatoes with her feet, and she would cut her children's hair with her feet. So I had that image, and I knew that anything could be done." In fact, in the early years after Olivia was born, Claire spent a lot of time being ill. They had a king-size bed that became the center of home, and later Olivia and her friends learned to push and play on Claire's wheelchair, which has become just another part of their family landscape.

Finding the Time

Time often seems to be the most limited resource of all. We are having children because we want to watch them grow, participate in their discoveries and achievements, guide them through their mishaps, and give them all the conversation and cuddling they need. How can we be there to do that if our careers demand long hours and weekends?

One single gay man decided not to pursue parenthood at present because the small business he owns affords him virtually no time at home. "When the second adoption agency turned me down, I had to admit that they were right. Until the business can manage without me, I really can't give a child what it needs."

When we consider how much time our future children may require, we are usually imagining the needs of a normal, healthy child. But some of us may be thinking of adopting a child with special needs, and all of us planning to have children biologically must consider the possibility that they may be born with special needs. A child with learning disabilities, emotional problems, or physical challenges is going to need more of your time. If you are adopting, you can decide ahead of time how much you have to offer.

Barry and Tony were prepared to adopt a child with problems, even very significant problems, as long as the child's condition didn't represent a total disability. They wanted a child who they knew would someday be able to live independently. Barry recalls, "Profound retardation or autism were things that we felt we couldn't deal with. Having backgrounds in special education actually suited us to become parents of a special-needs child, but on the flip side we also knew what was required. We could not afford for one of us to stay home and be a full-time parent."

In evaluating our resources, we are of course concerned with the things our children will need. It is equally important, however, that we take stock of our own needs when we consider parenthood. It takes time to nourish our lives and our relationships. It is unrealistic to suppose that we will comfortably do without the things that matter most to us. While we may imagine being willing to sacrifice everything for the sake of our children, the truth is that the less we sacrifice, the easier a time the whole family will have.

Emotional Resources

Raising a child challenges your emotional resources like nothing else on earth. As prepared as I felt I was for parenthood, it was a shock to find myself pushed to the limits of my maturity. Time and again, dealing with life as a parent has forced me to grow. Sometimes I have delighted in the opportunity, but on occasion I have been dragged painfully to the next level of awareness. Working in a helping profession, I thought I knew all there was to know about putting my own needs aside to care for someone else. Parenthood has taught me more. After years of my own therapy and exploration of my family history, I thought I would never repeat the mistakes my parents made. Yet I have found my parents' hurtful words on the tip of my own tongue, sometimes too late to stop their emergence. Being a sensitive person and a psychologist, I thought I would always be able to understand my children's emotional experiences, but sometimes I find myself bewildered by their angers and upsets, and often I don't have a clue about how to help.

Prospective parents all share concerns about whether they can provide the essential nurturing a child requires. Do we personally have the emotional maturity to give generously and compassionately, over twenty years or more, even when it conflicts with our needs for sleep, social life, career goals, etc.? Will the negative feelings that we may have developed about ourselves in growing up get passed along to our children? Will we cause our children the same kinds of pain or damage that our parents' limitations caused us? Will we pass along our fears? Our bad habits? Will our own conflicts about intimacy, about anger, about dependence become problems in a relationship with a child?

Sally worried about whether she could be the kind of parent she wanted to be. She recalls, "I started seeing all the bad things about myself. At a very young age I took on this awful criticism thing that my mother brought me up with. I was worried that I was too critical a person because I was raised that way. All the things that I'd seen from my own childhood, and from seeing other children grow up, made me very, very nervous. I wanted to be the perfect parent."

The emotional bonds of parenthood may be the precise reasons one wants to raise a child, and yet they are not always fun, and not always welcome. There is the pervasive, twenty-four hour a day sense of responsibility for someone's life, safety, nutrition, emotional well-being, education, moral development, health care, and happiness. Not everybody greets such a prospect with open arms.

Wendy was frightened of becoming a parent. When her fears came out in the open, she revealed, "I don't know if I can do this—if I can handle a commitment to a kid. I don't know if I'll freak out and have to run away. What if the child gets sick? It would break my heart if anything happened to the child. What if the baby died? I don't think I can make myself vulnerable like that."

"Vulnerable" is a key word here. You have never been so emotionally vulnerable as you will be as a parent. That vulnerability opens you up to love you've never imagined, and also to comparable pain. How you feel about such intense emotional connection will depend, in part, on your temperament. The more easygoing and flexible you are by nature, the more easily you are likely to ride the emotional roller coaster. A constitution which gets overwrought by emotional turmoil may find parenthood a tougher road. My lover is vastly more clear-headed and efficient in a crisis than I am. Afterward, however, I bounce back fairly quickly, while she may reverberate for days or weeks from the emotional stress. And though she is far more competent than I in arranging practical, everyday logistics, her lower tolerance for the children's noise and arguing often make parenthood more stressful for her.

In evaluating our emotional resources for parenthood we should also imagine having a child who is more difficult than the Gerber baby. We all hope for children who sleep through the night at four weeks, are allergic to nothing, are easily soothed, and have cheerful, flexible temperaments. Unfortunately this is reality for only a few. Child-development specialists recognize that a child's disposition is only partially dependent on the parents' care-giving styles. Much of it is simply innate. Children are who they are, and we must deal with it as it comes, acknowledging that we have only so much influence. The truth is that a child with a temperament very different from yours will be harder to handle, and some children are hard to raise no matter who you are.

Some lesbians are concerned about whether they could feel comfortable raising a boy. The gay men I have spoken with had their preferences, most for boys and some for girls, but didn't express any real anxiety about not getting their preference. Most women preferred girls, and some were afraid that their ability to bond with and love a boy might be affected by their feelings about patriarchy.

Harriet, mother of Jed, said, "I wanted to be prepared if I was going to have a boy. I really always thought that I would have a girl. I knew that if I was to have a boy I'd have to prepare, because of just general feelings about men. It was really just a fear that I wouldn't be as connected with him."

If you feel very strongly that you only want to raise a child of one gender or another, adoption will allow you the opportunity to choose. For most of us, however, the concerns we have about raising boys or girls will dissipate with some self-exploration. It helps to talk over your reservations with someone you trust. Try to articulate your fantasies of what raising a boy or a girl might involve. They may well be based on fears which derive from your experience in your family of origin, and which need not be repeated in the family you create. Once you actually have your child, however, you are going to fall in love regardless of its gender.

Single Parenting

Though parenting is hard for anyone to do, it is certainly tougher for a single parent. For starters, the economics of single parenting are more challenging. You have only one income, and you probably have to pay for child care during your working hours. If you do not live with other adults, you have sole responsibility for all the chores of maintaining a household and earning the money, on top of parenting your child. In addition, unlike a couple, you can't get your needs for adult companionship met just by staying home. You have to work harder to arrange a social life, overcoming babysitting obstacles and your own reluctance to leave your child when you already have too little time together.

The key to single parenting is support. You simply cannot do it in isolation. Even if you have a great deal of money and can afford to hire nurturing, live-in child care, you will need concrete help from friends and family. Children in single-parent families need to have stable relationships with other adults, so that their parent isn't the only one in the world they can depend on. Single parents need people to share the load with them, so that they can keep their good humor and give their best to their children. The larger your support network, the better it will be for both you and your child.

On the plus side, single parenting need not be just a second-best solution to becoming a parent in the absence of a partner. Though Miriam has had several loving relationships, she basically sees herself as a single person, preferring not to live with her lovers. "I wanted to be a parent and share my life with a child, but not necessarily to have to share the work of parenting. It's nice to know that I don't have to negotiate with someone else about my decisions for my child. I like being in charge." If you want to be a single parent and have a reliable circle of people available to help, it can certainly be done.

Decision Making in a Couple

Relationships are guaranteed to change with parenthood, and change is almost always anxiety-provoking. We all worry about whether we have the kind of relationship that will not only survive the pressures of parenthood, but thrive. Will our home life be a happy and nurturing atmosphere for our child? I can't encourage couples enough to talk at length about their expectations and fears. If the communication in your relationship is already excellent, you have the tools to do that talking on your own. Many couples, however, find that seeking counseling before embarking on parenthood is a good way of anticipating feelings and addressing concerns. Spending a few months ahead of time talking, as a couple, with a knowledgeable counselor or therapist may help avoid the need for crisis management later on.

A couple's decision to bring a child into their lives will obviously have to incorporate the feelings of each of them. They may both be stricken with equally intense baby-lust, and picture their roles as parents in mutually compatible ways. More likely, though, there will be some differences between them, simply because they are individuals. Even when both partners feel decidedly positive about wanting children, each will have different reservations and concerns. The greater the number and intensity of those differences, the more talking that has to be done. It is not necessary that you feel the same way about things. It is necessary that you talk about, understand, and accept your differences.

If you and your partner have very divergent visions of family life, emotions may run high. It is often hard to understand why someone feels so differently from you. You may also feel threatened that those differences could stand in the way of your happiness. It may require hard work to listen to each other in a genuinely open and accepting way.

For example, sometimes only one partner feels a strong desire to parent. The other may be reluctant, anxious, or adamantly opposed. For someone who hasn't experienced an intense passion to have a baby, it may be very hard to understand. Judy, a lesbian in a relationship of six years, said, "I feel like Ellen wants a baby more than she cares about me. We've managed to negotiate every other issue in our relationship, but there seems to be no way to compromise on this one. It makes me terribly sad and very angry. If I decide not to raise a child, she'll leave me. If I decide to go ahead and become a parent, I think I'll still be angry. I would feel that the baby was more important to her than I am."

The fact is that two partners may love each other very deeply and yet be diametrically opposed on this issue. However they resolve it, there will be some pain involved. If you are thinking of suppressing your needs for a child for the sake of the relationship, you will have grieving to do. Sadness and anger may recur over time. Both partners will have to be patient and sensitive to those feelings when they arise. Similarly, if you decide to go along with parenthood primarily out of wanting to preserve your relationship, with no real positive interest in parenting of your own, both of you should be prepared for a difficult time. And if you should decide that you cannot come together on the question of parenting and must end the relationship, it doesn't mean that your love wasn't strong enough. It means that two mature people who genuinely love each other made a realistic assessment of their needs and arrived at a difficult decision.

Often, though, the differences between members of a couple are not so extreme as all or nothing. Though one partner may have serious reservations, there is a margin for working out a solution. Many times when couples are able to come to terms with their differences and acknowledge the depth of each other's concerns, they can begin to see a solution.

Dana and Wendy, who worked together on their finances, also worked hard on their different feelings about becoming parents. In Dana's words, "I was the one who wanted children. For Wendy, having children and being a lesbian were mutually exclusive. Though she liked children, and taught swim classes to kids at the Y, she could never picture herself as a parent. Wendy sort of enjoyed fantasizing with me about it from time to time but would say 'I just can't make that decision.'"

So Dana initially made the mistake of trying to convince Wendy to want a child. "Just the little one-liner things. When kids were around I'd say, 'Oh, wouldn't it be nice? Wouldn't you like to do this?' I would also try more in-depth conversations, like 'Maybe when you were twelve being a mom and being a lesbian didn't go together in your mind, but you're different now and things are different and you can have whatever you want.' Wendy never said no. She just said it would take her a long time to think about it. She said she just didn't know if she could make that kind of commitment. She was afraid of the degree of dependency that a kid has."

After attending a conference on lesbian parenting, Dana had a revelation. "Something dawned on me: that I needed to come to terms with the question 'If I have the choice of never having a child at all or being a single mom, what do I choose?' I thought about that a lot, and felt if I had to, I would choose to be a single mom. Realizing that made me stop pressuring Wendy. It made me stop feeling that I was waiting for her. Until that time I was spending a lot of energy trying to convince her that it was a good idea. I was so focused on her feelings that I wasn't able to focus on my own."

Dana came to see that her pushing the issue was forcing a polarization of their two positions. She backed off, giving Wendy more time and space. Instead of trying to change Wendy's feelings, she was able to finally hear and understand Wendy's concerns. At the same time, Wendy realized that having a child was something Dana simply had to do.

Dana concludes, "As we got closer we realized we would have to respect each other's dreams. It didn't seem impossible for both of us to have all of our dreams and still be together."

Sima and Millie were even farther apart on the subject of parenting when they started discussing it. As the oldest of four children, Millie had experienced the responsibility and deprivation that come with the arrival of babies, and it wasn't the way she wanted to live her life. Being an artist requires that she put in many additional hours just to earn a living, and to her, "It seemed like, Oh, God, one more thing to add to my list: Now I have to be a parent."

For Sima, there was no question that she had to have children in her life. "It was really clear that I was the person who wanted to become a parent and that Millie was not interested in being a mom. It went so far that we weren't sure that we would stay together. It was very painful for us to look at each other and say we wanted two different things. I wanted so much for us to stay together, and at the same exact time I wanted so much to be a mother, and it was a very terrifying experience to face the possibility of us having to break up."

When Sima was able to acknowledge Millie's feelings, however, the conflict loosened. Millie wasn't forced to defend her position all the time, and started to think of alternative ways of making the situation work. She came to understand that Sima's need to have a baby was the equivalent of her need to paint. They decided to go ahead, with the understanding that they would not share equally in the work of parenting. The baby would be Sima's "project," and painting would be Millie's. It is a solution which requires continual talking and negotiating to make it work, but their respect for each other and for their differences makes it possible.

Being Out

The more open we can be about being gay or lesbian parents, the easier a time we will have. Every arena in which we feel we have to watch what we say is a source of stress. Denying or omitting who we are may feel demeaning, and we may worry about the messages it sends our children. On the other hand, there is stress involved in coming out all the time, especially to people who are strangers or only casual acquaintances. When we have to interact with the heterosexual world, our personal needs for privacy may conflict with our needs to affirm our pride in our families (see Chapter Twelve: Out in the World). Roz and Jane, who live in a small southern town, said, "We've been as open as we could be here, but it hasn't felt good. We're planning to move to a city where we can really be ourselves, so our son can feel comfortable about having two moms."

It is worthwhile assessing how much support you have for being open. The social and political climate of your neighborhood, the availability of open-minded schools, your proximity to a community of gay and lesbian parents, your openness about your sexuality at work, and the degree of acceptance from your family of origin will all have substantial impact on you and your children.

Supporting Our Cultural Identities

If, in addition to planning on becoming lesbian or gay parents, we are also members of other minority cultures, we need to assess the opportunities for providing ourselves with a sense of community. If we are in an interracial couple or are planning to adopt a child of a different race from us, we need support from people who share our family's racial and cultural identities as well as from other lesbian and gay parents. It may be hard to get all of our support in one place. There is still racism in the gay and lesbian communities, just as there is still homophobia in communities of people of color. We may have fewer places where it all comes together, but the more people we have in our neighborhoods, our families, and our friends who can affirm and validate our identities, the easier life will be for us and our children (see Chapter Twelve: Out in the World).

Dealing with Negative
Reactions to Our Plans

The issue of gay men and lesbians becoming parents evokes strong feelings in people, and we may not get the support we need from everyone. If we have to deal with other people's anxieties, shame, homophobia, anger, or envy, those negative responses may get in the way of our clearly evaluating our own concerns. We may get caught up in having to defend ourselves against criticism, at the expense of staying in touch with our own feelings. Or we may find ourselves discouraged by the negative predictions of a friend or family member and succumb to self-doubts, which again interfere with our decision-making process. The place to consider our decisions is in a supportive atmosphere. When people are negative, we have to evaluate whether their criticisms are destructive to us. If so, we may need to limit our discussion with them until we feel more secure about our own choices. In considering the questions they raise, it is important that we don't adopt a negative attitude toward ourselves.

Even if we feel secure about what we want to do, we may feel frightened about doing it in the presence of family or friends who seem to be disapproving. It may be particularly difficult when the negative responses we get are from other gay people. It is not at all uncommon, though, for lesbians or gay men to have misgivings about gay parenthood. Some gay men or lesbians who are closeted may feel threatened by the fact that parenthood makes us so visibly "out." If they carry around a lot of internalized homophobia, they may not be able to envision a healthy, happy lesbian or gay family. If they have buried their own desires to parent, they may resent your opportunity to have something they may have wanted themselves. If they simply don't like children, they may feel that your having children will ruin their friendship with you.

When Sally was considering becoming a single lesbian parent in a small midwestern town, she encountered some opposition from a lesbian separatist. Sally remembers, "She gave me a really hard time. She was very critical of my wanting to become pregnant. She said, 'Do you realize what is going to happen if you have a male child? and what control do you think you have over that? If you decide to go to bed with a man do you realize what the lesbian community is going to do to you? You will not have straight friends and you will not have lesbian friends.

The child will be a total outcast.' I got a lot of discouragement, and I had some really hard feelings about it. I began to wonder, God, can this be true?"

Sharon recalls telling one lesbian friend that she and Kathy were planning to have children. She recounts, "She was not supportive. She didn't think it was fair. She didn't think it would be easy. She didn't think we'd be able to do it. She was very deflating about it, and to this day she has distanced herself. I think she really thinks it's the wrong thing. I think it was threatening to her because she's been in a lesbian relationship for six years and they have never told a soul. They're completely closeted, and they could never have children."

Getting this kind of response from other lesbians or gay men may make us frightened that we could lose our community if we become parents, and the truth is that the makeup of our friendship circle will change somewhat with parenthood. People who are not at ease with our parenthood may fade out of our lives. However, there are many lesbians and gay men who, though they may not want to be parents themselves, are delighted to see children come into our community and enjoy being part of our families.

Even in her isolated town, and despite one woman's disparaging remarks, Sally realized that she could find what she needed. "I did a little bit of research, just asking questions of lesbian women. I found that there were quite a few out there who enjoyed children."

Of the people who criticize us for wanting to become parents, there may be some people whose approval means a lot to us. Sometimes it is our parents or our siblings who have the harshest words to say. In addition to our hurt at not being supported, and the anxiety about our children-to-be that may get touched off by their comments, we also may have concerns that we will lose the love of our families if we go ahead with parenthood.

Sally remembers, "I also got pressure from my mother. She gave me a hard time, saying, 'What do you think it's going to do to a child to bring it up this way?' She was basically telling me that it would be unfair to a child, that the child would go through a lot of ridicule, that it would be emotionally unsettling, that it would be setting the child up to become emotionally unstable. She said I would just be giving a child too much to overcome: 'Kids have enough trouble just worrying about being kids. Why do you want to throw in having a lesbian mom? The other kids aren't going to want to play with them. The other parents aren't going to let their kids play with them. They will assume that the child is also gay or lesbian, and it's not the right thing to do. If you want to go through this with your life, that's one thing, but how can you go and put somebody else through it, too, and somebody who doesn't have a choice?'"

Sima said, "My mother had her fingers crossed that I wouldn't get pregnant. My parents have never really been able to welcome me as a lesbian, or to welcome me and Millie into their home as a couple. So, on top of that, I'm telling them that I'm getting pregnant. I mean, they almost had a heart attack. My mother, who feels that being gay is sick, felt 'How could you do that to a child, to be a gay parent?' It was clear to me that I wanted to do it and that wasn't going to stop me, but it was very painful because I knew there was a chance I would lose my family."

In reality, it is a rare family that actually cuts off contact with a child. Of course, we all know terrible stories of some families who react very badly when their daughters and sons come out to them. With some exceptions, though, even those very negative families eventually go through a process of adjustment which leads to reconciliation. When there is a grandchild in the picture, it appears that the adjustment process is facilitated. It may take time for our parents to get used to the idea of our being parents. It may take time for them to get over their shame about what to tell the neighbors. It may take time for them to resolve issues of racism if we are an interracial couple or if we adopt a child of a different race. But it rarely takes much time for them to fall in love with the new grandchild. That love, accompanied by our sympathetic but firm response to their reservations, will support our families of origin enough so that, within their limitations, they will grow into the situation. (See Chapter Eleven: Our Families of Origin.)

Deciding to Live Child-Free

It should be noted, lest we forget, that for a long time lesbians and gay men have found creative, satisfying, and productive ways to arrange their lives that do not include parenthood. The fact of lesbians and gays not raising children contributes to our being able to do extensive political and community work, to devote ourselves to our careers, to develop and explore personal interests and creative talents, to nurture our relationships, and to have time and energy to volunteer to help others in our families and in our society. We should not allow the baby boom to lead us to believe that raising children is the only way to go.

Women, in particular, have been oppressed by the belief that their worth and femininity depend on their fulfilling the duties of motherhood. I would hate to see the wonderful options opened to us by the gay and lesbian family boom turn into one more source of oppression for lesbians. That is, it would be sad to think that a lesbian who does not want children might now have to feel defensive about that preference because all around her lesbians are choosing motherhood.

What the baby boom can help us to do, however, is eliminate homophobia as the reason for choosing child-free living. The fact of hundreds of thousands of lesbians and gay men being open and visible proves that it can be done, and that it can be done comfortably. We may have many good reasons for not wanting to become parents, but homophobia shouldn't have to be one of them. When parenthood is completely accessible to lesbians and gay men, we become able to make true choices about what we want for our lives. The choice not to parent can and should be based on the same factors as the choice to parent, namely, whether it suits your needs, wants, and circumstances.

If your choice to live child-free comes as a result of weighing powerful ambivalence, there will be some grieving to do. Even though you may feel resolved and satisfied that you decided not to parent for lots of good reasons, both practical and emotional, you still have to contend with the part of you that wanted a child. Like any grieving, it is a process which will take time. No matter how happy you are with your decision, be prepared to comfort yourself for the sadness of giving up whatever parenthood would have meant to you. The sadness will fade eventually, as your life becomes more richly committed to the path you've chosen.

The critical factor here is choice. The more you feel you have truly been in charge of a decision-making process, the more you will feel that the life you are living is the right one for you. Psychologist Ronnie Lesser studied fifteen lesbians who chose not to become parents.[7] She found that those women who felt that the choice not to parent was in their hands were also most resolved about their decision. Their grieving could go on without bitterness or regrets, leaving only the healthy experience of sadness about a loss. They had an easier time than those women who attributed their decision to something external, like finances or being single. The feeling of being in charge of one's choices allows us to get on with what we need to do.

Finally, loving children and enjoying having them in your life does not necessarily mean having to parent them. There are many ways to form special bonds with children and have lifelong relationships with them which don't involve having to change diapers or making sure they've brushed their teeth. Especially now, when the gay and lesbian community is bursting with children, there are countless opportunities to connect with them.

As lesbians and gay men, we have always defined family in our own ways. We have formed families of friends to offer us social networks, companionship, and help in hard times. Many of the families I speak with say their main supports are other gays and lesbians who do not have children of their own. You can become the friends, honorary aunts and uncles, godparents, role models, and mentors to your friends' children. Lesbian and gay communities are in a position to combat the isolation of the nuclear family structure and to create extended family networks that include children. For lots of gay men and lesbians who like children but don't want the role of parents, forming relationships with the children of other gay men and lesbians is a way of affirming and supporting all of us.

2

LESBIANS CHOOSING PREGNANCY

When I told my mother that I wanted to have a baby, she replied in horror, "But do you realize that you'll have to be pregnant for *nine months?*" My mother is a biologist, with unsentimental notions about the gestation of humans and the attendant miseries of morning sickness and swollen ankles. By contrast, I am enchanted with the magic of a new soul forming in my belly. There are clearly very different strokes for different women. For some of us pregnancy is a means to an end; for others it is a spiritual experience. Whichever way you view it, pregnancy is a pretty intense time.

For many women the desire to bear a child seems to come from an inner place of primal intensity. There may be something about the idea of pregnancy, the wonder of it, that draws us to it powerfully. Rebecca, who is planning to begin inseminations soon, said, "It's not explainable, really. But when I have thought of why, I come to the basic fact that I believe conception and birth are the most incredible God-given miracles on earth. I regret nothing in my life thus far, but would definitely regret not having at least tried to conceive and start a family this way."

There is no question that if pregnancy is what you want, deep in your bones, nothing else will quite substitute. You may want so much to conceive and carry a child that you would have serious mourning to

do if you were unable to get pregnant. There are many women, however—and my mother is probably among them—who find the prospect
of carrying and delivering a child to be decidedly unappealing. It may
feel frightening, burdensome, or downright loathsome. It may be an
unwanted impediment to athletic training or other physical pursuits.
The alterations in body shape during pregnancy may be disturbing. Or
pregnancy may simply be inconsistent with one's self-image.

As women, we have been socialized in a society that idealizes
pregnancy as a state of holiness. The other, unspoken side of the coin is
degradation, as witnessed by the practical realities of the poverty and
lack of concern for women and children in our society. Adrienne Rich,
in her classic book *Of Woman Born*, articulates these complexities and
their profound political implications: "The woman's body, with its
potential for gestating, bringing forth and nourishing new life, has been
through the ages a field of contradictions: a space invested with power,
and an acute vulnerability; a numinous figure and the incarnation of
evil." The idea of pregnancy touches our most primitive associations.
We have been led to believe that a "real woman" is one who glows as
she stands there peacefully swollen with child. Psychoanalysis has been
a major culprit in promoting the idea that maturity and mental health
for women involves the acceptance of their "natural" desires to bear
children. Because of that, women who don't want to experience pregnancy sometimes feel they have to defend a desire to avoid that state of
beatific bliss. The truth, however, is that while your leanings in this
respect may have had many cultural and emotional influences, and may
reflect complicated and highly individual personal feelings, there is no
particular virtue in either wanting or not wanting to be pregnant. It has
nothing at all to do with your maturity or your emotional health. It
certainly has nothing whatsoever to do with how much you may want
to parent or how good you will be at parenting. Like our sexual orientation, it is nothing more and nothing less than a preference. It is just
what we feel.

Some women have told me that they chose to become pregnant
primarily because they felt it was simpler than adoption. Lena said,
"Aside from the emotional reasons, we felt it was easier. People would
ask fewer questions. There would be less expense. We felt we'd be more
likely to have a healthy child. We'd have fewer problems later."

There may be other advantages to having a biological child. Some
extended families care very much about biological ties, and a lesbian or
gay parent who is concerned about family reaction may feel that a child
genetically related to the family will have an easier time. As Georgia

said, "We were afraid my family would have a hard enough time with the idea of a child raised by lesbian parents. If it had the family resemblance, they might get used to it faster." This might be important to you if your extended family is not comfortable with the idea of adoption in general. However, this is your child and you are creating your own family. Your extended family will ultimately respond to the ties of love between you and your child, with or without biological connections, so you should do it your way.

For some women it matters very little whether the child is related to them genetically, and there is no question that a child we adopt is just as much adored as one we carry in our bellies. But parenthood is a matter of very personal feelings. Rhea, a prospective parent, has strong feelings about the genetic connection to a child. She said, "I want to see a part of me in the child. I want a biological tie with the child. I would like the child to have similar looks and my family's characteristics."

Many women feel that being biological mothers gives them legal protection from the risk that an adopted child could be taken from them. There is a certain reality to this. In all adoptions there is some risk until the actual finalization, and as lesbians and gay men we feel especially vulnerable. Making babies can be done without involving the courts in our families.

Biological parenthood is not without its own risks, though. Instead of fear of not being approved by the courts, or of a birth mother changing her mind about an adoption, we have fears of infertility, miscarriage, prematurity, and birth defects. You may find yourself unable to conceive, perhaps after many frustrating and expensive years of trying. If you are able to conceive, you have no guarantee that all will go well, and there is always the potential for heartbreak. So becoming a parent is going to involve some anxiety, no matter how you arrive at it. We choose the risks that we feel we can live with, and the route that seems to suit our needs and personalities.

In general, I think, lesbians who don't want to experience pregnancy have an easier time acknowledging it than heterosexual women have. We are already used to defining ourselves differently from the roles society has in mind for women. Perhaps this makes us less vulnerable to feeling that we "should" want to be pregnant. Meanwhile, lesbians who want to get pregnant now have access to support, information, and semen from a wide variety of sources. Getting pregnant as a lesbian has never been easier.

Heterosexual Sex

Some lesbians choose to get pregnant by having sexual intercourse with men. As Livia put it, "I'm kind of earthy, and having sex with a man to create my baby had a spiritual meaning to me." For some lesbians, having heterosexual relations feels like the most natural way to make a baby, while for many others, nothing could be more unnatural. If, in order to conceive, you are planning to have sex with someone you know and trust, you must plan at least six months in advance. He should be tested twice, for HIV and other sexually transmitted diseases, with a six-month interval between tests, because it may take several months for HIV infection in the body to yield a positive test result. You must be sure that between the first time he is tested and the time you have intercourse, he has not engaged in any activity which could involve risk of acquiring a sexually transmitted disease. You should also inquire carefully about his genetic background, general health, and substance use (see below on screening a donor). If you wish, you can also arrange for his semen to be analyzed to insure that he is fertile. UNDER NO CIRCUMSTANCES SHOULD YOU EVER HAVE UNPROTECTED SEX IN ORDER TO CREATE A BABY WITH A MAN WHOSE HEALTH YOU HAVE NOT VERIFIED. The risks of sexually transmitted diseases, including AIDS, are very serious. Both your future child's life and your own could be at stake. What this means is that you cannot have anonymity from the biological father if you are planning to get pregnant through heterosexual relations. You must know the man with whom you are having sex. And he must know why you are doing this, so that he can fully cooperate in evaluating his health status.

In addition, there are legal ramifications of sexual intercourse in many states. Creating a baby this way probably insures that the man will be considered by the courts to be the father of your child, not merely a sperm donor. If he ever pressed the issue, he would probably be granted full paternity. You should consider making a baby through sexual intercourse only if your intention is to grant him full parental rights to your child. In that case, you and he should come to some agreement—carefully thought out, discussed, and written down—about what his role will be with respect to the child, should you become pregnant. The question of his future role is complicated, and has many legal implications (see Chapter Six: The Legal Issues).

Alternative Insemination

Most lesbians planning a pregnancy choose to conceive via alternative insemination. The medical mystery that once surrounded this process has fallen away. By now we are all pretty much aware that the task of putting semen into the vagina requires amazingly little knowledge or equipment. It is simple enough that you can do it yourself at home, or have a nurse or physician do it in a doctor's office. Alternative insemination seems to be about as effective as intercourse in achieving pregnancy, and does not increase the likelihood of miscarriage or birth defects.

There are just a few facts to grasp. The vessel that holds the semen should be clean, and should be made of glass or plastic (metal is not good for sperm). It is preferable to use something which will squirt, like a syringe with no needle, or the legendary turkey baster, but you can also pour the semen from a test tube or similar vessel, if you wish. A speculum is useful to hold the vaginal walls open during insertion. The semen is usually placed just outside the cervix, in the cervical mucus. If you are using fresh semen (page 51), it should be kept at approximately body temperature until use, and used within one to two hours of collection. With frozen semen, you should carefully follow the sperm bank's directions for thawing. Sometimes women are advised to lie quietly for a while with their hips up after the insemination, but there is so far no empirical evidence that this increases your chances of conception. That's basically all there is to it. While there is some specialized equipment available (syringes designed specifically for insemination, cups that will hold the semen against the cervix, and sponges designed to help retain the semen within the vagina), these items are not essential, and it is not known whether they actually increase the effectiveness of the insemination. They are readily available and can be mail-ordered from Milex Products, Inc., 5915 Northwest Highway, Chicago, IL 60631; Tel. (312) 631-6484.

Despite the simplicity of the procedure, there are numerous reasons for deciding to have alternative insemination carried out by a physician. For one thing, many state laws are such that if you do not intend the donor to be a participating father with full rights, you must carry out the insemination as a medical procedure in a doctor's office (see Chapter Six: The Legal Issues). Therefore, whether or not the donor is someone known to you, you may want to have the insemination done on a physician's premises. For another thing, you may want to employ the services of a physician to obtain donor semen for you. If you want anonymity and the protection of frozen sperm screened by a sperm bank facility, you will probably have to go through a physician. Finally, even if you are choosing a donor who is known to you, you may want the medical safety of having the sperm frozen and quarantined through the medical facility's procedures while the donor is tested and retested for HIV.

The drawbacks of going through physicians are the costs and the necessity of finding physicians who are genuinely supportive of women's reproductive freedoms. A 1987 government survey reported that there were approximately 11,000 physicians in the country doing alternative insemination. Of those, about half were willing to inseminate single women, and 37 percent were willing to inseminate lesbians.[1] That would mean that there are more than 4,000 physicians out there who are agreeable to doing alternative inseminations on lesbians, but you have to find them. In the process, you may get a few doors slammed in your face. Even those who are willing to help may not provide the atmosphere of warm acceptance you want for your baby's beginnings. Some physicians feel entitled to administer a battery of psychological tests to assess a woman's fitness for parenthood. Sometimes only single women are evaluated for suitability this way. Not only can this be degrading and discriminatory, you will be billed for it. On the other hand, many physicians will respect a woman's right to self-determination. There are enough doctors out there that you don't have to put up with unsupportive treatment. See the Resources section at the end of the book for lesbian and gay parenting groups and other organizations that can help you find a physician in your area.

The same 1987 survey estimated that the average cost per pregnancy through alternative insemination was about $1,000.[2] That figure is likely to be low, since it includes inseminations performed on married women using the husband's sperm, which eliminates a major expense. Donor semen samples cost as much as $75 to $150 each. The cost of shipping frozen semen is additional. There are also likely to be initial screening fees to cover consultation and medical evaluations. Depending on what's involved, these initial fees can range from less than $100 to well over $1,000, with the latter including costs of the education and counseling that some programs provide. In addition, the physician may charge for a regular office visit, from $50 to $100 or more each time you go for an insemination. There may be extra fees for lab tests. If it takes you a long while to conceive, you could end up spending several thousand dollars. Physicians report that about half of existing insurance policies cover some portion of these expenses.[3] However, expenses which are unequivocably for the purpose of achieving conception, such as the cost of semen samples, are rarely covered.

Determining Fertile Times

If you are attempting to get pregnant, you will save a lot of effort by restricting your attempts to the two or three most fertile days of your cycle. To do this you have to become aware of when you ovulate. The average cycle of twenty-eight days, with ovulation occurring on day fourteen (the first day of the menstrual period is counted as day one) is just that—an average. It varies for different women, and it may change from month to month for any one woman. It is therefore useful to spend several months observing the changes in your cycle to get an idea of when you are fertile.

One good indicator of ovulation is the quality of the mucus discharge in the vagina. At the time of ovulation, the cervical mucus becomes clear, stretchy, and runny, and in most women plentiful enough to notice when going to the bathroom. This quality of mucus is the most favorable environment for sperm. The last day of this wet mucus is considered the most fertile time. After ovulation the mucus becomes thick, tacky, opaque, and generally hostile to sperm. Some perfectly healthy, normal women don't have sufficient cervical mucus to make these observations, however, and they may have to rely on another method.

Another way to assess fertility is by using a basal body thermometer (available at your drug store, this is not the same as a fever thermometer) and keeping temperature charts. Take your temperature every morning before moving around or getting out of bed. Though there will be daily dips and rises as a matter of course, in general the body's temperature is low (below 98 degrees) before ovulation. There is commonly a slight dip just before the egg is released, followed by a rise to above 98 degrees. The temperature then stays high until the menstrual period, when it drops. If there is a pregnancy, it stays high.

There are also ovulation predictor kits which can be purchased at your drug store. You use them at home to test your urine to determine fertile times. Their drawback is that they tend to be expensive.

It is generally considered advisable to inseminate two or three times a month, once about forty-eight hours before ovulation is expected, again on the day of ovulation, and once more a day or two later.

Fresh or Frozen?

If you choose your own donor and get inseminated without the protection of a medical setting, you will be using fresh semen. In doing so, you are taking the same health risks you would if you were having unprotected heterosexual intercourse. You must be comfortable with your knowledge of your donor's HIV status, sexual practices, and general medical health, and you must trust that he has not had exposure to any sexually transmitted organism since he was last tested. If you can be sure of your safety, you have the advantage that fresh semen seems to be somewhat more effective in achieving pregnancy than frozen semen.

The primary benefit of having semen samples frozen by a sperm bank (you cannot freeze them yourself) is that they can be quarantined. That means that the donor can be tested for HIV when the semen is first collected, and then tested again six months later. This protects you against the possibility that HIV exposure occurred before the sample was collected but had not yet had time to register on the tests. If the donor is still free of disease or HIV antibodies six months after the sample was frozen, you can feel pretty confident about its safety.

Since February 1988 the American Fertility Society, the Centers for Disease Control, and the Food and Drug Administration have all recommended that physicians performing donor insemination use only frozen semen; if you are using a donor obtained through a physician, you are probably better off using frozen semen. The physician has no way of knowing if the people who are donating fresh semen for his or her practice are in fact avoiding all high-risk behavior. In fact, in some states it is now illegal for physicians to use fresh semen.

Another advantage of frozen semen is that it is always available when you need it. There is no need to make sure that the donor you have chosen, or who has been chosen for you, is in town and available when you become fertile each month. You may want your second child to be conceived via the same donor's sperm, and with frozen samples you do not need to worry about whether your donor is still willing to participate two or three years later.

Still another advantage of frozen semen is that the recipient has the option of using sperm bank facilities anywhere in the country. Frozen semen can be flown in, packed in dry ice or liquid nitrogen. Liquid nitrogen will keep about a week, but you will have to pay a rental fee or deposit on the special tank it comes in. Dry ice will last about forty-eight hours, and can be replaced to extend the life of the sample over your fertile days. Sperm banks which give the sperm directly to you will provide you with information on how to preserve, thaw, and use the frozen specimens. If you are not concerned about the possible legal advantages of having a physician conduct the insemination, there is no particular medical reason why a physician has to receive the sperm first. (One lesbian was told by a righteous medical assistant that women couldn't defrost frozen sperm themselves, because it had to be defrosted in the hand of the doctor!)

On the down side, freezing seems to cut down by about one-third on the effectiveness of the sperm.[4] That is, it is likely to take you approximately 30 percent more inseminations to become pregnant with frozen sperm than with fresh sperm.

Boy or Girl?

Alternative insemination (AI) increases your chances of having a boy. The statistics suggest that about two-thirds of the children conceived through AI will be boys.[5] It is apparently possible to improve your chances of having a girl through careful timing of the insemination. The theory is that the male-producing (Y-chromosome) sperm, while they are faster swimmers, are more fragile. They do not fare well for long in the acidic environment of the vagina. When insemination occurs right at the time of ovulation and the sperm are placed directly at the opening of the cervix, the male sperm are likely to get to the egg first. The female-producing (X-chromosome) sperm are slower but hardier. If insemination is done a day or more before ovulation occurs, the female-producing sperm will be more likely to survive and be present when the egg is available. Placing the sperm farther away from the uterus may also help, as a longer swim favors the more resilient X-chromosome sperm. Additionally, a mild vinegar douche (one or two tablespoons in a quart of water) will increase vaginal acidity and may favor conception of girls, though tampering too much with the vaginal environment could reduce your chances of getting pregnant. There are also laboratory techniques which attempt to separate the male-producing sperm from the female-producing sperm to achieve a greater certainty. These techniques are expensive and imperfect, however, and may result in lowered effectiveness of the sperm. The reality is that no method guarantees the gender of your offspring. If raising a child of one gender or another is extremely important to you, adopting a child is the only way to be sure. Most of the lesbians I know who want to get pregnant have been primarily concerned with doing it as quickly and safely as possible, and are less concerned with wanting to control the sex of the baby.

The Donor's Health

If you choose a donor known to you, it will be your job to gather information about his medical history and family background. If your donor is being selected through a sperm bank or medical facility, it will do the screening for you. However, sperm banks differ with respect to how much information they collect about a donor, and how much they will make available to you. You can inquire about their screening procedures. A medical history is important in case the child develops health problems. Other information about the donor's personality and family background may be desirable as part of your child's heritage.

Information should be obtained from the donor about his age, race, ethnicity, religion, education, occupation and work history, and physical characteristics such as height, weight, hair color and texture, complexion, and bone structure. You, or the sperm bank, should find out whether his sperm has ever created any offspring and, if so, how many. The purpose is both to assess his fertility and to insure that he has not contributed to the creation of so many children that the offspring are likely to meet and marry. In addition, his sperm can be analyzed directly for fertility.

It might be advisable to ask about his diet and exercise habits. You may also want to know about his eyesight without corrective lenses, his dental history, and a list of things to which he is allergic.

A thorough inquiry into the donor's exposure to environmental agents such as toxic sprays, asbestos, lead products, Agent Orange, radiation, and pesticides is important. In addition, detailed information on the frequency of use of all recreational drugs, alcohol, and prescription and nonprescription medications should be obtained. It is also advisable to find out the donor's history of sexually transmitted diseases, including herpes, hepatitis B and C, syphilis, gonorrhea, CMV, HIV, chlamydia, and any others.

The donor should be asked about the incidence of a wide variety of diseases and birth defects in his own and his family's history. Appendix III reproduces the list of medical problems that one sperm bank uses to assess donor health. If you obtain the health history yourself and are unsure about whether the occurrence of something in the donor's history represents a significant risk for your offspring, consult your physician.

Finding Donors Through Physicians and Sperm Banks

While many physicians will choose a donor for you, based on your physical characteristics—race, height, coloring, etc.—some sperm banks offer a catalog of donor profiles which allow you to choose your own donor. The profiles may include information on a donor's hobbies, talents, and interests. Some even provide a personal statement by the donor, in his own handwriting, though his name and address are withheld.

In general, the majority of physicians performing AI tend to be opposed to the idea of donor offspring having rights to communicate with their genetic fathers when they are adults.[6] About half the physicians who do inseminations keep records that would make identification possible, but most say they would not release those records to anyone, under any circumstances, including by judicial request.[7]

Some facilities, however, are offering a wider range of options for mothers, children, and donors alike. One of the few that does is the Sperm Bank of California (see the Organizations list in the Resources section), which has a feminist orientation and is responsive to the needs of lesbians. (The program also ships frozen semen anywhere in the country.) When donors are screened for their program, they are asked if they are willing to be contacted by any offspring that result from the insemination once the child is eighteen. (While the child is still a minor, the donor is anonymous.) Those who agree to the release of their identifying information to the grown child are called "Yes" donors. Women are given a list of donor profiles to choose from, and can decide whether or not they want a "Yes" donor. This is a very important consideration. With this option, a mother can have the legal safety and family privacy of an anonymous donor arrangement throughout the childhood of her offspring, while still providing her child with the opportunity to meet his or her biological father later. The child may decide not to pursue contact, but at least he or she has the option.

In selecting a physician or sperm bank to work with, it is a good idea to do as much research as you can. Join a group of lesbian mothers and find out how they've gone about it in your area. Benefit from the information they have already gathered. As a group, lesbian mothers are quite generous about sharing their resources with others in the community. Contact the women's health centers and gynecologists in your area, and find out if they do inseminations for single women and lesbians. Ask them what their fees are, and what is included. Find out what screening procedures are used for donors. Find out what kind of help you can get if a fertility problem arises. Make sure that they are comfortable with lesbians, or at least with single women. See what restrictions they place on providing samples. Can you arrange to have samples sent to you directly? Will they send samples only to a physician? If so, will the physician allow you to pick up the specimen and inseminate at home, or must you have it done at the medical facility? How much notice do they need? Are they available on weekends, when you might be fertile? Do they offer any educational program or support groups? Find out how much information is available on the donor.

Take charge. Inform yourself and make your own decisions. Don't be afraid to ask clinics and doctors and sperm banks to do things in a way that meets your needs. We no longer need to be timidly grateful to the few brave and maverick physicians willing to help us. In many parts of the country, insemination has become quite a business, and as an informed consumer you are in a position to have it your way, within reason.

Choosing Your Own Known Donor

Women who find their own donors generally do so because they do not want an anonymous arrangement. They want to see and know the donor, and may even want the child to have contact with him while growing up. The issues involved are complex and require extensive thought before going ahead. You must be certain that you want all of what a relationship with a known donor might involve (see Chapter Three: Donors and Coparents), and you must feel very good about choosing this particular man as the one.

Most lesbians choosing a known donor ask someone they already know. Many gay men who have tested HIV negative are in demand as potential donors. They get requests from friends, colleagues, and by word of mouth. Women who don't know a good candidate or who don't want to use someone living in their part of the country may advertise in gay papers or in the newsletters of lesbian and gay parenting groups.

Needless to say, you must screen the health of a donor you choose as thoroughly as you would expect a physician to screen an anonymous donor. He must be tested for HIV, ideally at six-month intervals while his sperm is frozen and quarantined in a sperm bank, unless you can feel very sure that he is risk-free.

Finding an Anonymous Donor Through a Go-Between

Though sperm banks and physicians are the best way to find anonymous donors, it is also possible to arrange for anonymity through a go-between or intermediary. A go-between acts as a liaison between the lesbian mother(s) and the donor, and accepts responsibility for maintaining everyone's anonymity if that is what they request. Often the go-between is a lesbian—a friend or acquaintance of the mother-to-be. In the early days of lesbian inseminations, there were very few physicians willing to help us, and the use of go-betweens was the only anonymous route available to many women. In those few areas of the country today where physicians still won't inseminate single women, a go-between may still be necessary. Also, some women who don't want to involve the medical establishment in the creation of their families prefer the more personal atmosphere that a home insemination through a go-between may provide. For some people, however, the primary reason for using a go-between today is financial. Using a go-between can save many hundreds of dollars in physician's fees; however, it adds more risks to the maintenance of anonymity. While a few experienced go-betweens are very professional in their record-keeping and in maintaining everyone's privacy, others are just pitching in to help in an individual situation and don't necessarily have experience in handling potential difficulties.

Jennifer and Mindy's story is an example of what can happen when a go-between is well-meaning but not in control of the process. The go-between they used was a lesbian they did not know; she had heard they wanted to inseminate and volunteered to help. They trusted her to locate a sperm donor and transport the semen to them. They also trusted her to preserve the anonymity of everyone involved. They have a wonderful daughter, Molly, but some parts of the process have not worked out as they had wished.

Jennifer reports, "It's very touchy, actually. [The go-between] didn't realize how careful she needed to be. She didn't understand the ramifications. We set out believing we would know nothing other than what we needed to know in terms of health stuff, and we now know more than we want to."

Jennifer and Mindy found out too many details about the donor and, living in a small community, they put two and two together. They now know who he is. Jennifer explains: "All of a sudden it was evident to us. The go-between was really sloppy with it. I think we could have been clearer with her, too. I mean, we were on the verge of wanting to know more, so we didn't stop her when she said things that were too much. I wish we'd had the clarity and the discipline to stop her from talking as much as she did. I wish we had been clearer that we did not want to know names, we did not want to know details. All we wanted to know was could he do it, would he do it, and the health stuff. We didn't even want to know where he lives."

Jennifer continues, "In one way I'm glad, because she couldn't have picked a better person for a donor, in terms of his way of being in the world, his reasons for doing it, his intelligence, his way of living his life. I just think he's terrific. Everything about him is very appealing to me. I don't know if I would seek him out as a friend, but I like what I know about him. But it's a protection thing I'm concerned about."

In retrospect, Jennifer thinks they would have done things differently. She says, "Probably if we had known her better, we wouldn't have chosen her for a middle person. I think for the middle person you should have an idea of their sensitivity in general, and I think that we kind of blew it there."

Jennifer is concerned now about what will happen. She says, "I am worried about protecting the donor, because we agreed to do this anonymously, and about protecting my daughter. This takes it more out of our control. The original plan, if Molly ever asked who her father is, was to say 'Well, we don't know, but he's a very good person who helped us.' Now we really don't know what to say. You never want to lie to your kid, and we're kind of at a loss now as to what to do. Should we lie? Because we do have a responsibility to him. So we're in a big dilemma."

Jennifer and Mindy are not worried about the donor intruding on their lives. He is older and has finished raising his own family. They feel comfortable that he would not attempt to interfere with them. They do, however, feel conflicted now about having to either keep a secret from their daughter or risk jeopardizing the privacy of the donor.

Jennifer concludes, "The big message that I hope to communicate is that women must be very clear with the middle person about how this could affect people's lives. It could potentially hurt people—the kids, the parents, the donor, the donor's family."

The go-between will be responsible for keeping the secret from both the donor and the recipient for the offspring's entire childhood. If you live in a small community, it can be a difficult task. It may be made harder if either donor or recipient brings any pressure to bear on the intermediary in the ensuing years to disclose the identity of the other party. You, of course, want protection from the donor deciding he wants to be part of your family. An anonymous donor, meanwhile, wants the assurance that you and your child will not intrude on his life or his family. Leaked information could have painful consequences for one party or another. Having a physician or sperm bank maintain the records of the parties involved is likely to afford more protection.

In addition, in many states using a go-between instead of a physician may have legal consequences. For one thing, there are some places where using an intermediary for alternative insemination is illegal. More important, however, is that some states will afford you the legal protection of having the donor designated as a donor only, with no parental rights, only if you comply with their required procedures. Those procedures often specify that an insemination must be carried out under the supervision of a physician. Even if your state does not have such a statute now, it may adopt one later, and you will receive the benefit of that protection if you have gone through a physician. As with anything else about creating our families, however, legal risk is only one factor to be considered, and choice or necessity may lead you to opt for some greater legal uncertainty.

The go-between should be responsible for insuring that the proper medical tests are carried out (screening for HIV and other sexually transmitted diseases) and obtaining a full medical and genetic history. In addition, she must have contracts signed by the donor and the recipient, stating clearly that the recipient is purchasing the donor's sperm, for money, and that it is the intention of both donor and recipient that the donor will have no parental participation in the child's life. Appendix I contains a sample donor-recipient agreement form.

Deciding Who Carries the Baby

Lesbians who are in couples where both women are fertile are in a unique position: When they want to make a baby, they have a choice about which one of them will conceive. Having the option that either or both of them may conceive can be a distinct advantage. It may also create dynamics which are unique to lesbian families. Unless one of the women has no interest in being pregnant, a decision may have to be made about which of them will do it. If both women are eager for the experience, one of them may either have to forgo it (if only one child is planned) or defer it until after her lover has given birth to their first child.

If both women plan to conceive, they will have to decide which of them will go first. They may consider their relative ages (the older one deciding to go first), or the demands of their respective careers, or their respective salaries. Jennifer and Mindy had expected Mindy to bear their first child but had to change plans because of finances. Jennifer explains, "We were really broke. Mindy was working as a carpenter, and she made more money than I did. We had been going along on the assumption that Mindy would get pregnant first, and I hadn't even considered it. Then all of a sudden the light bulb went on that perhaps I could do it. We talked many hours. We did lots of crying. It was painful for her to give up being the first, and it took us a while to get through it, but once the decision was made we were together on it." If both women really want to be pregnant there may be some feelings of jealousy or sadness on the part of the one who has to wait. Anticipating and acknowledging those feelings can keep them from causing problems.

Sometimes the decision about who goes first is made in anticipation of the responses of a woman's parents. Sooner or later, most extended families will accept a grandchild, even one conceived by their daughter's lesbian lover. However, some families will get used to their daughter's lesbian parenthood more easily if they have a biological connection to the first child. As Lena expressed it, "We felt that Betsy's father, for emotional reasons, would find it easier to accept a first child if she gave birth to it."

When one lesbian in a couple chooses to be the nonbiological mother, whether reluctantly or by preference, it is not just the experience of pregnancy which is being forfeited. Becoming a nonbiological mother to your lover's biological child may mean having to tolerate being invisible, as attention is being lavished on your pregnant lover. It may mean being left out of the nursing relationship and the powerful bonding that entails (though nursing is not the only way to bond and is not required for bonding).

Unfortunately it also may mean becoming a nonlegal parent (except in the not-yet-common situation where the state allows a second mother to adopt without the biological mother having to relinquish rights). That is, it may mean being excluded from all the legal rights and privileges of a biological or a legal adoptive parent. There are many things that can be done to create protections for the nonbiological mother in the case of future custody issues, but there are still legal insecurities to contend with. Altogether, the lack of social and legal recognition of one's role as a parent may make for some difficult feelings. Talking them over, repeatedly, with each other and with other people, will help to make them livable (see Chapter Eight: Family Life).

With some hindsight, I can see that in my own relationship with my lover, Susan, the decisions we made were, at least partially, our attempts to avoid the feelings that might arise if either one of us was left out of the first pregnancy. We wanted at least two children, and we each wanted the opportunity to give birth to one of them, so we made the decision that we would get pregnant at the same time. A certain amount of reasonable thought went into it, but it was tempered with more than a dash of madness. In retrospect I can see how defensive we were about both of us getting the status of "real" mother. I think we hoped that giving birth simultaneously would leave no time lag before one of us gained "real" mother status. We also hoped that the children's closeness in age might insure that they felt like siblings, despite the lack of biological relationship. We envisioned it as having twins.

In general, though, I wouldn't recommend this as a solution. If we were doing it today, with the support that exists for lesbian mothers, I doubt very much we would do it the same way. With hindsight I know that we needn't have worried about our children feeling like true siblings, but then the worries one anticipates in life are rarely the problems that come to pass. It's obvious, from our own family and from every lesbian and gay family I've observed, that what makes you feel like a real parent, or what makes kids feel like real siblings, has nothing whatsoever to do with biology.

Conveniently, though, it seems that in most couples only one of the women may want to experience pregnancy. Some nonbiological mothers say that they get the pleasures of expecting a baby without having to gain thirty pounds. Many women who have no desire to be pregnant themselves find that they thoroughly enjoy being a part of their lover's pregnancies. For them, pregnancy and childbirth can have a wonder and a magic once-removed that it would never have firsthand.

Sperm Meets Egg

An almost universal aspect of bearing children in our society is that we will have to deal with medical personnel. Even a home birth with midwives involves some contact with the medical establishment. Dealing with health facilities requires us to make decisions about whether, when, and how to come out to them. If we don't come out to them, we will have to deal with the consequences of invisibility. If we do come out to them, we will have to deal with their reactions to us. At the very least, we have to deal with their attitudes toward women. From what I have seen, the responses lesbians get range from sexist and homophobic to joyfully supportive and feminist, with a lot of variation in between.

Sharon and Kathy each wanted biological parenthood. They decided that Kathy would go first because she is five years older than Sharon. Sharon soon found herself uncomfortable that Kathy seemed to have all the control over the process of getting pregnant. They went into couples therapy to work on it. Sharon explains, "I couldn't get her to make the phone calls and get the ball rolling. When I offered to do it, it was very difficult because I couldn't plan her schedule and make appointments for her, and I couldn't talk about her body. I was feeling very frustrated that Kathy wasn't doing anything to get this show on the road. It finally came out in couples therapy that she was intimidated. She was so unsure of what she would meet when she started contacting professionals, doctors, or what have you. She didn't know what kind of questions would be asked and it was frightening her."

Kathy recalls, "I had heard a couple talk about going to doctors for inseminations and having to fill out psychological evaluations and going through all this screening, and the doctors deciding if you were fit to be a parent. I was so offended by that. I thought it was so invasive that I was procrastinating because I just didn't want to deal with that. When I finally let out that that's what I was afraid of, our therapist said, 'Well, my gynecologist is a lesbian who has a child by artificial insemination. Why don't you go to her?' The next morning I called her and made an appointment, and it was really easy."

Issues like this may not always be resolved so simply, however. Some physicians are more concerned with protecting societal mores than with respecting their patients' decisions. Women without men, whether single or with other women, are suspect. Not only some male physicians but some female professionals as well may have trouble accepting that a lesbian or a single woman can be as good a parent as any other woman. There are some physicians who perform alternative inseminations but nevertheless have anxiety about its unconventionality. They may be insecure about potential court actions or malpractice questions. They may worry about community response if they practice in a region where there is violent opposition to women's reproductive choice. Avoid these physicians if you can. If they are not comfortable with the process, they are not likely to treat you with the respect you deserve. The fertility business is just that—a business. As much as we may feel desperate to become pregnant, it is important to remember that our doctors are not doing us favors. We are hiring them to do a service for us. We have a right to service without sexism or homophobia, and there are plenty of physicians out there to choose from. Talk to other women. Network. Find out who's gone where and what their experiences have been.

Susan and I went looking for a physician to inseminate us in 1980. Our own gynecologist didn't do fertility work at the time, so we started calling ads in the Yellow Pages for infertility specialists. At first I did not say I was a lesbian. I lied and said I was a single woman wanting to have a child. Even so, the staff at many of the places I called were bordering on outrage when they announced that they would not consider helping a single woman to get pregnant.

The infertility clinic we finally found could not have been nicer. They were warm and positive, and indicated that they did this often. The only thing I was asked to sign was a consent form stating that it was entirely my choice to become pregnant as an unmarried woman, and that I would not hold the physician responsible for any consequences of my decision. The doctor eventually came to know that we were a lesbian couple. Perhaps he knew long before we told him. At any rate, he did not seem to have any particular feelings about it one way or another. We will always be grateful to him for his respectful manner and his help.

The donors were part of a pool: an organized fertility service through which a fertility specialist could order semen for his or her patients. The service screened potential donors from among the physicians at a major local hospital, then provided fresh semen to the fertility specialist according to the required specifications. There was little awareness of AIDS in those days (1980), so it was not a concern. I was asked to choose race, height (short, medium, or tall), and complexion (fair, medium, or dark). I was also given the option to choose religious background, and to write in a few preferences for other characteristics. I don't think they were actually considered, though, because I know that the sperm specimens they ordered for me were coded only as ABA, meaning Caucasian, medium height, fair complexion. We could, I suppose, have insisted on the additional characteristics we had requested (like curly hair), but we didn't care that much and just wanted to maximize our chances of a healthy donor being available at the right time. We were far more anxious about whether we could actually get pregnant than whether our children's hair would curl.

The choice of donors, then, was out of our hands. (Today there are some facilities which allow a woman to have more control over the selection of donor characteristics, though most still do not.) It was even out of our doctor's hands. The fertility service running the donor pool was making the choice. Having no more control than that was frightening for me. We simply had to trust that people we didn't know, and whom even our physician didn't know, were in fact being conscientious about their medical histories and good health.

The plan was that I would try to get pregnant first, because we were concerned that my irregular periods would create fertility problems. As soon as we knew it had worked for me, Susan would try.

The mechanics were simple enough. I had to start charting my basal temperature. I was put on Clomid, an oral fertility drug, to regulate my cycles and make it possible to time an insemination. Making a good guess about when ovulation would occur, I was to schedule one insemination for the day or two before, and one or two more in the following few days. If I wasn't pregnant within six months—the time by which most people have achieved pregnancy—we would do some testing to see what the problem was.

I have known a few women trying to conceive who have had the serenity to just let nature take its course. Between inseminations they just go about their lives. The rest of us, however, find it very anxiety-provoking to be utterly dependent upon processes and people beyond our control for something so crucially important to us. I tried visualizing my ovum in a state of receptivity (whatever that might look like). I cheered the sperm onward and upward to their destination. I charted my daily temperature meticulously and obsessively.

The donors never came to the clinic. Two miles away, near the hospital, a jar of semen would be handed to a taxi driver. When the specimen arrived, the nurse would examine it under the microscope to make sure the sperm were still alive and active. The semen was then drawn into a syringe, which either the nurse or the doctor inserted through a speculum. A plastic-covered sponge was put in my vagina to retain the semen, and I was left to lie quietly for a little while. Sometimes Susan came with me, and sometimes not. The actual moment of insertion didn't seem all that important to us as a couple, perhaps because it occurred in such a medical atmosphere. What we did do, though, was make love at home afterward. It allowed us to reclaim a certain privacy and intimacy to the process of starting these new lives.

I got pregnant in the second month of trying. I should have realized my hormones were different when I found myself weeping at the sight of the Thanksgiving Day parade on television. Marching bands had never been so poignant. The test came back positive and we called everyone with the good news.

Susan began trying right away, and she also conceived in the second month of trying. So the beginning of 1981 found us expecting one baby in August and another at the end of September.

In contrast to our experience, many women feel that the insemination itself is a moment of ceremony with a lot of significance. For Sharon and Kathy, going through the mechanics of the insemination together was extremely important. Sharon, who had to postpone her own childbearing, struggled with feeling left out of her lover's process of conception. She tried hard to make sure she was included. She recalls, "It was very important for me to identify a role for myself. I went everywhere with [Kathy], to assert my role and have a place in this pregnancy. The doctor's office was very receptive to me. In fact, the doctor made sure that I pushed the plunger on the syringe. I wouldn't have said, Gee, can I do it? but she turned to me and said, 'This is your job, Sharon.'"

When their son, Jake, was two, Sharon started trying to become pregnant. This time the experience was quite different for them. For one thing, life had changed dramatically; the things that were issues the first time around simply didn't matter. Both Sharon and Kathy now felt like fully participating and titled parents to Jake, so no one felt left out. Their primary concern was no longer how to include the nonbiological mom. Instead, their concerns shifted to how to work the whole process into their busy lives as parents and professionals.

They also did things differently the second time. They purchased the frozen sperm directly from the sperm bank, which they felt gave them more control than having to go through a physician. Sharon explains, "We paid the owner of the sperm bank to store it for us. When I was ready for it, I simply had to call him up and say, 'Defrost one for me.' He was wonderful to us. There was one time he met us at his office at six o'clock in the morning because we had a seven o'clock flight that we had to catch out of town. He even gave us a room where we could just go and do the insemination and then leave."

In addition to their busy schedules, which took some of the romance out of insemination, Sharon and Kathy had anxieties about their supply of semen. They wanted their second child to be conceived using the same donor they had used for Jake, but the donor was no longer available, and there was only a limited quantity of his frozen sperm left. Sharon had not conceived after several months of trying. "We were running out of sperm. I got very scared. I decided it was time to go to a fertility person because if there was anything even slightly wrong we'd better know about it before I used all the sperm. He started me on a regimen where I was only inseminating with one vial a month. I got pregnant when there was only one vial left."

Sima and Millie performed the insemination at home on their own. They used a syringe without a needle which was provided by a friend who is a nurse. Sima recalls, "I went to my gynecologist before I got pregnant. She checked me out and said I was in good health. I said, 'That's great because I'm planning to get pregnant by artificial insemination.' She said, 'Oh, where are you doing that?' I said, 'We're doing it ourselves.' 'You can't do that,' she said. I answered, 'I can't? I thought most people got pregnant by themselves.' She said, 'You can't do artificial insemination by yourself. You have to go someplace.' I said, 'Well, we're going to do it,' and that was the sum total of our medical advice."

They used Millie's brother as the donor for Sima's pregnancy. He lived in another state, which necessitated flying back and forth when the time was ripe. The first month he flew in when Sima's temperature chart indicated ovulation. The three of them—Sima, Hal, and Millie—

met together. They felt more than a little awkward about the whole thing.

Millie remembers, "I was nervous. We were all nervous. So we went out for Chinese food. Then we came home and did it. We worried, 'How is this going to work? What if something goes wrong?'"

Sima continues, "Hal masturbated in the bathroom. It really felt awkward, with him going in there to masturbate. We gave him a little dish or cup or something, and he put his semen in it and gave it to Millie."

Millie goes on: "This was new. I mean, the first time we just didn't know what we were doing. So it was step by step, and every step took some thought. I didn't know how I would feel walking from the bathroom with the little glass into the bedroom to Sima. And then actually inserting it, and Sima keeping her pelvis tilted up. We really hadn't talked with anybody about the 'how to.' We had just heard that you use a turkey baster. But we worried about what if something happens to the semen when it hits the air? Or what if there's no semen? Did enough come out? Did it go up all the way? Did enough semen get in there?"

It didn't work that month, but the next month it did. Sima flew out to where Hal lived, while Millie stayed home because it would have been too expensive for both of them to go. Sima recalls, "When I did the insemination the next month I was directly on target with my ovulation. I felt then that I was pregnant. About a day or two later, I spotted. I thought, 'Well, this is when the egg implants in the wall,' and I thought it was really true. I kept taking my temperature the whole time and thought, 'It just has to stay up.' On the fourteenth day, when I went to the bathroom, I stained. I thought, 'Oh, no, I got my period. I can't believe it. I was so sure I was pregnant.' I must have taken my temperature ten times in that hour. It was still up. For the next two days I took my temperature every hour on the hour and it stayed up. So we knew. Later we took the test, but we already knew. It was so exciting."

Nine Months

How you end up experiencing the state of pregnancy appears to be unrelated to how much you wanted to be pregnant or how easy it was to achieve. Pregnancy seems to have surprises to offer some of us. I have known many women who were on a "hormonal high" for the entire nine months. They had no anxiety. They felt wonderful. They went about their preparations for parenthood secure in the likelihood that all was going to turn out well. This was not my experience. Like many women, I found much to worry about during pregnancy. Though it was an exciting time, I knew I would not fully relax until a healthy baby was in my arms. Many women also find that they experience physical discomforts which may make them cranky and irritable.

Sima was one of those women who are blissfully pregnant. She remembers, "It was wonderful. I was delighted. I loved it. I felt different. I felt special. I was aglow for nine months. I loved that I got to have this opportunity. I felt very lucky."

By contrast, I sat on the edge of my seat for nine months. My expectation had always been that I would adore being pregnant. I expected to be continuously tickled by the combination of having a very private and wonderful secret going on in my body, and at the same time having the public attention that is special to pregnant women. Was I surprised.

For one thing, I was scared. I worried about miscarrying. I worried about the health of the baby. I worried about the unknown, and what could go wrong. Whatever help some women get from their hormones during pregnancy did not come to me. Every little thing became huge. Once in my second trimester I got a nasty pain on the lower right side of my abdomen. There was no doubt in my mind that it was appendicitis. My pregnancy bible said that major surgery during pregnancy would probably kill the fetus, and my fears went out of control. I was already grieving. Over the phone my gynecologist diagnosed the problem correctly as gas, and within a short while I was restored to sanity, albeit feeling a bit foolish. Worries like that came up several times.

Susan was pregnant at the same time, and I worried about her pregnancy as much as mine. When she was supposed to have her amniocentesis, the sonogram revealed that the baby was smaller than it should have been, given the date of conception. The radiologist tried to reassure her by saying she must have just mistaken the date, but we knew better. We were both terrified. Together we *both* wolfed down every nutritious and appetizing thing we could stand to eat, in the hopes of making the baby in *her* belly grow. A few weeks later, our unborn daughter had managed to progress, on her own timetable, to the size she was supposed to be, without benefit of the extra weight I'd gained.

I also found that I did not enjoy all of the public attention. Some of it was lovely, of course. Friends and family offered very welcome encouragement. But enduring the comments of strangers was not much fun. It was intrusive (people I'd never met feeling entitled to put their hands on my belly) and, on occasion, obscene. Even worse, for me, was the experience of having everyone regard me as heterosexual. I was tempted to get a maternity blouse inscribed with the words "How dare you presume I'm heterosexual!" It felt uncomfortable to walk past a lesbian couple and fail to get the ordinary flicker of recognition and kinship I was used to getting. A pregnant woman evokes a constellation of traditional associations for most people, and my nontraditional identity was not being affirmed. This is a feeling I have heard echoed by a number of other women.

When Susan and I walked down the street together, holding hands, with our swollen bellies ahead of us, the stares we got were also more than we were comfortable with. In our largely gay neighborhood, we had often felt at ease holding hands on the street. With both of us pregnant, however, we elicited gaping confusion from gays and straights alike, and the effect was inhibiting. Though we knew intellectually that our unusual condition would evoke reactions from people, the emotional reality was a little more stressful than we had anticipated.

Of course, I did get tremendous pleasure out of the pregnancy as well. It was wonderful to be pregnant at the same time as Susan. When I felt the baby kicking, it was very special to know she could feel exactly the same thing. We did lots of joyful planning and shopping and learning. There was an intense feeling of bonding with each other and with both babies.

Susan and I were fortunate enough to have an obstetrician who supported us as a family, and our general experiences with the medical end of things affirmed our togetherness in this process. Medical professionals, however, are not always sensitive to the needs of our lesbian families during pregnancy and delivery. Sharon and Kathy had one unpleasant experience. Sharon felt a strong need to be recognized and included as the other parent during Kathy's pregnancy. When Kathy went for a sonogram at twenty weeks, they expected to share a special experience. Sharon said, "We had talked about it as the first time we were going to meet our baby. Unfortunately for us, we had built it up to some extent. So we got there, and we were waiting. A lab technician told Kathy she had to come into this room. Kathy said, 'I want Sharon to come with me.' The technician said, 'Well, we'll come and get her.' They went into the room, and a good twenty minutes passed by. I was standing in this closet of a changing area where Kathy had changed her clothes, waiting for someone to come for me. I was getting furious."

Sharon finally just barged in and said she really wanted to be there during the sonogram. "The woman was very hostile to me, as though I had no right to be there. Kathy was trying to let her know that she wanted me to be there, but she was sort of overwhelmed because she'd already been through most of the sonogram and she'd already met *her* baby. It really ruined the whole thing for me because I had missed this opportunity to be with Kathy when she saw the baby for the first time. Kathy later wrote a letter to the hospital about it and realized that because she was in that patient position she had been intimidated by the professionals. That's something that has never happened again. We are both extremely vocal now where we never used to be. We've just realized that people are going to walk on us if we don't speak up for ourselves."

Jennifer and Mindy used a midwife practice, and they ultimately had a very good experience with the medical personnel. The midwives had not worked with a lesbian couple before. Jennifer explains, "They didn't know what to do with us at first. We were so scared. The receptionist and support people were a little bit abrupt at first. I remember Mindy starting to go into the room with me one time and one of the nurses stopping her, and me saying, 'No, no, I want her to come.' I had put her name on the sheet as my partner, but I don't think they got it." By the end of the pregnancy, however, things had changed. "We were kind of the stars of the place. They looked forward to us coming. We kind of pat ourselves on the back about it, that we were gentle but constant about who we were."

The midwives came to respect them as a family. Even more special, there was an incident in which the midwives affirmed them as lesbians. Jennifer was ten days past her due date. She and Mindy went for a checkup with one of the midwives. Jennifer recalls, "I was feeling depressed because I'd had some false labor the day before. The midwife said, 'Well, listen—and she closed the door—'This is what you guys can do. If Jennifer has orgasms it will help bring on labor.' She was wonderful, telling us we should have lots of sex. Ugh, at that point it was the last thing I wanted to do, but she really acknowledged us. It was great."

Mindy, like many nonbiological mothers, found that going through Jennifer's pregnancy was hard for her. There is no established role definition for the nonpregnant woman in an expectant lesbian couple. In Jennifer's words, "Mindy felt like an invisible person throughout this pregnancy. Everyone was always asking me how I was doing. She felt like here she was having a baby and it sure didn't look like it. She felt funny saying to people 'Yeah, well I'm going to have a baby in two months.'" At one point early in Jennifer's pregnancy, Mindy actually found herself blurting out to an acquaintance that she was pregnant, and later had to correct the statement with a lengthy explanation. Other people will not always readily grasp that the nonbiological mother is very much a part of the pregnancy, and there are times when that may feel uncomfortable. Both women may have to work harder to publicly affirm their partnership in this process, to insure that the nonbiological mother is included in the social experience of pregnancy.

Delivery

Most of the women I know have been able to arrange for a birthing situation which supported them as a family. Before you decide on which midwife or obstetrician you will use, find out about the hospital in which they practice. Even if you are planning a home birth, a hospital backup is necessary in case something goes wrong. Hospital policies about labor and delivery differ enormously from one institution to another, and they can greatly influence the kind of experience you have. Obstetrical units in hospitals commonly give tours of their facilities, during which time they answer questions. You are likely to tour with several expectant heterosexual couples, and may want to wait for a private moment to ask the tour director if members of the medical team are likely to be comfortable with your family situation. Most hospitals will allow you to have a woman with you in labor and delivery as your birthing coach. In addition, some hospitals, especially in urban centers, are familiar enough with lesbian families that you won't necessarily have to blaze new trails if you come out to them. It will help a great deal if your midwife or doctor is aware of your relationship and expectations. The labor and delivery staff will take their cues from the doctor or midwife about how to regard your relationship. A supportive midwife may allow the nonbiological mother to catch the baby during delivery, and staff may put the baby in her arms right away. This will only happen if they know you are a couple. In addition, if a Cesarean section is necessary, unrelated birthing coaches are generally excluded from the operating room, whereas your lesbian partner, if she is recognized as the baby's other parent, may be allowed to be present.

In addition to the hospital's response to your lesbian parenthood, you will want to find out their policies about labor and delivery in general. Some old-fashioned hospitals exclude family members from the delivery, leave a woman lying immobile during labor (a position which tends to retard the progress of labor), require that a woman remain hooked up to monitoring machines and IVs even when the labor is normal, forbid food or drink, and generally view delivery as something the physician, and not the woman, accomplishes. By contrast, other hospitals and birthing centers provide a friendly homey-looking room in which to labor, encourage you to bring several coaches and supportive friends, as well as food and music, and opt for minimal medical intervention in the birthing process.

In addition, hospitals have very different rates of Cesarean sections. Those whose percentages of C-sections are lowest are usually the ones which take the most care to help a woman labor and deliver naturally. Make sure to ask questions about all of these issues. Depending on where you live and what facilities are available to you, you may have to settle for something less than what you would ideally want. Sit down and prioritize which features are most important to you. You may like hospital A better than hospital B, for example, but feel more accepted as a lesbian couple by the midwives who work at hospital B. There will probably be some compromise involved in your decision.

Sharon felt very connected to Kathy at Kathy's delivery. She recalls, "The midwife responded wonderfully. She was so warm to me. It was a very hard labor, and during a stretch of about seven or eight hours Kathy wouldn't let me leave for a second. I couldn't go to the bathroom. It was very, very hard. I probably had been up for about twenty-seven hours already. I was exhausted. I had been massaging her back for most of that twenty-seven hours. I could see Jake's head for about five hours and the labor was not progressing. At one point I was about to sit down in the rocking chair and Kathy didn't know where I was, and she started saying, 'Where are you? Where are you?' So I hopped right back up and started massaging her back again. I was literally falling off my feet. While I was massaging

Kathy's back the midwife started to rub my back, and I just felt she was so warm and sweet.

"And she had prepped everybody on the floor about us. Kathy was eventually brought in for a Cesarean, which was sort of a blessing, like okay, do it already, just do it. I had to wait in another room because they had to put her under general anesthesia. Within twenty minutes the midwife brought me Jake, while Kathy was still under anesthesia. As I was waiting in the recovery room for Kathy and holding Jake, one of the interns on the floor walked by and congratulated me, so I knew that the midwife must have told all these people the story. We were featured in a newspaper article some time later and the article had a picture of the three of us. We hear that the article was posted on the wall of the birthing room. They were proud of us."

Coping with Infertility

So much decision making, effort, money, and arranging goes into a lesbian's plans to become pregnant. By the time we are ready to have the sperm meet the egg, the last thing we want is for nature to fail us. We all know about the lucky ones who got pregnant on the very first try, and we hope we will be one of them. On average, it takes about six months for most women to become pregnant through whatever means. That may be no big deal to a heterosexually married woman who is going about her life and continuing to have sexual relations with her husband. For lesbians, though, each month that goes by means more difficulty. It may mean flying out of town to meet a sperm donor. It may mean paying hundreds of dollars for more sperm samples. It may mean canceling business engagements and taking off time from work in order to inseminate. It may mean imposing on your donor's time and good will, yet again. It may mean absorbing the disappointment when he decides to be away on vacation that cycle.

Barbara Raboy, director of the Sperm Bank of California, says that it is very common for women to give up on inseminations after the first two or three cycles haven't worked. Many are unprepared for the frustrations of trying, month after month. Because of that, their program lowers the price of sperm samples progressively, at intervals of a few months, as incentive to continue. The statistical expectation is that most women will conceive within a year of consistent attempts.

If you don't happen to be among the fortunate, however, it can be extremely painful. Infertility is heartbreaking, and infertile lesbians are a decidedly unsupported group. The same people who were supportive of your desire to get pregnant may not understand why you would persist when nature presents obstacles. They may not comprehend that a lesbian's desire to conceive can be as impassioned as anyone else's.

My own experience with infertility came after our son Michael died at four and a half months of age of Sudden Infant Death Syndrome, leaving us desperately grief-stricken. (For a description of what happened, see Chapter Ten: Crisis and Tragedy.) Our daughter, Emily, was three months old at the time. The family we'd envisioned was shattered. Michael was a special and wonderful baby, and we knew he could never be replaced in our hearts, but we still wanted a family with two children. We decided to try to have another baby. Six weeks after Michael's death we went back to the fertility specialist who had inseminated us. That began a nightmare period of infertility which lasted for two years.

What I had was called secondary infertility, which means that I had been able to conceive and carry to term once. It is a somewhat different experience from that of the woman who has never gotten pregnant, and who finds her attempts not working, month after month, with no idea of why. I, at least, started out with some faith that my body could accomplish the miracle, but it dwindled as the months went by. I believe now that my infertility was caused by my emotional and physical state, though I did not want to recognize it at the time. I was grieving, crying a lot, heartbroken over the loss of Michael. I was parenting Emily and still suffering the sleep deprivation of nightly feedings. I was also working full-time. My body was simply not ready to take on a pregnancy under all this stress.

But while my body did not want a pregnancy, every particle of my consciousness did. I wanted another child so badly. I needed to restore some of my faith in the goodness of life, which had been dealt a terrible blow by our tragedy.

In addition, when your child dies there is always a level on which you ask yourself, "What did I do wrong?" There were no rational answers to that question. We had done nothing wrong. We had given Michael everything there was to give. Yet on some irrational plane I felt a terrible biological inadequacy. What was wrong with me that I couldn't make a baby who could survive? I needed a pregnancy to repair the sense of damage in my body, to affirm my wholeness.

I began taking Clomid again, the fertility drug I had been put on the first time around. Without it, my periods were so irregular and infrequent as to make ovulation almost impossible to predict. Using Clomid, I had conceived Michael on the second cycle. I expected it would be the same this time and began calculating probable due dates. This time, however, my body didn't always ovulate, despite the Clomid. Sometimes when it did, there would be no cervical mucus. We would do the inseminations anyway, hoping every time. The physician augmented the Clomid with shots of human chorionic gonadotropin (hCG) and tried to improve the mucus with estrogen pills.

Every month when ovulation looked like a possibility, I would have to suddenly cancel patients and race across town to the clinic. Waiting there for the sperm to arrive could take forever, and sometimes when it got there the sperm would be dead from the long trip through traffic. The nurses would call for another specimen to be delivered, and I would get on the phone and cancel more patients because I would be delayed several more hours. More than once I sat in the clinic waiting room unable to fight back tears. Susan was rarely with me, because she had to be home caring for Emily. Though she supported me completely in this, neither of us had as much to give the other during those two painful years.

My doctor's laid-back, quiet manner drove me crazy. I needed answers about why this wasn't working. I wanted him to be aggressive about what the next step would be. He, however, seemed to take his cues from me. When I blurted out my desperation he agreed calmly that perhaps some further tests would be a good idea. It became clear to me that I was running the show, and I had no idea how to do that. There were further medications to consider, intrusive and painful tests, and surgeries. I read books on infertility, and became much more assertive about what I wanted done. Still, the decisions were hard to make as the steps got more invasive. All of this took place against a backdrop of depression and anguish.

Over the course of two years of inseminating, two and three and sometimes more times a month, I went through batteries of hormonal tests. I had consultations with other specialists. We switched to a different, more powerful fertility drug, Pergonal, which cost a fortune and whose side effects—most seriously, the risk of multiple births, increasing the chance of losing another baby—scared the daylights out of me. I was scared of not getting pregnant but equally scared of having drug-induced quintuplets. Susan gave me daily injections of the Pergonal, and it made me irritable and anxious. Eventually I had laparoscopic surgery, not knowing whether I was crazy to be going through all this or whether I was stupid not to have done it earlier. The surgery confirmed that I had cystic ovaries, which accounted for my irregular periods, and showed that nothing else was really wrong with me. Sonograms had to be taken to determine if follicles (structures in the ovaries that produce the eggs) were ripening. The whole intense focus on one medical procedure after another completely distorted any semblance of normalcy in our lives. My psychotherapy practice was continually disrupted. I was moody beyond toleration. Susan was forbearing and sympathetic, but I was hard to live with.

In desperation, I called a phone number I found on the bulletin board at the clinic. The organization was called Resolve (see the Organizations list in the Resources section), and it provides help to people dealing with infertility. My local chapter offered support groups. I can't say that the idea appealed to me. The thought of exposing my pain to a room full of heterosexual women was truly frightening. I didn't want to be that vulnerable in a place where I expected not to be understood. I thought they would resent me because I had already had a child, that they would recoil from the reality of my having lost a child (as many people did), and that they would reject me for even wanting a child as a lesbian. I went anyway, because I saw that my daily distress was putting an awful burden on Susan. I needed help from another source.

At first I was tense and unfriendly in that room of nine women. It seems to me now that we were all very tentative with one another initially. For me, it was one of the hardest coming-out situations I'd ever encountered. Somehow, though, over the next several weeks, it began to work. The other women there were also in great pain. If they judged me adversely for being a lesbian, I never knew about it. They gave me genuine sympathy and concrete help.

Besides emotional support, the group was an invaluable source of networking about the efficacy of various treatments and the reputations of several specialists. The cost of inseminations, Pergonal, sonograms, and time lost from work, plus other expenses, had reached close to $2,500 per cycle for the past two months. Our meager savings was going to be completely depleted in two more months. The group encouraged me to grapple with the difference between my need to bear a child and my need to parent another child, and I was able to come to a resolution. I would continue inseminating for the remaining two cycles; if it didn't work, I would give up. Susan would then start trying to get pregnant, so that we could have another baby and get on with our lives. It felt like a plan I could live with.

The calendar was not in my favor that month. Ovulation would have occurred on a Sunday. Since the clinic would be closed that day, the doctor had me inject an extra dose of Pergonal to postpone it. We inseminated on Monday, but by Wednesday there was something wrong. My overstimulated ovaries had blown up to the size of honeydews. I was sent immediately to bed, because any movement, even a sneeze, could cause a rupture. As luck would have it, I was also pregnant. The positive pregnancy test was less than joyful, because my chances of keeping the pregnancy didn't look too good. For the next three months I was confined to bed, not knowing if surgery would be needed. The hope was that the placenta would start producing hormones at the end of the first trimester, which would allow the ovaries to recede. Mercifully, it worked. The rest of the pregnancy was tense but basically healthy, and our son Jesse was born big and beautiful.

Infertility is painful. Women who have children feel uncomfortable offering you support, and women who don't want children can't understand why you would go through all that. People who are supportive about our becoming lesbian mothers often think we have gone too far if pregnancy isn't quick and easy. The people who can best understand are other women going through it. If you are struggling with infertility, don't try to go it alone. Contact Resolve, or ask your specialist if there is a group for infertile women in your area. You might try to locate other lesbians who have suffered infertility by putting a notice in the newsletters of gay parenting groups (see the Resources section). Meanwhile you might gradually explore your feelings about nonmedical options for parenthood by talking with women who have become mothers through adoption.

If you are the partner of a woman going through infertility treatment, you will also need support. You will find it hard to go to a support group for "husbands," and your lover is likely to be too stressed out herself to provide much help for you. Don't underestimate your needs in this situation. Her infertility is your loss, too. Her emotional unavailability is also your loss. You are going to need to talk to friends, and perhaps a counselor as well, about your feelings in all of this.

There are different routes to pregnancy for lesbians; like any other path to parenthood, they are all emotionally intense. The decisions along the way—about which partner will conceive, how to affirm the other partner's participation, how to become pregnant, what kind of medical involvement you want in the process of conception and delivery, and so on—have to be based on your personal needs and preferences. But you also have to prepare yourself for the unexpected: Nature has her own ideas. Your willingness to examine your feelings, to seek help, and to change course, if necessary, will help guide you through the ups and downs of this incredible endeavor.

3

DONORS AND COPARENTS

Defining the Family

Most of us have been raised to believe that a family has one father and one mother who live together and are involved romantically and sexually. The other family configurations society has witnessed are usually the result of divorce and remarriage. They are adaptations to mishap, not what the parties planned from the outset. Our lesbian and gay families, however, have completely broken the mold. We start out with a variety of options for structuring the family according to our preferences. We are breaking such new ground with the families we create that our language does not yet have words to name all the potential parties involved. Here are just a few of the parenting possibilities we have when we start out to construct a family:

- A single parent
- A primary parent, plus that parent's partner, who is also considered a parent of some sort, but not fully a mother or father
- Two equal mothers, or two equal fathers, with no one else having a parental role
- One or two mothers plus one or two fathers sharing parenting

In addition, the living arrangements can be whatever we choose. There are lesbians and gay men who choose to live together to share parenting, as well as families that choose to parent from two separate households. Sometimes two separate homes are a block away from each other, sometimes hundreds of miles.

The parenting arrangements that suit us may have nothing to do with the biological relationships between any parent and the child. Theoretically, we could construct our families any way we want even when the child is being adopted. However, most often our creative family structures are prompted by the logistics of biology. As lesbians and gay men, we are in a unique position with respect to creating families. If we are going to make babies (as opposed to adopting them) we need the cooperation of someone of the opposite gender to whom we are not romantically committed. We have to make choices about how much involvement he or she will have in our children's lives and in our lives. These are very important decisions. Each of the options has complicated legal and emotional consequences. No one solution is ideal for everyone, but careful thought should go into which way would work best for you.

At present, most of the families opting for primary biological parenthood, that is, making babies and having sole custody of them, are headed by women. Women need the services of a biological father for conception, and beyond that can decide whether they want him to function solely as a donor of genetic material or to be an active part of the family constellation in some manner. The men in these situations must decide what level of involvement suits their needs, and choose lesbians to work with whose needs with respect to biological fathers match their own.

The parallel situation, in which men opt for primary biological parenthood through the services of a surrogate mother,[1] is relatively less common, because of the greater participation required of a woman in the creation of a child. (Chapter Four is devoted to a detailed discussion of gay men becoming primary biological parents through surrogate motherhood.) Because of this, the following discussion focuses on the situations in which lesbians are planning to become the primary parents. The majority of the issues raised in the discussion of how lesbian mothers interact with biological fathers, however, are comparable in the case of gay fathers and biological mothers.

I'm going to make a distinction here between "donors" and "fathers." I will define a donor as someone who helps in the biological creation of a child but who has no parental involvement. The family, including the child, may know who he is or they may be anonymous to each other, but he does not participate in raising the child. A father, by contrast, has an ongoing relationship with the child which involves care and decision making. The amount of actual contact he has may vary from occasional visits to full-time custody. (I will use the more neutral expression "biological father" to refer to the man who has participated in the genetic creation of the child, whether he functions as a donor or as a parent.)

When lesbians and gay men are interested not only in creating children together but also in sharing the responsibilities of parenting together, they want more than a donor or surrogate mother. They are opting for a mom-and-dad coparenting arrangement. Occasionally the mother and father live together, but usually the family has separate residences from the beginning. They agree to divide up the time spent with the child, the financial burdens, the work and decision making of child rearing, in any way that suits their needs and wishes. The last section in this chapter, "Mom-and-Dad Coparents," deals with men and women forming a parenting team together.

The distinction between donors and fathers, between sole parenthood and coparenting arrangements, is somewhat arbitrary. There is a continuum of cooperative involvement, which parents will ultimately define in their own ways. A man may have virtually no contact with the child, for example, yet be referred to in the family as "Daddy." A man may also have regular contact with the child, yet be considered just a family friend with no parental role in the child's life. Furthermore, the titles and positions that are assigned at the time of conception may change over the years. A sperm donor may become a father as a relationship with the child develops. The fluidity of family roles makes them hard to slot into categories, but I think the distinctions can be useful in clarifying the issues.

Donor or Father?

For lesbians, the question has to do with how they see the family unit. Do the women see themselves as their children's only parents, having sole custody, financial, and decision-making responsibilities? Is it important to insure that they will remain the sole parents throughout the child's lifetime? If so, what they want is a donor, not a father. They may or may not want the donor to be known to them, and to the child, but they do not want him to have a parental involvement. That is, they intend that he will never be in a position to make decisions for their child, to contribute money to the child's upbringing, or to actually do the work of care-giving. This is a decision lesbians make because they consider it to be in the child's best interests, as well as their own.

Lesbians who want a father in the family unit, however, are envisioning a different family constellation. They, too, are considering their child's best interests, but may feel that their child should have parents of both genders in his or her life. They may also feel that a coparenting arrangement, which entails sharing the work load and responsibilities of parenthood, suits their circumstances and preferences. Whether they are expecting to have primary custody, with the father participating infrequently, or to arrange custody with the father on a more equal basis, they intend to negotiate the complex dynamics of shared parenthood throughout the child's life. They are opting for the richness that coparenting can provide for all involved.

For gay men, the question of whether to become a donor or a father is also very personal and very important. Gay men considering becoming donors should expect to have the opportunity to contribute to the biological creation of a child, while relinquishing all rights to make decisions and participate in the child's upbringing. Your motivation may be to help out a lesbian or lesbian couple in need of a donor. You may also have some interest in seeing the offspring you help produce, and perhaps even in having a relationship with him or her once the child is grown. You are opting, however, for an extremely passive role with respect to the child's upbringing.

If, on the other hand, your interest in making a baby as a gay man has to do with a desire to be a parent in some capacity, you do not want the noninvolvement of a donor. You want to become a father, and may be looking for an opportunity to coparent with a lesbian or lesbian couple.

Choosing which arrangement is right for you is a very complicated decision. There are legal issues to consider, as well as your personalities and your individual beliefs about what a child needs.

How Important Is Biology?

Lesbians deciding whether to opt for anonymous donors, known donors, or fathers in their family structure will be influenced by their personal beliefs about the relative importance of biology in the making of parental bonds. If you believe that genetic bonds are also emotionally compelling, you may expect your child to want a relationship, at some point, with his or her biological father. In part, our beliefs about this will be based on very personal visions we have of what a child needs, and on our own histories and experiences.

Twenty years ago, when I was in graduate school in psychology, we tended to assume that almost everything about a person could be explained on the basis of how they were treated by their early caregivers. Since then, however, more and more evidence has accumulated to support biology's role in the inheritance of a great many characteristics. It is not just body type and coloring that are passed along in the genes. Temperament, preferences, styles of thinking, and other personality characteristics are now thought to be much more under the influence of genetics than was once supposed. Elizabeth Noble, in her book *Having Your Baby by Donor Insemination,* argues strongly that biology creates powerful emotional connections. She believes that the genetic tie results in what she calls a "cellular consciousness," binding the child and biological father together. One mother I spoke with described how her toddler slept through the night for the first time after meeting her biological father, attributing a significant power to that connection.

The relevant question is whether you believe the biological tie is of such a nature that it is important for your child to grow up with or be raised by the people who created him. Or do you think it's sufficient that the child be able to contact the donor someday, without necessarily needing to know him during childhood? Keep in mind that it may be possible for you to choose a donor arrangement that excludes him from the family system during your child's minor years, yet allows him to be contacted once the child is grown. This is a way of respecting the child's right to a link with her biological father while maintaining the safety and simplicity of a single-household family.

Lesbians who are considering excluding a donor from the family system are understandably concerned about whether the child is likely to be unhappy because of it. They worry about whether the child will have a sense of personal sadness or anger, and feel deprived of something, and whether the child will have a harder time socially because of the absence of an identifiable father.

There is no way to predict for sure whether your child will feel a strong desire to have a biological father in her life. If your child is born looking and acting like you, the absence of a known donor may feel irrelevant. If, however, your child clearly shows physical and temperamental characteristics that are unfamiliar to your genetic line, you will find yourself more aware that there is a biological "other" in the picture. The stronger your child's resemblance to a biological father, the more you or the child may want to have contact with him, though the contact your child wants may involve anything from a brief meeting to an ongoing parental relationship. The reality is that there are offspring of donor insemination who want very much to meet their biological fathers while they are still children, and children who either never care or aren't interested until they are young adults. You obviously can't anticipate what your child will feel—that will depend upon the individual psychology of your particular child. If you choose a family arrangement that results in some sadness for your child, however, you should keep in mind that this need not be psychologically harmful; with your support, it can become a normal part of your child's maturational process.

With respect to the social difficulties of not having an identifiable father in the picture, a lot will depend on how you feel about the situation. When the parents are truly comfortable with the facts of alternative insemination, the children tend to be comfortable also. If, in addition, there are other children around who are being raised without contact with their donors, your child will have a social reference group which affirms the completeness of a family without a father. If, on the other hand, you feel defensive or guilty about creating a family which does not include a father, your child may get the message that there is something missing in the family. You have to create a family that ultimately you can feel good about.

One of the motivations for designating biological fathers as parenting figures is the desire for a man in a child's life. It may be useful here, though, to think of separating biology from sociology. That is, do the men who become role models and mentors to our children necessarily also have to be biologically related to them? Some women feel that their social circles and living circumstances leave them no opportunity to include men in their lives, and therefore the biological father is a good candidate for the role. Other women, however, prefer to rely on male relatives and close friends to contribute to their child's environment.

There are legal and emotional consequences of involving biological fathers in the family system which must be taken into consideration. How you feel about those consequences must be weighed against the beliefs you have about the importance of biological ties. The whole package then must be measured against your personal vision of family.

The emotional issues require a very personal evaluation. There is no right way to feel. One consequence of having a father in the picture is that a nonbiological mother may feel more insecure about her role. The nonbiological mother in a lesbian family often has difficulty getting recognition of her status anyway, and the presence of a man outside the household who has legal and social privileges which she doesn't possess may make it even more difficult. In addition, the dynamics of negotiation and decision making are greatly altered by the presence of a father in a lesbian family. How comfortable you can be in such a situation is a very individual matter.

Keep in mind that you cannot give your child everything in life, no matter how well you plan or how much you love. Nor do children need everything; they just need enough. There is no one family constellation that is best for children. The healthiest family for a child is the one that the parents feel good about and can function in comfortably. My own children are best off in their family structure, because of who my lover and I are. Yours might be best off in something completely different.

Men who are considering becoming sperm donors must also think about what that biological connection to a child is going to mean for them. As such a man, perhaps you have been approached by a lesbian couple and asked if you would be willing to help them inseminate. You may be eager to do a service for lesbians in general, or you may have an affection for these particular women and want to help them out. You may also think the idea of creating a child from your genes is appealing. It is very important, however, that you think through your feelings before agreeing to something as serious as baby making. You don't want to be surprised later by feelings that could be extremely painful to live with. Try to picture as realistically as possible that the child is already born. Imagine that you know its gender and its name. Suppose the mothers are in your city or even your social circle. If you are expected to remain out of the picture, would you feel that you wanted to see the child? Would you want to be able to tell your friends that you were this child's donor? Would you find yourself wanting your parents or siblings to know that you had created a child? Imagine this child getting older, going to school. How much would you long to see whether it looks like you, and whether it has interests and talents similar to yours? If you expect to have contact with the child but not be identified as a father, what would it feel like to keep that secret? What if the child asked about his or her father and you were still supposed to keep it secret?

If you are intending to have some nonparental connection to the child, think carefully about the fact that you will have no control over the child's upbringing. What if you disagree with the way the mothers want to raise "your" child? How painful might it be to have to keep your feelings to yourself? What about the fact that the mothers will expect to make all the decisions about when and how often you see the child? Or that they might choose to move far away? What if your child develops illnesses or other problems that you don't think the mothers are handling well? What if you see signs of relationship problems between the mothers, or alcohol abuse, or other behavior that concerns you? How would it be to have to stay out of it?

If you find yourself uncomfortable with the idea of having no decision-making control over the child's environment, consider your alternatives. One possibility is that you may really want to become a father, and not a donor. You may want to enter into a mom-and-dad coparenting agreement with a lesbian mother and have a full share in your child's upbringing. Or you may realize that you want to parent without having to include a woman in the family unit. In that case, you can opt to create a family through adoption or via a surrogate mother who does not participate in the child's life.

Another possibility is that you may want to be a friend to a child to whom you are not biologically related. Sometimes it is easier to have an ongoing relationship with the child of a lesbian family when neither you nor they have any tension about what a biological connection might mean.

The Legal Considerations

The law recognizes and grants legal rights and privileges to biological fathers. Any man acknowledged to be the biological father of a child is entitled by law to considerations of visitation and possible custody. In terms of the law, there is nothing in between a completely non-participating sperm donor and a fully privileged father. When a woman chooses to identify her child's donor as the biological father, she opens the door to the possibility that he may want more involvement than she or he imagined at the time of conception. Should he bring the issue to court, his parental rights will carry considerable weight, and there is a chance that the family environment which was originally intended will undergo major changes. At the very worst, of course, is the dreadful, though unlikely, possibility that a lesbian mother could actually lose custody of her child. For that to happen, she would have to be seen by the court as unfit to parent. In most states, her lesbianism alone would not be enough to make her unfit, but there are some states in which it would. If the courts declared a lesbian mother an unfit parent, the biological father could conceivably be granted custody.

More likely, a lesbian mother runs the risk of having to share custody or accord regular parental visitation to a biological father who presses the issue in court. Even if she intended him to have informal visitations with her child, ending up in a legal dispute could put visitation on his terms, not hers.

In addition, the law does not accord any legal rights or privileges to a nonbiological lesbian mother whose lover has inseminated. If the biological mother becomes incapacitated or dies, for example, a known biological father may have rights to the child which the nonbiological mother does not have. He could potentially take custody of the child, with resultant suffering on the part of both the child and the nonbiological mother. The courts are supposed to make these decisions in the best interests of the child, but courts tend to believe that children need their genetic parents.

These are serious considerations. Men who agree, in good faith, to be uninvolved sperm donors often find that reality hits them differently. Even the presence of a contract won't guarantee that your family plans will remain intact if the man changes his mind. In addition, even though everyone intends for the biological father to be merely a known donor, and not a father, once the child is three or four or five, and establishes an independent relationship with him, the child's feelings for him may determine a designation of "father." Gradually, what started out as a lesbian family with a known donor may become a mom-and-dad coparenting arrangement, with emotional consequences. Though it might all work out well, it also happens that very decent, well-meaning adults end up in ugly disputes, simply because their feelings and perceptions are in conflict. The consequences for a child can be extremely painful.

The only way to insure that a lesbian family will not suffer the disruption of a donor suing for parental rights is to use an anonymous sperm donor and have the insemination done as a medical procedure through the auspices of a physician or sperm bank which guarantees the anonymity of the records. Any other arrangement whereby you and the biological father are known to each other involves some legal risk.

On the other hand, there may be good reasons for deciding to incur some legal risk. Your feelings about a child being able to know his or her biological father, as well as your personal preferences about having a father's active participation, may lead you to decide to accept the legal uncertainties and hope for the best. Choosing a donor carefully, for his attitudes and feelings as well as his genetic potential, and spending a lot of time talking with him to make sure you all understand each other, will help to insure that all goes well. The reality is also that very few disputes between lesbians and sperm donors have actually gone to court. Given that many thousands of arrangements with participating fathers exist, the vast majority clearly manage to work it out.

(See Chapter Six for a fuller discussion of contracts, guardianship, and the position of the courts and laws.)

Adding Ingredients to the Family Stew

Depending on the degree of involvement you expect the other biological parent to have in your family's life, the interpersonal issues that are raised can be very complex. Having both biological parents involved in the family, especially where there are also other nonbiological parents, means complicating the family network. Each of the parents, biological and nonbiological, will have some relationship to the child. Additionally, they will each have ongoing commitments to each other, because of shared parenting. If couples break up or establish relationships with new partners, those new partners will join the family as well. And the possibilities multiply if you start to include relationships with extended family members.

When it works well, a child gets to have several different parents and extended families, all of whom participate cooperatively in the child's life and enjoy the rich complexity of the family relationships. It can be wonderful for everyone. Children I have spoken with who had many parents—two dads in one household and two moms in another, for example—all of whom got along well together reported feeling very lucky to have so much love and attention. The parents, for their part, benefited from having more people to shoulder the financial and emotional responsibilities of child rearing. As one mother coparenting with two fathers put it, "Nobody ever burns out on this kid."

However, there is no such thing as a relationship without conflict. Whether this type of arrangement will work for you depends, in part, on how much emotional complexity you are comfortable tolerating. The very fact of two people being different means that there will be some areas in which they disagree, or misunderstand each other, or fail to meet each other's needs. Many people are undaunted by adding all the extra ingredients to the family system. Indeed, some people are downright delighted by the variety that such complexity affords. Those are the people who can more or less gracefully negotiate the inevitable conflicts and differences that arise without having their blood pressure skyrocket or their sleep ruined. Their ability to be comfortable working around the schedules, opinions, needs, and resources of several people enables them to reap the best of what the added relationships contribute to the family, without paying too high a price for the difficulties which accompany them.

Other people, and I count myself in this group, are inclined to want to limit the interpersonal entanglements of their lives. I find the dynamics of family life with my lover, myself, and our two children in the family unit to be quite as much as I can handle. My lover and I are poor candidates for a coparenting arrangement with a biological father, because we would be likely to feel threatened or distressed by every disagreement with him which required renegotiating our situation. We would worry over things that might not necessarily trouble someone else, and that would not create a good atmosphere for our children or for us. On the other hand, we are delighted to have men who have no parental rights involved in our children's lives as role models and friends.

Some people don't necessarily relish the added work of relating to a biological parent of the opposite sex, but don't particularly dread it either and feel the benefits are worth it. Your assessment of your own temperament is just one of the factors to weigh along with the other costs and benefits of mom-and-dad coparenting. Lesbians and gay men who don't want to deal with the complications of the other biological parent, however, should keep in mind that biological parenthood is not the only way to create a family. Adoption is a viable alternative which can allow you to become primary parents without having to use anonymous sperm donors or surrogates (see Chapter Five).

Known-Donor Arrangements

If you are thinking of using or being a known donor (not a father), there is a lot of negotiation that must take place. A known-donor arrangement presumes that the mother(s) will be the sole parent(s). The donor accepts the fact that he will have no decision-making power, as well as no financial or care-giving responsibilities for the child. However, there are still many other things to be negotiated before going ahead with inseminations. You must come to agreements about what the donor is allowed to reveal to friends and family members, and you must do a lot of talking about how it will feel for everyone to live with those arrangements.

JoAnne and Gwen opted at first for the safety of an anonymous donor arrangement but then realized that it didn't suit them. It was worth it to them to make it work with someone they knew and cared for. Their story describes some of the difficult feelings and conflicts that can arise even in a basically good working situation where everyone involved is caring and committed.

Gwen recalls, "We discussed every aspect of this and what its implications would be for at least two years before we even started trying. Deciding whether we should go with a known or an unknown donor was probably the longest discussion because we were going back and forth. Our attorney friend said to us, 'You don't want a known donor because that can cause too many problems, and from a legal perspective it just doesn't seem like a good idea.' But JoAnne and I really wanted Moira to know who her father was. At the same time we didn't really know anybody who we could ask. So by the time we started the process, we went to a fertility clinic to do it with an unknown donor.

"We tried for about eight months before a friend of ours told us one evening that he'd been tested for AIDS and the test was negative, and his lover's test was negative, and everybody who they had slept with had been negative. The following week we asked him if he would be the donor.[2] He didn't even hesitate. He was really excited about the prospect of being a donor.

"We then called our attorney who told us that this was the worst idea that we had ever had in our entire lives, that it was a mistake, but that these are the things that we needed to do. She went through a list of the things that needed to be considered, and how we had to talk with the donor and his lover about who the parents were going to be and what his role was going to be. We had an unending number of conversations with them about what their role would be in Moira's life—how we wanted to set the contract up. Though we briefly discussed their being coparents, we quickly settled on wanting them to have no parental rights or responsibilities. That was what we wanted and basically, we were calling the shots and they were agreeing to them. We're talking about a donor here who is quite possibly the most generous person on the planet, and what he wanted to do was help us have a child. For him, what he described was that he wanted to see what his offspring would look like, without necessarily having a role. He just wanted to see. We discussed with him what the possibilities were for what could happen, because we had never had children and they had never had children. We went through things like, 'Okay, you have no rights and responsibilities. The child is born and all of a sudden you realize that's not the way you want it. You want to see her all the time, and we're not available, or we're leaving town, and you don't get to see her much at all. What is going to happen here? Is this going to destroy our friendship?' We went through all the worst-case scenarios. He and his lover discussed it with each other. I think it was a very difficult thing for the donor to do—to imagine giving up the child.

"We were terrified. I, in particular, was terrified. I mean, this was going to be JoAnne's biological child but not mine. And the father of the child would be somebody who lives in our community and sees her all the time. I was sure that the biological connection was going to become strong and emotional, and that he just didn't know that was going to happen.

"He said he wasn't anticipating that. At the very least he thought he could deal with it. When we discussed the possibility that he might not be able to deal with it, he thought that we were threatening him and not trusting him. He said, 'I'm such a trustworthy person, don't you trust me?' And we kept saying to him, 'This is not an issue of trust, this is an issue of you suddenly realizing what this baby means, and what is going to happen?'

"He was not denying that he would have some feelings about this child. He kept saying, 'You're going to have to accept the fact that I am going to have some feelings about it, but you're going to have to trust me to be able to deal with them within the context of the relationship that we've agreed upon.'

"The agreement was not signed until after JoAnne was pregnant. Then issues started coming up. It was very clear that they were talking to their close friends, and either what they were telling their friends wasn't an accurate representation of what we had agreed on, or their friends were completely misunderstanding. At dinner, when JoAnne was about eight months pregnant, one friend of theirs asked, 'Is the birth going to be a family affair?'—meaning were all four of us going to be there. He was presuming that the family of this child was more than just two parents. We were flabbergasted that he would even suggest that. JoAnne even asked him to clarify what he meant.

"At that point we went back to them in a panic and said, 'What's going on here?' We had a number of emergency meetings with the donor and his partner where we were just completely freaked about something that had happened. What made us nervous was that we wanted him to see himself as just a sperm donor. He was getting very angry with us that we were not allowing him more emotional involvement than that, not necessarily with Moira but just in terms of his feelings about it. The things that happened to cause these emergency meetings were oftentimes misunderstandings, and each one required a rebuilding of trust afterward, but the last one almost resulted in the end of the friendship."

JoAnne describes what happened: "Moira was six or seven months old, and the donor and his partner were having an anniversary party. They'd invited thirty close friends from all over the country, some of them people we had never met. That afternoon I wasn't working and I went over to drop something off. Three of the friends were there. Moira did something and one of them (the same man who had made the comment about the 'family affair') said, 'Oh, you must have gotten that from your father.' It was crossing a boundary. It was suggesting that he had an effect on her life equal to ours. Then that night at the party, it was clear that everyone knew so much about Moira that the donor was telling them all sorts of things."

Gwen remembers that she found this all very threatening. "I was asked questions about the father repeatedly, throughout the evening. I went from one group to another, the entire evening, hearing the same incredible comments about Moira's father."

JoAnne agrees, "I mean, they all knew who the father was because they were all his friends, but it was this constant reminder to Gwen that she didn't have this biological tie. Gwen wrote them a letter afterward saying, 'You must not be telling them what we've agreed to because the comments that we're getting are totally inappropriate.' They were just beside themselves when they got it. We finally said they should think about a heterosexual couple who is unable to have children, and finally is able to adopt a child. They love the child with all their hearts, and yet all someone wants to ask them about is the biological parents. And they tell them how wonderful the biological parents are that they could do that for the adoptive parents, giving no credence to the feelings of the parents who were raising the child. I think that when they understood that, they calmed down."

Despite the endless negotiations, and the stormy path to get there, JoAnne and Gwen and Moira have preserved the integrity of their family, while managing to maintain good friendships with the donor and his lover. The men come to visit, and they occasionally babysit for Moira. She gets very excited when they come in the door. Observing the realities of parenting during Moira's first months of life convinced the donor and his lover that they didn't want to be parents, and at present everyone seems to have gotten what they want out of this situation. Moira does not call him Daddy, and their intention is that she not know about her biological connection with him until she is older, though there are clearly many people through whom that information could leak. If JoAnne and Gwen were going to do it again, they would do it the same way, and would like to be able to use the same donor.

As JoAnne and Gwen can testify, having a known donor makes life more complicated. Their lawyer friend was right, from a strictly legal standpoint: Using an anonymous donor is the simplest way to go about things. But like all decisions which have powerful emotional consequences, the heart has to take precedence. If it is important to you to have your donor be known to the family, then you will be willing to negotiate the complexities.

Using a Family Member as Biological Father

A number of lesbians have used members of their partner's families as sperm donors for their children. The purpose is to create a child who combines the genetic characteristics of both women's families. This is obviously a decision based on strong feelings about the importance of biological relationships. It carries with it some potentially complex dynamics, however, and must be thought out and discussed very carefully.

Most commonly, one woman's brother becomes the donor for her partner's pregnancy. The resulting advantage is that the nonbiological mother is actually the biological aunt. The child may actually look like both women.

The disadvantages, however, have a lot of potential for outnumbering the advantages. If having a donor be a known part of the child's life complicates the emotional picture, having the donor be the brother of one of the mothers adds even more wrinkles to the situation. The donor then becomes both the child's father and the child's uncle. The biological mother is then connected to her lover's family not just through affectional ties, but through having a child with her lover's brother as well. In one family in which the women split up amid very bad feeling, the fact that they used the nonbiological mother's brother as a donor exacerbated the problems. The biological mother then felt she had angry relationships with both her ex-lover and her child's father, who understandably sided with his sister.

In addition, the child's connection to both biological parents, which sometimes leaves nonbiological mothers out in the cold, may elicit long-standing sibling rivalries between the nonbiological mother and her brother when the brother is her child's donor. Jenna and Ruth used Jenna's brother, Matthew, as the donor for their daughter, Leaura. Though things had been friendly among them for years, hostility began to erupt between Jenna and her brother when Leaura was a toddler. It was largely attributable to the fact that Jenna, as the nonbiological mother, felt replaced by Matthew when he was around. Though the sibling issues between Jenna and Matthew dated back to childhood, they got exacerbated when Leaura was excited about Daddy coming to visit. Jenna's position was particularly vulnerable since she never wanted to be called Mommy, preferring that Ruth alone have that title. That meant that Jenna was neither Mommy nor Daddy, a fact that was highlighted when Matthew was present. Leaura's primary parents are unquestionably Jenna and Ruth, but Jenna frequently felt left out. Ruth was in the middle. It has required considerable emotional effort on everyone's part to make the situation work.

The problems these families encountered should serve as cautions if you are considering using a family member as a donor. Before you go ahead, think through the possible feelings that might arise, and talk them over thoroughly with everyone involved.

The Donor of the Second Child

When the couple is planning a second child, they may have preferences about whether the two children share the same biological father or not, and there are arguments that support both sides of the proposition. Susan and I felt strongly that we did not want our two children to have the same donor. We were concerned that if our children had the same sperm donor, he might become a great deal more psychologically important in our lives than we intended. The children would be biologically related to each other through the sperm donor, deriving from the donor a link that we could never give them. It felt more comfortable, then, to have different donors, and let our children's primary ties to each other be based on our love for them and their love for each other.

As with everything about parenthood, though, there are other ways to look at a situation. Sharon and Kathy, who are both attorneys, at first thought they would use different donors for their two children, but then changed their minds. Sharon said, "Kathy's got blond hair and I've got brown hair. We figured that I'd conceive by a blond-haired donor and she'd conceive by a brown-haired donor, and we'd have a nice mix of kids that could pass for either one of ours. But when we thought about it we thought it would be nice for the children not to be biological strangers. As it turns out we're very happy with that choice because we see that in New York State the Court of Appeals recently decided a case where they called the nonbiological mother the 'biological stranger' to the child, and denied her rights to visitation. One of the things we realized in our thinking was that since the children are biologically related they will never be 'biological strangers.' Therefore there will always be a right on the part of each of these children to see one another that will be recognized in court. And therefore, this family can never be disturbed. If anything happened to Kathy or me they cannot separate these children. It's really something that makes me feel a lot more secure.

"Kathy and I do have contracts with each other, and we have often discussed the fact that we would never be in a situation where we would be denying each other rights to see the kids. We both feel that what's best for the child comes first and it's never best for the child for divorced parents to have that kind of tension. So I never worried about Kathy keeping me from seeing Jake if we split up, but I did worry about Kathy dying, or being incapacitated. Being the biological parent of Jake's biological sibling just gives me a little bit of an edge. I feel like no court would take Jake out of a home where he's with his biological brother, and they can't take the brother away from me."

Mom-and-Dad Coparents

If having a known donor requires a lot of careful planning, setting out to have a gay father and lesbian mother parent together requires many times that amount of talking, thinking, and negotiating. You are embarking on a parenting project which will require that you make hundreds of thousands of joint decisions, overcoming your different perceptions, backgrounds, expectations, resources, needs, and even the fact that you live in different places. On top of that, you have to do it with someone who is not in a sexual or romantic relationship with you. You can't make love to ease the tension or reaffirm your trust for each other—you have to rely on talking.

The better you know each other before you start, the fewer surprises there will be. Lesbians and gay men who have been close friends for years are starting with the optimal foundation for coparenting. They have already had occasion to deal with conflict in their relationship, and to learn how to resolve differences. They already know each other's emotional languages. They are aware of each other's individual temperaments, including their weaknesses or peculiarities—someone's tendency to procrastinate, for example, or to withdraw when upset, or to be anxious about things. If they have negotiated a summer house between them, taken joint vacations, supported each other through personal and family crises, they will have come up against some of the challenges which sharing parenthood will present.

However, not every gay man or lesbian who wants to make a coparenting family has such a friendship available. Many people find that they are drawn together as coparents by the simple reality that they both want to be parents and time is ticking. You may have found each other through mutual friends, or you may have responded to ads in gay publications. You have a lot of work to do to get to know each other as thoroughly as you can before inseminations begin. If you have misgivings during the negotiations, you can pull out at any time, but once the baby arrives you are in it together, one way or another, forever.

Roger, a single gay man, considered becoming a father through a surrogate mother, but then rejected the idea because he felt he was not equipped to be a single parent. It made more sense to him to find someone with whom he could share the work of parenting. Roger had heard that Fay, a woman he had known peripherally for many years, was also talking about wanting to have a child. He recalls, "We'd never been really close friends, but I kind of liked her and admired her. She was intriguing to me."

Fay was thirty-six, a single lesbian, and felt it was time to go ahead with parenthood. She describes, "I really wanted my child to have an identifiable father. It was a normalcy that I wanted to be able to give her. I hear stories of people who are adopted who go to great lengths to find their biological parent. It seemed to me that the biological bond is really strong. And I wanted to have a man in her life. At a minimum, I wanted the father identifiable. Beyond that, my ideal was that there would be regular contact."

Roger picked up the phone and called Fay. He explains, "It's really hard to call someone and say, 'Do you want to have a baby?'" Fay remembers that he said, "Well, you're probably wondering why I called you after a couple of years like this, but I was talking to [their mutual friend] and asking how you're doing and she told me that you really want to have a child, and I just wondered if … I've always wanted to have a child, too, and I wanted you to know that I could be a potential father."

Roger and Fay live in different cities. They spent the next year and a half traveling back and forth, trying to get to know each other in preparation for coparenting. Roger explains, "We would spend the weekend together, talking about what it would be like. It was important to me, and to her, to establish the level of my involvement." Fay recalls, "At the beginning we were both very careful. It was like going on a first date with someone, where you're on your best behavior and the relationship gradually develops and becomes more open. As the process evolved, the issues started surfacing around feelings of control over this future child. I found myself in the position of reassuring Roger that I wasn't going to interfere with his relationship with this child, while at the same time making clear that I was going to have custody. We were trying to make concrete decisions about a whole new life, and we didn't know how it was going to work. Roger wasn't sure how much involvement he wanted. On the one hand, he didn't want to feel pressured. On the other hand, he didn't want to feel that his relationship to the child was totally dependent on me. We both pushed at each other to see where the limits were."

Roger felt that "no matter how much you talk about it, no matter how much you try to anticipate what you might feel in the situation, when you get right down to it, you just don't know. It's a leap. I had a lot of anxiety about what was going to happen. I didn't know whether I would take a trip to see the child and come back on the train tortured about having to leave her, or whether I'd feel, 'Whew, God! I'm glad that's over!' I didn't know if it would feel like a great joy or a burden."

A major conflict surfaced when Fay was five months pregnant. They had agreed early on that the child would have Fay's last name. Roger's first name could become a middle name, or even a first name for a boy. As things progressed, though, Roger realized he wasn't happy with that arrangement. "The more I thought about it, the more I felt it had a symbolic meaning to me. Giving the child Fay's last name was saying to the world that Fay was the primary parent. There were a lot of practical reasons for it, because the child would be living with her, but it really meant a lot to me to have our two last names hyphenated. I didn't care which was first, and I realized that for practicality mine would probably be dropped, but I wanted it officially there. When I brought it up, Fay was really angry about it. She felt I was breaking our contract."

Fay's feelings on the issue were strong, rooted in her feminist ideology and her personal experience. "This was an issue I was not flexible on. Children grow up with their father's last names. I have my father's last name. But this child was going to be brought up in a lesbian household. If I couldn't have a child who has my last name, then who can? Part of my fear was that some teacher would figure out that was the father's name and would start to tell my child that it was really supposed to be her last name. I had fears of relatives and society not recognizing the family my child was in."

Negotiations on other issues had gone very well. Finances, custody, and visitation arrangements had all fallen into place, with no one feeling threatened or uncomfortable. The name issue, however, became a real sticking point.

Roger's analysis of it is that "Fay was very focused on my breaking our agreement. She felt betrayed. I was just having a lot of feelings and needed to know they were being heard or understood. I felt that if we could really understand how important it was to both of us we could probably come up with something we both could live with. But I think she never got over the feeling that she couldn't trust me, that I was not reliable. And I never felt heard, which confirmed my feelings that Fay was out for herself and didn't care about me."

Fay recalls, "I tried to hear what he was saying. He continually thought I didn't understand. I felt like he would never think I understood unless I agreed to change my mind. It was very frustrating. He wanted to talk about it, but he also didn't want to bring it up because it was upsetting. He had started coming to the breathing classes, but at some point said maybe he wouldn't come anymore. It was all involved with this name issue."

They ultimately reached a compromise, with Roger's last name becoming their daughter Leigh's middle name. In the process, though, they learned a lot about the kinds of conflicts they could expect in their future together, and how to work with them. Roger reflects, "It's an ongoing issue that I feel Fay is ultimately in control of what happens with Leigh. Even in the most incidental things, Fay is the authority who will determine how things should be done, and I feel kind of inhibited and reluctant. It's a very unusual situation for me, because I'm used to being in control of my own life. It's been hard, and I swallow a lot, but I feel Fay goes out of her way a lot to make things easier for me."

Fay concurs, "I put a lot of effort into making it work. In the beginning I felt like I was walking on eggshells with him, that whatever I said was somehow controlling. He felt uncomfortable talking to me. I felt like I couldn't disagree with him without him closing down. I wanted to be able to be upset or get angry and have him get angry back."

Fay and Roger had come up against the kind of differences that occur in any relationship. The coparenting agreement they had written together contained a provision for seeking counseling if either one of them wanted to. They entered therapy together, which helped to increase their respect and tolerance for each other. In the course of working on things, they discovered that they each had different visions of what the family would be.

Fay recounts, "One of the surprises to me was that Roger seemed to want a totally separate relationship with Leigh, in contrast to my wanting a family that included all of us. It's reflected in the fact that his pictures are of him and Leigh, but in my house the pictures are of all of us together. I was disappointed in that. I wasn't sure whether it was a personal rejection of me, or whether he just felt he couldn't have a relationship with Leigh when I was around."

Roger adds, "I think Fay really wanted a family with a Mom and Dad. My motivation was more to be a father and daughter. My favorite times with Leigh are her and me. When I go down there I prefer to take her off for the day."

They continue to work on these issues, and to get support from other people. Roger has formed a group of gay fathers who are coparenting with women. "It's helped a lot because it's made me realize how really terrific Fay is with me. She's going out of her way to help me. When I arrive there it's like 'Daddy's coming!' and it's obvious that Leigh has been primed. Leigh thinks I'm important and wonderful, and a lot of it is because Fay is always encouraging that kind of thinking."

The one continuing discomfort they all share is that they live in different cities. As time goes on, Roger's feelings about fatherhood have intensified, and the geographical problem has become more difficult. Roger reports, "When Leigh was a baby I would feel involved with her while I was there and excited by it, but I found I didn't miss her very much when I was away. I didn't feel so intensely bonded with her. Now it's changed. It's amazing to me the emotions that come up for me when I'm with her now—a welling up of all sorts of feelings. We can talk on the phone now, it's fulfilling. She just had the chicken pox and I felt really sad, longing to be there." Neither Fay nor Roger can relocate without major difficulty, however, so this is a discomfort they will have to endure.

Fay is no longer single, and her new lover, Patty, has also become a fully functioning parent to Leigh. Roger likes Patty and welcomes her presence in the family. In fact, he finds his relationship with Patty refreshingly easy, since they have none of the power issues between them that make for insecurity and tension. The four of them take vacations together, along with two male friends of Roger's who are designated uncles. Fay, happy to have men in her life and in Leigh's life, would definitely do it this way again. She says, "I like Roger. We have gotten to the point where we know each other and respect each other." Leigh is now four years old, very secure and very loved.

Fay and Roger are not necessarily representative of every coparenting family. There are many possible family constellations, with as many different issues to be resolved as the personalities which present them. The struggle about their child's name that surfaced for Fay and Roger might not be the issue that comes up for you. It could just as easily be money, or time spent together, or whether the child will wear dresses. Conflict is inevitable when two people, who are different by definition, do something together in which each of them has tremendous emotional investment. It is not a lack of conflict which indicates a good working relationship, but the ability to deal with differences in a way that increases mutual understanding.

Keep in mind, also, that the agreements you make at the outset will have to be modified by the child's developing needs. It is all well and good to say you plan to share custody on a 50-50 basis, but what your child requires will have to take precedence. An infant who is nursing will need to be with its mother. A baby or toddler will need the continuity of a familiar environment, routines, and care-givers to develop a sense of basic trust. Trying to shuttle an infant back and forth in split custody may be very disruptive to its development. It may be necessary for one parent to have primary custody, at least initially, while the other parent spends time visiting in that household. Keep in mind that even if you do not have physical custody of your child, you can develop a strong parental bond during the time you spend with him or her. You can also have a full parental input into the decisions that are made about your child's care.

As your child matures and shows evidence of being able to tolerate longer separations from the primary care-giver, you can evaluate how well he or she handles changes in the home environment. Some preschoolers and early elementary school-age children do very well living in two different houses, while some feel confused and distressed by being here on Tuesday and there on Friday. Furthermore, a child who handles split custody well at three and four and five may start to experience difficulty with it as school pressures make life more complicated. Other children may do fine in the early school years, but may find split custody taxing as their social lives become more active.

While we undertake parenting because we have strong personal needs to care for and raise a child, in a coparenting arrangement we have to be willing to modify our vision of our parenthood to suit the child's developing needs and capacities. You don't know who your child is going to be. Even knowing what your child can handle this year doesn't completely predict how she or he will react to things next year. There has to be a willingness on the part of all the parents to continually reevaluate what is best for the child, and to seek guidance and counseling if they are not sure about it.

To make mom-and-dad coparenting work, you must go into it with an overriding dedication to supporting the family structure you create. It is not enough to just want the child, you have to be willing to champion the whole family constellation, knowing that it is in your child's best interests to do so. Fay and Roger's story is a good example of the kind of maturity, caring, commitment, and outside support that have to go into this. If you can see yourself putting in this kind of effort, and you have picked a coparent who shares your vision, your child will benefit from the richness of having two or more devoted parents with a lot to offer.

GAY DADS MAKING BABIES

What Is Surrogacy?

The phone rings, and Georgeanne tells Stefan that Lila is in labor. It has just started, they don't need to rush. Stefan, still on the phone, signals to his lover, Raphael—"This is it!" The men finish their breakfast slowly and deliberately, afraid to be elated, not wanting to rush lest their excitement jinx it all. They remember the camera, the music tapes, the champagne, and their jackets. On the way to Lila's they stop for flowers. Later, at the birthing center, Lila will deliver a baby boy, hold him for a few minutes, and then hand him to his parents, Stefan and Raphael.

Lila, a lesbian, conceived via alternative insemination with Stefan's sperm. But Lila never intended to function as a parent. She wanted very much to be pregnant, however, and to have the satisfaction of knowing she could bring joy to a gay couple who wanted a child. Throughout the pregnancy she was delighted by the growing life inside her, but always thought of it as Stefan's and Raphael's baby. She and Georgeanne expect to see the child with some frequency, as the two couples have been friends for many years. They look forward to being godmothers to the child, and to watching Stefan and Raphael become the parents they have always wanted to be.

Stefan and Raphael, like some other gay couples aching for a child, arranged for this pregnancy with Lila in an informal way, without contracts, based on years of friendship and trust. In doing so they took substantial legal risks. If the parenting arrangement ceased to be agreeable to either Stefan or Lila at any point, the law would offer little guidance or protection. In their case, however, they felt that they were on pretty secure ground given how well they knew each other. It has, in fact, worked out happily for everyone. Two years later they are discussing plans for Lila to conceive again, this time using Raphael's sperm.

Not every gay man who wants to parent, however, is so lucky as to have a friendship of long standing and deep trust with a woman who wants to bear a child for him. Nor would every man who does have such a friendship want to incur the legal risks of such an arrangement without protection. Some gay men are therefore turning to paid surrogacy contracts, entered into with the help of lawyers, with women they have never met before.

Surrogate motherhood is the route to parenthood chosen by gay men who want to be primary parents to a child biologically related to them. Some gay men have employed surrogates because they did not know that adoption was an available route to parenthood for them (see Chapter Five). Surrogacy is often expensive and sometimes difficult, but not necessarily more so than the other routes lesbians and gay men take to become parents. Socially and legally it is controversial, but as lesbians and gay men none of us are strangers to controversy. It represents a valuable option for gay men who want to be both biological and primary parents.

Surrogacy as a solution to infertility has been documented since as early as biblical times. Throughout history in many cultures there have been women who bore a child for an infertile relative, for example. Commercial surrogacy, however, in which a woman agrees to perform a reproductive service for someone she may never have met before, is relatively new in our society. A 1988 newspaper article[1] reported that there were 1,000 such births in the previous decade; some experts I have spoken with believe 2,000 is more accurate. In the most common surrogacy arrangement, a woman agrees to be inseminated with the sperm of the man who intends to parent the child. The agreement specifies from the outset that she will never be the parent of the child she delivers. She is merely offering the use of her reproductive services to create and bear a child for the biological father. The contract usually specifies how she will care for herself medically during pregnancy. The father agrees to accept the child as it is born, whether or not it has unforeseen problems. He also agrees to pay the surrogate's expenses—medical, legal, living, and whatever else is agreed upon—and usually a fee for her time and efforts as well.

Variations on the surrogacy theme include situations in which the egg from one woman is fertilized with the sperm of the man intending to parent the child, and the resultant embryo is gestated in the womb of a second woman. That woman, the surrogate, gives birth to a child who is not genetically related to her. The medical technology for this is expensive and more complicated than alternative insemination, since it involves either *in vitro* fertilization or embryo transfer, which have not yet become simple techniques. While this procedure is primarily used when the woman who intends to be the child's mother can produce eggs but cannot carry a pregnancy to term, there are gay men who have gone this route. One advantage of having the egg contributed by an ovum donor and then carried by a different woman is that it separates the complex emotional issues of being a genetic donor and being a gestational mother. In addition, the gestational surrogate does not have to meet as many specific criteria, other than being healthy enough to carry a pregnancy, since her genetic characteristics are irrelevant.[2]

Such sensitive interactions between strangers and concerning highly emotionally charged events can easily lead to conflicts, misunderstandings, and difficulties, if not outright tragedy. It is therefore important that a surrogacy arrangement be made extremely carefully.

A Murky Area of the Law

The constitutionally protected right to privacy guarantees each individual's freedom to reproduce and create a family as he or she chooses. The government is not permitted to interfere in such private matters, unless it can demonstrate that such interference is necessary to prevent harmful activities. Legislators of the past did not envision commercial surrogacy, however, and the federal government has as yet taken no stance, legislative or judicial, on the issue. Passions run high on the debate about whether paid surrogacy contracts are, in fact, harmful to anyone, and so far there has not been a constitutional challenge. Meanwhile, the states are rapidly introducing legislation to address the problems they anticipate from surrogacy, and some such laws have been passed (see Chapter Six: The Legal Issues). Some seek to regulate surrogacy so that it can be carried out with the best possible outcomes. Others seek to make entering into a surrogacy contract a criminal act.

As long as it isn't a crime in your state to hire a surrogate mother, the government won't interfere. In reality, according to a government survey, "the majority of surrogacy arrangements proceed without judicial involvement, with few reported instances of parties reneging on their agreements."[3] In fact, some experts believe that no case has ever ended up in court in which a surrogate mother was adequately screened and the sponsoring parents were fully informed. There have, however, been a few cases in which surrogate mothers changed their minds and decided to keep the babies, or where a sponsoring parent refused to take a child. Should something go wrong, the parties will find themselves in a legally foggy area.

Where no state laws have been enacted which regulate and protect surrogacy, the courts are on their own to determine the legality of a surrogacy contract. In general, the courts have little to rely on except the existing laws that govern adoption and custody, which are not adequate to handle the unique circumstances of surrogacy. The result is that it's difficult to predict the outcome of a surrogacy case.

Controversy

The "Baby M" case in New Jersey brought the potential problems of surrogacy into the public view. The biological mother, Mary Beth Whitehead, contracted to bear a child for William Stern and his wife, Elizabeth. When the child was born, Whitehead claimed that she could not part with her and asked the court to grant her custody. The initial court decision awarded the child to the Sterns on the grounds that the surrogacy contract was valid and should be respected. On appeal, the decision was overturned. The surrogacy contract was invalidated, and surrogacy in general was declared to be baby selling, as well as degrading to women. Custody, however, was given to the Sterns on the court's consideration of the child's best interests. Mary Beth Whitehead's parental rights were reinstated; though she would not have custody, she would be entitled to parental visitation.

The trial was a media event. It became a rallying point for spokespeople on both sides of the surrogacy question. In general, most of those opposed to surrogacy are political conservatives who see it as a violation of traditional family proscriptions, whereby sex and reproduction are always supposed to occur together within the confines of marriage. Yet feminists have been divided on the surrogacy issue, with some feminists siding with conservatives to condemn surrogacy as harmful to women.

The controversy around surrogacy brings into question our basic definitions, legal and moral, of what parenthood is. It questions the legal status of biological ties, and whether contracts which seek to override those ties can be valid. Is a woman who enters into a surrogacy agreement illegally selling a baby? Or is she merely renting her reproductive system, over which she has legal domain? Are the prospective custodial parents exploiting women in poverty by using their wealth to buy babies? Or are they exercising their constitutional rights to create families for themselves with the informed consent of the women involved?

In the antisurrogacy camp are feminists like Barbara Katz Rothman, who argues that parenthood should be determined solely on the basis of relationship, and not on the basis of genes and gametes.[4] According to this reasoning, a sperm donor is not entitled to parenthood, because the donation of semen involves no relationship with the offspring. The surrogate mother, by contrast, has a relationship of nine months with her offspring in utero. That should make it hers and hers alone to decide, at any time, whether to keep or relinquish her baby. Therefore, a contract she signs before that relationship begins should be subject to her complete revocation, at her will, whenever she chooses. This would effectively render all surrogacy contracts unenforceable. Furthermore, Rothman argues, it is questionable whether a potential surrogate mother can even be considered to have free choice in the matter. Economic considerations put the mother at risk for exploitation. The parents seeking a child through surrogacy are almost always from the upper classes, while the surrogate is almost always in need of money. One of the surrogate's motivations for conceiving a baby is to get paid. What, then, would protect poor women from becoming the wombs of the rich?

On the other side of the debate are feminists who feel that to ban surrogacy in order to protect women from the dangers of exploitation is to adopt an attitude that women do not have the ability to determine for themselves and to contract for themselves the ways in which they will use their reproductive capacities. Such a ban risks portraying women as helpless victims of their hormones and emotions, whose maternal instincts must take precedence over their rationally stated intentions. Carmel Shalev, a feminist lawyer, feels that a woman should absolutely be allowed to enter into surrogacy contracts for payment, and should be required to honor those contracts.[5] Not to do so, she argues, would be to continue the patriarchal "protectiveness" of women that has kept them and their reproductive capacities under male domination for centuries. Giving women the right to contract for surrogacy insures their privacy and control over their own reproductive power. If, in addition, this right were coupled with the opportunity to have visitation with her offspring, as is more commonly done in open adoptions these days, the interests of everyone are best served.

The issue, as the proponents of surrogacy see it, is not whether surrogacy itself is an abuse of women or children, since clearly many surrogate births have occurred to everyone's satisfaction. The problem instead is how to regulate surrogacy so that people are free to make the reproductive collaborations that they choose, while avoiding potential exploitation of women and children because of poverty or lack of truly informed consent.

The Question of Money

Much of the debate around surrogacy centers on the issue of payment. Adoption laws uniformly ban the payment of a fee to a birthmother. The purpose of the prohibition is to prevent baby brokers from coercing poor pregnant women into selling their babies. It helps insure that babies are placed for adoption in accordance with the mother's wishes and the child's best interests, and not merely to the highest bidder. Surrogates, meanwhile, customarily receive a fee of $10,000 or more for their services (though that is not the total cost to the prospective parents; see the section on costs, below). Opponents of surrogacy have called it reproductive prostitution. They say that payment constitutes the purchase of a child as if it were a commodity. However, surrogacy and adoption are fundamentally different. A woman with an unwanted pregnancy is in a crisis in her life, and therefore vulnerable. Surrogate mothers, by contrast, set out to do this deliberately and consciously, fully able to make a choice about the prospective risks. Furthermore, the surrogate is not giving the baby to a stranger but to its own father. In addition, the father pays the money to the surrogate even if the baby does not survive. The money, therefore, is clearly not for the sale of the baby, but to compensate the woman for her considerable work and investment of effort in this endeavor. Nor is the father merely hiring the woman's womb in a depersonalized way. The surrogate is making a choice to use her time, her body, and her energies to accomplish an end.

Though some surrogate mothers have been willing to incur the significant risks and hardships of pregnancy and delivery for no compensation, other than the intrinsic satisfaction of altruistic desires to help a childless couple, in truth this is hard work. The surrogate deserves to be paid. Few women would be able to do the job without payment. In fact, $10,000 seems at best a token payment for the surrogate's role, which includes many months of negotiations, screening, and inseminations; 24-hour-a-day child care over the course of nine months; countless hours at medical appointments; time lost from work; and health risks, emotional upheaval, and possible permanent bodily changes. The reality is that if you ban payment, you essentially render surrogacy unworkable.

Choosing a Surrogate

In addition to the ethical, legal, and emotional complexities of surrogacy, there are logistical difficulties. Finding a suitable surrogate mother is no easy task. A lot is asked of such a woman. She may spend a year or more leading up to the pregnancy, and then nine months of gestation. During that time she has to explain her pregnant condition to her family, neighbors, and employer, knowing that she will have to account later for the absence of a baby in her life. She will have to deal with the reactions of her other children, explaining to them that this baby belongs to someone else. She will have to go to prenatal care and listen to people's comments on her pregnant status. She undertakes the health risks and discomforts of pregnancy, followed by labor and delivery, with a risk of major surgery if a C-section is necessary. She will have to live with the permanent changes to her body that pregnancy and delivery may leave behind. And she will have to separate from a baby she has known and carried and birthed, which may not be emotionally easy.

It will take some hard looking to find a woman who is interested in such an ordeal, who meets your criteria for genetic contribution to your offspring, and with whom you think you can feel comfortable working. Yet there are women who want the job.

Most gay men find surrogate mothers through advertisements in local newspapers. Other private sources may include word of mouth—asking friends if they know someone who might be interested. There are also a number of commercial services throughout the country which will screen potential surrogate mothers and match them with a suitable father or couple, as well as handle the legal work. These agencies vary in the quality and extent of screening and follow-up they do; some are extremely professional and conscientious, while others are less thorough or less involved in the emotional concomitants of surrogacy. Some are merely law offices, which do not provide psychological support for the parties involved. Others may offer a range of services and supports. It is therefore important that you interview a surrogacy service carefully to assess what they have to offer.

In addition, surrogacy agencies differ in their receptiveness to gay men as applicants. Noel Keane, an attorney whose advocacy for surrogacy has made him an international spokesperson, has changed his stance on the issue of gay applicants. A few years ago he wouldn't consider it, not because of personal prejudice but because the legal and social problems involved with surrogacy made it so precarious that he did not want to add fuel to the arguments of conservative opponents. Now, however, he assists gay men seeking to become parents via surrogacy "because of my feeling of strength in what I am doing—my absolute conviction that it is our right of privacy."[6] While I was on the phone with him, a call came in from a single man in Canada who represented a group of thirty single men interested in becoming fathers through surrogacy. Keane notes, however, that finding surrogates comfortable working with gay men is problematic. It is not just the surrogate but the surrogate's husband, if she is married, who must feel at ease with the arrangement.

Other surrogate-matching centers I spoke with also indicated that they had no problem with gay applicants. Services I spoke with in Kentucky and Kansas indicated that they would be happy to assist gay men but did not believe they could find willing surrogates. Attorney Steven Litz in Indianapolis, however, has a file of thirty-five surrogate mothers recruited from all over the country and asserts that half of them would be willing to work with a gay applicant. Litz finds that women who are interested in being surrogates tend to be open-minded to start with and thus more likely to feel comfortable with a nontraditional family, despite the fact that most of them are themselves in very traditional families.

Some of the services that accept gay applicants are listed in the Resources section of this book. A few of the agencies who do work successfully with gay men, however, did not want their names listed as resources. That position, while less than satisfying, is understandable, given their concern about not arousing controversy that could put them out of operation. Networking through gay parenting organizations is one way to locate those resources. Another is simply to call surrogacy agencies in your state and ask their policy.

Dr. Hilary Hanafin is a psychologist specializing in surrogate parenting who works with attorney William Handel in Beverly Hills. Though their service will not accept gay applicants out of a concern with the fragile legal and political status of surrogacy, they are willing to offer private information, education, and consultation to gay men who want to become parents. Hanafin, who has done research on the characteristics of good surrogate mothers, shared with me some of the criteria that make for a successful arrangement. She asserts, "This is a long-term relationship. It isn't going to be over and done in the hospital. You should only make a baby with people you like and trust." Hanafin feels that this edict is even more important when gay men are involved, because the surrogate will be the child's only female parent.[7]

An important criterion for surrogates is that they should already have children of their own. The assumption is that only a woman who has already been through pregnancy, childbirth, and the bonding relationship with a baby and child can enter a surrogacy contract with truly informed consent. The potential for tragedy for everyone involved increases significantly for a first-time mother, who may be unprepared for the emotional experience of motherhood. In addition, Hanafin asserts that a surrogate mother should have "a financially stable situation, a good pregnancy health history, and good self-esteem. She also must be between the ages of twenty-four and thirty-five and be bright enough to handle a complex forty-five page legal contract and sophisticated psychological dynamics."[8] The surrogacy screening program that Hanafin directs rejects nineteen out of twenty women who apply to become surrogates.

The director of another surrogacy service I spoke with described surrogates as "very special people" who tend to be motivated strongly by sympathy for the pain of an infertile couple. In their experience, they are not giving their own child away but having someone else's child for them. They love the child without feeling a sense of parental ownership, and are very concerned about the quality of home the parents will provide. Many maintain personal relationships with the child's parents, including visits together, for years to come. Hanafin suggests that lesbians who have children from a prior heterosexual marriage may be good candidates as surrogate mothers for gay men. They have the advantage of not having a husband in the picture who has to give consent, and may in addition have a particular sympathy for gay men who wish to parent.

For some surrogates, the money they receive for their services seems to be a secondary motivation. Though few could devote the necessary time without some compensation, and many are pleased that the money will help with their children's education, for example, the money is not the primary reason for undertaking a surrogate pregnancy.

For a woman to choose to bear a baby for someone else in our society today is an act of courage as well as generosity. Most surrogates come from Christian backgrounds and traditional family situations. It takes a great deal of originality and personal integrity to expose themselves to potential criticism. For a surrogacy situation to work out well, therefore, it is important that the surrogate have support for what she is doing. Some centers offer, and even require attendance at, support groups for surrogate mothers. In a private surrogacy arrangement, counseling or therapy might provide an important avenue of support. The benefits of having the opportunity to thoroughly explore and anticipate all of the feelings that arise will accrue to everyone in the situation.

As with adoption, the degree of openness that couples desire varies significantly in commercial surrogacy arrangements. Some matches are kept entirely anonymous. The sponsoring parent or couple may meet the surrogate near the baby's due date, and on a first-name basis only. Up to that point, the screening, contracts, and inseminations may be carried out with no contact between the two parties. The surrogacy contract provides for whether or not identities will be revealed when the child comes of age.

At the other end of the spectrum are the matches that are made with complete openness from start to finish. Attorney Litz says of his program, "I don't allow anonymity. A woman doing this is doing it because she wants to help someone. It's only fair to allow her to meet the couple." Furthermore, there is only so much he can tell either party about who the other is. It takes only a twenty-minute meeting for everyone to feel more secure. Besides, he says, "For me it's the most rewarding part of this whole thing—to see them meet and care for each other."[9]

The Costs

The family that Stefan and Raphael created cost them almost nothing to arrange. Lila's insurance paid for the medical costs, and the agreement was done out of love. In general, however, the expenses of surrogacy are high. The payment to the mother is frequently about $10,000, though it may be twice that or more. In addition, if a surrogacy center does the screening, legal work, and support, a fee of another $8,000 or more will be required. There may be additional advertising costs, physician's fees for screening and inseminations, maternity clothes, fees to establish paternity, travel expenses to and from medical appointments, the surrogate's legal fees, and other costs. The total, can come to $20,000 to $30,000 or more, although it may not have to. The expenses of any given situation are quite variable.

John and Brendon's Story

John and Brendon had no support network of gay families when they began the process. At present they are the fathers of sixteen-month-old Sara, and they are proceeding with a surrogate contract for a second child. They both wanted children very much, and had talked about it on and off for many years.

John recalls, "I think turning thirty was a catalyst. Okay, now I'm thirty. I'm grown up. We finally started saying, 'Let's figure out if there's anything we can do to have children.' The first thing we did was put an ad in our local gay paper. Our ad read something like 'We're a loving long-term gay male couple, and we want to be dads. Do you have any knowledge of or interest in adoption or surrogate parenting? Please write our box number.'" There was only one response to their ad; as luck would have it, it was exactly what they needed.

John and Brendon were extraordinarily fortunate. Their ad contained only a post office box number, and in general that is a poor way to get a response. Very few people will take the initiative to write. Your chances of success are better if you include a phone number. You may wish to have a separate telephone line installed in your home for this purpose. That insures that when you hear it ring, you can prepare yourself for the possibility that it is a surrogate mother. First impressions are important, and she has to like you as well as you liking her.

Gay papers are also not necessarily the best or only places to advertise. The local free papers that get distributed in supermarkets are often the best way to reach women who might be willing to be surrogates. You needn't mention in your ad that you are a gay man. You can reveal that information when you screen people on the telephone, or you can put it in a letter written after the initial phone interview.

John and Brendon were astonished to have gotten a letter from Leslie, a potential surrogate. "She wrote a very nice letter. We were very eager to meet her, and arranged to meet her and her [lesbian] lover for dinner. It was Friday night. We had to wait on line at the restaurant. We didn't know how we were going to meet these people. We didn't know what they looked like. It felt awkward. You're just feeling so wound up and excited, and your adrenaline's coursing through your body.

"I remember vividly that I had some sort of vision in my mind of what a woman who would be a parent to our child would look like. This woman doesn't look at all like that. She's not incredibly attractive, and I don't think she pays a lot of attention to her appearance. She's tall and athletic-looking. She and her lover were wearing matching sweaters.

"I remember thinking, 'There's no way Brendon's going to go for this.' Then when we got out of the restaurant and compared notes, he said, 'Let's go for it.' She had an interesting story. She was in the armed forces, and had been the victim of a lesbian witch hunt. For a cover, she had married a gay man from a foreign country who wanted his citizenship. It turns out that one of her motivations for surrogacy was that if she got pregnant she had the option of getting out of the armed services. She never wanted to talk about the money. She always felt very awkward about that part of it. She genuinely wanted to help us.

"Our lawyer was a gay man we had used for a house settlement. He didn't have any family law experience. In retrospect that was terrible. We did hear of one surrogacy specialist, but he wouldn't deal with us because we were gay. He thought it was too complicating, in addition to all the factors in Leslie's life like possible trouble with immigration and possible trouble with the armed services."

Over the course of the next three months both biological parents got medical evaluations. John had a sperm count done. The mother had psychological evaluations done. The lawyers did their part. Brendon and John decided that John would be the sperm donor.

John explains, "It was largely because I was the initiator in all this. We felt that I should get that privilege. I was the one who really wanted the biological connection, and was really intrigued by making all this happen. Then we also looked at it in a very cold rational fashion. We would sit down and say, 'What's the worst thing that could happen?' The worst thing that could happen, we decided, was if the child was born and we did not get custody, and there was all this messy legal wrangling, and we were required to pay child support. Because Brendon makes a lot more money than I do it made a lot more sense to limit our financial liability. That's a cold rational way of looking at it, but we got a lot of security out of it. You feel so emotionally exposed doing this, especially because we had no support and didn't know anyone who had done it."

While the evaluations and paperwork were being done, John and Brendon met several times with Leslie and her lover. It is extremely important in a situation like this that everyone talk about what they expect to feel at every step along the way. It's useful to keep in mind that a woman in need of the surrogacy payment may not have the same resources that the prospective parents have. It would be worth exploring with her where her support comes from, and making sure that she will be helped with the psychological stresses of a surrogacy arrangement. The prospective fathers should be willing to pay for professional counseling support for the mother, from a counselor of her choice, if she wants it.

John relates, "We met just to get to know each other. You wonder, is she the right person to do this? Can she stick to the bargain? You have to make sure they understand the psychological ramifications."

They had some negotiations about whether John and Brendon would be present at the birth. John describes, "It was a moment of some awkwardness in our relationship with Leslie. She said it was fine if we wanted to be there, but while we were thinking about it, her lover got jealous of us. Leslie then decided the birth was something she wanted to do just with her lover. That was fine, because frankly it seemed too personal for me anyway. I know if I were the mother I wouldn't want what is virtually a stranger in there with me."

As it turned out, Leslie's labor was short and easy. John was in the waiting room, but Brendon didn't even have time to make it to the hos-

pital. Their baby girl, Sara, was born in perfect health. John got to help
the nurses clean her up. Together he and Brendon watched her and
took pictures. Within twenty-four hours, they bundled her home. It
was not the end of things with Leslie, however. Some ongoing emotional issues, exacerbated by difficult legal wranglings, complicated the
picture for a while.

Leslie chose a lawyer who bills herself as an expert in gay families.
John and Brendon were not happy with her choice. "We felt her legal
expertise wasn't good and she wasn't helpful, and she made things a lot
harder for Leslie emotionally." As the sponsor of the arrangement, you
are naturally paying for the surrogate mother's legal expenses, yet she
must have the complete freedom to choose the lawyer she wants to represent her. With the selection of a lawyer, as with her selection of a therapist or counselor, you do not want in any way to be construed as
coercing her decision. As a consequence, you are dependent on the
expertise and professionalism of whomever she chooses. I have heard of
incompetent lawyers delaying the process for a year or more while the
fathers paid their fees.

John describes the trouble he and Brendon had with the legal
arrangements. "Leslie's lawyer started encouraging her to get visitation
rights in writing, which was something we had never agreed to. We
were the parents. If she wanted to have a relationship she knew she
could be a friend to our family. But her lawyer tried to put all that in
the contract and it got very awkward."

A number of dynamics fueled the conflict. John continues,
"Leslie's biggest problem was that she wasn't out as a lesbian. At work
she used being married as her cover story. She told co-workers that her
husband was going to stay home and raise the baby. As she got closer
and closer to her due date, people started buying her gifts, and women
would talk about the pregnancy in ways that women do. It just made
things harder and harder. She really allowed herself to be swayed by a
lot of these people. She felt a lot of pressure to bring the child in to
show to them.

"At one point she said she wouldn't sign the parental termination
papers (giving up her rights as a parent) unless she got some side agreement on visitation. She decided that the way she would handle this
whole thing emotionally was to make us the villains. She wanted to
have a relationship with the child, but it was too awkward to have a
relationship with us. So she wanted a relationship with the child that
didn't include us. We said, 'You have to do it through us. We're not
going away. We're not the bad people, we haven't done anything

wrong, and we're not going to be treated like that.' She made some threats. She said if she didn't get unsupervised visitation she would go to court, and that was no good for us. She didn't want a lot. She wanted maybe one hour a month."

John and Brendon were eager to avoid a court scene. They wrote Leslie a long letter detailing their feelings and how they had been consistent all along, had welcomed her as a friend to the family, and were hurt by the antagonistic approach she was taking. However, they said, they were reluctantly agreeing to what she wanted. They stressed that in addition to her getting to visit the baby alone, they wanted her to come and talk with them over dinner, or go to a therapist with them, or open some form of communication that would help repair the feelings and reduce the stress for everyone.

John continues, "That was in August. We never heard from her again until Christmas. She said, 'I'm sorry for what I did. I had a lot of emotional problems. I finally found a therapist who has been helpful and things are better now. It's probably better that I don't see the child.' We didn't hear from her again until Mother's Day. She came to visit, it was nice, and we haven't heard from her since."

John has learned from experience, and says that he would never again choose a woman who wants to keep her surrogacy such a closely guarded secret. He also would not choose a woman who has not had a child before. The contract they are now drawing up for their second child is with a different woman who has already had children.

Brendon and John did the paperwork to arrange for a second-parent adoption of Sara (for a discussion of second-parent adoption, see Chapter Six: The Legal Issues). Their case was the first in the country involving a gay male couple who became parents via surrogacy. Hopefully, the trail they blazed can open options for other families.

It is not likely that surrogate motherhood will ever become as easily available an option for gay men as donor insemination is for lesbians, as the logistics are significantly more complex. However, as an increasing number of gay men consider becoming parents, the availability of surrogacy resources, both private and commercial, may increase accordingly. If becoming a primary parent of a child who is biologically related to you is what you want, don't give up. It takes perseverance and careful planning, but it can be done successfully.

5

ADOPTION

Why Adopt?

If adoption is right for you, it is a wonderful way of forming your family. It provides a loving home for a child in need and a loving solution for birthparents who are unable to parent at this time in their lives, as well as the opportunity for you to raise a child.

Despite the much-publicized shortage of adoptable healthy newborns, there are tens of thousands of children in need of homes at this very moment.[1] This includes healthy newborns, though it also includes healthy older children, and babies and children who need special help of one kind or another because of physical, intellectual, or emotional disabilities. When you adopt a healthy baby, you can become the parent you have always wanted to be, with the satisfaction of knowing you have helped a birthfamily solve a difficult crisis. Furthermore, the families I know who have adopted children with problems or disabilities find that the special quality of their parenting interactions can be particularly gratifying. Many of them know that without their love, their children might have fallen through the cracks of the child-welfare system and languished in institutional settings.

Lesbians and gay men are in a unique position with respect to adoption. Most heterosexuals consider adoption after long years of medical infertility workups, disappointments, and grieving. For them, adoption is something to adjust to when all else has fallen through, and it often requires that they overcome a sense of loss and failure. By contrast, lesbians and gay men often choose adoption first, out of pride in themselves and in their desire to give love to a child who needs it. In addition, because of our experience of being different from the dominant culture, we bring to our commitment to parenting an ability to embrace diversity in our families.

No matter how we create our families, we usually start out prepared for the fact that at least one parent in a couple will have no genetic connection to the child we raise. We have therefore already overcome the bias which presumes that parenting a child means having a biological relationship.

For lesbians who prefer not to experience pregnancy, adoption bypasses the medical and physical trials of conceiving, carrying, and delivering a child. For gay men, adoption is often the easiest route to parenthood, avoiding the costs and complications of surrogacy. In addition, some lesbian couples and gay male couples like the idea of neither partner being a genetic parent, so that both parents will have equal status with respect to the child. As one mother by adoption said, "Neither of us wanted that badly to be a biological mother, but we each expected to feel insecure if the other one was and we weren't."

In addition to those of us who are preferential adopters, there are lesbians and gay men who choose adoption because, like many heterosexuals, they suffer from infertility or carry genetic diseases or traits they do not wish to pass on, or because biological alternatives like surrogacy are not available. If adoption is your second choice, you should spend some time and effort working through your sense of loss about the biological child you would have wanted. Talking with other adoptive parents, especially in lesbian and gay parenting groups, as well as getting professional support from a lesbian- and gay-affirmative counselor, can help you arrive at a positive and joyful outlook on the prospect of becoming a parent by adoption.

Willa is a single lesbian who came to adoption for several different reasons. She first thought of it when she was twelve or thirteen years old. "My Mom and I used to talk about kids, and she'd say she wanted to be a grandmother. I said, 'I think I'm going to adopt because there are so many children out there who don't have homes.'" After growing up and coming out as a lesbian, Willa tested her desire to parent by caring for a foster child. The experience convinced her that "it wasn't that important to have a biological child."

Willa also felt that being a single mother made adoption a good choice for her. "I was doing it by myself, and I had the feeling that being pregnant by myself would be very lonely. There would be no one in the middle of the night to turn to and say, 'Did you feel that kick?'"

In addition, Willa was concerned about passing her genes on to a child. Several relatives suffered from alcoholism, and there is a lot of cancer in her family as well. But ultimately, she says, "It really wasn't that. It's just that adoption seemed the absolute natural thing to do." Willa is now the delighted mother, through adoption, of nine-month-old Sam.

Can We Do It?

It is absolutely possible for lesbians and gay men to adopt. We have become parents through every one of the various adoption routes that exist. While most gay parents have presented themselves in the system as single men and women, there is a growing trend toward adoptions in which full disclosure of sexual orientation is made during the process.[2] As we are becoming more visible in the system, word is getting around that we are good parents. Many social workers who wouldn't have dreamed of placing a child in a gay family ten years ago now do so without hesitation. More agencies are happy to facilitate adoptions to openly gay applicants. More pregnant birthmothers are choosing open lesbians and gay men to raise the children they are carrying. Catherine Unsino, a social worker in New York who specializes in adoption, feels that while government policies and adoption bureaucracies are still clinging to biases against lesbians and gay men, individuals in the adoption world are becoming more accepting. She notes that gay and lesbian parents increasingly find themselves welcome at adoption conferences. When she gives talks to prospective heterosexual adopters, she uses lesbians and gay men in her examples. She says that "at first I thought they would be startled to hear about gay applicants, but I haven't found that so. They nod and listen and think." Felix

Fornino, the president of the New York chapter of a fairly traditional mainstream adoptive parents support group, wrote, "It seems to me, that with over 70,000 children in New York under the protection of our child-welfare system, every effort should be made to recruit and support nontraditional families who wish to adopt. The marital status, sex, or preference of potential parents should not be an excuse used to prevent an adoption."[3] Despite continuing discrimination in many areas of adoption, there is momentum in our favor. It is already easier than it was five years ago, and possibilities are likely to increase in the next decade.

What Do We Need to Know?

As every parent by adoption knows, there is a tremendous amount to learn about what adoption means and how it works. It is a very complex process, and there are numerous decisions to make about what kind of child you are prepared to parent. Based on those decisions and on your financial resources, there are many options for finding your child. Each of those avenues entails different procedures and requirements that are regulated by different laws in each state. For lesbians and gay men in particular, there are different implications, both procedurally and legally, depending on where you live and the adoption route you choose. You will have to investigate and become an expert on the system.

In addition to learning the mechanics of adoption, it is important to begin the process of understanding how forming a family by adoption differs from creating a family biologically. The three main participants in an adoption are the birthparents, the adoptee, and the adoptive parents. Each member of that triad has his or her own psychological needs and experiences in the adoption situation. It is important to understand the motivations and circumstances of birthparents, so that we can feel we are in a cooperative relationship, not an adversarial one. Our children, too, will have some different experiences as adoptees from those of children raised in their biological families. Finally, our own experience as parents will include some unique features as a result of becoming parents by adoption. The more we understand about the feelings of everyone involved, the more successful the experience will be.

Where Do We Start?

There is no single, centralized source for all of the information you need about adopting your child. You may end up gathering information from books, from heterosexuals who have adopted, from lesbians and gay men who have become parents by adoption, from agency social workers and personnel, from private adoption educators or counselors, and from attorneys.

As you learn about your options, you will become clearer about your needs. Some people start out thinking they want a healthy newborn, for example, yet realize as they speak to other parents that they are more flexible than they thought. Others assume they will only be able to adopt the kind of child they want if they maintain privacy about their sexual orientation, yet discover there are ways that they can safely adopt as openly gay and lesbian parents. The information you piece together will become your individual treasure map, marking the route that seems right for your needs. This chapter is not intended as a substitute for the investigative work you will have to put in. It merely offers some basic outlines, along with the stories of some lesbians and gay men who have done it successfully.

You might start by contacting the lesbian and gay parenting group near you (see the Resources section). If no one in your area has adopted, try contacting a group in a larger city. You can write to Center Kids, the parenting project of the Gay and Lesbian Community Center in New York, for their information packet on adoption.[4] Finding one lesbian or gay adopter will lead you to another, and you will learn from each of them. For the most part, people who have negotiated the adoption system are astonishingly generous in giving time and information to other people just starting out. Don't stop just because you have learned something useful, as there may be options you haven't discovered yet.

Some of the adoption resources for gay men and lesbians are available only by tapping into the gay network. There are agencies and social workers who are friendly to lesbian and gay adopters but who do not publicize that fact about themselves. They are not necessarily where you would expect to find them. Some of them are tucked away in conservative states, and some are run by religious organizations. Though you may stumble upon them on your own, you are more likely to find them through the recommendations of lesbian and gay parents. In addition, there are some private adoption educators and counselors who are eager to help lesbians and gay men. They, too, may be found through other parents, and can direct you to services around the country and the world which will work with you. Furthermore, private counselors may help to educate you about the psychological issues in adoption for you, your child, and your child's birthparents.

Aside from pursuing specifically lesbian and gay sources of information, it is a good idea to begin to contact the adoption community in general. Starting with your Yellow Pages, you should consider finding an adoptive parents support group and attending their meetings. You can gather information there about conferences and other support organizations, and get put on mailing lists for newsletters. The contacts you make will enrich your understanding of the varieties of adoption experience available, and may also provide some wonderful personal support.

Wayne Steinman, a founder of Center Kids, tells prospective parents that adopting a child should become a driving force in their lives. He recommends that you be proactive and aggressive in pursuing adoption, and not just wait for agency personnel to get around to things. He also suggests that when you start this process you buy a loose-leaf notebook and keep notes of everything that goes on. When questions occur to you in the middle of the night, write them down. Note every phone conversation you have in regard to this process, detailing time, date, person, and content. When you are dealing with multiple agencies and many different people you may get confused and forget who said what to whom. This may be a long process, and it will help to keep things in order.

How Does Adoption Work?

Adoption is a legal proceeding whereby the parental rights of birthparents are terminated and the adopting parent is declared the legal parent. This means that every adoption must go through a court to be finalized.

The process of locating a child may be conducted by an agency, public or private; alternatively, in the states that permit, you may do it yourself. If you go through an agency, sometimes the birthparents' rights will already have been terminated and the agency will have become the legal guardian of the child. In other situations, the agency does not take legal custody of the child, and rights pass directly from the birthparents to you once the adoption is granted.

If you contact an agency to locate a child for you, you will probably be invited to a series of orientation meetings to learn more about the adoption process and what the agency has to offer. You will then be asked to fill out their application. It is likely to be extensive, requiring documentation about finances, references, and other matters. The agency is required by law to let you know in some reasonable period of time if they have accepted you.

Regardless of whether you intend to find your child independently or have an agency search for you, you will have to have a home study done before a child is placed with you. This is now mandatory in every state. If you are working through an agency, they will conduct the home study themselves. If you are adopting independently of an agency, you will have to arrange for your own home study to be done. In some states it is legal for independent licensed social workers to conduct a home study. In others, you must have a licensed agency conduct it for you, even though the agency may have no further role in your adoption process.

The purpose of the home study is twofold: It evaluates whether you could acceptably meet the needs of a child, and it presents your parenting strengths in a way that facilitates the adoption. The home-study process should not be adversarial. Home-study workers are eager to see children placed in loving homes. They want to observe and understand what you have to offer a child.

As part of your home study, you will probably attend one or more meetings at the agency office, and a worker will make one or more visits to your home. Everyone who lives in the home will be interviewed about their feelings about the adoption, employment, extended families, social lives, interests, religious activities, and so forth. The worker will also want to see where a child would sleep, and the general quality of your home. The physical environment of your home does not have to be elegant, just adequate and safe.

When a child becomes available through an agency, you will be offered the opportunity to decide if you want to parent him or her. If you agree, the child will be placed in your home. If you are adopting independently or through some private agencies, the birthparents will place the child with you directly or through an intermediary, like a lawyer. In international adoptions, you may have to go to the child's country of origin, or an intermediary may escort your child home to you.

Once you have the child in your home, you can petition the court to adopt. (Some international adoptions are final in the child's country of origin, though you have the option to readopt here. Some states require that you readopt here.) Following the petition, there is usually a waiting period before you can go to court to finalize the adoption. During this time, in an agency adoption, postplacement supervision visits are usually done by the home-study agency or worker. At this time, postplacement visits are not generally required for nonagency international adoptions. The waiting period, which is mandated by law, differs from state to state, varying from no time at all to over a year, (the average is one to six months). The number of postplacement visits is also regulated by state law.

At the end of that time, you go to court. The judge reviews your home study and the agency's recommendation, and approves the adoption. You then become the full legal parent to your child, with all the rights of biological parents, and can resume life without further intrusion from public officials.

What Kind of Child Do You Want to Parent?

All kinds of children are available for adoption. They include healthy infants of all races, and older children, some with serious problems. Because of the intense demand for healthy white babies in the private adoption system, children not in that category are often considered harder to place or are classified as having special needs. These may be healthy babies or children of color. They may also be healthy older children, who might have been stuck in the child-welfare system for years for bureaucratic reasons, such as delays in getting their parental rights terminated. There might be groups of two or more siblings who need to find a home together. Having special needs may also refer to having some physical, mental, or emotional disability. For some this may mean physical problems which are easily correctable or emotional difficulties which can be adequately dealt with in a loving home. Others may have serious limitations which skillful and loving parenting will surely improve but never correct completely.

Opening yourself up to the broadest possible range of children will do a lot to increase your chances of having a child placed with you, but this is a very personal decision. There is neither virtue nor shame in whatever choice you make. The child has to fit into your family, and your extended family, forever. It would be foolish to say you are prepared to parent a child with special needs if you couldn't lovingly and proudly embrace the child for who he or she is, or if you couldn't provide the extra attention or help the child might need.

On the other hand, if you have considered only a newborn because you believe a toddler or preschooler would never really be "yours," or because you believe that a child who has had transitions or hardships in early life can never be emotionally healthy, it might be worth talking to parents who have adopted somewhat older children. Similarly, before you say no to a child with physical problems, find out what they actually consist of. Learn about the specific medical problem and the additional demands it might or might not make on your family's resources. You may discover that many children who need homes have difficulties that you can live with comfortably. Ultimately the joy in parenting comes from seeing your children make progress, and it often doesn't matter where they start from or what levels they can eventually attain.

Different Types of Adoption

There are many various routes to adopting a child, but they can be broadly categorized as public, private agency, independent, and international. They differ in costs, options, and procedures. It is worth understanding something about the way the different systems function. The following is a brief and simplified sketch of the features of each type of adoption.

Public Adoptions

Public adoptions are done through a state-sponsored public child-welfare agency. For the most part, children come to the attention of public agencies through reported incidents of child abuse or neglect. It is the state's job to arrange for foster placements for these children, and to work with the birthparents, helping them to get services they may need, with the ultimate goal of reuniting the family. If the parents have died, or if they are not able to resume parenting and there is no extended family able to step in, the state agency will arrange for the parental rights to be terminated. The child then becomes available for adoption. Because of the public system's role in the protection of children whose families lack the resources to care for them, it encompasses a large proportion of older children, sibling groups, and children with emotional and physical problems. Though there are healthy newborns in the public system, the wait for healthy Caucasian infants is often many years. Healthy African-American and Latino infants in the public system are generally readily available to families of color.

The children in the public system are predominantly children of color. All state agencies will attempt to place children in families of their own race before considering a transracial placement. Some public agencies have policies which all but prohibit transracial placement, preferring to keep the child in foster care if no suitable family of color can be found. Other agencies will give preference to families of color, but will not hesitate to place a child of color with a loving white family if that is the best available option. If you are a white adopter and are interested in adopting a child of another race through the public system, you have to find out what your public agency's policy is.

The main advantage of the public system is that it is virtually free. The state pays the bill for the initial home study, for obtaining the termination of parental rights, for the services required to place your child with you, for postplacement supervision, and for finalization of the adoption. In addition, if your child has a condition which requires medical or psychological treatment, the state will provide a stipend or a medical service card for your child's care. If you are eager to parent a harder-to-place or special needs child and have limited funds to put toward the adoption process, the public system may be a good option.

It is not, however, your only possibility. Because the public system is so overwhelmed, many public agencies are now contracting with private agencies to assist them in finding families. Private agencies may be better equipped to provide you with attention and services with less red tape. Though they are expensive, their fees will often be waived if the child they place with you comes through the public system. You will also still receive the state's stipend for a special needs child if he or she comes through the private system.

Foster-Adopt Programs

Many states have programs allowing you to take a child into your home for foster care who is likely to then become legally free for adoption. This may happen directly through the public child-welfare system or through those private agencies which contract with the public system. The children involved are in permanent foster care. That is, their families are not expected to be able to resume caring for them. In addition, it is expected that at some time in the future it will be possible to obtain a termination of parental rights.

The advantage of a foster-adopt program for the child is that she may not have to get bounced around from home to home before being adopted. For the adoptive parents there are no fees at all. There is a stipend for the child's care until the adoption is effected, and this can be a wonderful way for a child to come into your family. The risk, however, is that the parental rights may never be terminated. Having a child removed from your home after years of caring can be devastating, so try to be as well informed as you can be about the circumstances of your child's birthparents and the likelihood that they will be able to resume parenting.

If you are interested in a foster-adopt program, contact the department of social services in your state and apply to become a foster parent. Let them know that you only want to care for a child who is potentially adoptable, and find out what your options are.

Private Agencies

Private agencies usually work with birthparents who come to them to make an adoption plan for their child. Because of this, adoptable newborns are much more likely to be found through private agencies than through the public child-welfare system. Most often a birthmother will approach a private agency during her pregnancy. Agencies may also recruit pregnant women with advertisements in newspapers and on radio. The agency provides birthparents with counseling about their options. For those birthparents who decide to pursue adoption, the agency will handle the costs of pregnancy and delivery, and help the birthparents with a variety of services. A suitable family will be found for the child, honoring the wishes of the birthparents.

Private agencies run quite a gamut with respect to their attitudes toward the adoption process and their requirements for adoptive parents. At one extreme are very traditional, conservative agencies that control the decisions about which babies get placed in which homes, with a primary concern for maintaining the secrecy of all parties. These agencies usually work only with traditional adopters (white, middle-class married couples below the age of forty).

At the other end of the spectrum are less traditional agencies that allow birthparents and adoptive parents to have a great deal of information about each other; sometimes such agencies facilitate open contact between the two parties so that they can truly choose each other. Agencies are increasingly offering a less traditional approach in response to a growing demand in the adoption community for a more humane process. Many of these agencies also welcome single adopters, and some are happy to deal with openly gay and lesbian couples.

Because they can limit the number of placements they handle, private agencies tend not to be overwhelmed like the public system. This leaves them freer to provide personal contact and quality adoption education and counseling.

Private agencies are sometimes expensive, especially for the process of adopting a healthy Caucasian infant,[5] though their fees vary enormously depending on their other funding sources, and on the breadth of medical, psychological, legal, and other services they provide to birth and adoptive parents. The range is from a low of about $5,000 to more than $30,000.[6] Some of the money you pay supports counseling and other services for the many birthparents an agency serves who do not choose adoption.

In many agencies, the fee will vary depending on the needs of the birthmother. You may be able to specify, for example, that you can only afford to work with a birthmother who has medical coverage or one whose family takes care of her living expenses. If you are adopting a child from an ethnic minority these fees are often reduced. Children of color are often considered harder to place through the private agency system, primarily because many families of color have not easily been able to afford high fees. If you are a family of color, the fees may even be waived in order to support same-race placements. As stated earlier, sometimes it is possible to adopt a state-subsidized special needs child through a private agency; in such an arrangement, you can virtually avoid all fees and still benefit from the private agency's atmosphere and services.

Independent Adoptions

In an independent adoption, there is no agency involved (except, perhaps, to do your home study). The job of finding an available child is yours. You may put ads in newspapers around the country, or on bulletin boards, informing pregnant women that you can offer a loving home to their child. There are lawyers who specialize in being intermediaries, advising you on placing the ads and getting through the process. Some people also find children through word of mouth or through recommendations from physicians or social workers they happen to know. Each state has regulations regarding whether and where you can advertise. (In fact, some states do not permit independent adoption at all, and adoption laws change quickly. Your state department of social services can tell you exactly what is legal in your state, or you can obtain a copy of your state's laws from the National Adoption Information Clearinghouse, listed in the Resources section.)

When you make contact with a birthmother who wants to work with you toward an adoption, you will be responsible for taking care of her medical expenses (if she does not have coverage) and all legal fees. Where the law permits, you may also have to pay her living expenses and possibly other costs. The costs of a private independent adoption vary a great deal, depending on the circumstances of the birthmother and laws of your state which may restrict the kinds of expenses you can cover. If she should change her mind about completing the adoption, you may have to forfeit money you've already paid.

Paying for birthparents' expenses which your state doesn't permit may make you guilty of a punishable crime and may void your adoption. States are concerned with distinguishing between adoption, a caring solution for all parties, and baby selling, which is exploitative and illegal. Sometimes birthparents request additional money to live on, for example, either because they are truly in need or because they are trying to capitalize on your eagerness to become a parent. Do not, under any circumstances, consent to any payment which is not strictly permissible in your state.

An advantage of independent adoption is that as long as you receive an acceptable home study, no placement agency has to approve you. This bypasses agency requirements about age, marital status, and sexual orientation. A further advantage is that you may have as much or as little contact with the birthparents as you and they choose to have. A disadvantage of adopting independently is that you may not have the benefit of valuable counseling and educational services, which are usually provided by an agency and are often crucial to making the process work successfully.

The decision to place a child for adoption is a difficult one for the birthparents. It requires resolving conflicting and painful feelings during a period when their life may be in tremendous crisis and judgment may be clouded. It may also occur at a time when hormonal surges may intensify and distort the emotional issues. The sensitive screening that an agency usually does helps to insure that placements are made only when the birthparents are comfortable and positive about their choice. In a good agency placement, it is less likely that a birthmother will change her mind at the last moment than in a situation in which she has not had adequate counseling and support for her decision. It may be possible and advisable to arrange for private counseling in an independent adoption, though you must be careful because some states prohibit this. In this and all matters relating to adoption, you should be thorough in investigating the possibility of any legal risks you may be taking.

The advice of a knowledgeable lawyer will help insure that you are adhering to your state's adoption code every step of the way. Attorneys are also essential for filing termination of parental rights petitions for birthparents, and for finalization of the adoption for adoptive parents.

International Adoptions

Because of widespread poverty and political problems, many countries are unable to provide adequate homes from among their own citizens for children in need. Some of them are willing to allow people from more affluent countries to adopt. Most of the countries permitting international adoption are in Central America, South America, Eastern Europe, and Asia. The availability of children in those countries, as well as the acceptability of unmarried adopters, may vary from time to time, as these countries' governments and laws sometimes change rapidly. The International Concerns Committee for Children publishes the *Report on Foreign Adoption*, updated nine times a year, which contains information about sources, requirements, and support groups.[7]

The laws and procedures of international adoption are quite complex. You must comply with the laws of your child's country of origin, the state in which you live, and the federal laws of the U.S. Immigration and Naturalization Service. There are many forms to fill out, and you will have to be fingerprinted.

It is less likely that you will be able to get a newborn by adopting internationally, because there are usually delays between the time a child becomes available and the time the child may leave the country. In some places it is possible to get a child as young as a couple of months, but more often they are somewhat older. You are also less likely to get detailed information about the birthparents through this route, and the children of an impoverished country are often malnourished. Try to find out as much as you can from your agency and from other parents about their experiences with different countries.

Once an adoptable child has been located for you, you will usually receive a picture and some information. When the adoption has been processed in the child's country and it is time for him to come home, you may have to travel there to pick him up. You may be required to stay for a week or more, or to make more than one trip. Dealing with the government of a foreign country may be an ordeal, especially if you do not speak the language. Some agencies, where the country permits, will arrange everything for you. A few will escort the child home.

The advantage of an international adoption is that children who need homes are readily available. They are often in desperate poverty, and adoption may be lifesaving. International adoption is also an opportunity to become part of another country's culture. If you have a particular affinity for, or relationship to, the culture of a country that allows international adoptions, that should govern your choice. Deciding where you want your child to come from is a good first step.

Agency fees in international adoption are comparable to those in private domestic adoption. Additional costs of international travel with air fare, hotel stays, and time off from work can add a considerable amount. On the other hand, you will not have the added expenses of paying for the birthmother's medical and living expenses. All in all, with the rising costs of domestic adoption, international adoption is not necessarily more expensive.

Can We Be Open About Our Sexuality?

Depending on the type of adoption you are doing—public, private agency, independent, or international—there are different factors involved in whether or not to disclose your sexual orientation. How open you can or should be also depends upon the laws of your particular state, your personal feelings about it, and whether you are asked directly. Lesbians and gay men who want to present their relationships openly and proudly are managing to adopt. At present, the options are limited, but they do exist. As we become more visible in the system, new opportunities will open up.

If you are adopting through the public child-welfare system and you live in New York or California, you are legally protected against discrimination in adoption. In those states it is illegal for a public agency to turn you down as a prospective adoptive parent on the basis of your sexual orientation. That means that if you want to adopt through the public system as an openly gay person, and you live in those states, you have some protection. It does not, however, guarantee that you will not experience discrimination, which can appear in many guises. Homophobic social workers may simply not find your family suitable, ostensibly on other grounds, for the children in their care.

In Florida and New Hampshire, openly lesbian and gay prospective adoptive parents are expressly prohibited by law from adopting. Lesbians and gay men have certainly adopted in those states but are likely to have presented themselves as single adopters, remaining private about their orientation.

Other states have no particular laws which either protect lesbian and gay adopters or preclude them from adopting. Some families in those states have successfully adopted as openly gay men or lesbians. Since adoptions are processed county by county, the feasibility of being open in your home study will be influenced by the political and social climate of the specific county in which you live. Networking among lesbian and gay adopters in your area is the best way to get an idea of the kind of reception you will get.

Another influential factor may be the kind of child you are requesting. If you are offering a home to a child with very serious medical or emotional problems, your sexual orientation may be considered less of an issue. It is, of course, ironic that the same bureaucracies which feel that lesbians and gays are not suitable parents will place with us the children who require the most highly skilled parenting of all.

A private agency may establish its own criteria for the parents it serves. Some are happy to place a child with a lesbian or gay family, and some will accept applications only from heterosexual married couples.

The policies of adoption agencies friendly to lesbians and gay men may differ about how they will present your family in the home study. One agency I spoke with[8] insists that lesbian and gay applicants present themselves completely openly to birthparents. They also require that adopting parents submit a photograph of themselves for birthparents to look at when selecting a family for their child. Advertisements which this agency directs to birthparents might read: "We have two women who would like to adopt. Please call this number." In reference to the adopting parents' sexual orientation, the director of this agency said, "We're establishing it from the beginning so we don't have to backpedal later on, and we have found that to be very successful." If you live in a state or county where you are legally protected, the home study that is prepared will discuss, in writing, the fact that you are a loving and devoted lesbian or gay couple.

Some birthparents have chosen openly gay households for their children. A recent case this agency handled involved heterosexual married birthparents who met the lesbian applicants and were delighted. Some birthparents even specifically request a lesbian or gay couple once they know they are available. Sometimes this is because the birthmother has had painfully negative experiences with men and wants a family of women for her child. Once it was because a woman felt it would be harder to let go of her child to another woman and thus preferred the idea of two men. This agency has completed five successful adoptions for lesbians and gay men, and has two more in process.

Other private agencies who are friendly to lesbian and gay applicants may feel it is advisable to be more discreet about sexual orientation. They will approach the adoption from the standpoint that you are a single adopter, legally,[9] since the law does not recognize gay and lesbian unions. Though they are fully aware that you offer a loving, two-parent home, their omission of any mention of your sexual orientation will rest on the fact that they deem it irrelevant to your parenting qualifications. Your partner will appear in the home study as another adult in the home who will share the work of caring for the child.

In an independent adoption, you can decide for yourself what will work for you. Keep in mind, however, that if you are open and honest from the beginning, and the birthparents choose you with full knowledge of your sexual orientation, you are in the most secure position with respect to having your adoption finalized in the courts. In addition, one of the major advantages of independent adoption (or private adoption with a progressive agency) is the opportunity to have contact with the birthparents, and the value of an open relationship is marred by having to keep a secret. Independent adopters have found that they could come out to birthparents in their advertisements, in the initial telephone contact, or upon first meeting. Though many birthparents will reject you, you only need to find one who is comfortable with you.

If you are adopting a child from a foreign country, you may be dealing with an agency or a contact person in this country to locate your child for you. There are some sources who will work with an openly gay applicant, though many won't consider it. In international adoption, however, it is not advantageous to present yourself as an openly gay or lesbian family to the foreign government you are dealing with. The countries which need to place their children for adoption overseas tend to be religiously conservative third-world countries which are not yet at ease with the idea of lesbian and gay families. In these situations, you should always present yourself as a single adopter, omitting mention of your sexual orientation as part of your constitutional right to privacy, even if your source in this country knows that you are gay.

One critical point in all of this: *Do not ever lie at any time in the adoption process.* Though it is completely legal to omit any mention of your sexuality, it is illegal to lie about it when directly confronted. If you are asked a direct question, you must tell the truth. Failure to do so could be considered fraud. If discovered, it is grounds for taking your child away from you and nullifying the adoption, even though you may have loved and raised your child for years. It doesn't happen often, but when it does it's devastating. Do not take this chance with your family. It is far better to risk being rejected by an agency or turned down by a birthmother because you've acknowledged you are gay. If you are turned down, there are probably other agencies or birthmothers you can work with.

Open vs. Closed Adoption

Adoption laws change with the social and political climate. At one point in our history, adoption records were open in most states. That meant that any adopted child, at the age of eighteen, could have access to her original birth certificate and learn who her birthparents were. The social conservatism of the postwar 1950s changed all that, however. During that era, staying home and producing babies in the context of a heterosexual marriage became about the only way a woman could achieve social respectability. It became a source of shame to be infertile, unable to produce the required offspring. It also became a source of tremendous shame to become pregnant outside of the bounds of marriage. In the context of all this shame, adoption became a secretive business, and adoption records became sealed. During the 1960s and early 1970s, as a result of the progressive social values of the times, many states changed laws, and records once again became available and open to adoptees at eighteen years of age. The conservative 1980s unfortunately produced a time when legislators reversed decisions of earlier decades. Records now remain closed in all but three of the fifty states. Currently, in more than twenty-five states there are laws pending to reopen adoption records.[10]

During conservative periods, birthmothers were sent away to relatives or "maternity homes" to have their babies. Mothers were not allowed to see their children or even know what gender they were. The prevailing view was that these women would forget and go on to live normal lives; no one would need ever know about their "mistake." Infertile couples also had to hide their circumstances. Adoption agencies tried to match the baby's characteristics with those of the adoptive parents, so no one would know about their infertility. They were encouraged to believe that maintaining the family lie would be best for everyone.

The adopted children, meanwhile, often suffered. Though parents tried to keep the adoption a secret, children often discovered it later on and felt betrayed and disoriented. To prevent that occurrence, parents were advised to tell their children they were adopted but that their birthparents had died. Alternatively, they told them they were specially chosen children, with no reference to their ever having been born or having birthparents at all.

The deceptions spawned by the sexism and sexphobia of the time led to a lot of heartbreak. Birthparents found that they had pathological grief reactions; they were unable to adequately mourn and let go of a child they had given birth to but had never seen, and about whose fate they knew nothing. Many birthmothers, encouraged to deny all feelings about having had a child, suppressed them for years until the subsequent birth of another child or some later loss in life brought up intense pain and sometimes severe depression. Many adoptees grew up feeling angry at both the system and their adoptive parents for having lied to them. They longed to know about their origins. Adoptive parents saw their children suffering and felt inadequate to help them, due to the inaccessibility of information about their child's birthparents.

The adoption reform movement was an outgrowth of the fallout of closed adoption. Beginning in the 1960s and 1970s, adoptees and birthparents began to lobby for open records. Independent adoption facilitators and some private agencies began to help birthparents and adoptive parents choose each other, knowingly, in open-adoption arrangements. The children adopted this way can be raised with awareness of their origins, free to come to terms with their dual heritages. The birthparents can help insure that the child they love will have the home they cannot provide themselves, proud of their responsible and caring decision. With the knowledge of their child's birthparents and the circumstances of the adoption, adoptive parents can more readily help their children deal with the realities of who they are. No one has to feel guilty or inferior about the plans that are made by both sets of parents in the best interests of the child. As lesbians and gay men in a homophobic world, we know the kind of psychological havoc that carrying a "shameful" secret can cause. Openness and honesty in adoption is obviously much more humane than the old ways of secrecy and denial.

The amount of contact birthparents and adopting parents have in an open arrangement can vary from a mere exchange of nonidentifying information through an intermediary, to a close relationship during the pregnancy, with the possibility of continued contact thereafter. Occasionally birthmothers have even lived with adoptive parents before the birth, and adoptive parents have often been present at the delivery. Most commonly, the relationship after the adoption becomes a yearly, and in some cases more frequent, exchange of greeting cards and photos.

Open-adoption arrangements are increasingly available through private agencies, and are common in independent adoptions.

While the public adoption system does offer some opportunities for relatively open adoption, it is less common because of the way in which children in that system become available for adoption. Children in the public system have often been placed there because of neglect and abuse, and may need protection from birthparents who could be destructive to them. There are a growing number of adoption professionals, however, who feel that as long as a child is not in danger, it is better for her to have honest information about what happened to her, painful though it might be, than to deal with concealment or misinformation.

With international adoption, there have been only limited opportunities to know who the birthparents are. Hopefully, as attitudes toward adoption evolve all over the world, the option to make contact with birthrelatives will become increasingly available.

Transracial Adoption

If adopting a child, any child, carries with it the responsibility to educate yourself and your child about what it means to have a dual heritage, in a transracial adoption this task becomes much more involved and extensive. Babies of every race and color are cute and adorable, and anyone who wants to parent can fall in love with a baby who looks different from them. Love alone may not be enough, however. Trying to be "color-blind" does a tremendous disservice to both the child and the culture he comes from. Raising a child from another race and culture requires conscious awareness of that culture's presence in your life, and a willingness to embrace becoming an interracial family forever.

In addition to providing your child with access to his culture or race of origin, you will have to be prepared, if you live in the United States, to teach him how to deal with prejudice. If your child is of African descent, there may be extra prejudice to overcome. The history of slavery and black-white race relations in this country has left so many deep and continuing wounds that raising a black child in a white family carries additional responsibility, over and above raising children of color from other racial backgrounds. In the early 1970s, in response to difficulties arising in transracial placements and the emerging sense of black consciousness, the National Association of Black Social Workers (NABSW) issued a position paper decrying transracial adoption of black children as tantamount to genocide. Since then, some agencies have adopted policies which prohibit white families from adopting children of color. Other agencies, however, feel that a child in need of a home should not wait an inordinately long time in temporary foster care because a suitable same-race home cannot be found. In the two decades since the NABSW policy statement on transracial placements, it has also become apparent that Caucasian families who are prepared to raise their children of color responsibly, living fully integrated lives and providing access to their child's cultural and racial heritage, can do an excellent job of raising healthy, self-aware children with intact self-esteem and racial identities.

Before adopting a child of color, it is imperative that you look at your own lifestyle. Consider whether your neighborhood and your available schools are sufficiently racially mixed. If not, would you consider moving? Drs. Derek and Darlene Hopson, psychologists and authors of *Different and Wonderful*, assert that the key to learning to live in a racist society is having pride and self-esteem. These are encouraged by role models who can teach your child effective means of dealing with the world. Can you find a pediatrician, for example, and teachers and clergy of your child's race? Will you be able to provide some situations for your family in which whites are in the minority and people of your child's race the majority? Can your extended family embrace your child's culture as well?

If your geographic location, extended family, lifestyle, or anything else would make it difficult to provide the necessary components of successful transracial parenting, consider it carefully. Chances are you can find a child of your own race who needs a loving home. If, however, the prospect of becoming an interracial family appeals to you, as a lesbian or gay man you may be in the best position to do so. Those lesbians and gay men who have addressed their own internalized homophobia, and who are willing to address the racism we have all been raised with already have knowledge of how to create self-esteem in the presence of adversity. This can translate to knowing how to both embrace and value diversity in our own families.

A Public Adoption: Barry and Tony's Story

Barry and Tony were a perfect gay couple to try a public adoption in New York. They had met when they were barely in their twenties and both were teaching school. After thirteen years together, during which time they went through their process of deciding to become parents, they were ready. They wanted to adopt through the public system both because of their social consciousness—they were aware of how many children in that system need homes—and for financial reasons. Barry recalls that even if they could have afforded the costs of private or international adoption, "I would rather use the money for a child's education."

Barry is an activist in the gay community, and the two men had always been public about their relationship. So right away, he remembers, "We knew we were going to be open about being gay throughout the adoption process." In doing so they expected to experience some discrimination, and they decided they would be ready for it. Barry recalls, "We wanted to weigh all the options, all the what-ifs, to make sure that, in applying, we had every question answered beforehand. We didn't want any surprise questions thrown at us—anything that we would not have taken into account."

They started with the phone book, calling the city's adoption hot-line. They were referred to a Catholic agency which subcontracts to the city child-welfare system. They felt initially discouraged. Barry notes, "We felt there was no way we were ever going to be able to adopt. We'd just never get past square one." However, they filled out the application. The agency accepted it and called them in for an orientation. They found themselves in a room with other potential parents—two single black women, two married white couples, and them. One of the married couples was shortly dismissed when it became clear they were looking for a healthy white newborn. Barry and Tony, anxious about their own acceptability, finally asked cautiously about the agency's religious affiliation. Barry recalls, "The person conducting the orientation, who turned out to be the adoption supervisor, said, 'We do not discriminate on the basis of sexual orientation or, for that matter, on race, creed, color, marital status, handicaps, or all the other things that one can't discriminate against. We receive some of our money from public funding and some from private. Now, to answer your question, yes, we're part of the Catholic diocese and Catholic Charities.'" A little taken aback at their question having been so transparent, Barry has to admit that they were pretty easy to spot, "I mean, you kind of can't miss—we were wearing matching greens and we do stand out."

Barry and Tony presented all the characteristics of a model couple. Both have extremely stable work histories, including having been special-education teachers. They are warm and personable. They also demonstrated that they knew what kind of children were likely to be available; that they were knowledgeable and competent about finding support and services; and that, because of Barry's employment with the city, they knew a lot about how to access the social service systems. Barry reports, "I think the worker realized how serious we were, and that we were looking at it very appropriately and realistically. So being gay became a nonissue. The issue was just the best interests of the child."

The home-study process took about six months. Barry recalls, "It was a relatively young, newly educated social worker who did the home study. She was very politically correct. Instead of asking about the 'marriage' she would talk about the 'relationship' and 'significant other.' She fully understood and had no problems with the fact that we were gay. Whether she was chosen purposefully or this was just the luck of the draw, I don't know. To my knowledge, none of the people handling the adoption were gay."

Barry and Tony had prepared for this process like athletes in training. "We worked out everything! We knew which school a child would go to already. We knew how much it would cost, and we had the school application before we went to the adoption agency. If we had to act rapidly, we would have the answers. You never know, you might suddenly have a child who has to go to school. We kept copious notes. It's not unlike what we've done in life in order to succeed. We have to run at about 125 percent in order to be given equal treatment. There are more hurdles to jump over, and you have to be that eager in order to be given equal treatment."

Barry and Tony knew that the children available would be likely to have problems. He remembers, "We were trying to be realistic. Instead of saying we wanted a child who was four months old and had green eyes and would grow up to be an Einstein, we said we wanted to open ourselves up to the broadest possible choice because we were not that picky. Gender was not an issue. I was leaning a little bit more toward a boy because it would be easier running around naked in the house. Having never personally experienced what it's like to go through one's first menstrual period, I felt a little insecure about a girl. On the flip side, though, we wondered what would happen if we had this very macho little boy and we're both the world's worst baseball players. So we weighed it both ways and decided there was no issue there. We didn't care if it was a boy or a girl.

"We said we would consider any race, religion, or any ethnic background. We said we would consider a child with a handicapping condition, as long as that handicap was not a total disability." Tony and Barry drew the line at profound retardation or autism, feeling that they didn't have the resources to provide for the needs of a child with those conditions. "We also told them we would take a legal-risk child, that they should let us have the say, yes or no, as long as the risk was tilted in our favor."[11]

In addition, Barry and Tony did not insist on an infant. They said they would accept an older child, with the specification that they wanted one who was not yet in school. They wanted to have at least a year or so to transmit their own culture and values to a child before the child was exposed to the school environment.

Once they were certified to be preadoptive foster parents, they began aggressively searching the public system on their own. Even though it is the agency's job to find the child, it may help to add your own efforts to the search. Many states have lists of waiting children which can be found in the library and are open to the public.[12] Barry remembers how painful it was to look at those pictures. "It's gut-wrenching. It just tears you apart to see some of the children, especially those who are severely handicapped, with physical abnormalities. I almost resented going through the books because it felt like I was playing God. Tony and I knew that we would provide an incredibly good, warm, loving home for a child, yet who were we to pass judgment over a child who didn't photograph well or whose social worker wrote a bad caption?"

Painful as it was, they continued, and over the next eight months identified twenty-four children they were interested in. "We took a very proactive stand, and said to our agency, 'We're interested in these children. Please find out more information about them.' The agency was so overworked and understaffed that it would take weeks to get information, so they gave us the number of the adoption hotline in Albany, which is like a central registry. We did our own phoning, finding out where the child was. We spoke to the children's social workers. In fact, it worked out better because we were our own strongest advocates. No one can tell our story better than we can."

Barry and Tony explained that they were a gay male couple who had been approved for adoption. Despite New York's nondiscrimination law, they had many doors slammed in their faces. Pursuing the twenty-four children they were interested in, they were told twenty-three times either that they were inappropriate for the child or that the child had already been placed. This was an emotional roller coaster, because they developed feelings of attachment to several children they were looking into. Barry recalls, "There was the first child, his name was Julio. We still have his photo. You know how you fall in love with a picture? Julio was ours. We wanted Julio. There was no question in our minds. This was the perfect child. Unfortunately, he had been placed before we could make contact. On a few occasions it clearly was the wrong placement. One birthfamily wanted the child to remain in a certain region of the state. There was one where the social worker recommended a strong female presence in the home. That clearly was something we couldn't provide. On the flip side was a child who needed a strong male presence in the home. How much stronger can you have than two dads? But we were 'inappropriate.' Clearly there were many instances where the social workers were right, but it was very frustrating, especially after all this time and not even a nibble from our agency. We were seeing what we thought was systemic homophobia and we felt we were not going to succeed.

"Somewhere around the sixth or seventh month after the home study, they did ask us if we were interested in a baby we turned down. The child was severely autistic, and although we knew what to do and how to do it, the issue was that we're not full-time parents, and the child needed daily interventions in order to reach some ability to deal with the world. We could not provide that amount of time. The other issue was that we wanted a child who would grow up and be able to live independently, and there was no guarantee on that. Then, finally, we got the call, would we be interested in a little girl?"

Carla had been abandoned in the hospital, and she tested positive for cocaine at birth. She had some degree of physical impairment, for which she was receiving physical therapy. She was in a temporary foster placement, but the foster mother would not keep her any longer, so a decision had to be made quickly. The other two families who had been approached about Carla had turned her down. Barry and Tony felt anxious about the impact that the cocaine might have had on Carla's development. They got permission to call the facility where she was receiving physical therapy and ask questions. It appeared from the information they were able to gather that there was nothing which would prevent them from being able to care for her, but they wanted to see her first.

Barry explains, "We fell in love immediately. They said her muscle development was not quite up to par for her age, but when we saw her we couldn't imagine what they were talking about. It was not anywhere as pronounced as they were making it out to be. It was love at first sight." Like many new parents with a sense of style, they immediately began planning her wardrobe. "She was wearing some very chintzy frilly pink polyester thing that we couldn't wait to get her out of." For bureaucratic reasons, however, they had to wait until after the weekend to bring her home.

Barry and Tony began their new life as a family. The legal process, however, which should have taken two to three months to complete ended up taking two and a half years. This was in part because the process of terminating the rights of the biological family took a year longer than it should have. Delays like this are common in the adoption process, but the excessive delay Barry and Tony experienced had another reason. The irony is that their being such a perfect gay couple was responsible. As Barry remembers ruefully, "Three days before the adoption was to take place, the judge canceled it. He said that he had searched the records and there was no openly gay adoption in New York State, and he wanted to make our case a precedent. He wanted to go on record as being in favor of placing children, in their best interests, in gay and lesbian homes. So he canceled the adoption because he had more work to do to make this happen. He had to make sure that he had an ironclad rationale and that he couldn't be second-guessed."

Barry and Tony had no choice in the matter, and it turned out to have frustrating consequences. "The court chose a retired judge who is known to be ultraconservative to be the guardian *ad litem*.[13] He taught at a Catholic university and had a reputation for being incredibly methodical. What was supposed to take two weeks took months. They investigated us inside and out. It was horrendous. We became mentally incapacitated with fear that Carla was going to be taken away from us."

Carla was two years old at this point and had been in their home her whole life. Barry remembers the day the guardian *ad litem* visited their home: "He came into our home and sat down and said, in front of Carla, 'If I had my way she wouldn't be with you. However, I can find nothing wrong. You are, in fact, caring for this child better than anyone else would be.'" The adoption was finalized with his approval.

Meanwhile, however, the original judge who wanted to write the precedent that would put gay parents on the map never got around to it. His good intentions put Tony and Barry through months of agonizing insecurity and thousands of dollars of legal fees which would not have been necessary otherwise. This public adoption should have cost them $300 at most; however, with the increased investigation of their home, Barry and Tony had to hire a private adoption attorney to be safe. The total cost came to about $3,000.

When Barry and Tony went through this public adoption process, they were among the very first gay adopters the system had dealt with. There are now a number of counties in different states where gay and lesbian adopters are well known to public agencies, and many families encounter fewer difficulties. It seems that almost every adoption process is likely to include some drama or insecurity, however, regardless of the sexual orientation of the parents. The memories of that tension remain, but the experience, like childbirth, fades with time and parenthood. Carla is now a beautiful, joyful five-year-old. The anxieties Barry and Tony went through to get her are in the past, and she is everything they ever wanted in a child.

Jeff and Peter: Another Public Adoption Story

At about the same time that Barry and Tony were adopting Carla, Jeff and Peter, in another state, were deciding to adopt an infant with AIDS. Though their state does not expressly protect lesbians and gay men from discrimination in adoption, they decided to access the public system as an openly gay couple. For years they had joked and talked in a light vein about adopting a child, never really believing it was possible.

Jeff says, "It was just a silly fantasy, because we figured if we went to any adoption agency in the country and said, 'We're two gay men,' we'd be turned away."

Then Jeff, who edits a newspaper, began reading press releases coming in to his paper from the Division of Youth and Family Services in his state. The articles talked about the desperate need for foster and adoptive parents for addicted and HIV positive babies. Jeff called up the Division office in his county, and told the worker that they were two gay men who wanted to adopt a baby with AIDS. The worker asked if he wanted to take six babies or a dozen.

The home-study process was initiated. Like Barry and Tony, Jeff and Peter also continued to network on their own. Through a contact who worked in a hospital, they heard of an abandoned baby who tested positive for HIV. If they liked him, the baby could be theirs as soon as the state approved them as foster parents. The next day they drove to the hospital to see him.

Jeff recalls, "Daniel at that point was just four months old. He was in seemingly perfect health. He was gorgeous, he had the most beautiful brown eyes, he was the happiest child. He was in a stainless steel crib with a thick plastic cover on the top that looked like something an animal would be caged in, in a room with big HIV posters out front that said, 'Warning, AIDS precautions, bodily fluids, wear gloves, masks,' whatever. He was born drug addicted and HIV positive.

"We'd have taken any kind of child, any level of illness. The little baby they brought to us—it was the most amazing experience of my life to see this baby. They all said he's perfectly healthy. He tests positive but he's perfectly healthy.

"We used to come to the hospital and see the nurses feeding

Daniel. He was sharing a room with a little girl who was HIV positive, and the nurse would be standing in the middle of the room with a mask on and gloves on, with a bottle in each hand and her arms extended, feeding Daniel on one side of the room and the other baby on the other side of the room. There was no contact."

It took four weeks for Jeff and Peter to get approved as foster parents, during which time they were at the hospital with Daniel every day, feeding him and caring for him. Finally, they got the call that they could take Daniel home. They had been unwilling to acquire baby supplies, except for a car seat, before getting approval, for fear it would jinx things. Then, suddenly, they were instant parents and didn't even own a diaper.

Jeff describes, "On the way home we stopped and bought diapers and formula. We had a modular sofa in our living room. We rigged it up, put cushions around it and made it into a little crib for him."

The next morning both Jeff and Peter had to go to work. Peter, who owned his own shop, took Daniel to work with him. Jeff went to the newspaper office.

"When I got into work my desk was covered from one end to the other with diapers and formula and bottles and everything you could imagine. It was the most unbelievable sight. They basically, overnight, gave me a baby shower. People came into the office that day who weren't even working, but who had stopped at Sears and picked up a little sleeper set or a little wash set, or this or that. The customers at Peter's shop were even more overwhelming. We got so many things and so much support. Everybody thought it was absolutely fabulous. I remember this one straight woman who had adopted a child herself, and she said, 'Oh, he's young enough that he'll learn your smells and he'll really be your child.' It was the most amazing thing. And gay people were so touched and overwhelmed. They just dumped baby goodies on us."

As family life went on, the legal proceedings to disentangle the biological family's rights from the child were in progress. Finally, when Daniel was about eighteen months old, the case was transferred from the agency's foster-care division to the preadoptive office. Throughout the whole process, Jeff and Peter were known to everyone, officially and on all the paperwork, as a gay couple.

Jeff recounts, "Well, then all of a sudden they said, 'Okay, Daniel's cleared for adoption. You can get a lawyer, we'll get a date in court and you'll adopt him. But we think it would be easier if Jeff did the adoption just by himself, as a single man.' We had been on pins and needles that whole eighteen months. We loved Daniel dearly, and any thought that we might lose him was devastating, so we didn't want to rock the boat whatsoever. This is one area where I feel truly oppressed as a gay man. I think the state was wonderful in allowing us to do this, though they wouldn't let us take any old child; it was only an AIDS baby they'd let us take. Nonetheless, they let us do it, and I was very happy and appreciative of that. But then when it came time to adopt him, I really do feel we were denied due process or something. We felt so vulnerable to losing him, so we didn't push the issue."

Jeff became the legal adoptive parent of record because of his salary and position. "It was really sad on the adoption day. When we went in, we were there together as a couple. But it was me who walked up and swore the oath and answered the judge's questions. Peter was sitting out in the audience, and I really felt sorry for him."

Jeff and Peter opened their hearts to a baby who was born HIV positive. They, like the others who have done this, went into the experience with the raw courage it takes to give your heart, knowing it may well be broken. There are, however, some happy endings in life. At sixteen months, Daniel's regular monthly blood tests converted to HIV negative. Though it is now widely known, medical personnel at the time were not aware that the majority of children testing HIV positive at birth have probably acquired only the antibodies to the virus from their mothers and not the virus itself. In time, the antibodies pass out of their systems and no longer yield a positive test result. Daniel is now in perfect health, with a perfectly normal expected life span, and all the potential in the world.

Marty and Earl: An Independent Adoption

Marty and Earl, both in the entertainment industry, at first thought they would go through the public system, but after being sent to many different agencies and enduring numerous orientations, they felt frustrated. Here is Marty's appraisal of what happened: "When we actually presented ourselves we got great feedback—the people we met at each place were bright and caring and supportive—but when the bureaucracies behind them found out about our situation, they were more reticent to help out." The result, as they educated themselves about their options, was that they decided to bypass some of the bureaucracy by doing an independent adoption. The more they learned about adoption, the more it was important to them to do an open adoption, and to do it their way. As Marty puts it, "I didn't feel that it was appropriate to have a governmental body running interference between the birthparents and us. It seemed that we could act as our own advocates more readily, and it seemed that it was easier to be intelligent and not be a victim in the adoption process."

They went to lawyers who specialize in arranging independent adoptions. A few turned them down, saying they didn't want to take their money because there would never be a birthparent who would choose them. There were also lawyers who took their money and then said that a birthparent would never choose them. They were then referred to an adoption facilitator (who was not a lawyer) who helped them get going.

They placed ads in papers around the country. In some of the papers the ads said that they were a gay couple; in others it didn't, but they revealed it in the very first telephone contact.[14] Marty says, "It was opening ourselves up to a lot of crank calls, but it also cut to the chase. We would offer to meet them immediately, rather than spending weeks on the telephone."

Like most people entering the adoption process, they were initially focused on just getting a baby. However, they quickly found that they had many offers, and they could afford to do some more thinking about what was important to them. As Marty recalls, "We were thrown for a loop. We backed off and thought, 'Whoa, we have more power here than we thought.' Because of that, we felt we had a responsibility to figure out what our needs really were."

Among the birthmothers they turned down was one who seemed to have a lot of ambivalence about letting go of her child, who was already eight months old. Marty says, "I think she was looking for a babysitter." Earl adds, "She seemed to be looking as much for a new family for herself as she was for her baby." That wasn't what they wanted.

Some birthmothers wanted two men because they envisioned two incomes. Some wanted two men because they didn't want to be replaced by another mother, but Marty and Earl were concerned that the latter were situations in which the birthmother might never reach emotional closure on the placement. A number of the birthmothers who called were too early in their pregnancies. Marty notes, "We had been advised not to begin before six months of pregnancy." They referred those women to the facilitator who was helping them.

What they came to realize, in the midst of so many options, was that they needed more than a birthmother who would give them her baby. They needed a birthmother they could feel good about. As Marty puts it, "I needed to respect the birthmother. I wanted to like her, so that at some point I could tell the child it was planned for. If I had worked with a birthmother that I didn't like and didn't respect, and was just keeping a relationship going to get a child, I was going to have feelings about it which I would then project onto the child."

They arranged to meet with one of the most promising birthmothers. Their first glimpse of Dora, in a crowd at a shopping mall, was dramatic for Marty. "I said, 'That's her, I know it is! And this is it!' There was an immediate, very intense connection." The meeting confirmed the feeling—they all liked each other.

Dora had noticed their ad, one which stated specifically that they were two men, despite the fact that it was hidden in an obscure part of the paper. She was not quite eighteen, single, headed for college, and not interested in parenting. Marty and Earl describe her as a person of great bearing and presence. The three of them met a number of times, and they met with some of her extended family. Marty recalls that they "went into it keeping everyone else at bay. It was our dance. All communication was directly between the three of us. It didn't go from lawyer to lawyer—it wasn't like that. We didn't send medical forms; we said 'Tell us your medical history.' It was just very trusting. I remember saying, 'If you change your mind, that's fine. You'll be a great parent.' I did not want to parent a child that was taken through coercion. If it was meant to happen, it was going to happen, and I wanted her to be very clear that this was what she wanted to do."

Marty and Earl were present at the delivery when their daughter, Joy, was born. Marty recalls, "Dora turned to me in the delivery room and said, 'I feel so good about all of this.' That was the first thing she said to me when I was holding Joy."

Beginning life with the baby they already loved, Marty and Earl kept all the options open about what kind of ongoing contact they would have with Dora. Marty says, "We decided not to make a rigid plan. We felt we couldn't know what we would need in the future, or what life was going to be like, so we decided that we were going to trust each other to do the best we could."

Shortly after the birth, Dora came to visit, and Marty realized that the bond Dora felt was more with them than with Joy. He adds, "I have tremendous love and respect for this person, who really went out on a limb for us."

Though telephone contact was maintained, Dora did not come to visit again until Joy was two and a half. Marty recalls that they were involved in bonding with Joy, and so the distance from Dora was welcome during those first years. Especially in an open-adoption situation, it may take time for the adopting parents to fully believe that they are *real* parents, not just custodians. Marty discovered that "there's an entitlement that comes with being thrown up on, and being the bottom line twenty-four hours a day."

Dora's visit when Joy was two and a half laid to rest any lingering concern that Marty and Earl may have had about being the parents. Dora and the babysitter happened to walk in at the same time, and Joy responded immediately—to the babysitter. There have been several subsequent visits, and though Joy knows that Dora is her birthmother, there is nothing particularly intense about their connection. The adults feel they have been through a very intimate experience together, yet they don't really know each other very well. The result is a certain awkwardness in their meetings, offset by mutual warmth and respect.

Lynne and Pearl; Andrew and Don: International Adoptions

Lynne and Pearl adopted their daughter, Rosa, from El Salvador. Later, they adopted another daughter from Peru, and provided telephone support to Andrew and Don when the men adopted their baby, Chad, from Peru also. Both families speak with the relief of people who have been through an ordeal. Both families, also, couldn't be happier with the final outcome.

In each family, one of the couple presented herself or himself as a single adopter to the agency. Their partners, though fully participating in the parenting, were merely supporting players in the background as far as the bureaucracies were concerned. The first time around, Lynne and Pearl came to international adoption because they feared that a birthmother in this country could track them down and expose their homosexuality. Andrew and Don came to international adoption after a domestic adoption, poorly handled by a private agency, had fallen through. Many other families, however, including Lynne and Pearl for their second adoption, choose international adoption for more positive, and more political, reasons. Among those reasons are the awareness of the painful conditions of poverty and political unrest in some countries, where the children's need is truly desperate.

The number of documents required in international adoption can be daunting. Andrew remembers what he had to put together. "I had to have a report from a psychologist saying I was of sound mind, my passport, a letter from the bank stating how much money I had in the bank and whether I was a good customer, a complete physical, an AIDS test, a budget statement showing our monthly expenses, five recommendation letters from friends, tax returns for the last three years, a completed home study, local police clearance, and an FBI fingerprint check."

Andrew and Don were especially concerned about getting as young a child as possible. Though Andrew had expressed his preference for a girl, he was told that it would not be possible. Peru is a Catholic country, and a single-father adoption is not a familiar scenario. They had already cleared the fact of Andrew's being a single man with the judge in Peru, but there would be too many questions of impropriety if Andrew wanted a baby girl. If he were adopting twins or siblings and one of them was a girl there would be no problem, but otherwise they would best understand a man wanting a son. Lynne and Pearl wanted a daughter.

Lynne got the call one night that there was a little girl in El Salvador available for adoption. She recalls, "They said she was beautiful and happy, that she'd had some malnutrition but nothing that was going to be long term. She was a year old, and had just been brought by her birthmother to foster care. They needed to find a family right away. I remember trying to think of all the questions I wanted to ask. I didn't feel I could say yes on the phone, because I had to talk to Pearl. I said, 'She's a bit older than I expected. Let me just think about it overnight.' Pearl was completely calm. When I asked, 'What are we going to do?' she said, 'Well, she's going to be our daughter.' I hardly slept and could barely restrain myself from calling the social worker before seven in the morning to say, yes, I wanted her." They made the decision to adopt Rosa without ever having seen a picture of her.

Over the next six months, while the adoption was being processed in El Salvador, they got more information about Rosa. Though initially some of the material they got was confusing and contradictory, they eventually found out that Rosa's two siblings had died of measles and malnutrition. When she was brought to foster care, Rosa also had measles, an illness which is frequently fatal to children in the conditions of El Salvador, and her mother was afraid she was going to die. Two pictures finally arrived, which Lynne and Pearl kept on their refrigerator. Lynne recalls, "We made copies of the picture and sent them to everyone we knew, and carried them around. We were definitely glued to those pictures."

Andrew got a call from the agency director in the United States saying that there was a three-week-old boy available in Peru. He remembers, "I said I would love to meet him and bring him home. She said, 'Can you get on a plane to Peru by next week?' I have a business to run, and I said, 'No, I can't pull it off in one week. I need two weeks.' In two weeks we got it all together."

Their source in Peru required that they make an initial trip to the country, and then return in six to eight weeks when the adoption would be finalized. Lynne and Pearl, following El Salvador's rules, had to make only one trip to get their child, but had to wait longer before that could happen. Both families found it very disruptive to have to be available for international travel on very short notice, whenever the call came. When Lynne and Pearl were ready to go, they were told that El Salvador had just changed the requirements, and they would need more documentation, necessitating further delay. When the women finally went, they went together, with Pearl acting as an interested friend. Andrew, for his trip to Peru, did not want to arouse suspicions by taking Don with him. He was also advised not to take the Spanish-speaking woman friend who had offered to go with him, as it would not look appropriate for an unmarried man and woman to travel together. Instead, he took his mother.

Both families recall being overwhelmed in their children's countries by the combination of breathtaking beauty and horrifying poverty. Andrew had never traveled much, did not speak the language, and was quite anxious the whole trip. He recalls, "I was scared of the whole thing. At that point, without Don there, I thought, 'What the hell did I do? I really pushed it this far and now we're stuck.'"

The birthmother brought the baby to him in his room in the mountain village. "She had this baby wrapped up, covered in layers and layers of stuff. I was scared. I was scared that he didn't look as good as I wanted him to look. But really I was just scared of the whole situation. She started to unwrap him, and the more I saw of him the more I started to fall in love with him.

"We talked for a while, as best we could. Even though there was a language barrier, the mother and I communicated, and we cried. I'm so glad I met her, because she knows that he's going to have all the love in the world, and I know that he came from love.

"We spent about an hour together. Then they left my mother and me there with the baby, and I was suddenly thrown into parenthood."

The plan required that Andrew care for the baby in his hotel room for the week, during which time he would appear before the judge, pay money, sign papers, and be fingerprinted. At the end of the week, the Peruvian lawyer would introduce Andrew to his babysitter, the woman who would care for Chad during the next eight weeks while Andrew waited in the States. Andrew had brought eight weeks worth of diapers and formula to turn over to the sitter.

"After a week of being there with him and living the way we were living, I was torn between how badly I didn't want to leave him, and how much I wanted to get the hell out of there and go home to Don and a normal life. We weren't prepared. We didn't bring enough books. There was no radio or TV. My mother got very ill with altitude sickness. She was in bed for three days, and I was caring for her as well as the baby. I wrote Don this long letter saying, 'I can't believe I'm doing this. What did I get us into now?'

"But then it was horrible when I had to leave. Because of everything that was going on, I didn't realize the bonding that was taking place. When I went to leave him, I couldn't stop crying. We were afraid we'd never see him again. We were afraid they'd switch babies on us. We were afraid of a million things. In that eight weeks the mother can change her mind and we were afraid of that, too."

The return trip to Peru was fraught with mishaps, delays, and miscommunications. Everything took longer than it was supposed to. While they were in the mountain province, the authorities wouldn't let Andrew see Chad. Andrew was dreadfully anxious.

"On the way to the airport, to fly from Lima to the mountains, we got into our cab with a married couple from New York City. You know, you're very cautious about how much you say or what you say, but we figured out what we were both there for. We discovered that our babies were born the same day and they're both little boys. Can you imagine how I felt? I thought they were getting my baby."

Andrew's mother got sick again. Andrew got angry at the officials and threatened to leave without the baby if they didn't hurry up the process. Finally, though, everything was done and they were met at the airport by their baby.

Andrew felt, "Thank god it was him. We knew it was him. And he was beautiful. He was dirty, but he was beautiful. The feeling on that plane going back to Lima was incredible. I knew I was going to be safer in Lima, and I just let the tears come out."

In Miami, Chad was given his green card (his permanent resident immigration status). Back home, Don met them at the airport, and family life began.

Andrew notes, "He's still a Peruvian citizen until I have him naturalized. It takes six months to a year. I'm in the process of filling out all the forms, but I'm not doing it as quickly as I did everything else because I don't have the energy right now. He's not in a hurry to vote, anyway. In six months I'll raise his little hand and say the oath for him."

Though Andrew had found the whole adoption procedure to be difficult and painful, he would do it again. "I think it's like carrying a baby and giving birth to it—you forget a lot of the pain."

Lynne and Pearl were eager to learn all they could about their child's country. Though they were required to spend only a few days in El Salvador, they decided to stay longer so they could take pictures and travel around. The pictures and memories would help Rosa learn about her origins.

Rosa was eighteen months old by the time she was free to be taken home. Unlike a newborn, Rosa had formed strong attachments to her foster family, and the transition to Lynne and Pearl was extremely painful for her and wrenching for everyone. The foster mother and the lawyer brought Rosa to the hotel room and announced to her that Lynne was now Mama. Rosa screamed, 'NO!' Mama was the foster mother she had lived with and loved, and she clung tenaciously to that reality. Lynne would have preferred to be called by her name at first, but the damage was done. She recalls, "Rosa screamed in fury for nearly an hour when her foster mother left."

The next few days in El Salvador were intense for all of them. Lynne remembers, "At around six o'clock every night, when Rosa would hear cars, she'd look out the window and say, 'Papa?' because that's when her foster father came home from work in his car. She was clearly grieving. She cried herself to sleep every night."

The early adjustment with a child in the family is intense no matter how the child arrived there, but when the child is not a newborn, child and parents both have to come to accept their new life together. Rosa's malnutrition had caused a lactose intolerance, with resultant calcium insufficiency and dental troubles. In two trivial falls on the grass a few months apart, she broke two bones. When people teased Lynne and Pearl about child abuse, they were not amused. They were still trying to feel secure about being Rosa's parents.

One night, some months after being adopted, Rosa was looking through a magazine. She saw an ad for a car, looked at it, and said, 'Papa?' She then threw it across the room in a rage. She did the same thing when she was shown a picture of her foster mother. On another occasion, Lynne and Pearl were playing some Spanish music and dancing around with Rosa, who was laughing and giggling, when she suddenly began crying hysterically.

Lynne and Pearl subsequently adopted their second daughter from Peru. Teresa, at age two, was also severely malnourished and required extra medical attention as well as sensitive help with the emotional trauma of abandonment and change. Lynne noticed, "With both kids, after about six months at home, it suddenly became clear that they had been waiting for another shoe to drop. There was this visible transformation, almost overnight, where they somehow decided that this was home." The girls have become very attached to each other, and the four of them are now truly a family in everyone's minds and hearts.

Meanwhile, Lynne and Pearl have developed a deep respect for and interest in the countries their children come from. They have become active in Central American politics, in an effort to give something back to places toward which they feel gratitude. While adoption saves the lives of many children who are transplanted to richer soil, it does not solve the problems of poverty and disease which made adoption necessary. Lynne and Pearl feel that their growing involvement in Central and South America is a natural extension of their parenting of two beautiful children from those lands.

Whether you choose to adopt through the public child-welfare system, go through a private agency, find your child independently, or adopt in a foreign country, you will need stamina and patience. You may find yourself hungry for information, frustrated by bureaucratic delays, worried if it will ever happen at all, anxious about your child's well-being, and generally fatigued by the demands of a complicated process. If adopting a child is what you want, hang in there. Find support from other lesbian and gay adopters, and from the adoption community in general. Talk to knowledgeable people who can help you rethink your options, if necessary. Once your child is in your home and heart, the struggle you may have gone through to get him will be quickly replaced by joy.

6

THE LEGAL ISSUES

Heterosexuals who are planning to become parents do not usually consult with lawyers first. They don't have to. The laws which protect the families they create are already in place. When we create our families as lesbians and gay men, however, we are in a very different position. Our life partnerships have no legal status. In addition, our parental relationships with our children, if we are not the biological parent or the legal parent by adoption, also have no specifically designated legal status, despite all the love and care that go into those relationships.

First, let's be clear that it is not *illegal* for lesbians and gay men to create families with children. There is a big difference between doing something illegal and not having legal recognition. What this means is that if all goes well, and there are no conflicts between the parties involved which end up in the courts, the government will not bother us. Unfortunately, however, no one can ever be sure that all will go well.

For one thing, there are homophobic laws. Lesbian and gay relationships are denied the legal benefits of marriage in every state. Additionally, two states have laws which expressly forbid lesbians and gays from becoming parents by adoption.

For another thing, laws which are not specifically homophobic may simply be ignorant of the realities of our families. The laws and precedents about inheritance and custody were written with nuclear heterosexual families in mind. They have not kept pace with changing reproductive technologies and changing sociological trends. Applying those laws to us, the courts will tend to interpret our families along heterosexual lines. In the process, they may ignore the realities of our very different family structures.

Furthermore, judges are human. Many are ill-informed about or unfamiliar with lesbian and gay families, and some are even overtly homophobic. The overwhelming majority of judges are white males over the age of fifty who went to law school before the gay and lesbian movement gained prominence.[1] Even in situations where the laws would allow them to respect our parenting intentions, some judges will decide against us simply because they harbor prejudices against lesbians or gay men.

The overriding principle of family law is supposed to be the consideration of the child's best interests. While there is ample evidence from research and mental health professionals that a child's best interests are always served by the continuation of a relationship with any good care-giver, judges are still free to impose their own views. A parent's homosexuality may be seen as creating an immoral environment, for instance, and therefore to be not in the child's best interests.

Finally, there are those areas of the law where we suffer discrimination even if we don't end up in the courts. Discrimination in health insurance, tax and inheritance law, housing, and employment affect our families on a daily basis.

Family law is state law. Individual states have very different statutes about what constitutes a family. The political climates of those states will influence how narrowly or broadly those statutes are interpreted. Court decisions in one state which favor the recognition of lesbian and gay families may have an impact on decisions in another state, or they may not. It is therefore impossible to give a list of general principles which apply equally to everyone.

This chapter is by no means intended to be a comprehensive legal manual for lesbian and gay parents. Instead it is an attempt to describe broadly a variety of important areas to consider. There may be any number of additional legal concerns which are specifically relevant to your county, state, family structure, or means of becoming a family. In addition, the legal picture in your state may have changed by the time you've finished reading this. You are likely to need the help of a lawyer who is knowledgeable about your state's family laws and supportive of the type of family you want to create. Familiarizing yourself with the issues in this chapter will enable you to ask your lawyer the questions that most concern you. In addition, there are some things you can do on your own to help provide the maximum protection for your family.

What Is a Parent?

Traditionally laws and courts have viewed a child's parents as consisting of one heterosexual father and one heterosexual mother, usually legally married to each other. Some states have legislation which expressly limits the legal definition of a parent to someone who is a biological or a legal adoptive parent. Even where the laws don't specify, however, the courts are inclined to view parenthood in this narrow way. This tradition continues, despite the fact that only a minority of families today reflect this constellation.

New definitions of parenthood are needed which recognize functional parenting that involves a relationship of care, support, and responsibility for raising a child. So far, the state legislatures have been reluctant to enact laws protecting functional parenting relationships, but legal scholars like attorney Nancy D. Polikoff, of American University Washington College of Law, as well as organizations like Lambda Legal Defense and Education Fund, the National Center for Lesbian Rights, and the American Civil Liberties Union are attempting to change the way families are interpreted in the courts. Polikoff proposes that the "courts should redefine parenthood to include anyone in a functional parental relationship that a legally recognized parent created with the intent that an additional parent-child relationship exist."[2] She elaborates that "a parent under this new definition would be the child's parent regardless of how many other parents the child has or what sex those parents are."[3] This would comprehensively recognize all parents in the family structures created by lesbians and gay men. It would also exclude from legal parenthood other people who might claim rights through biology alone, for example, or through a caregiving relationship with a child that was never intended to be parental, such as that of a live-in babysitter.

The wheels of social and legal change grind slowly, however. In a recent New York decision, the court referred to the nonbiological mother as the "biological stranger" to the child, a phrase which negates the validity of a parental relationship, despite the fact that both women clearly planned to have and raise the child together. There continue to be court decisions which reaffirm outmoded definitions of family, to the detriment of the children, even while more humane courts are overcoming archaic prejudices and supporting more realistic perspectives on family law. The balance, we hope, is shifting.

Things Do Go Wrong

We don't like to think about the possibility that one of us could die or become incapacitated, that a loving relationship could break up, that an agreement made in good faith between decent, caring people could result in bitter disputes, or that extended family members could try to hurt us, but these things can and do happen. For the most part, even when these problems arise, lesbians and gay men manage to find ways of resolving them that do not involve the courts. However, sometimes conflicts do end up in court, where we are subject to a judge's interpretation of the statutes. It is important to think ahead of time, before any disputes arise, about what the probable outcomes of a legal battle might be under any of several circumstances. That way, you can make choices which might help safeguard your child's best interests.

When the Parents Break Up

Courts are hesitant to do anything which might impinge on the rights of the legal parent. Polikoff writes, "The significance of parental status in custody and visitation proceedings is profound ... When the dispute is between a parent and a nonparent, not only is the parent usually considered the preferred custodian, but the nonparent may even be found without standing to challenge parental custody."[4] As long as the legal parent is alive and competent, he or she is in control of the nonlegal parent's relationship to the child. (By "nonlegal," I mean anyone who is functionally a parent but who is neither a genetic parent to the child nor legally a parent by adoption. A nonlegal parent may be the lesbian or gay male partner of the legal parent, another adult of either gender in the same household, or an adult with a separate residence who has a parental role in the child's life.) In other words, the legal parent generally has the right to exclude the nonlegal parent from contact with the child. If the adults' relationship falls apart, the legal parent can take the child away and forbid visitation by the other parent. Nonlegal parents, then, are in a very vulnerable position. If a custody or visitation dispute ends up in court, the nonlegal parent's prospects are poor.

When a couple breaks up, it may be very tempting for a legal parent to exercise his or her rights to exclude the other parent. Except in situations where a nonlegal parent is abusive or potentially dangerous to the child, preventing him or her from continuing to parent the child is destructive. On a human level, it is harmful to the child and painful to the nonlegal parent. On a political level, attempting to use the laws to exclude a nonlegal parent is bad for the establishment of lesbian and gay families as legal entities. Polikoff, discussing cases in which biological lesbian mothers attempted to use their rights to exclude nonbiological mothers from visitation after a breakup, is emphatic about the ethics of such action. She writes that these biological mothers "have asserted reprehensible positions. Perhaps in each case, the biological mother wished she had never formed a family with a nonbiological mother. In this respect, she would be no different from vast numbers of divorced parents who wish they did not share a child with a former spouse. Courts do not preserve the bonds of parenthood when a family dissolves because it is easy for parents; they preserve the bonds because courts consider it critical to a child's well-being to protect the child from the traumatic and painful loss of a parent.... If any of the biological mothers can prove it is in the child's best interests to deny contact between the child and the other mother, she should litigate the case on that basis. Attempting to avoid such litigation on the merits by equating the nonbiological mother's legal status with that of a babysitter or family friend does not demonstrate a principled defense of either parental rights or of the best interests of children. Rather, the technique is a bad faith assertion of a definition of parenthood that is no longer adequate to recognize contemporary family forms."[5] Paula Ettelbrick, legal director of Lambda Legal Defense and Education Fund, urges, "We've got to create a lesbian and gay ethic if we're going to do this. Rule number one is if you agree to parent a child with your partner, you've got to follow through on that agreement."[6]

There are several steps you can take to help insure that you stay out of the courts. First, prepare a coparenting agreement before you have a child. The document itself has no absolute legal power, but the process of drafting it forces all of you to discuss in detail what you have in mind. (It also indicates to the court, should it come to that, the original intentions of the parties involved, which may count for something.) Include in your coparenting agreement some method for seeking help with resolving a dispute should one arise (see Coparenting Agreements, page 174).

Second, when conflicts occur which might threaten the ongoing relationship of the child with one of his or her parents, seek counseling together. See a therapist, marriage counselor, lawyer, member of the clergy, divorce mediator, or anyone you trust who is comfortable supporting lesbian and gay families. In some cities, such as New York, Los Angeles, Chicago, and San Francisco, lesbian and gay mediation projects are being developed to provide a place where families can work things out with a trained mediator.

When the Legal Parent Dies

A nonlegal parent has a much better chance of getting custody of the child in the event of the death of the legal parent than in a dispute with a living legal parent. While the courts generally want to protect the rights of a legal parent during his or her lifetime, when the legal parent dies they will be more concerned with protecting the child's ongoing home environment. The type of dispute that has come to the courts most frequently is a challenge to custody brought by the biological family of the legal parent. Grandparents have attempted to take a child away from their daughters' lesbian partners.

In Florida, for example, a legal mother died when her child was five years old. A year after the death, the grandparents sought and obtained custody, taking the child away from the surviving mother. Grief-stricken from the loss of the child, the surviving mother was unable to mount an appeal. Fifteen months later, unbeknownst to the surviving mother, the grandparents adopted the child, terminating visitation. When the mother found out, she was able to challenge the adoption, get it overturned, and gain custody. Unfortunately, the completion of this legal battle took five years. The court ruled in the surviving mother's favor not because it wanted to legitimize the parental rights of a nonlegal lesbian mother but because it was clearly in the best interests of the child, who showed obvious signs of distress at the grandparents' actions.

The older the child is when a legal parent dies, the more the relationship between child and nonlegal parent can be demonstrated. This is a relationship which the courts will be inclined to consider important. If the legal parent dies when the child is very young, however, it is harder to make a case that the bond between the nonlegal parent and the child is of such strength and duration as to be harmful if discontinued. In such cases, the documents which support the parents' original intentions may be your best protection in the courts.

In Vermont, a biological mother was killed in a car accident when her child was fifteen months old. The biological mother had indicated clearly in her will that she wanted her partner, who was the child's other parent, to have guardianship of the child. Her parents tried to invalidate the will and take the child away from her. Despite the fact that this child was very young, the court refused to allow the grandparents to have custody. The court respected the biological mother's decision to appoint her partner as guardian and awarded legal custody to the surviving mother.

The moral of this story is that having correctly executed documents makes a difference. You never know when a tragedy will happen, so it is important to have a properly executed will in place before a baby comes into your home.

Adopting Your Partner's Child

Second-parent adoptions, in which the lesbian or gay partner of a legal parent is granted full parental rights to that child, promise, at the moment, to be an answer to the legal vulnerabilities of lesbian and gay parents. They allow a nonlegal functional parent, with the consent of the legal parent, to adopt the child they have been raising together, thereby acquiring all the rights and responsibilities that parenthood entails, while the legal parent retains all of his or her rights as well. It makes no difference whether the legal parent is a biological or adoptive parent. As of this writing, more than 200 second-parent adoptions have been granted[7] in a total of eight different jurisdictions (Alaska, California, Minnesota, New York, Oregon, Vermont, Washington, and Washington, DC).[8] Cases in other states are pending, and the next few years should witness an increase in the availability of this option. This is a very exciting legal development for several reasons: It provides the child with the security of ongoing relationships with functional parents in the event of the breakup of the parents' relationship or the death of one parent. It allows the child to be covered on either parent's health insurance. It also permits inheritance to fall under the regulations for family members instead of strangers, which has definite tax advantages.

When a court grants a second-parent adoption, its motivation is to protect the ongoing relationship of the child with the nonlegal parent. You must therefore be able to establish that there is a relationship of parental quality and, in most places, some duration between the nonlegal parent and the child. The longer the nonlegal parent has been raising the child, the easier it is for the courts to understand the importance of the bond.

Whether a second-parent adoption can be done where you live depends upon the attitudes toward lesbians and gays in your county, as well as the statutes of your state. Extensive legal arguments, based on lengthy research and documentation, will have to be made to provide the court with a means of overcoming any objections. Much of the material that has been used in prior cases can be obtained by working with Lambda Legal Defense and Education Fund, the National Center for Lesbian Rights, and the American Civil Liberties Union.

Protecting Lesbian Families from Claims by Sperm Donors

Alternative insemination is relatively new, and states are just beginning to enact laws to deal with it. The critical legal question is how to distinguish between a sperm donor and a father. This is a vital issue for lesbians. If the donor is considered a legal father, he is entitled to all the legal rights and responsibilities of parenthood, including custody, visitation, financial support, and decision making with respect to the child's education, religion, geographic residence, health care, etc. If he is legally a sperm donor, he has no parental rights whatsoever.

At present, thirty-three states have some form of legislation that attempts to make the distinction between donors and fathers. Other states are currently considering insemination laws, and many states are expected to revise the specific requirements of their statutes, in both more liberal and more conservative directions, as fervor over these issues grows. The legal picture in your state may have changed by the time you are ready to begin inseminations, and it is worth checking with your lawyer.

Many of the statutes dealing with alternative insemination require that the insemination be performed as a medical procedure by a licensed physician, usually on the physician's premises (there are variations on specific details) in order for the genetic father to be clearly seen as a donor and not a father. Regardless of whether or not your state regulates alternative insemination, if you want to feel as legally secure as possible, you'll want to seriously consider carrying out your insemination according to the most conservative criteria, in case the legal climate changes.

What the artificial insemination statutes mean for lesbians is not entirely clear. The intent of most of these statutes is not, generally, to sever the rights of the donor per se, so much as it is to protect the parental rights of a heterosexual woman's husband. When the inseminated woman is not legally married, as is the case with lesbians, the laws may not apply at all, though a judge might choose to interpret the law in a way that favors a lesbian mother. The statutes of a few states provide for the donor's rights to be severed regardless of the mother's marital status, as long as the insemination is done as prescribed. Even if your state requires that you be married for a sperm donor to lose parental rights, conducting the insemination according to the statutory requirements will add some measure of protection.

To help insure that a donor will not have the rights of a parent, it is advisable to get a signed contract from him, stating his intention to sell his semen for a fee and to relinquish all claims to parental status (see Donor-Recipient Agreements, page 173). If you are using an unknown donor, your physician or sperm bank can obtain the document. If you are using a donor who is known to you, you can obtain the agreement yourself and have him donate his semen to the physician, who can then supervise the insemination as legally specified. These donor-recipient agreements are not legally binding contracts. A court may or may not respect them. They do, however, demonstrate everyone's intentions at the time.

While lesbians plan families with varying degrees of involvement from the biological fathers, the law recognizes only two possibilities: He is either a donor, with no rights at all, or a father, with rights to everything. If your primary concern is legal safety, you will want to insure that your child has only a donor, and not what the law might consider a father. Maria Gil de Lamadrid, an attorney with the National Center for Lesbian Rights, states that "there are no gray areas in the law here, and when in doubt, the courts tend to grant donors full parental rights in cases involving single mothers. From the lesbian mother's perspective, unless she is prepared to fully coparent her child with the donor under court order, she is much safer if the donor remains strictly a donor in the eyes of the law."[9] Any contact the donor has with the child could be interpreted as fathering. The longer the contact goes on, and the older the child becomes, the more likely he is to be viewed as a father. As Paula Ettelbrick of Lambda says, "If you use a known donor and you don't want him to be a father, then don't let him develop a relationship with your child. Once you do, you can't limit that relationship."[10] Any deviation from your original agreement, which stated that he would have no parental involvement, could be construed by a court as changing his status from donor to father. If the donor should change his mind and decide he wants rights to your child, a court would probably grant his petition.

Of course, legal protection isn't the only thing we value in our families, and we may want to incur certain legal risks so as to include a known donor in our child's life. In that case, while we cannot get absolute protection, we can increase our chances of things going in our favor. In addition to the donor-recipient agreement in which the donor states his intention to relinquish his parental rights, you should draw up a second document, indicating precisely the extent and nature of the contact you intend him to have with the child. Gil de Lamadrid recommends that this second document state that any time the donor spends with the child is completely at the discretion of the mother. This agreement should not use words like "visitation," "custody," or "father" in describing the kind of contact the donor may have with the child, as these terms may be construed to indicate a legal parental relationship.[11] While this document, like coparenting and donor-recipient agreements, has no legally binding status, it may be useful in preventing a paternity suit. And, as with the other agreements described here, should a dispute come to court, it also clearly states the original intentions of the parties involved.

Disputes Between Biological Mothers and Fathers

When a lesbian and gay man have agreed to create and raise a child together, acknowledging each other as having full parental status, the courts will regard them as a heterosexual family unit. They will consider both parents to have equal rights to custody and visitation. While any two legal parents should attempt to resolve their differences without court battles, lesbian and gay parents should try even harder. Despite the fact that both parents have legal rights, the courts will still not understand our different intentions. They will often misinterpret the roles of any nonlegal parents, such as the legal parents' partners. In some homophobic courts, the presence of a lesbian or gay partner in the home may even be taken as evidence of an improper moral climate for the child. Unless there is a situation of abuse or neglect, try to find another way to get help with the conflict.

Again, drawing up a parenting agreement ahead of time is a useful ounce of prevention; it encourages the parents to think clearly about what their expectations are, and it can specify a means for resolving disputes should they arise.

Gay Men and Surrogate Mothers

Surrogacy arrangements are contracts for the sale of reproductive services. Like alternative insemination, surrogacy is so new that the legal issues are still confusing and conflicting. In Arizona surrogacy is a crime, and you can go to jail for contracting to have a woman bear a child for you. In Kentucky, Michigan, and Utah, surrogacy is a crime only if you pay the woman, because it is thus regarded as "baby selling," whereas there is nothing illegal about it if you don't pay her. Some states that ban payment of a surrogacy fee will allow payment of various kinds of medical and other expenses to the birthmother. Attorney Lori B. Andrews, an expert on reproductive medicine, feels that bans on payment should be deemed unconstitutional. She makes the analogy that "our right to get an abortion wouldn't be worth much if there was a ban on doctors ever getting paid" and feels a constitutional challenge could be brought on that basis.[12] So far, however, such bans are untested.

There are currently eleven states in which surrogacy is not a crime, but the laws explicitly state that paid surrogacy contracts are not legally recognized.[13] Five of the states go one step further and void unpaid contracts as well.[14] There is an important distinction between statutes which criminalize surrogacy and statutes which simply do not automatically uphold surrogacy contracts, although the media often lumps them together: In the latter case, you are not breaking any law by contracting with a surrogate, and you do not risk going to jail. The statute simply means that if the surrogate changes her mind, the courts will not throw her claim out without considering it.

If all the parties involved in a surrogacy arrangement are satisfied, there is nothing to worry about. The legal problems crop up in situations where either the surrogate mother changes her mind and keeps the child, or the genetic father is unwilling to accept the child once it is born. The major legal concerns for a gay father via surrogacy are to establish that he is indeed the legal father of the child, and to enforce the mother's contractually stated intention to give up her parental rights.

It would seem that there should be no problem establishing the biological father's rights as a parent, since blood tests can determine that he is the genetic parent. However, the fact that conception occurs through alternative insemination means that, ironically, the same statutes which may protect a lesbian mother against an unwanted intrusion by a sperm donor may make it more difficult for a gay father via surrogacy to establish parenthood. He may be considered a sperm donor, making the woman's legal husband the child's official father. However, when surrogate mothers have challenged the father's paternity on grounds that he is a sperm donor, the courts have overridden the challenge, so this should be seen as an initial stumbling block and not a barrier. Your lawyer should know what action to take in your state to bypass this hurdle.

Enforcing the surrogacy contract is more complicated, however. This is what lawyers I've spoken with call a "fascinating" area of the law, which means that it is contradictory, largely uncharted, and has far-reaching implications for many other issues. What this means for gay dads, however, is that we just don't know which way a given case will go. In the worst-case scenario, a gay father could conceivably risk ending up with financial obligations to support a child he is not permitted to raise. Where the father's claim to custody is upheld, there are still complex legal and ethical issues about whether the surrogate mother should be entitled to visitation, based on a consideration of both her interests and the child's interests. Because of the legal complexities, it is important that the lawyer you choose for a surrogacy contract be knowledgeable in this specific area. You should look for a lawyer who is open-minded toward gay parenting and has proven expertise in family law and surrogacy.

At this writing, two gay men who are parents via surrogacy are applying to become the first family of that nature to be granted a sec-ond-parent adoption. If successful, the biological father's partner will then become a second legal parent to the child, adding one more achievement toward the goal of gaining legal recognition of our creative family structures.

Homophobic Relatives

Assuming your relationship does not break up and no sperm donor or surrogate mother challenges your right to custody, it is still possible that your parents or other relatives could make trouble. If they wanted to take your child away from you, however, they would have to demonstrate that you are an unfit parent. Grandparents and other fam-ily members have attempted to take custody of a child away from a legal parent on the grounds that the parent's homosexuality is contrary to the best interests of the child. In most places, even in conservative states, you are fairly secure. Because of the law's preference for a bio-logical parent's rights to his or her child, there is a large burden on the relatives to prove that the home is unsuitable. The contention that a child will be harmed merely by being in a lesbian or gay environment is insupportable, given the existence of a great deal of research to the con-trary. If you do face a challenge to your parental rights you may have to go through the pain and expense of having to educate the judge about lesbian and gay families, and present the case for your parenting. You will need help to do this. The National Center for Lesbian Rights, Lambda Legal Defense and Education Fund, and the American Civil Liberties Union can provide materials and guidance to your lawyer.

Adoption

Adoption is the legal proceeding whereby parental rights to a child are transferred from one set of parents to another. It is governed by numerous and complex laws. Individual states have very different legal requirements. What one state permits in an adoption arrangement might even be criminal in another state. In addition, when you adopt a child from a different state there are interstate regulations with which to comply. When you adopt internationally, there are your state's restrictions, the laws of the foreign country, and the federal immigration laws to which you must adhere. Choose a lawyer experienced with adoptions who knows the complex legalities that have to be considered. You don't want to risk doing something wrong when so much is at stake.

While many courts would avoid *taking away* a biological parent's rights on the basis of sexual orientation, they may be much more reluctant to *grant* parental rights by adoption to a lesbian or gay man. Every adoption must go through the courts. At present, there are twenty-two states plus the District of Columbia in which sodomy is illegal. Judges in those states may refuse adoption petitions to lesbians and gay men on the grounds that the criminal activity of sodomy is likely to occur in their homes. (This is blatantly discriminatory, as the same sexual acts are likely to occur in heterosexual families as well, but the laws are not applied against them.) Other courts may not cite sodomy laws but may consider homosexuality per se as an indication of an environment unsuited to raising children.

State laws and the regulations created by the state's child-welfare administration, which the courts are supposed to interpret, vary on the issue of sexual orientation. In two states, Florida and New Hampshire, lesbians and gay men are expressly forbidden by law from adopting. In New York and California, however, lesbians and gays are explicitly protected from discrimination in adoption and foster-parenting. In Ohio, the Supreme Court interpreted the adoption law to allow a gay man to adopt, refusing to let the fact that he was gay stand in the way. The remaining states have no specific legislation regarding gay men and lesbians as adoptive parents.

In most states, adoptions are processed county by county. This means that in more liberal counties, even in conservative states, judges may be favorably inclined toward our families. It also means that, even in liberal states, in the more conservative counties judges may find ways of impeding our adoptions.

A critical rule in adoption is never to lie. Lying about your sexual orientation constitutes fraud and is grounds for taking your adopted child away when the fraud is discovered. This is a tragedy for everyone, and it has happened to gay families.

Some agencies may choose not to ever ask directly about your sexual orientation, deeming it irrelevant to your ability to parent. In that situation, you are not required to volunteer it, though you may choose to. In all cases, though, a partner who lives with you must be part of the home study, however he or she is identified. Some agencies may insist that the nature of your relationship be fully disclosed in the home-study document. In most cases judges will accept an agency's recommendation in the home study that a child be placed in a gay or lesbian home, but the judge does have the ultimate authority and may question the appropriateness of this placement.

Your best protection, then, is to be prepared to educate the social workers and the judge about the issues they may raise. In considering the best interests of the child, judges who aren't familiar with gay and lesbian families may presume that the parents will sexually molest the child, the child will grow up to be lesbian or gay, or the child will suffer terrible social stigma because of having gay or lesbian parents. There is a huge body of writing and research articulately refuting each of these claims which your lawyer should be prepared to submit to the court, should it be necessary. The material you need can be obtained from the National Center for Lesbian Rights and Lambda Legal Defense and Education Fund (see the Resources section).

In independent, open adoptions, where the birthparents choose the adoptive parents for their child, the birthparents' choice is likely to be respected by the courts. In situations where birthparents have signed an affidavit saying that they are aware that the adoptive parents are in a lesbian or gay relationship, and that this is the home that they feel is best for their child, the placements have been approved, even in conservative states.

At present, except in a few places, only one member of a lesbian or gay couple will be permitted to become the legal adoptive parent. Even with a home study which clearly states that the adoptive parents are a lesbian or gay couple, parenting together in a committed partnership, in most places only one of you will walk out with the legal rights of parenthood. A handful of joint adoptions have gone through in California,[15] and it is hoped that more will follow, but this is new territory. As described earlier, second-parent adoptions (where they are being granted) will confer parental legal rights on the other parent once the initial adoption has been finalized.

Finding a Lawyer

The legal issues that arise with respect to gay and lesbian parenting are unique. When you choose a lawyer, therefore, you are ideally looking for someone both knowledgeable about and supportive of lesbian and gay families. The best place to start looking is to ask other lesbian or gay parents for references. Your local lesbian and gay parenting group (see the Resources section) is, once again, a prime resource. If you have no access to a parenting group, look in the "Legal Resources" list in the Resources section for an organization which will provide you with a referral to someone. If you cannot afford a lawyer, most big cities with active gay communities have legal clinics with sliding-scale fees which could at least help you write your will and may actually be able to help in a court dispute.

Many state bar associations will offer some pro bono (free) services. In addition, if you are a member of a labor union, your benefits may include basic legal services, such as the drawing up of wills. The problem with these options, however, is that attorneys found through these routes may not be sensitive to the special needs of a lesbian or gay family.

It is a good idea to interview more than one lawyer, either on the phone or in person if he or she will offer a free or low-cost initial consultation. Ask about their experience with your type of situation. Ask about their hourly fees and get an estimate of the total cost of their services. Get a sense of what their approach to your situation would be. Do not hire a lawyer with whom you don't feel comfortable.

Don't ever put yourself passively in a lawyer's hands. The attorney is your employee. It is your job to know what you want from her or him, and to communicate it. You should inform yourself, and stay on top of whatever legal work is being done. Make sure that you read the papers you sign. You are ultimately the one responsible for the results of your lawyer's efforts.

Wills and Guardianship

You will need a lawyer's help to write a will. The laws governing wills are very specific and vary from state to state. Using the wrong language or failing to adhere strictly to the legal requirements of your state in drafting your will could render it invalid. Especially if there is any possibility that your biological family would challenge your will after your death, you need to make sure that it is in perfect form. Therefore, even if you want to draft a do-it-yourself will, make sure that you have an attorney review it. As with any document, the more thinking you do on your own about what you want it to say, the less money you will spend on attorney's fees. For guidelines about how to do an initial draft, you can consult *A Legal Guide for Lesbian and Gay Couples,* by Hayden Curry and Denis Clifford, an easy-to-read self-help law book that contains many useful sample forms. It is available from Nolo Press, in Berkeley, California; Tel. (510) 549-1976. The book is not a substitute, however, for legal advice specifically tailored to your location and circumstances.

In many states, a will is the place you can name the person you want to be the guardian of your child in case of your death. In some places, you may need to write a separate document nominating a guardian. If you have a child, you must make arrangements for guardianship after your death. Not to have one could mean that the state will impose its ideas of what is best for your child.

However, while you have the legal right to assign your property to whomever you want, a child is not the same as property. In most cases, a court will respect your choice of guardian, but it will impose the standards of the best interests of the child. If you are nominating your partner, a nonlegal parent, as guardian, you should include in your document a statement that you believe it is in your child's best interests to continue a relationship with the person with whom they have resided in a loving home.

Judith Turkel, an attorney in New York who specializes in lesbian and gay families, also suggests setting up a trust for your child. She points out that in a heterosexual family it is common for one spouse to leave all of his or her property to the other spouse, who is also the guardian of the children. In our families, however, leaving all our property to our partners may appear to the courts as if we've left everything to a stranger and failed to provide for our child. We don't want a court to say, "This parent is irresponsible and therefore we are skeptical about his or her designation of guardianship as well." Even if your assets are small, leaving a portion of them—part of a life insurance policy, for example—in a trust for your child may prevent a challenge of that nature.

Finally, your will is valid only if you were clearly in possession of your mental faculties when you wrote it. If you have been diagnosed with AIDS or any other disease which could potentially result in dementia, you may wish to get a certificate from your physician to the effect that you were of sound mind at the time you signed your will. This will prevent a later challenge on those grounds.

Life Insurance

Term life insurance policies are inexpensive, and in the event of your death they can help protect your family from financial disaster. You have the right to name whomever you want as the beneficiary on a life insurance policy. On occasion, insurance companies will reject a designation of a nonrelative on the grounds that there is no "insurable interest." You can indicate on your designation that the person you name is the guardian of your child, which is a clearly insurable interest. If your insurance company rejects your designation of your partner as your beneficiary, put down someone they will accept—a relative, for example. You have the right to subsequently change beneficiaries to anyone you wish without penalty. However, don't neglect to make the change.

Donor-Recipient Agreements

These documents are not legally binding but are important both as preventive clarification for both parties and as a means of demonstrating the intent of everyone at the time of conception. The purpose is to protect the biological mother from a claim to paternity by a sperm donor, as well as to protect the donor from obligations to support the child financially. A sample donor-recipient agreement can be found in Appendix I. You do not need a lawyer to draft this document, though it is not a bad idea to have your lawyer review it for you.

The agreement should be a contract for the sale of the donor's sperm to the recipient, indicating that a fee has been paid. It should include the marital status of each party, and should state that artificial insemination was carried out, ideally (from a legal standpoint) under a physician's supervision. It should state that the donor is relinquishing all rights and responsibilities to the child, and that the recipient will have full authority to name the child, appoint a guardian, and determine the amount and nature of future contact between the child and the donor. If there is to be ongoing contact, a second document could spell out the details, leaving all control in the hands of the mother.

Coparenting Agreements

Coparenting agreements are documents drawn up between any two people intending to raise a child together. The coparents may be a lesbian mother and a gay father, both of whom are biological parents to the child. They may be one legal parent and that parent's partner, or any other person designated in your family structure as a parent who does not have legal parental rights. The basic structure of a coparenting agreement is the same whether or not both parties have legal rights to the child, though the specific provisions will have to be tailored to your family structure. The sample coparenting agreement that appears in Appendix II presumes that the parties are one legal and one nonlegal parent.

Coparenting agreements generally are not legally binding documents. They provide what attorney Turkel refers to as a "belt and suspenders" addition to the protections of a nomination of guardianship. In a court dispute, a coparenting agreement will further demonstrate your intentions at the outset of parenting.

The main value of a coparenting agreement is preventive. It forces the parents to articulate their expectations about child care, finances, decision making, and custody, so that misunderstandings do not later turn into battles. The responsibilities of child rearing, financial and otherwise, do not have to be equally divided, but the intended division should be spelled out. Generally coparents presume that decision making will be equally shared.

A coparenting agreement should clearly indicate that the couple is going forth with the intent to parent together, that the nonlegal parent is a psychological parent to the child, and that guardianship goes to the nonlegal parent in the event of the legal parent's death or incapacitation.

The agreement should spell out what visitation, custody, and support arrangements will be made if the couple should split up.

Perhaps the most important provision of a coparenting agreement is a statement of how disputes will be resolved, should they arise. You can agree, for example, that if either one of you feels it is necessary, you will both consent to see a counselor or mediator together. Having a plan for conflict resolution in place ahead of time is not only useful when you need it, it is psychologically reassuring ahead of time and can therefore help prevent insecurities from escalating into major conflagrations.

If you and your partner have separated, regardless of whether you wrote a coparenting agreement when you began parenting together, you should write one now to reflect your new circumstances. The difficult emotional atmosphere at the time of a breakup makes it even more important, for your child's sake, that a structure be in place to help guide you through rough spots that may lie ahead.

Powers of Attorney

The concept of a conventional power of attorney is that you can designate someone of your choosing to act on your behalf in decision making and the signing of documents. This is generally used to allow someone to handle your finances for you in your absence. It is legally recognized in every state.

While conventional powers of attorney are useful for lesbians and gay men who want their partners to have some of the rights of spouses, they are limited in what they provide. They terminate when you become incapacitated and therefore will not help in circumstances of serious medical illness. The Sharon Kowalski case was an example of what can happen. Kowalski was seriously injured in an automobile accident. Her parents, who were upset that their daughter was in a lesbian relationship, would not allow Kowalski's lover, Karen Thompson, to visit her or to make decisions about her medical care. What is needed to prevent tragedies like this is a *durable* power of attorney. A durable power of attorney provides that the person you designate can continue to act on your behalf even if you become medically incapacitated. (It can also be written to take effect only if you are incapacitated.) This is especially important if you are a legal parent, as you may want someone to have the right to make decisions on your behalf in your child's best interests, should you become unable to.

Durable powers of attorney are legally binding documents in only some states, though the number is increasing. Even in states where they are not officially recognized, it is important to execute them as a demonstration of your intent. You can designate that your partner or another responsible adult of your choosing will have the authority to make financial and medical decisions for you and your child if you are not able to. You can also designate your partner to make educational decisions for your child and to travel with the child. You may want to execute separate documents—a medical power of attorney and a separate authorization for educational decisions, for example. Some states require that medical powers of attorney be separate from any other powers of attorney. Separate documents may also lend support to your intentions. In addition, they allow you to designate different people for each function, if you wish. The person you designate should keep a copy of the document in an accessible place. In case of emergency, it can be taken to the hospital, school, bank, or other locations, as needed.

Conventional powers of attorney can be easily executed on your own, if you wish. There are forms available in many stationery stores. Durable powers of attorney, on the other hand, should be drawn up with the help of a lawyer, as state codes vary and must be adhered to.

Birth Certificates

If you are a lesbian who has conceived by alternative insemination with a known donor, do not put his name on the birth certificate unless you intend for him to be a legal father. If your donor is unknown or you want him to remain a donor, you can put "Unknown" or "Name withheld" in the space for the father's name. Some lesbians have put their partner's names, or their partner's first initial and last name, in this space. This is technically not legal, although rarely does anyone care. Doing so does not, however, entitle your partner to any additional legal standing whatsoever.

In an adoption, a new birth certificate will be issued indicating the name of the adoptive parent, as well as the child's name as chosen by the adoptive parent.

In a surrogate mother arrangement, what is done depends on the laws of your state. In most states, the birthmother via surrogacy is the legal mother on the birth certificate, though a later adoption proceeding may issue a revised birth certificate.

In some states, you are free to give your child the last name you choose. You may use a hyphenated combination of your name with your lover's name or any other name you want. Some states, however, prevent an unmarried woman from using anything but her own last name for the child. In that case, you are limited at the time of the child's birth, but later you can institute a legal change of name proceeding for your child.

Health Insurance

Health insurance is something no one should be without, yet it is expensive and, for many people with pre-existing medical conditions, hard to obtain. As lesbians and gay men, we face discrimination in health insurance because we are not permitted to legally marry. A small but growing number of group health policies recognize a spouse-equivalent of either gender. For most people, however, being in a lesbian or gay relationship means that your partner cannot be covered on your health insurance policy. It also means that any children you are raising can be covered only under the policy of the legal parent.

Discrimination against lesbians and gay men in health insurance can make getting benefits very expensive. My lover and I, for example, both self-employed and each a biological mother of one child, had to purchase two separate family policies, doubling our health insurance costs.

If your policy specifies that only your biological or legally adopted child is eligible for benefits, it is fraudulent to claim a child you are not legally related to. Don't risk it. If there is a medical catastrophe, an insurance company is likely to investigate. Not only would your claim be denied, your policy could be canceled.

Anger and Insecurity

Don't underestimate the emotional consequences of all the legal uncertainties. When you find yourself angry or insecure in relation to your parenting, it may be that at least some of your feelings stem from suffering the effects of discrimination under the law. A situation in which one parent has no legal rights is a powerful source of anxiety which may profoundly affect family dynamics. The restrictions on our families are demeaning to us. They cost us money, time, effort, and emotional energy.

As Millie said, "I get very angry at the inequity of it. The insurance stuff. You can't get all the legal rights. You can't get married. You can't get joint taxes. I've become much more aware of those things, and they aggravate me."

Candace added, "We got powers of attorney for Jill to have access to Ethan's school records and to get medical treatment for him. But it's a real drag to have to do that stuff legally. In order for her to be able to take him to the emergency room when I'm at class or something, she has to take this dumb piece of paper with her."

Joel also feels the effects of discrimination: "We have all the legal documents done, but there's only so much we can do. If I were to die, there's no way that I can be one hundred percent sure that Glenn would be her parent. He's named as guardian, but if somebody protests that, it's the court's decision, not my decision. That upsets me."

For Tina, since the breakup of her relationship with Rebecca, not having legal rights to their daughter is excruciating. "When Rebecca says I can't see Rachel, all I can do is sit there and cry. It's the one aspect of my life that debilitates me within thirty seconds."

It helps to know that we're angry, sad, and frightened, and what we're upset about, so that we don't take it out on ourselves, our partners, or our children. The legal picture is changing, slowly, and we can look forward to a time when our families will have the rights they deserve.

Part II

MAKING IT WORK

7

RAISING OUR CHILDREN

What Do We Tell Them?

Lynne overheard her three-year-old daughter, Rosa, discussing their family with another child, Katie. Rosa was explaining that she had two moms. She said, "I just have two moms, you know, and some people have two moms, and some people have two dads, and some people have just one mom...." Katie said, "Boy, wouldn't it be funny if you had two moms *and* two dads?" and both girls giggled. Then Rosa said, "What if I had three moms and three dads?" and they giggled some more. Then Katie tried, "What if you had four moms and four dads?" Lynne, listening from the next room, heard dead silence. Then she heard her daughter answer, in a solemn tone, "*That* would be too many." The children in nontraditional families are clearly able to grasp the concepts, talk about them, and even have some fun with them.

People often ask what we tell our children about their family constellations, about our sexual orientations, about who their genetic parents are, and about how they were conceived. The universal answer among the families I know is that we tell them the truth. Lesbians and gay men who choose to raise children seem to be dedicated to truthful parenting, respecting the rights of our children to know the realities of their origins, and trusting ourselves to provide them with the resources to comprehend those realities.

Because we are open with our children from the beginning, we don't ever have to formally sit them down and tell them the story of what their family is about. Instead, teaching our children about who we are and what their families are is part of the ongoing process of imparting culture that occurs in every family. The story of our children's arrival in our families, whether via adoption or alternative insemination or surrogate motherhood, is told and retold in many different contexts over the years. The nature of the family our children are being raised in is also described and discussed repeatedly, over years of bathtime, bedtime, and dinner conversations. The reality of our children's families is often reflected in the music we listen to, the books on our shelves, the events we attend, and the conversations we have at home and with our friends and family members. An ongoing dialogue about diversity in our families enables our children to learn a wonderful perspective on human relations and society with the same ease and familiarity with which they learn to speak and read.

Of course, truthful parenting must also be sensitive parenting, with information geared to the child's age and level of development. There's an old joke about a child who asks, "Where did I come from?" and then endures a lengthy and awkward recounting of a birds-and-bees story, only to clarify, "But Johnny came from Cleveland. Where did *I* come from?" We don't want to let our anxiety about these issues cause us to blurt out more than the child is ready to grasp. As parents who are intent on doing everything right, we may get concerned about how much or how little to do around these issues. Marty, a father by adoption, says he tends to give too much information. "I need to realize that I should just answer the question, and when I see her eyes glaze over, shut up." Mona also struggles with how far to push things. "Shana came home saying that she was building Lego things with mommies and daddies in them. I said, 'That's fine, and do you ever build them with mommies and mommies like what you have at home?' And she said, well, yeah, she does that. What's not clear to me is whether she's saying it to please me. Is she doing mommy and daddy stuff because that's what all the other kids in school are doing, or do I need to do more work with her around being comfortable about having this kind of a different family?"

None of this requires being perfect. A missed opportunity to discuss something will appear again later. Anything you say can be amended in another conversation. In fact, everything you say will have to be repeated and elaborated, many times over, as children hear the same things in new developmental contexts. What constitutes the whole relevant truth for a three-year-old will need to be expanded at age five, and again at eight and ten and fifteen, as cognitive maturity and life experience make for a more sophisticated understanding of the concepts of family and sexuality. Our children will tell us, directly or indirectly, when and how much they want to discuss these issues. Meanwhile, we can be prepared with some ways of presenting things.

The suggestions I offer here are condensations of what many families have found useful. They may not necessarily fit your family structure, your child's needs at a given time, or your own preferences. There is no one right way to do this, and when in doubt, trust your own best judgment. You know yourself and your child better than anyone else.

"Where Did I Come From?"— Biological Origins

The facts of life are different in our families if we formed them biologically. The egg and the sperm still meet, of course, but the story usually does not include the coincidence of sex and procreation. Some lesbians and gay men considering parenthood have concerns about how they will explain alternative insemination to their child. So far, it has not been a problem for any child I know. Last year I asked my son, Jesse, then age seven, what he says if anyone in school asks how he was born without a father. He replied calmly, "I say it was alternative insemination. I explain it to them. I say my mom went to the doctor's office to get sperm because she wanted to have me. After I explain it to them once, they get the idea." Both of my children adored the movie *Look Who's Talking* because of its whimsical depiction of the meeting of sperm and egg, and because the mother, to cover up her affair, describes it as having been artificial insemination. They comfortably tell their friends, all of whom have seen the movie, that they were made by alternative insemination.

A simplified version of the conception story in our families, suitable for preschoolers and younger school-age children, generally runs something like this: A baby is made when a woman's seed, called an egg, and a man's seed, called a sperm, get together. In a mommy and daddy family, the mommy usually provides the egg and the daddy usually provides the sperm. In a two-mommy family, they can use an egg from one of the moms, and get sperm from a man who doesn't live with the family but who wants to help women have babies. (Here the story varies depending on whether the donor is known or came through an unknown source.) The man who is helping the woman gets the sperm out of his penis and gives it to the woman (or her doctor) to put into her vagina. The sperm then swims up to the place where the egg is waiting. The egg and sperm meet and grow into a baby in a special place in the woman's belly called a uterus until it is time for it to be born. When it is ready, it comes out through her vagina, and both women are the baby's parents.

In a two-daddy family, a woman sometimes helps the men have a baby to raise. One of the fathers can get his sperm from his penis and give it to the woman (or the doctor, etc.). The woman puts the sperm into her own vagina (or has the doctor do it, etc.). When the baby is born, she gives it to the dads who are going to be its parents.

Obviously, the story can be modified to include other kinds of family constellations, and you can include more or fewer details, about either the biology or the emotional aspects of it, as fits your nature and your child's needs at any given age. I personally found that explaining conception through alternative insemination was easier than having to explain conception and heterosexual sex at the same time. In my family, we have always talked about sexual activity not as something that grownups do to make babies, but as something that everyone, even children, engage in. As children, having sex consists of enjoying the feelings they have when they touch their own genitals. Later on, when grownups love each other, they can get together and make each other's genitals feel good. (This gets away from the definition of sex most of us were raised with that equated it with penis-in-vagina penetration only.) It was a very simple transition from there to include the fact that in heterosexual sex, the man's penis can go into the woman's vagina and deposit the sperm directly.

The important thing to emphasize when telling a child about her conception and birth is that it was just one of the normal ways that children arrive here on earth, and that the decisions to do things that way were done with planning and love. In the same casual way that you may point out, "That's the hospital where you were born," you can point out, "That's the doctor's office where we went to get sperm to make you," or, "That's the place where we first met your birthmother," while your child is still very young. This helps to make it an ongoing dialogue that everyone is at ease with. The point of the discussion is to both impart the information to the child about his birth story, and also to communicate that it was a normal and healthy way to come into being. The latter is conveyed by your relaxed tone of voice, and by the fact that you do not mention or emphasize it any more or less often than you would talk about a child's circumstances of birth in a more traditional family.

"Where Did I Come From?"—Adoption

Many of our families were formed by adoption, and the children need to hear a story of their origins that includes information about who their birthparents are and how they came to be adopted. The words you use in describing the people involved in an adoption are important. You are your child's parents. There is no need to qualify your role by saying "adoptive parents." When you want to explain how you came to be a mother, for example, try "mother by adoption," instead of "adoptive mother," as the latter may carry the implication that your mothering is in some way different. You may want to refer to a family "formed by adoption" rather than an "adoptive family," as the latter also suggests that there is something different, and potentially inferior, about the kind of family it is. Similarly, the child was born to "birthparents" or "biological parents," not "natural" or "real" parents. One mother described feeling understandably offended when she was asked about her daughter, "Is she your real daughter or was she adopted?" She answered by saying, "She's my real daughter. She was also adopted." Another mother replied angrily to the question "Are you her natural mother?" by saying, "There's nothing unnatural about how I am her mother."

The birthparents "made an adoption plan" for the child. They didn't "give up" or "put up" the child for adoption. This emphasizes loving intention, rather than rejecting behavior.

Your child should be told from very early on, in a relaxed and casual way, that she was conceived by an egg and a sperm from her birthparents, grew in her birthmother's uterus, and was born the same way any child is born. If your child was adopted at birth, her story might go something like this: Her birthparents were not prepared to raise a child at that time in their lives, while you were ready to be a parent and wanted a child very much. So it was arranged that she would come to live with you, and you would be her parent(s) forever. You are the ones who will take care of her until she is grown. Lois Melina, author of *Making Sense of Adoption*, suggests that you add that you are sure her birthparents felt sad to have to say good-bye to her, and that your child was sad, too, though she doesn't remember it. The point of doing this, says Melina, is to introduce the idea that there are feelings associated with what happened.

George and Philip had an open adoption, and can tell their son, Brett, about his birthparents. George describes, "He's being raised by two men and he has no mother, which I think is even a more serious issue than a child not having a father. Everyone has a mother. So it's always been a focus for us to make sure he understands. We say, 'You know, Brett, you were adopted, and Stella and Hal are your birthparents. They're the ones who got together and made you, and Stella delivered you. She's your birthmother.' So if someone asks, 'Why don't you have a mommy?' Brett clearly states, 'Well, I have a birthmommy, but Daddy George and Daddy Philip are my parents who raise me.'"

Jeff and Peter don't know Daniel's birthmother, but they use some of the information they have about her. "We refer to his mother by name, Jacki, and we say, 'You look like Jacki. She was beautiful, too, just the way you are. We told him that his mother was ill and wasn't able to take care of him, but that she loved him very much and she let us adopt him. Jacki was short, and Daniel seems to be growing tall, so we talk about that, too. We point out the medical center where he was born. One time he wanted to go back there and see his mommy. We said, 'Well, your mommy wouldn't still be there. She was just there when she gave birth to you.'"

Parents whose children come from difficult or painful backgrounds, where the circumstances of adoption included neglect or abuse, have a harder task. As important as it is to be truthful to a child, the information about her origins should be presented in a way that does not evoke deeply disturbing fantasies that a young child is not ready to deal with. There is no perfect way to handle things, but Pasqual describes their attempts with their son, Jaime: "She abandoned him in the hospital. She was homeless and on drugs. To begin with, we'll just say that his mom was sick and could not take care of him, and that because she cared about him she wanted him to have a home and that's why we adopted him. We feel he has the right to know that he has a brother and a sister, but we sort of don't know how to do that. If his brother or sister are into drugs or bad situations, we may not want him to get involved with that. We would like to tell him as much as possible so that he doesn't feel totally lost in the world, and certainly we'll try to do it in a caring way that he can relate to. By the time he's sixteen or so he might be able to handle the truth as it is. It's difficult to know what to do. We're still asking and researching and finding out what other people are doing." While it is important not to lie or keep secrets about your child's adoption or the existence of biological relatives, it takes sensitivity and timing to convey painful details of your child's origins. As your child matures and can grasp more difficult realities, she will be able to handle more information.

Your child will undoubtedly have feelings about having been adopted. Fantasies about why her birthparents gave her away are common in the younger school-age years. An adolescent will have strong feelings about identity and heredity, especially when she is racially different from her parents. Sadness and anger about having been separated from birthparents, which may be present at any time, are normal and natural. They in no way reflect badly on your efforts as a parent. It is important to communicate to children that feelings are welcomed without being pushy about it. Some children bring up issues of adoption daily, while others put the topic on the shelf for long periods of time or even refuse to discuss it. As long as the family atmosphere encourages talk about the past and about emotions in general, and makes gentle references to the fact of adoption in the course of ordinary family living, your child will probably become ready to raise these issues in his own time. Many families formed by adoption find it helpful to make use of support groups and organizations. Contacting the National Adoption Information Clearinghouse can help you locate such groups (see the Resources section).

"Where's My Daddy? Who's My Mommy?"

When the children raised in lesbian households ask about Daddy, and the children in gay dad homes ask about Mommy, it's important to get a sense of what it is they are asking. There are several different things the child could mean. For one thing, some questions about the "missing parent" are emotionally neutral requests for information. A preschooler in a lesbian family who asks, "Why don't I have a daddy?" is not necessarily expressing a desire for one. She may be asking, "Why is our family constellation different from that of Janie's family?" It may be an attempt to gather knowledge, presenting you with a wonderful opportunity to tell her about diversity. When these questions first appear, a good response is something like, "There are lots of different kinds of families. There are families with a mom and a dad, and families with two moms, or two dads, and families with just one parent, and some families who have three or more parents. Ours is a two-mom (or whatever) family, and we think that's pretty wonderful. How do you feel about it?"

If your child grows up knowing other lesbian and gay families, she will easily get the sense that her family constellation is healthy and ordinary. George is able to use their community of lesbian and gay families as a reference when talking to his son, Brett. "We say, 'Well, a lot of people have a mom and a dad, but some people like you and your friends Christopher and Sara have two dads as parents.'" One mother in a large community of gay families noted, "Until Alison was four, she thought most children had two mommies, a few had two daddies, and only once in a while did a child get one of each." Exposure to more of the world through school experiences will undoubtedly impart a more realistic perspective on the relative proportions of different family structures. Meanwhile, though, these children's sense of rightness about their own family is firmly established from the beginning.

"Why don't I have a daddy?" may also mean, from a somewhat older child, "Why isn't the man who created me biologically one of my functional parents?" This is a more sophisticated question, one which requires a knowledge of the basic biology of reproduction to conceptualize. By the time your child asks this, she has gotten the idea that biological fathers are parents to most of the children she sees. She will be looking to you to make sense of the different situation in your family. If the biological father is known to the child and has some role in the child's life, you can tell her that "Joe is the man who gave sperm to the moms to make you." It can be made clear that Joe never intended to become a parent himself, only to help you make a baby. You can emphasize that Joe likes her, but that his role does not include caregiving or responsibility. The kind of relationship your family has with Joe will be apparent to your child, and she will grasp that making a child and raising a child don't have to be done by the same person.

If the donor is unknown, you also want to convey that it was never his intention to become a parent, only to help in the creation so you could parent. Rebecca's and Tina's daughter, Rachel, at age four, is quite content to answer, "I have two mommies and a grandma" when someone asks about her family. But Rebecca and Tina had some concerns about what to say if Rachel started asking, "Do I have a daddy?" As Rebecca describes it, "My feeling was that I was going to say 'Yes, you do,' and Tina's instinct was to say, 'No, you don't,' and we were at odds." They consulted with a child-development specialist and came up with a story that sat well with both of them. It was: "Rachel, there are daddies who make you and daddies who take care of you. You have a daddy who made you, but you have two mommies who take care of you."

You can use terms like "daddy who made you," "birthfather," "donor daddy," and so on to designate the biological father, if you want. In our house, and in many others I've learned about, we are inclined to reserve the term "daddy" to mean a man who has a parental, care-giving role in a child's life. My own children understand that they had "donors" or "biological fathers" who helped create them, though they don't have "daddies." I have told them that the doctor who gave us sperm got it from some generous, caring men who wanted to help women have children. They understand that although we don't know who those men are, we feel gratitude toward them. They comprehend also that whatever we feel toward the donor, whether gratitude, respect, interest, curiosity, or whatever, does not include a sense of his being part of our family unit. The place the donors' existence will occupy in our children's consciousness is for them to determine as they mature.

Whatever information you have on an unknown donor, a surrogate mother, or the birthparents of the child you adopted belongs to your child, ultimately, because it is part of his heritage. It might be helpful to allow that information to come out gradually, as an easy part of talking about who your child is. For example, you may say that your child has brown eyes like the donor, or that the birthmother was a musician and your child has such a good sense of music. Your child may have fantasies of other characteristics of her genetic parents, for example, that they were royalty. Though you can and should temper them with gentle reality, fantasies are a normal part of development and shouldn't cause you too much worry.

When a donor is anonymous now but knowable later, the parents have to decide when to communicate that information to the child. The early questions about why they have a family of moms may not require lengthy explanations about the fact that their donor has agreed to meet them when they are eighteen. A three- or four-year-old has no concept of what being eighteen means, anyway. More likely, her focus is just on what makes families different. You can take your cues from the child about what she really needs to hear. For some children, the request to meet the donor may be raised because other children in their lesbian family peer group are meeting or interacting with their donors or fathers. Your child may be asking, "Will my donor be a part of my life at some point, too?" Before you answer, take the time to find out what your child imagines. For example, your child may be wondering, "Will I have to start living in two houses like Tommy does?" Or your child may be thinking, "Will I get someone to take me fishing like Mary's dad does?" You can ask, "What are your thoughts about that?" and "Is that something that you would want?"

Depending on your family's situation, you may say something like, "When the donor agreed to help us make you, we all understood that your parents would be just your two moms. While you are growing up and living with parents, you will only live with us. We are the ones who will take you fishing [or whatever], and do all the other things that parents do. But the donor said that when you're all grown up, if you wanted to meet him, he would also be happy to meet you. That's a decision you don't have to make until you're an adult. How do you feel about that?" If your child indicates that he feels sad about it, you can let him know that you understand why he would feel that way.

In a gay-dad family, the question "Where's my mommy?" also has to be understood for what it means to your particular child at this moment in her life, but there is an added dimension. For one thing, children are culturally inundated with the idea that every child has a mommy, whereas they may be able to go for some time without noticing the role of fathers in heterosexual families. Though people may ask about who a child's father is, they will often ask a parenting dad *where* the mother is, implying that since every child has one she must be missing. Because of this, a child may develop some concern that perhaps something *is* missing in her family. If that is what is behind her question, what she needs is your reassurance that the family she has is the one everyone planned and chose to have, and that it is just one of the many ways a family can be. Exposure to other families like yours will help to normalize things.

An added dimension to the mommy question in a gay-dad family is the fact that the mother's role in the biological creation of a child is more involved and will be known to the child from an earlier age. While it may take a while for a child to grasp that a man's sperm is necessary for reproduction, the fact that babies grow in women's bellies becomes a topic for conversation as soon as they see pregnant women at the playground. A surrogate mother or a birthmother in an adoption arrangement is quite different from a sperm donor. She has had intimate knowledge of the child over the course of the nine months of pregnancy, and she was there at the birth.

If a surrogate mother is a part of your child's current life, you can explain the facts of biology, teaching your child that the person who creates you or gives birth to you is not necessarily the parent who raises you. You can say, "Yes, you have a birthmommy. You grew in her tummy just like everyone else grew in their birthmother's tummies. But we always planned that you would be raised by your two daddies. She knew how much we wanted to have a child, and she wanted to help us. She loved you and took good care of you while you were in her uterus. When you were born, she thought you were beautiful, and she was so happy to see you in your daddies' arms, and to see how happy we were together as a family. What do you think about all of that?"

If the birthmother, either through surrogacy or in an adoption situation, is a part of your lives, your child will take her cues from all of you about how to relate to her. You needn't worry that your child will want her more than you. Children's attachments are to the parents who care for them on a daily basis. If she is not a part of your lives currently, it will help to have a picture and a description of her, to give more reality to your child's experience of her birth story.

Reading books to your child about lesbian and gay families will both stimulate discussion and normalize the family structure. Leslea Newman's stories *Gloria Goes to Gay Pride* and *Heather Has Two Mommies,* Susanne Bosche's *Jenny Lives with Eric and Martin,* Rosamund Elwin and Michele Paulse's *Asha's Mums,* and Michael Willhoite's *Daddy's Roommate* are all excellent for younger children. *How Would You Feel If Your Dad Was Gay?* by Ann Heron and Meredith Maran, is useful for children from about age eight and up. An annotated bibliography of more than seventy books for children in gay and lesbian families is available through Gay and Lesbian Parents Coalition International. Send $1 and a stamped business-size envelope to GLPCI, P.O. Box 50360, Washington, DC 20091.

"I Wish I Had a Daddy/Mommy"

What happens if your child is not merely asking, "Who is my father (or mother)" but is lamenting, "I wish I had a father (or mother)"? Many lesbian and gay parents understandably feel some anxiety over this possibility. We are all working so hard to be the best parents we can be, and it's painful to think that our children might feel deprived by the family we give them. Our anxiety isn't helped by the fact that we may hear some negative opinions expressed by rigid people in society, who assure us that boys shouldn't grow up without fathers and no child should grow up without a mother.

At ages eleven and eight, my own children have not expressed any particular interest in daddies, whether biological or otherwise, beyond curiosity about the story of their origins. Other than that, the daddy question has been a nonissue at our house thus far. Though we are open to discussions about what it means for them to have biological origins outside of the family and to have no male parents within the family, these issues are clearly not prominent in their minds at this time in their lives. When I have raised these issues in conversation, their response has been mild interest, quickly replaced by more pressing concerns over what's for dinner.

Not all children feel the way mine do, however. Some children do express an intense longing for the other biological parent, talking about it frequently and emotionally. Children are individuals, and there is a wide range of what you can expect from them. It is also true that what is unimportant today may surface tomorrow with urgency. Adolescents take particular interest in both their heredity and in gender-specific role models. In their teenage years they are forging identities out of understanding what makes them look, act, and feel the same as and different from other people. It is reasonable to expect that adolescence is a time when our children will feel most keenly the desire for a parent they don't have. Again, they are individuals, so while one teenager may go through a significant mourning process about not having a particular kind of parent, another may cast it a few passing thoughts and let it go. We have to be prepared to accept whatever the feelings are with understanding.

When a child expresses a wish to have a daddy or mommy that he doesn't have, it might mean many different things. It is important to try to get a sense of what your child is feeling when she makes that wish. Your response to it will vary enormously depending on what you perceive to be the issue at the time. To make matters more complicated, children are rarely able to put into words what their emotional motivations are. You will have to feel it out, perhaps by giving them multiple-choice options for what they might mean, or by playing it out with dolls or stuffed animals, allowing your child to ask and answer questions through the toys' personas. (This is a very useful technique for talking with children about feelings. It happens often that my daughter has no idea why she's cranky, but her stuffed walrus can clearly tell me that he is anxious about an upcoming event at his school, for example.)

Some, but by no means all, of the possibilities for what "I wish I had a daddy/mommy" might mean are:

—"I wish I had another parent in the home to give me attention. It wouldn't matter whether that parent was a man or a woman, or whether or not they were biologically related to me."

This is especially common in single-parent families. A child with one lesbian parent will say, "I want a daddy," but really be expressing in conventional terms the wish for another adult. Zachary, at age eleven, was able to say it directly. "I'd like it if there were another adult because sometimes my mom works a little late. It's difficult having only one parent around. It helps to go over to Beth's [his mother's former partner, who still has a parental role], but it's not really the same as having two parents in the house. I stay alone most of the time, and it gets a little lonely. It wouldn't really make a difference if it were a man or a woman, just another adult."

If your child seems to be lonely, see if there are family or friends who could provide companionship while you are out. Beyond making practical changes, however, the best response is a nondefensive, sympathetic ear. You can validate your child's feelings about wanting more attention and about the realities of your work schedule, for example, while also pointing out the positive things that your family enjoys and does together. You can begin to convey the idea that a family, like everything else in life, is a mixed bag. No one's family is perfect, but most families have good things to offer.

—"I specifically wish I had a parent of the other gender from my parents because I have some ideas about what it is that fathers (or mothers) do with children, and it sounds good to me. Whether that person is related to me biologically or not is unimportant. It also doesn't matter whether or not that person lives in the home with me. In fact, if my own parents did those things with me (whatever they are) that might solve the problem."

Marty and Earl's three-year-old daughter, Joy, was injured one day shortly after starting preschool, and Marty took her to the emergency room. She began calling Marty "Mommy." Marty recounts, "I said, 'What's all this mommy stuff?' and she said, 'I want my mommy.' I asked, 'Do you know who that is?' (Marty and Earl have an open, ongoing relationship with Joy's birthmother, whom Joy has met.) She said, 'Yes.' I asked, 'Who?' and she named the housekeeper. So I asked, 'Are you saying that because she's a woman?' and she said, 'Yes.' I said, 'Honey, mommies are parents, and daddies and poppas are parents. Your parents happen to be Daddy and Poppa. Do you mean a mommy who does stuff for you?' and she said, 'Yes.' I said, 'Well, that's my job.' She said, 'Can I call you Mommy?' and I said, 'Sure.'" What Joy wanted in a mommy was something Marty was fully prepared to provide. Her feeling that it was mommies who take care of you when you get hurt was probably sparked by seeing them at preschool. She wanted to make sure she wasn't missing out on anything that mommies do. Marty's ease in letting her call him "Mommy" allowed her to realize that she had the same parenting that other children have.

The things an older child wants may be more specific. One seven-year-old girl I know who wished for a father was responding to the fact that her friend's father, in a divorced family, took her to Disneyland, while her moms had never taken her. Kiya, an eleven-year-old girl, said, "I wish I did have a dad. I think dads are different in some ways. They maybe would take you different places than your mom would. Like, they might take you to a football game or to a movie that your mom wouldn't want you to see. I just see my friends' dads and they look like a lot of fun." Carter, a twelve-year-old boy, said, "Sometimes they have contests where you and your dad go, and I can't really do stuff like that." However, he had only minor feelings about it, because "most of the time men teach kids sports and stuff, but since my mom already played baseball and knew how to do all that stuff it's okay."

Letting your child know that you are interested in what she feels she's missing, and in seeing if there is any way to provide a workable substitute, will be a help. Keep in mind, though, that no one gets everything in life, and we are providing our children with wonderful, loving homes. Mike struggled with this issue: "When Ben was younger he said he wished he had a mother. It made me feel bad. But you know, you have to put it all into the bigger picture. I think our boys have it pretty good." If you start out feeling good about the family you offer to your child, you are in the best position to help your child with her feelings about it. Correct any misapprehensions she may have about what her family has to offer and be realistic about what you can't offer. Ask her if it makes her sad or angry. Tell her you can understand why she might feel that way and that you are sorry she feels bad. Sometimes it is more important that you offer a sympathetic, nondefensive ear about your child's laments than that you solve the problem.

—"I specifically wish I had a parent of my own gender (when he or she doesn't) because I am looking for a role model for myself. Whether or not that person lives with me, or is biologically related to me, is unimportant."

The same boy, Carter, who was happy that his moms could teach him sports, also said, "I feel like I need a male in my life, to talk about certain things that you wouldn't feel right talking about with your mom, because a male has experienced stuff like that before." It's clear that this male doesn't have to be his donor, nor does it have to be someone with a parenting role in his life, just a man he has access to on a personal level. Carter has solved this problem for himself. "Actually, my best friend knows who his dad is and spends a lot of time with him, and I spend a lot of time with him and his dad. He's like the male in my life."

Zachary, at age eleven, also said, "Sometimes I feel like I need a man to help me grow up. My uncle helps. He's kind of like a dad."

Barry and Tony are the parents of Carla, age four. Barry recounts, "It started with my mother and Tony's sister showing her that women often wear makeup and this is how you put it on. This was the first time I questioned whether or not the absence of a woman in the house was having any impact on her. I mean, I'm intelligent enough to know how to put on makeup and, after all, I'm a gay man—I know this stuff. But I realized she runs more readily to her grandmother and her aunt to help her with these very strongly woman-identified things."

Barry goes on, "I have my public persona which says that we're more than capable of providing everything she needs, and there are enough warm, loving, successful women in her life to give her the role modeling that she needs. But there's another side of me that says that there are things that I just can't do for her. This issue of the makeup is one of them, and it hurt me very much. It's Jewish guilt. I can't be perfect. The rational thing is that there may be some things I can't provide for her and there's nothing wrong with that."

—"As a girl with lesbian parents (or a boy with gay dads), I just wish I had a chance to have a relationship with an adult of the opposite gender. That person wouldn't have to be a relative or live with us."

Just as a boy in a lesbian family, for example, may want a male role model, a boy in an all-male family may sometimes want a "woman's influence" in his life. A girl with two moms may want the opportunity to relate to men. In general, though, this wish is not likely to be quite as intense as the desire for a same-gender role model. Unless you are living in a very isolated area or tend to relate only to people of your own gender, there are ample opportunities for children to have contact with adults of the opposite gender. The interactions they have with grandparents or other relatives, teachers, and their friends' parents are likely to provide what they need. As with many other things your child feels, helping her to put into words what she's feeling may solve half the problem.

It is clear that our children need people of both genders in their lives, though not necessarily in their homes. As our communities of lesbian and gay parents become more organized, hopefully we will create more avenues for the gay men and lesbians who never wanted to be full-time parents to take active roles as friends and role models to our children. Big brother/big sister and foster grandparent projects in the gay and lesbian community are very much needed. In the meantime, however, most of the families I know manage to find a way of including other adults in their children's lives.

—"I wish I had a parent of the other gender who lived with us so I could have a family that wasn't different from other kids' families. If I knew better how to deal with the kids at school, I wouldn't have a problem with my family the way it is."

If you get the sense that your child's wish for a father, for example, has to do with social discomfort, you can point that out to him. Remind him that within the family, he is very happy with the parents he has. The problem, then, is not that there is anything wrong with his family, but that there are people outside the family who don't understand. He may need more contact with other lesbian and gay families. Or he may just need some sensitive talking about what having a different kind of family feels like for him. Some children really enjoy a sense of being "special" because of their family constellation, while others would prefer to fade into the woodwork. You can validate your child's feelings, letting her know that you understand how she could feel that way, while also offering her the reassurance that you feel pride in the family and that being different gets easier as you get older.

Offer to talk with his teacher, if that would help. If there is one child in particular who is persistently giving your child trouble, perhaps it would help to invite the child over to meet you. If the problem is that your child is being overly cautious about revealing her family situation and is therefore isolating herself, it might help to role-play some ways of being more open, letting your child choose what feels comfortable to her. Our children need our help about how to present themselves to others (see below, as well as Chapter Twelve: Out in the World). You can also reinforce for your child that his experience in your family has given him an understanding of difference, diversity, and tolerance which some other people do not have, and which deserves to be a source of pride.

—"I would like to meet the actual person who helped to create me biologically. It doesn't matter whether I ever live with him (or her) or even do things with him (or her), because I have what I need from my family. I would just like to see who I came from, and what I may look like someday."

Many children who were adopted benefit from the opportunity to meet their birthparents during childhood, when that is possible. It allows them to integrate their dual heritages while they are growing up, without having to solve a mystery later on in life. The family who has adopted a child in an open relationship with birthparents can be secure in the knowledge that they are the legal and psychological parents of the child, while providing access to the genetic parents who made her (see the section on open adoption in Chapter Five).

If your child has a sperm donor, however, or a birthmother via surrogacy, the situation may be more complicated. Except in states which clearly regulate alternative insemination and surrogacy, that person may potentially have legal rights to your child. The more contact there is between them and the stronger the relationship that develops, the more likely they are to be considered a legal parent. You have to decide, therefore, if your child wants to meet his or her other genetic parent, how safe you feel doing this.

In some families I know, when the child was old enough to want contact, the parents felt comfortable about providing it. Penny and Mara began with an anonymous donor arrangement for their son, Heath, but in the course of time discovered his identity. Meanwhile, Heath had been asking to meet his father. Penny recalls, "We thought, okay, we can handle this. He's a good guy, and we share some beliefs. We had been interested in finding a male role model for Heath for several years, and there just wasn't anybody out there interested in spending time with him. We knew that the donor didn't want kids of his own, so we thought maybe we could ask him to do this." They wrote him a letter, inviting him to meet Heath. "Well, as soon as he got the letter, all of a sudden he really wanted this kid, and wanted to know all about him." They met when Heath was in kindergarten. Now, six years later, Heath spends half his time with his father and half with his mothers. Penny describes, "It grew very slowly. Eventually he started spending one night a week, and for almost a year now they've spent half their time together. We all manage to remember most of the time that the reason we're doing this is for Heath, but it's been good for all of us."

Penny and Mara have yielded parental control and expanded the boundaries of their family because they were comfortable doing it, because Heath wanted it, and because they trusted Heath's father to participate cooperatively with them. They have acknowledged that he is no longer the sperm donor but a genuine father, and would have legal rights if a conflict ever came up, but they feel it is working well.

If they had wanted to instead, Penny and Mara could have allowed a meeting with Heath's donor but not supported the development of a full parenting relationship with him. As the parent, it is your job to make the decisions about what is best for your child. Even if your child should wish to increase the contact with the other biological parent, during her minor years you can determine the nature and extent of the contact you feel is best for your child and for the rest of the family. You might say to your child, for example, "Yes, we can go see Joe again sometime, and I'm sure he would like to see you, too. And when you're grown, you can decide for yourself how much time you want to spend with him. For now, though, Joe is a friend, and we have other friends to see, and other things to do as a family. We are the only parents raising you."

If you do not feel safe making contact with a donor, however, for fear of that person's jeopardizing your family structure, it is probably best to tell your child that the arrangement you originally made, in which the donor would not have contact with the child while she is growing up, is the one you all plan to adhere to. You can explain that the donor never had an intention of parenting, and you always had the intention of being sole parents, and that you will be happy to help your child meet the donor (or surrogate mother), if possible, when she is grown. It is not likely to be helpful to discuss the legal dangers with a young child, as you don't want to evoke fantasies that someone could come and steal her.

My own children's donors, like those of many other children in lesbian families, are unknown. Though I personally regret that I couldn't provide them with anonymous donors who could later be contacted, it is entirely possible that they, like many other children of alternative insemination, will feel no particular desire to make such contact. If, however, my children do care at some later point in their lives, and feel a sense of loss or pain about never knowing half of their biological roots, we are prepared to give them what we have to offer about any other emotional issue: our empathy and compassion. We expect that we will be able to hear their anger or sadness, should it arise, without guilt, defensiveness, or the need to "fix" it, because at bottom we feel very good about how this family came to be. Ultimately, we trust that if our children experience a period of mourning over this, it will eventually resolve itself in the context of our love and support.

What Do They Call Us?

For many people, the words "mother" and "father" carry with them more than just a designation of the parent's gender. They also connote something about the nature of the relationship with the child, and the kinds of parenting responsibilities that will be undertaken. "Mother" traditionally implies the one who has the primary care-giving responsibilities. "Father" is the one who comes home after breadwinning and provides a different kind of play or stimulation. Our use of language may get confusing when we use the terms "mother" and "father" to represent our parenting roles in our gay and lesbian families. Different families tend to use the terms in different ways, with a variety of results.

For example, though Susan and I intended to share child care equally, the reality has been such that I have increased my professional, income-earning responsibilities, and Susan has become a full-time homemaker. Though she spends a great deal more time with the children than I do, overseeing their homework, arranging their social lives, and being active in the PTA, we both consider ourselves to be mothers, completely equal in parenting status and responsibility. Our children call us both "Mommy." Before we had children I affectionately called Susan "Bear" and she called me "Seal." The concept stuck, and our children call us Mommy Bear and Mommy Seal. Similarly, we call them Emily Seal and Jesse Bear, names which they love. Our friends and family know about the bear and seal business, so the children call us Mom Bear and Mom Seal in any situation that feels familiar. When they are in school without us, they use our first names to distinguish us to classmates and teachers.

Many couples, like us, refer to both parents as moms, or dads, whether they share the work of parenting equally or not, and whether or not they entered parenting with an equal investment. They feel that they both want the title so that their role in the child's life can be recognized, both by the child and by the outside world. Jean and Evelyn both agreed that "neither of us wished Kay to call us by our first name unless it's Mommy Jean and Mommy Evelyn. We feel strongly that we're both providing the mothering."

When both parents are "Mom" or "Dad," the child will need a way to distinguish between them. Although most children think it's great fun to call "Mom" and have two parents turn around, fairly quickly the need arises for more specific appellations. In most lesbian families, it seems to be "Mommy" plus a first name. Some couples don't care for first names and want both parents to have official titles. The English language provides gay fathers with the option of dividing up "Daddy" and "Poppa" between the two parents. Women do not have two sufficiently different-sounding yet equivalent words for female parenting, though some have found that Mommy and Momma work well enough. Both Mommy and Momma, however, shorten to "Mom." I know of two families who use the term "Ima," the Hebrew word for mother, for one of the parents, and "Mommy" for the other. Other lesbian families have taken the name of the second parent and turned it into a title of its own. For example, one girl I know says, "This is my Mommy and this is my Lynnie."

Our best-laid plans, of course, are likely to be modified by our children to suit their needs anyway. For example, George and Philip both wanted the title of "Dad." George explains, "We decided to be called Daddy George and Daddy Philip, because we both hated the term 'Poppa.' What we didn't realize was that it easily gets truncated to 'George' and 'Philip.' It bothers both of us. We didn't realize how much we wanted to be called 'Daddy.' Last year I decided, 'Oh well, I'll be called Poppa, it's no big deal anymore.' But Brett [their son] wouldn't hear of it. 'No, you're not Poppa, you're Daddy George.' So now I would say that seventy percent of the time it's 'George' and 'Philip' and thirty percent of the time it's 'Daddy George' and 'Daddy Philip.'"

Some parents dispense willingly with parenting titles, finding it easier to be called by their first names. For some, it may reflect a dislike of the implicit power of such titles. As one boy in such a family put it, "They don't call me 'Son,' so why should I call them 'Mom'?" Other families may opt for the first-name solution simply because it solves the problem of who gets called what.

Lesbian and gay couples who decide to assign the parenting title to only one of them do so for several different reasons. On occasion, it's because the parents themselves are not at ease embracing the unconventional notion that there can, indeed, be two mommies. They simply feel they wouldn't be comfortable. As Dana reported, "Wendy feels very strongly that a baby has just one mom, that mom is a unique and special category. Wendy is a parent but not a mom."

Other families expressed concerns about their child's potential feelings. Petra describes, "She calls me 'Momma' and she calls Adrienne by her first name. We thought that life was going to be confusing enough knowing she has one Mama and one Adrienne, and that we're both parents." These couples voice the idea that it would be imposing too much on a child, who already had to deal with an unusual family constellation, to have to further proclaim that fact by calling two women "Mommy."

Some couples in which only one partner assumed the parenting title did so because the other partner entered the arrangement with more ambivalence and less investment. The less-invested partner sometimes expects to have a less-involved parenting role, both emotionally and in terms of responsibility and effort, and the couple wishes to reserve the term "Mommy" or "Daddy" to indicate the primary parental relationship. Our language so far does not include a parenting title that means, for example, "a woman who is indeed a parent, more than an aunt, yet not fully a mother."

Once again, however, our children do what suits them, and more than one child has started out with a mommy and another parent known by her first name, yet opted, on her own, to call them both "Mommy." Mona describes what went on in their family: "Shana, up until a year ago, called me 'Mommy.' Jamie had decided that she wanted to be called by her first name. When Shana turned four, she went to school with another child whose parents are lesbians. That child ran around talking about her two mommies all the time, and I heard her and Shana talk about this stuff. Shana came home from school one day and said, 'Since you're both girls like me, I have two mothers. So I want to call you both Mommy.' She let us know that something in her had shifted, so we said fine."

Shana was responding in part to peer pressure but also to the fact that Jamie, who had started out as a supporting player, had gradually eased into the role of a full parent. This effected a change in the whole family's dynamics which had to be addressed. Mona confesses, "It was hard for me to share that title. At the beginning it was really disconcerting and confusing to me, but it's been a year. I'm used to it and actually I get a big kick out of it now. When she calls 'Momma' and we both answer, we all laugh."

Martha, Joel and Glenn's daughter, worked out her own unique solution to the parent-title issue. When the family started out, Joel got the title of "Daddy," while Glenn was called "Uncle Glenn." Joel explains, "We made that choice specifically because early on in the relationship, we did not know where things were going. We weren't even living together until Martha was seven months old. I wanted him to be a part of her life, but I wasn't sure how much a part of her life he wanted to be at that point. We had heard of a few couples who both were "Daddies," but I thought that would be confusing to her. I guess we chose "Uncle Glenn" because that was a convenient way for her to feel a relational tie to him and also to clarify our true roles. It was also to help ease some of the homophobia of society by not raising questions from other people." That has changed. Martha decided to equalize the titles of her two fathers. Shortly before her third birthday, she announced that she was going to continue calling Glenn 'Uncle Glenn,' but she was now going to call Joel 'Uncle Daddy.'

It is important to remember that the titles Mother and Father, or their equivalents, though they may reflect nothing about the reality of who feels what about whom or who contributes what effort, have very powerful connotations. In families where the titles are unevenly distributed, there may be social and emotional consequences to deal with.

Though some parents have had no trouble feeling like fully vested, equal parents when only their partners had the magical title of Mommy or Daddy, others have felt left out. They found that not having the title meant that they often went unrecognized by the outside world. The result was sometimes that they failed to get the support they needed. It can be difficult for the nonbiological parent, the parent who is not the legal adoptive parent, or the parent who is less visible in the child's day-to-day life, to get full recognition of his or her parental status, and having the title can help.

What Do We Name Them?

My children, Emily and Jesse, have a hyphenated last name combining my name and Susan's. The result is a mixed blessing. On the plus side, it gives the children the same last name as each other, despite the fact that they are not biologically related. It also gives Susan and me the satisfaction of seeing both of our names represented in theirs. It has often felt helpful to each of us that we could introduce ourselves as either child's mother and not have to raise questions about why our name was different from our child's name. On the down side, the name they live with contains fifteen letters plus a hyphen, too much for most computer mailing labels to ever get complete, and far too much to ever fit on a basketball jersey, should the need arise.

There are certainly many families where the child has the last name of only one of the parents, often with a first or a middle name which comes from the other parent's family line. One family I know went through the process of changing the last names of both fathers to a hyphenated combination, so that the whole family now has a name that joins both sides. In another family, George and Philip changed their own last names to a name they picked from a book. The new name became their son's last name when the adoption went through.

There is no obvious, easy solution to the name question. In heterosexual families, the mother's name is consistently lost. In our families, one member of the couple may have to forgo the privileges of namesake or the child may have to live with a long handle—or else, like George and Philip, you have to get creative.

Growing Up with Gay Parents

All of us who have struggled with coming to terms with our identities as lesbians and gay men in a homophobic society know what a profound and often painful impact that has had on our lives. We may project that pain onto our children's lives and presume that they will have a similar struggle because of their parents' sexuality. There is a very big difference, however, between being gay yourself and having gay parents. Our being gay or lesbian has some impact on our children's lives, but not nearly as much as some people imagine. As Jeff said, "Maybe I'm just blind to it, but it seems to me that my having a radar detector in my car has had more influence on Daniel than my being gay."

Children have no trouble understanding love. They don't start out with preconceived notions about who should love whom. The affection they see between their parents feels unquestionably right to them, and always will. As Andrew said, "I don't think we're going to have to tell him a lot because I think he's going to just see it. I mean, he will see that Don and I are in a relationship. There will be no hiding anything. We are perceived as a couple by our neighbors, our friends, and our family, and he's our son. That's how it is." Our children do not have to be taught that their parents' love is acceptable. It's taken for granted.

What they do have to learn about, however, is homophobia. We will eventually have to explain the realities to our children. That explanation could go something like this: "There are other people in the world who don't understand that love is the same no matter who feels it. Those people think that men shouldn't love men and women shouldn't love women, just because it's different from what they are used to. They may not have had the chance to know any gay people personally, so they don't understand that gay men and lesbians are good people like everyone else. When we march in Gay Pride, or just while we are going about our lives, we are trying to show people who don't understand, but it sometimes takes them a very long time to learn."

While our children are young, we are usually in a position to shield them from experiences of other people's homophobia, and to promote a view of the world as a place in which there is plenty of acceptance and support to be found. It is not important that every family in the neighborhood be comfortable with us, only that some are. Our children need to know that there is always *enough* support to be found. From that secure foundation, they can gradually acquire a perspective of cautious sympathy for those people who are handicapped by homophobia (see Chapter Twelve: Out in the World).

The tools they need to deal with homophobia start with their own unshakable knowledge that the love in their homes is good. From there, they will pick up your style of handling things, which will vary with who you are and where you live. Sally is a single lesbian, raising her six-year-old daughter, Anna, in a small town in Ohio that has no real gay and lesbian community nearby. Though Sally has taken pains to read books affirming gay and lesbian families to Anna, and she comes out to everyone who takes care of Anna, she feels a need to teach her to be cautious. "She realizes that it's not something as comfortable for everyone as it is for her and me. I've tried to prepare her that someone may treat her or me badly because of it, so she is careful who she talks to about it. I don't want someone to ask her questions about my orientation that are none of their business. She's instructed to say, 'That's private.'"

Some other families, feeling safe in urban areas with active lesbian and gay communities, have been able to model openness for their children. I am fortunate enough to live in a neighborhood with a wonderful mix of races, ages, ethnicities, and sexual orientations, and very liberal attitudes. Though my children are older than most of the children in the lesbian and gay community here, and therefore have been the first and only ones in their school classes, they have never had a problem talking about their families. In fifth grade my daughter, Emily, said, "The kids sometimes ask if one of my moms is the real mom. I explain that they're both my real moms, that I live in a two-mom family. They usually get it." She has never encountered homophobia about her family but is prepared for it if it happens. "No one ever teases me, but I wouldn't take it seriously if they did. Who cares what they think? The only people whose opinions I care about are the people I ask, and my parents. Lesbians or gay people are people who love people of the same gender. They're not any different. What's the big deal?"

Olivia, a ten-year-old, said, "It doesn't feel any different having a lesbian mom and gay dads. They just feel like my parents and I'm used to it. Most of my really close friends know that my parents are gay. I just act as if it's usual, because it is."

The more our children are out in the world, of course, the more exposure they will have to people saying negative things about gay men and lesbians. They will learn to be selective about whom they discuss their family with. The process of learning to anticipate how different people may respond to things and to discriminate supportive from negative situations is an aspect of developmental maturity which may become refined at an earlier age among our children. On their own, they may devise ways of explaining their families to people they don't know well yet. We can help them by role-playing different options, gently encouraging as much openness as seems reasonable. There is nothing to worry about, however, if your child does not seem to have the same assertive gay consciousness that you have. Keep in mind that his techniques for dealing with these issues will develop over time, as will his feelings of confidence with his peers. Meanwhile, you may be asked to accommodate to his preference that you not hold hands in front of his friends, for example, or that you tolerate his wish to remain private in some situations.

Anders, in sixth grade, is in his first year at a middle school where he has to introduce himself to many new peers. His two mothers, Nell and Jo, separated when he was a baby, and each has a lesbian partner. Anders has always lived in both houses. He says, "Sometimes it's hard that my moms are lesbians. If they see Nell, and I've already told them that Jo is my mom, they ask, 'Who's that other woman?' They don't really understand. What I've been telling them lately is that Nell is my aunt. I say she's sort of like another mom who takes care of me. The kids sort of think that's strange, but they understand the aunt part."

Anders also has some trouble identifying his siblings. His mother Nell's partner has a two-year-old daughter, and his mother Jo's partner is expecting a baby. He also knows a girl in another family whose sperm donor was the same as his. He says, "It's confusing sometimes. Like doing a fill-out sheet, sometimes I can't really make up my mind how many sisters to put, two or one, or sometimes I just put none."

To put Anders's concerns in perspective, however, you have to hear the rest of what he says about his family. "I don't feel embarrassed or ashamed at all. I like that I have lesbian moms. I also like that they have partners. I feel I have a really nice and kind family. Instead of just two major people in my life, I have four.

"Some other kids know of only one way that a family can be, and they have all these rumors about what a lesbian mom does. I think they're the ones who have the problem. The kids who are my friends don't care whether my family is gay dads or lesbian moms, or a mom and a dad.

"I think that it's sometimes better to have gay and lesbian moms and dads. I think it might just be that difference makes people feel proud. I feel special, out of the ordinary."

Anders's feelings are echoed by many other children his age in lesbian and gay families. Carter, age twelve, said that his family "gave me a chance to see what it would be like to be different. I think that's been good for me."

Every parent seems to be afraid of adolescence. Pasqual worries, "I know they will go through teenage years and peer pressure. I wonder how it will affect them being raised by a gay couple. I hope we do a good enough job that they feel comfortable with the whole thing and that, instead of being a detriment, it's an asset. But you never know how it's going to happen."

Adolescence is just starting at our house, and we are fastening our seat belts. Every parent I know who has been through it says it had its rough spots. Lesbian and gay parents seem particularly concerned, however, that the teenage years will be the time when our children have the most intense struggles with the fact of being raised in nontraditional families.

To a large extent, we are dealing with an unknown here, because the baby boom is very young. There are not enough children born or adopted into gay-affirmative families who have grown to adulthood to be a representative sample. Those few who are now adults grew up at a time when their family structure was highly unusual and did not have the organized support of tens of thousands of openly gay families. We don't yet know how the adolescents of the current boom are going to feel about the families they grew up in. My guess, however, is that having gay parents is not going to be the major focus of their adolescent misery. I have no doubt that our teenagers will come up with many creative ways of being angry, difficult, worrisome, and negative. They will all go through the separation rites that may eventually make us glad to see them leave for college. My prediction, however, is that very little of their adolescent turmoil will center around the nature of their families. I think we are much more likely to battle over chores, curfews, standards of behavior, and general moodiness.

Isaac grew up with his mother, Roberta, and two other female parents. One is Roberta's lover, Elizabeth, and the other is Roberta's long-time friend and former lover, Shirley, who lives nearby and has continued to be a parent. Roberta recalls, "Sometime when Isaac was around ten or eleven he got very angry with me and said something negative about my lesbianism. I said that I thought that he should respect my sexual preference just as I intended to respect his, and that's what happened. He took it in, and reflected on it."

Through the adolescent years, Roberta notes, "Isaac had feelings about the fact that his life was so very different from the kids with whom he went to school, but it didn't prevent him at all from bringing his male and female friends home, and all his friends were fully aware of the relationship between Elizabeth and me. They sleep at our house. His swimming team visits. My relationship with Elizabeth is not a source of conflict for me in a social context, so I've never conveyed it in that way, and kids who come into our house don't respond to it that way. I also think that Isaac wouldn't have chosen friends who have those kind of opinions, anyway."

There have, however, been stormy times. Elizabeth explains, "Isaac went through a period of two years of being very angry and insolent with me over my insisting that he do certain chores and his reluctance to do them. One day a year ago when one of his friends was over, Isaac was very angry with me. His friend asked if Isaac thought I had done him wrong or been bad to him. Isaac responded that, no, I had only been good to him. He said what he couldn't stand about me was my essence."

Isaac, now eighteen, has just gone off to college. Things have settled down, and Isaac has a relationship of mutual love and respect with his family. Roberta concludes, "I don't think that being raised by lesbian mothers has been Isaac's issue. We've provided him with a very supportive family, and I think Isaac feels that way, too."

Will They Be Gay or Straight?

Our children will end up being gay or straight in the same proportion as children raised in any other families. The difference is that our children will never have to fear their parents' reactions about their sexuality. Lesbian and gay parents are universally accepting of their children's sexual orientation. Some parents have preferences, in their heart of hearts, that their children turn out one way or another, but all the lesbian and gay parents I know say that they ultimately believe they have no influence over it, which has been shown by all the research. Their primary interest is in their children's happiness. George said, "Dozens of times I've heard 'Aren't you afraid he's going to be gay?' I say, 'Well, first of all, we're not convinced that being gay is environmental. Second of all, if he turns out to be gay my concern is that he's happy.'" Sally concurs, "My mother and father raised me as a hetero-sexual woman. It had no bearing on how I turned out. I'm sure that raising her in a lesbian family is going to have no bearing on how she turns out."

Some parents, projecting their own painful experiences, think it would be an easier life for the child to be heterosexual. Rebecca, whose relationship with Tina broke up when their daughter Rachel was eigh-teen months old, says, "There's a part of me that would want Rachel to get married [heterosexually] and not have to go through all of what I went through. I'd like her to find someone who's devoted to her and going to stick by her and give her some security in a way that's been difficult for me. I think there's a part of me that doesn't believe it can happen with women, but maybe that's just because of my own personal experience." Unfortunately, the lack of visibility of loving, lifelong les-bian and gay relationships has deprived many of us of the role models that would reassure us.

Sally's experience living all her life in an isolated area in Ohio has been difficult. Though she wants to spare her daughter, Anna, that kind of struggle, she is also fully prepared to accept whatever turns out. "There is a part of me that does not want her to have this life. It's too hard. You know, you want the best for them. By the time she grows up this might all change, and society might see being gay as just another normal way to be. Whatever happens, I will support her one hundred percent."

Parents whose experience of being gay was not so difficult, how-ever, were not concerned about their children's orientation. John and Brendon, Sara's dads, have had an easy time being gay. John said, "We have straight friends who just announced their pregnancy to us by say-ing, 'John, when our baby grows up, if it's a boy, can he date your daughter?' Racing through my mind was the retort, 'If it's a girl she can date my daughter, too.' I think being gay is great. It's never been a problem for either me or Brendon. I hope life stays that way and I hope life is that easy for our child. I just want her to be happy."

Some parents had a slight hope that the child would be gay so as to share their experience. Lucy said, "I know it's not up to me, and I will welcome all her teenage boyfriends if that happens, but I would really enjoy it if Karen were into dating women and being a part of the lesbian community."

Like most parents, Mike and Armando want to have grandchil-dren some day. Mike said, "I like to think the boys' orientation is already set. I think they'll be straight. I hope they will be because I'd like to have grandchildren. If they're gay, the odds are that they wouldn't go on and do what we've done."

I, too, would love to have grandchildren. Perhaps I'm unduly optimistic, but my hope is that in twenty years the odds that our offspring will have children if they want them will prove to be the same whether they are straight or gay.

The children themselves, as of pre- and early adolescence, don't seem especially concerned about the issue. My daughter, Emily, announced at age six that as long as you can love anyone you want, she intended to marry a cow. At age eleven, she is leaning more toward humans but wants to leave the gender issue open. Ten-year-old Olivia said, "I wouldn't rather be one or the other. They both seem perfectly normal to me." Zachary, also eleven, thinks, "I might want to go out with girls when I get older, but it would be okay if I were gay or straight." Anders, age eleven, said, "If I do have a relationship with a woman or a man, it will probably be a really nice person."

Macho or Femme?

In the early days of the feminist movement, many of us assumed that we could raise our children to be immune to gender-role stereotypes. Our daughters could wear overalls, climb trees, and eschew glamour magazines. Our sons could be sensitive, expressive, empathic, and nurturing. As long as they got the right influences at home, we reasoned, they would be largely independent of society's sexist proscriptions. It has been a rude awakening for many parents to discover that very little of this is actually in our control. Lesbians in work shirts and hiking boots often find themselves parenting daughters who beg for nail polish. Parents of boys give them dolls to nurture only to find them used in aggressive games of good guys vs. bad guys. Not only is the cultural influence pervasive and powerful, but there are clearly aspects of gender-role behavior that are innate. While we can influence our children's attitudes and consciousness, we have little control over their preferences. It appears that they will want lipstick and trucks, Barbie dolls and Ninja Turtles, in about the same proportions as children raised in heterosexual families, regardless of what we feel about it.

Mona reflected, "I thought it was completely possible to raise a child in a totally nonsexist environment and I learned that that's a bunch of baloney." Sally observed, "Anna is attracted to young boys now and has very feminine qualities, none of which I possess. My mother looks at her and looks at me and just shakes her head. It just reinforces that we are who we are. It has nothing to do with how we are brought up."

Mona and Jamie worked to make sure Shana had a feminist environment. Mona elaborates, "She never wore dresses. We did a lot of physical stuff with her and a lot of sports, and she didn't just play with girl-identified kinds of toys. For her first four years we were doing a great job of raising her in a nonsexist environment, and I felt like 'Boy, this is great. This is a lot easier than I thought.' Then all of a sudden the shit hit the fan. She went to nursery school and got real interested in playing house, and started doing all the dress-up kinds of stuff that girls do. She would go to friends' houses and come back with makeup on and want fingernail polish and Barbie dolls. I held off on Barbie dolls for a full year. And then finally I thought, what the hell. She's playing with them at everyone else's house. Everybody that I knew with a girl Shana's age was going through this to some degree. So, yeah. She's playing with Barbie dolls, undressing and dressing them ad infinitum."

In general, lesbians with especially feminine daughters, though they may be surprised, seem to accept it with a sense of humor. For some, it's a kind of consciousness-raising with a twist. Mona explains, "I find myself more tolerant of certain kinds of traditional sex role-play that kids go through. I think I've had to look at that stuff in myself and come to terms with it in a way that I didn't before I was a mother, in the same way that parenting a black child made me look at my racism in ways I never had to before."

Some lesbians even take great pleasure in their daughter's feminine interests. Alicia said, "It's kind of a trip. I was never into it myself, but it's really fun to see how much she's into clothes. I get a kick out of when she asks me to help her decide which color nail polish would go best with the outfit she plans to wear to Grandma's. If anyone had told me I'd be doing this, I'd never have believed it."

Their daughters' femininity does not seem to trouble the gay dads I know. Barry says, "I refer to Carla as my little femme. She loves her frilly dresses, the frillier the better. She's into makeup right now. I was glad that she asked about it."

Not all daughters of gay parents go through a femme stage, however, regardless of peer and school influences. The only dress I've seen my daughter, Emily, wear in the last four years, despite my encouragement, was a costume for a school play, and she likes it better when I don't wear makeup. There's a frustrated ballerina in me that would have adored a girl in a pink tutu (my lover winces at the very thought), but I'm delighted to have the girl I've got.

Sophie's six-year-old daughter, Aria, has her own ideas about gender-role behavior. Sophie describes, "I have a little andro. She refuses to wear pants, is the best tree climber in the whole school, is rough, chooses to play with the boys, and wears nail polish." Aria, like other children who may not fit the mold, has not always found this easy. Sophie recalls, "One night before bed she had this look of confusion and shame, and she said she had a secret she couldn't tell anybody. All my alarms went off. She said, 'Well, I guess I can tell you,' and I said, 'Yeah, that's the best thing to do.' She said, 'Well, I'm half boy and half girl.' I was relieved that it wasn't something awful, and asked what made her think that. She said, 'Well, I like Cherry Merry Muffin *and* Ninja Turtles.' That was distressing to her because the girls are not into Ninja Turtles, and she definitely is, but she loves her dolls, too, which was confusing."

Our sons, also, become whoever they were meant to be, clustering toward the Superheroes end of the spectrum but, like the girls, running the gamut and incorporating the complex mixtures of interest and aptitude that we encourage them to pursue. My son adores aggressive video games and action shows, despite our consistent attitudes of nonviolence. He wants to fix or disassemble everything mechanical he sees, he thinks fast vehicles are truly important, and karate is his major passion in life. Though Susan and I were not originally prepared for dealing with such intensely "masculine" characteristics, we enjoy his competence in those areas. We are also happy to see that he loves being a tender daddy to his stuffed animals.

Leslie expected her son to be typically boyish, but she notes that at age five he doesn't fit the stereotype. The support she is able to give him is something many of us wish we had received growing up. She explains, "Alexander is very emotional. He is physically graceful, and I'm putting him in dance classes because he might enjoy being a dancer. So why not try it out? When he was three or four he seemed more typically feminine, but I think now that he was imitating me. Now that he's around little boys more I don't find that quite so much. But he is going to be a very gentle and romantic person. I would not be at all surprised if he turns out to be gay. It wouldn't bother me. I just want him to be healthy."

Though we accept our children's individuality, many parents want to make sure that they are also actively helping to combat the gender-role stereotypes that our children will pick up from the culture. Mona describes some of the efforts she and Jamie have made. "I noticed that Shana would see me making dinner and washing dishes and making lunch for the next day and doing all this caretaking stuff. I decided I had to start doing the other things that I like to do when Shana is around, so she doesn't just assume that women do all these caretaking things."

Recently, I saw my son, Jesse, wipe a tear away in an upsetting moment and claim that it was just his allergies. It was distressing to me that he had gotten the cultural message that boys shouldn't show their vulnerability. I was glad of an opportunity to tell him that crying is a good thing to do when you're sad, and that he should be proud of being able to express his feelings. His response—letting go and crying on my shoulder—gave me hope that our efforts do make a difference.

Parenting Across Racial and Ethnic Divides

Many of the children in lesbian and gay families are children of color. Parents of all colors are concerned about instilling a sense of racial pride and positive identity in their children, as well as giving them the tools to deal with the prejudice they will encounter in the world. When parent and child are of different races or ethnicities, it requires more effort. The children need access to their cultures of origin and attention to what it means to have a dual heritage. It may require a degree of assertiveness on the part of the parents to seek out members of other communities. Finding lesbian and gay families of color with children the same age as yours may not be feasible. You may find yourself gravitating primarily toward heterosexual communities of color to fill these needs.

Jean and Evelyn, an interracial couple, are raising a black daughter. Evelyn is a black but was raised in a largely white upper-middle-class environment. Jean, who is white, was raised in a working-class family in a more racially mixed neighborhood. Jean describes their situation: "Evelyn has been most comfortable in primarily white neighborhoods, and we live in a predominantly white middle-class community. Now that we have Kay, we are questioning that. We are talking about the need for Kay to have more racially mixed role models, and how to give her a sense of racial identity. I think that Kay will experience prejudice from many different perspectives, since she will always be a minority within a minority. I want her to feel strong enough in her identity to deal with what she may have to face."

Mike and Armando are raising their Mexican children to be bilingual. Armando is Mexican, and he and Mike have become very close to Armando's family. Mike explains, "Just the fact that they are around Armando's family all the time means that they hear Spanish. English is the first language for both of us, but we make an effort to speak some Spanish at home. And, of course, they're surrounded by the food and culture. We celebrate with Mexican traditions at Christmas and holidays. We talk about what it means for them."

Pasqual is Latino, but he and his partner, Robert, still have cultural differences to bridge in raising their two Latino children. Pasqual is Panamanian, while their son is Puerto Rican and Colombian, and their daughter is of Mexican background. Pasqual's plans include teaching them about the history and geography of all of Latin America. "We'll talk about the traditions, the folklore, the political background, and the stories of as many countries as we can. Geography is dear to me. I want them to be American, but I also want them to know that they have a part of them that belongs to another culture."

Jeff and Peter are also bridging cultural differences with their son, Daniel. Though all three of them are white, Daniel's birthmother was Jewish, while the dads are both of Christian background. When they adopted him, they decided to retain Daniel's Jewish last name, instead of giving him one of their last names.

Peter describes their efforts to impart Daniel's culture of origin. "I was Catholic and Jeff was Baptist, and we went to see the rabbi here and said, 'We are two gay men, and we have a Jewish baby. We would like to bring him up Jewish.' He said, 'So, join the temple.' So, we did. We are not religious at all. We are just exposing him to it. He can decide how he feels as he gets older. We have Jewish friends who help. They tell us about the customs and we have books on the subject."

Mona and Jamie are white, and their daughter, Shana, is biracial. With respect to Shana's African-American heritage Mona describes how they go about instilling racial pride. "There's not a day that goes by that I don't remember that my daughter is black. There's no way that I can have the same understanding and experience as Shana because I don't wear the same skin color that she does. Every weekend we're involved in activities outside our home where there are people of color.

It's very important for us to put ourselves in situations where Jamie and I are in the racial minority, so it's not just Shana always being in the minority. We switched school districts because the first wasn't integrated enough. The fact that Shana doesn't have a black parent or a black sibling at this point makes it very important that her school environment be totally integrated."

Mona gives an example of her efforts to impart her own Jewish culture to Shana while teaching about racial bias. "All the kids in Shana's Hanukkah books were white, so I colored in some of the people. We talked about the fact that most Jewish people in this country are Caucasian but that's not true in the rest of the world, and that the people who did the book made a mistake because they forgot to include people of color."

The success of Mona's and Jamie's efforts with Shana are apparent. Mona recounts, "Recently she sat down next to me and said, 'Mommy, how come you're different?' I was so happy that she said, 'How come *you're* different?' and not 'How come *I'm* different?' that I burst into tears. That let me know that we've done a very good job and that she feels total comfort and normalcy with the fact that her skin is brown. We couldn't do this if we didn't have people whom we love and who care about us who are African-American and who are willing to extend the experiences of their lives and their community to include us. I think that's critical."

Our children need our guidance to help them with their unique family constellations, their cultural identities, and the existence of societal homophobia and racism, the same way they need help with their homework or health care. You don't have to be an expert. Your family doesn't have to provide everything they may need. Instead, you have to be willing to listen to them, to communicate your love and respect for them, and to offer them opportunities to get some things from other people. With these tools, the children in our families are growing up strong and healthy.

8

FAMILY LIFE

Change and Stress

Looking back on how things changed when he adopted his daughter, one gay father put it this way: "When you have a child, it's the end of your life as you know it. And it took us about six weeks before we stopped feeling like we were walking through a hall of mirrors. Then the familiar started reappearing, but it was a new familiar, and we built on that."

The experience this gay father is describing has only minimally to do with parenting specifically as a gay man or a lesbian. Though there are aspects of parenting that are unquestionably unique to lesbian and gay parents, easily 95 percent of how our lives change has to do with the simple reality of parenthood in general. The demands placed on us by bringing a baby into the family will vary with the circumstances, and our ability to adapt to those demands will vary with our personalities and expectations. For some, the adjustment will be fairly smooth. Others among us will be profoundly shaken by the intensity of the experience.

Those who absorb the upheavals of becoming a parent calmly and gracefully have my considerable admiration. I am not among them. At first I thought people were simply lying when they said life with their new baby was wonderfully easy. Now I have come to realize that although some of them are lying, there are indeed a few parents who are barely ruffled by having their emotions, environments, schedules, and sense of control completely turned upside down. I am also relieved to report that finding parenthood easy is not a requirement for being a good parent. Those of us who struggle with it have just as much to offer our children, and we reap as many rewards. We're just on a bumpier train.

The stress that a family undergoes when a child is added to the picture depends on so many different factors. While a few of those variables, such as the quality of communication with our partners, how realistic our expectations are, or our personal preparedness to bring a child into our lives, can be influenced by our efforts, many of the relevant factors are beyond our immediate control. For those things we can't change, our best bet is a sense of humor.

Some of the forces beyond our control have to do with our individual temperaments. How well do we adapt to change in general? How quickly do we recover from disruption? How high is our tolerance for chaos, noise, sleep deprivation, intrusion, lack of solitude? We vary enormously in basic temperament, and there's not much we can do about it. Of course, never having been subjected to living conditions like those presented by a child, we may not know ahead of time what our capacities are. Before parenthood I thought I loved company around me all the time. It was a surprise to discover how much I long for solitude and how I become irritable when too much is going on. Fortunately, the role of parent comes in more than one size and shape, and can be somewhat tailored to suit your needs as you go along.

In addition to our own temperaments, it's largely the luck of the draw what kind of child we get. Though all babies are demanding, there is an enormous difference between the cheerful ones who sleep sixteen hours a day and seem to smile the other eight, and the active, fussy ones who interrupt their bouts of crying only with brief naps. It is not a coincidence that the people who claim to be breezing along with new parenthood are the ones to whom life has sent the former kind of baby. Our first son was deliciously happy and smiling, as long as he was being held and walked around. To put him down, even for a second, was to hear him scream. Our daughter didn't sleep through the night until she was two years old, and she had months of colic that nearly drove one babysitter to tears. Our second son nursed every hour and a half all night long until he was seven months old. Don't tell me about what we should have done to get them to sleep—we tried it all. A friend of mine has two children with allergies. For many years there was not a day of her life when she wasn't thrown up on. The experience of parenthood depends a great deal on whom you get.

In addition, the outside world has its stresses to add, and it may be largely luck that determines how heavy a load any one of us gets. Serious health problems, deaths of people close to us, job problems, and financial insecurities are major stresses that we usually cannot predict. Furthermore, for those of us who don't roll with the punches as easily as other people, stresses like the roof leaking, the neighbors playing loud music at night, the dog needing to go to the vet, and the washing machine breaking down may be enough to rattle us significantly. The trick, of course, is in not reacting so badly to events that it adds further stress to the family system. It's a trick I am sure I will have mastered by the time my children are grown.

Elise and Virginia had a truly blissful experience when baby Todd was born. Elise recalls, "Those first months at home were magical. I was just in awe of this infant. He was an easily consoled child. He nursed well. He was happy when he was held and happy when he was put down. He slept two or three hours during the day, and at eight weeks he started sleeping through the night, from seven p.m. to seven a.m. We felt, 'This is a piece of cake. What are people talking about?'"

Similarly Jeff and Peter, blessed with a placid, easygoing son, felt that "taking care of a baby just isn't that hard. It required a little organization, but we never felt stressed out by it."

Having a serene, joyful child doesn't guarantee you an easy parenting experience, but having a difficult child will insure tough times. JoAnne and Gwen went into parenthood with expectations of great enjoyment. They both had had a good time during JoAnne's pregnancy, feeling that they already knew the baby JoAnne was carrying. The pregnancy was a tremendous amount of fun. JoAnne was going to be home with the baby after it was born, while Gwen could get only two weeks leave from work. Gwen's main concern was that she did not want to miss out on the wonders of new parenthood.

When Moira was born, however, reality hit hard. Gwen recalls, "We're talking about a child who screamed twenty-four hours a day. When I came home she was still screaming. JoAnne was completely frazzled most of the time. I got phone calls at three o'clock in the afternoon begging me to come home. So, yeah, it was summertime and there was a new baby, but I was sort of glad I got to go to the office."

JoAnne remembers that "during the day, Moira would fall asleep in my arms or in Gwen's arms or in the Snugli, but if you tried to put her down in the crib she would start to scream. People said, 'Look, as long as she's dry and she's fed and there's nothing hurting her, just let her cry.' But it was continuous, and I couldn't do it. Eventually the doctor said to me, 'Look, some children just need to be held all the time. You have to ignore the fact that it's inconvenient and just do it.' She would cry slightly less being held than not being held and I preferred the slightly less."

Stress tends to multiply on its own and, as life would have it, the tension and the lack of sleep took its toll on Gwen's health. Gwen has epilepsy but hadn't had a seizure in years. Shortly after Moira's birth she had three seizures in the space of a few months. Gwen recalls, "It scared JoAnne because she wasn't sure she could trust me with Moira." This left JoAnne with the brunt of the child-care work, and everyone stretched to the breaking point.

A major factor that helped them through these hard times was that JoAnne's nephew had been born a few years earlier with the same temperament as Moira. JoAnne explains, "He was just a nightmare. And he turned into the most charming, delightful child when he was three or four years old. So we saw that Moira was the same way and we sort of held out hope." Moira did, in fact, settle down, but not until much emotional havoc had been wreaked in this family.

It doesn't take a difficult baby, however, to complicate the emotional adjustment to parenthood. Many other factors may make for feelings of loss, depression, loneliness, or frustration, even while you are absolutely and totally in love with your child. Not only does a baby not provide companionship in any adult sense of the word, but being with the child also makes you largely unable to do the things you habitually do for intellectual stimulation, amusement, physical exercise, or a sense of accomplishment. George, whose son is now four, encountered some feelings that may be especially relevant for male parents. He remembers, "It was hard. Philip and I were so excited and happy, but by the same token my life changed drastically. I felt very isolated because all of a sudden I was the primary caretaker of an infant, and there were very few males doing this. I didn't know anyone, man or woman, who had a baby at the time, so I had to go through a process of connecting with people. And even then, there were no men. It was always women, talking about pregnancies and varicose veins. When Brett got older, I religiously took him to the toddler playschools throughout the city so he could meet kids and I could meet parents, but it was all straight women. I was the only man, and the only gay person."

Philip, Brett's other dad, travels frequently on business for two or three days at a time, leaving George alone with Brett. George says, "There were times when I realized I didn't talk to one adult all day. Or that the only adult I talked to was the cashier at the grocery store. Now, four and a half years later, we have a network of people, and we share babysitting. There was a long process of developing a support network, but it wasn't in place at the beginning."

Many parents find that when the demands of a baby are added to the existing physical and emotional needs of the parents, there is just not enough to go around. Petra, who is parenting three-year-old Kim with her partner, Adrienne, feels, "Basically it's been a question of not enough time or enough energy or enough sleep. I feel lucky sometimes just to have gotten through the day. It's very hard to find time and energy to nurture each other because so much of it is going out to other people or to Kim."

How you respond to having an infant doesn't necessarily predict how you will feel about parenting a toddler. Some parents who stay on the periphery during the infancy stage, feeling less than enthralled with babyhood, will suddenly wake up and delight in their two-year-old's emerging independence. Other parents may find the blissful closeness of the nursing year painfully disrupted by the ensuing battle of wills. Rebecca confessed, "To tell you the truth, I don't think I thought much past the first year. I didn't realize that children become horrifically willful and uncontrollable."

Pasqual describes the struggles that arise now that James is a toddler. "He throws tantrums. He doesn't want to take a shower, he doesn't want to put his pajamas on, he doesn't want to take them off, he doesn't want to put his shoes on. I get impatient toward the end of the day, after I've told him something a thousand times. Robert reacts differently, and sometimes I don't feel supported by him. We're seeing a social worker to help us deal with this. We're both trying to do the right thing. It's just that sometimes we don't agree on how."

Pasqual continues, "It's hard not knowing whether what you're doing is the right thing or not. Especially during the time when you can't communicate with them. James is a little delayed in his speech because we're raising him to be bilingual. Sometimes he throws fits and I have no idea where it's coming from. I have to be on my toes and not let situations control me, although I'm a human being and he has to know I have a breaking point. Balancing all that is very difficult for me." Pasqual believes some of the stress has to do with being a gay parent. "I think other people don't worry about those things as much. Perhaps we're trying to prove that we can be good parents."

The toddler years are also really magical, though. I remember feeling that each new development made my children more fascinating and wonderful than they were the week before. There is little you could offer me, however, to make me want to repeat those years. They were hard. And although we have never completely lost the feeling of being overwhelmed, life has unquestionably gotten progressively easier as the kids mature. Of course, adolescence isn't in full swing yet.

Family Triangles

A relationship between two adults is complicated enough to nourish and sustain. There are always conflicting needs between partners, which require communication, negotiation, and some willingness to tolerate imperfection. When a child is brought into the picture, the interpersonal dynamics are made infinitely more complex.

For one thing, a huge amount of additional work is piled on top of the already full lives and jobs of the two adults. The increased workload must be divided somehow between two people, each of whom has his or her own idea of what their share ought to be. Laboring under the burden of so much to do, the partners will have less attention to give each other. Each may feel a little abandoned.

For another thing, one parent may end up doing the bulk of the primary nurturing, either because the couple plans it that way or because job schedules and breast-feeding dictate a modification of their original intentions to parent equally. Either way, the other parent may feel left out. Meanwhile, the child frequently becomes much more intensely bonded during the first couple of years to the parent who is doing the primary care-giving. Their unabashed love affair may further contribute to the other parent feeling shut out.

Furthermore, if the excluded parent happens also to be a nonbiological or nonlegal parent, stress may be added to the situation by the fact that the outside world often fails to recognize and validate that parent's role.

The physical exhaustion, sleep deprivation, and lack of privacy may all contribute to the reduction or deterioration of a sex life, and a loss of an important way of affirming an affectionate connection. Talking the problems over requires time and energy that the couple may not have, so communication may suffer.

In the most extreme situation, if left unattended the challenges presented by adding a child to a couple can be enough to end a relationship (see Chapter Nine: Breaking Up). Fortunately, for most families the situation is not so dire. More likely, we will find ourselves struggling to juggle the needs of everyone in the triangle, correcting our course in little ways when we get too far out of balance.

JoAnne and Gwen, whose baby screamed all day long and required constant holding, found their relationship strained almost to the breaking point. JoAnne describes what it was like during the first year. "What relationship? I think that the connection between me and Moira really came between me and Gwen. It created some major problems in terms of our ability to function as a couple. The only conversations we had were about the care and feeding of the baby. Everything that we did was centered around the baby."

Gwen remembers feeling very left out of JoAnne's emotional life. "I felt like JoAnne was capable of successfully maintaining only one relationship, and Moira replaced her relationship with me. There was no longer a relationship between us. We were both caretakers of Moira and that was it."

JoAnne elaborates on how hard things were. "It was very difficult to put any effort into nurturing our relationship. Moira was awake most of the time when Gwen was home in the evenings and on the weekends. By the time she would go to sleep, both of us were so exhausted that there was absolutely no energy left. And once I went back to work it was very hard for me to think of leaving Moira with a sitter for parts of the weekend as well."

Gwen tried to talk about the problems. "I kept saying, 'There has to be something wrong here. There has to be something wrong here.' But JoAnne was saying, 'No, there's nothing wrong, there's nothing wrong. This will get better. It will be okay.'"

JoAnne recalls that she was so overwhelmed by the baby's needs that she just couldn't think about the relationship also. "So it was easier to just say, 'No, it's going to get better, it's just a matter of time,' hoping that things would eventually balance out." They didn't. JoAnne remembers, "We reached a point where it was conceivable that the relationship was not going to survive. Both of us, in the midst of hating each other, realized that this was not something that we wanted to have happen."

They felt that they didn't have the means between them to return the relationship to a healthy course. They found a therapist who has helped them identify and tackle the problems. Perhaps equally important as therapy, however, was finding other parents whose experience reflected their own. JoAnne explains, "Recently we got together with some women that we met at Center Kids and discovered that they were having the same problems a year after their child was born. That was the first time anyone told us that what happened to us is something that happens to other people."

Isolation in family units is responsible for a lot of the hardships parents feel in raising their children. The danger is that we may believe we are the only family having such problems, and thus feel deficient and ashamed. A little reassurance from someone else who has been there can go a long way.

By now Moira is past her cranky period and has become a pleasure of a child, allowing both moms the relaxation to enjoy her thoroughly. JoAnne and Gwen, relieved of some of the stress, are doing much better. JoAnne says, "We have our good weeks and our bad weeks. We are both committed to surviving as a family."

Nonlegal Parents

Part of what helps support our roles as parents is the recognition we get from the outside world about the intense and wonderful path on which we have embarked. Unfortunately, in most lesbian and gay families one parent in the couple is likely to get less validation and support than she or he deserves. In a heterosexual couple, the father may not be the primary care-giver, yet he has a clearly defined role as a parent. Though he may feel somewhat left out of the bond between mother and child, no one ever questions whether he is a "real" parent. By contrast, the lesbian and gay partners of biological parents or the partners of legal parents by adoption who are not themselves legal parents may have to work overtime to assert their rights to the title of "Mom" or "Dad."

Sharon and Kathy decided that Kathy would have their first child because she is older. Sharon found that going through Kathy's pregnancy and their son Jake's first three years made her feel left out and unvalidated. Sharon has sometimes wondered if she was just imagining it, but now that she is pregnant herself with their second child, she sees how differently she is treated. She reports, "I have actually had people say to me—people who've been very nice and supportive and who should understand, many of them gay people who have kids—who say to me, 'Well, now you'll really know what it's like to be a mother.' And I just turn to Kathy and say, 'You see, it wasn't my imagination.'"

Sharon goes on, "There were people who would almost humor me by acknowledging my parenthood. It caused a lot of tension between me and Kathy."

Sharon's feeling of being invalidated outside the home was compounded by the dynamics inside the family. "Jake had very little use for me while he was breast-feeding. I felt I was the schlepper for the first year. I was the person getting up and getting this and getting that and moving this and moving that while the nursing couple were cuddled up happily. All of that was very trying for me."

Kathy describes what that time was like for them. "The difference between reality and our expectations created a lot of tension. We were both going to be equal mothers from the get-go, but I stayed home with Jake for four months and I was breast-feeding. Sharon complained a lot—she never suffers in silence. I felt put in the middle between the very legitimate demands and needs of this baby, and her feelings. I was trying to juggle the two."

Sharon agrees that she complained. "I was actually saying things to Kathy like, 'I wish you would stop breast-feeding because enough is enough, and I wish he would start to have eyes for me.' I wasn't really going to rob Kathy of her experience of breast-feeding, but it helped just to be able to say it."

Like JoAnne and Gwen, Sharon and Kathy were too isolated. Kathy says, "I think a lot of the problem was created by our own naïveté, and our lack of access to other women who were doing this. Once we met other lesbian mothers, we found that they all had the same complaints. If we'd had role models we would have adjusted our expectations."

Sharon found she did get some support from identifying with a friend of hers who is a father. She recounts, "We have very close friends, a straight couple who have a son four months older than our son. I remember traveling with them one weekend, and everyone was asleep in the car except the husband and me. We started to talk about it. He was feeling the exact same way I was. I do know that a lot of what I was feeling that first year does happen in probably every family where there is a baby."

With Sharon's pregnancy now, the feelings are very different. Kathy and Sharon have been through three years of working out their identities as parents. Their expectations have changed, and their needs have changed. In addition, being a nonbiological parent does not present the same problems for Kathy that it originally presented for Sharon.

Kathy elaborates, "I think two things are happening. One is that I'm prepared for being unrecognized, which Sharon wasn't, because we didn't realize that was going to happen the way it did. Secondly, our situation is different. We're already parents. We're dealing with a kid. I already have the title. Also, our lives are so full. This pregnancy isn't dragging on the way mine seemed to. Work is demanding. Jake is demanding. Running the household is a lot more demanding, and there's just not as much time to think about these things."

The dynamics created by nonlegal parenthood can arise even in families formed by adoption. Just the awareness of not having full legal rights to parent your child can create distress and affect your sense of security (see Chapter Six: The Legal Issues). How profoundly the lack of legal and social support impact on you will differ from family to family, as a function of many factors. Jean, for example, has a particularly hard time being viewed as the mother of her daughter yet finds it doesn't bother her that much. In addition to being the nonlegal parent, Jean is also white, while her partner, Evelyn, and their daughter by adoption, Kay, are both African-American. Jean states, "Kay easily looks as if she's Evelyn's biological child, and people see her that way. That's kind of hard." But Jean adds, "It helps that Kay is equally bonded to us emotionally." For Jean, the legal insecurities are more important than the social role recognition. "I'm only bothered by my not having legal rights to Kay in the event that something should happen to Evelyn."

Different Bonds

Though it may be hard to be left out of a child's primary attachment to the other parent, it may be equally hard to be the preferred parent. Petra's partner, Adrienne, works extremely long hours, so it was clear from the beginning that Petra would be the primary care-giver for their daughter, Kim. Petra says, "Sometimes I'll ask Adrienne to deal with her and Kim will have a fit. She'll say, 'No! I want Momma! I want Momma!' It's very exhausting for me, because I get tired of having to be the number one care-giver."

Meanwhile, though Adrienne says it hurts and she feels rejected by Kim's behavior sometimes, she handles it well. Petra continues, "She sees it as a developmental thing. Adrienne is really wonderful with Kim. Kim is separating from me, and fighting with me, and having power struggles with me. So Adrienne can be like the fresh air that comes home from work. They roll around and have all kinds of wild games."

Dana's and Wendy's daughter, Amanda, is one year old. Her primary bond to Dana is only mildly problematic for them. Dana explains, "If Amanda knows that I'm around, she'll squirm out of Wendy's arms and come to me. Most of the time Wendy feels fine about it. Sometimes, though, it's very frustrating to all of us, because Wendy wants to be with Amanda, I want a break, and it can't happen." Wendy says, "It's just so hard. I'm trying to do my best job and Amanda won't let me.'"

Not every child becomes more attached to one parent than the other, however. George is the primary care-giver in their family, while Philip earns the income. Their son, Brett, unlike the children in most other families I spoke with, didn't seem to have formed a stronger bond with George. George attributes it to the fact that "when Philip is home he takes over, because that's when I go to school or to study. He spends a lot of quality time with Brett, so I think from the beginning a bond developed between the two of them as well as between Brett and me." While it's true that the amount of time you put in with a child very much influences the strength of the attachment that develops, there is no formula for insuring that your child will become equally devoted to both of you in the early years. You simply have to play it the way it happens.

A child's tendency to be more bonded to one parent, when it exists, usually disappears during the second or third year. Eventually the child becomes interested in both parents, each for the different interactions they have to offer. Elise and Virginia's eighteen-month-old, Todd, is still more attached to Elise at present. Elise reports, "It certainly has been difficult for Virginia. She's expressed feelings of sadness or rejection or not being a part of it. But at the same time she made it clear from the beginning that infants are not her thing. She is glad that the total responsibility for dealing with him every minute is more on my shoulders than on hers because she just couldn't handle it. That's

fine with me, too, because it's when they get to be older and more verbal that I feel a little less confident about it, while she feels more confident."

Dividing Roles and Duties

Because lesbian and gay families are not laboring under the traditional proscriptions for heterosexual role divisions, we are free to
invent our own ideas about who does what in the nursery. In some
families, each parent does everything, alternating who gets up for the
night feedings. A number of families divide the total amount of child-
care work equally, but because of breast-feeding or other factors each
person is assigned different kinds of duties. In other families, the
demands of one parent's career make the workload of child care fall
largely to the other parent, though both share the emotional commitment to parenting. Finally, in some families, the entry into parenthood
is seen as one partner's venture, primarily, with the other partner playing a supporting role. Whether these role definitions will remain the
same over time or change with circumstances differs with each family.

Jennifer and Mindy agree that they share everything about raising
Molly. Jennifer says, "We both love that as parents we are very equal
and haven't deviated from what we set out to do."

Pasqual was raised in Panama, in a culture where the parenting is
left to the women. He says, "In my country the fathers are only
involved to a point. With us, we're both very involved. It's been quite a
learning experience for me."

Jeff describes how he and Peter divide the work. "I really and
truly feel that Peter and I have shared the responsibility for Daniel.
Common sense has been our guiding force, and as far as roles, well,
there wasn't anybody to breast-feed him. I wanted to give him his bottle as much as Peter wanted to, and I didn't want to change diapers any
more than Peter did. By the time he was three and diapers were a big
burden for both of us, we'd say, 'Well, I did the last one, you can do
this one.'"

By contrast, Jean and Evelyn had different expectations. Though
Evelyn was actually doing the adoption, parenting was primarily Jean's
project. Jean was supposed to be the mother, with Evelyn in the background. Jean recounts, "We went into this almost from the perspective

of the heterosexual couple in which the male worked and the female was the nurturer. Evelyn saw herself in the supportive role." It didn't work out that way, however, because Evelyn fell in love. Jean explains, "The moment Evelyn was handed Kay, she had this cataclysmic emotional response. She had gone into the agency with some pleasure about being able to get this baby *for me,* just because I wanted it so much, and she walked out a mother, saying, 'Look at me, this is wonderful, my daughter this, my daughter that.' Initially there was a little bit of jealousy on my part. I thought this was going to be *my* thing. But that very quickly dissipated, because there was just so much joy that we were sharing. I was relieved that she loved Kay."

Mark and Jon never went into parenthood as equal parents. Jon wanted to parent very much, and Mark was adamant that he didn't. They stayed together because of their love for each other and went ahead with parenthood because Jon had to. Though Mark is a parent and their four-year-old daughter Eva calls him "Poppy," it was understood from the beginning that her care was Jon's responsibility. Unlike some of the other stories in this book, where the ambivalent parent fell in love with the child once she arrived and became more interested in parenting than was expected, in this family Mark was predicting it accurately when he said he did not want the job of parent. It has taken a great deal of commitment and patience to work out this difficult situation.

Mark explains, "Jon says that he cannot picture life without Eva. I can. I wanted our lives to go on as they were. I still don't understand why anyone wants a child."

Mark and Jon were wonderful companions before Eva's arrival, doing a lot of traveling and often going out to dinner and the theater. Life changed dramatically, and both have had a lot of adjusting to do. "The qualities about Jon that I admire—that he was a sixties person, that he's very altruistic, very giving ... when he started being that way with Eva I resented it. Why can't he be more like me and just want to have fun and enjoy himself and travel and have dinner? Jon also resented that I couldn't be more like him, and why didn't I see all those things as being frivolous? One of the things we realized is that I get joy out of life by doing happy things, and Jon gets joy out of life by doing good deeds."

Even though Mark stated clearly that he was not interested in parenting, Jon had expectations of having more of a parenting partner. Mark feels, with hindsight, that they should have clarified much earlier what their explicit expectations of each other were. "It should have been abundantly clear that if Eva was sick, and one of us had to stay home, it was definitely him and that he had no right to expect that I would. If I volunteer that's one thing, but if I have a tennis game scheduled and Eva gets sick, he's the one whose plans get changed, and not mine. That should have been much more explicit."

For a while, Jon felt that if Mark loved him more, he would do more of the work, but couples therapy has helped them see the issue more realistically. They are gradually coming to accept the reality of their different needs and feelings.

Despite Mark's refusal to be a primary parent to Eva, he has a parental relationship to her. "I definitely have an attachment to her, though it's not as strong as Jon's. There are things that I do with her that Jon doesn't. I play tennis with her, and I do more sports stuff with her. The things that I don't like doing with her I just refuse to do. If she wants to play ring around the rosie with me, that's out. I will not do it."

Mark is aware that his feelings in this situation place him in a fairly unsympathetic position. "There are no groups for gay parents who don't want to be parents. It's like, you don't admit that to people. You don't say that parenthood is not all it's cracked up to be."

Mark's intellectual interests will likely be much more stimulated when Eva is older, and they will both reap the benefits of their relationship more as time goes on. For today, however, Mark and Jon have negotiated a very difficult situation, a process that required a tremendous amount of understanding and tolerance of their differences.

A Stepfamily

Couples do not always start parenthood as a new venture for both of them. Not infrequently, one partner already has children from a heterosexual marriage or a prior relationship. Sometimes a parent has finished raising his or her own children, and is now starting a new family in this relationship. This may put the partners at different stages of their lives with respect to parenting. They may have different needs, agendas, and expectations about their involvement with the new baby.

When Mona and Jamie met, Jamie was raising her two sons from her former heterosexual marriage. Thomas and Luke were ten and eight at that time. As is the case with stepfamilies, it took years for Mona to become a parent to the boys. She started out as their friend and gradually moved into a position of more responsibility with them. By the time they were teenagers, Mona was aware that she wanted very much to become a primary parent to her own child. Jamie, however, had had enough of parenting. She had put up with years of working out shared custody with her ex-husband, and she had supported the boys financially.

Jamie recalls, "I was at a point where I was beginning to look forward to both of the boys being gone and away at college and having that adult time again. I was concerned about starting over at age forty, the loss of a freedom that I thought I'd like to have, and financial concerns." But Jamie understood what becoming a parent meant to Mona and wanted to support her. She also thought it would be interesting to try parenting a child with Mona, without all the tensions of shared custody that she had experienced with her ex-husband. So when Mona adopted Shana their expectation was that Jamie would be a parent of some sort, but not fully a mother.

Jamie elaborates on what that meant to her: "I didn't want to be somebody's mother again, having to go to the doctor all the time. I remember saying very clearly, 'I am not taking her to the zoo.' Of course, I've since taken her to the zoo, but it was important to me not to acquiesce to something that I would resent later. We tried to get specific about what that meant, who got up with her at night, teacher conferences, etc. I said I would certainly participate in thinking about those things, but I didn't want to be the person who had to do them. I would do other supportive things, like I would cook a lot more. It wasn't like I wouldn't change a diaper, but I didn't want to have to visit all the adoption agencies. I didn't want the title of 'Mom.'"

Despite the support, Mona felt very much like a single parent that first year with Shana. The oldest boy, Thomas, had just left home. Luke was in his senior year in high school, and Jamie's energies were devoted to helping him apply to colleges. Mona remembers, "I was the one who got up with Shana five times a night ad infinitum. It was very hard. I felt a little deserted. We were in opposite places vis à vis children in our life. We had worked very hard at coparenting Thomas and Luke, but in that first year suddenly I was Shana's mother and she was Thomas's and Luke's mother. The reality of what it meant to have children of disparate ages got in the way. We ended up fighting rather than talking about it. It was pretty painful."

Once Luke went off to college, Jamie was freer to let her role as Shana's parent evolve. Mona recalls, "Things got better because our lives calmed down. Something really wonderful happened in that year. Jamie slowly let herself get close to Shana, and really fell in love with her." Mona had to gradually let go of her preferential position in Shana's life to make room for Jamie. Eventually, Mona relates, "We were really ready to figure out who we were as a threesome, Jamie, me, and Shana, and how we wanted to parent her. Actually, I am still in some ways the functionally primary parent, but I feel very confident, five years into Shana's life, about our commitment to each other as partners in parenting and about Shana's full relationship with both of us."

Jamie and Mona still find that it requires conscious effort to change the nature of their parenting patterns. Jamie sums up, "If I've been away a lot at work or something like that, sometimes Mona and Shana can be a pretty impregnable pair. Mona is aware that she might do it on purpose, and I'm aware that I might use a certain ambiguity in a situation involving Shana to duck out of having to do something. We see those as imbalances and inequities that we want to correct."

Communication, Arguments, and Negotiations

With a child in the house there is more to negotiate, even while there is less time to talk it over. You may find yourselves having more arguments or fewer, but the likelihood is that your characteristic patterns of communicating will be altered somewhat.

Petra notes she and Adrienne tend to argue more, because scheduling can often be so difficult. She says, "We have arguments about duty, about needing free time to get work done. We have to compromise more than we ever did. Before, we both went off and did our thing independently. And mostly, now, it's my independence that's been lost. That was a big adjustment for me, and I have a tendency to want to be paid back: Okay, you do this so now it's even. Well, it's never going to be even."

Mona recalls, "I'm not sure how we got through that first year with Shana—we certainly fought more than we used to. I remember many mornings when I was exhausted because I'd been up half the night with Shana, when Jamie would walk out the door going to work and say something on purpose to tick me off. And then I'd haul off and just get furious. We'd have a screaming match in the living room, with both of us crying, and Jamie going into work an hour and a half late." Mona reflects on what caused the intense conflicts: "It was like we didn't have room in our life for intimacy in the positive ways—spending time together or being sexual—so we developed a pattern of reaching out and touching each other quickly through fighting. It was like getting negative attention."

George and Philip find that their different ideas of how to parent cause a fair amount of friction. George recounts, "It hasn't been a pleasant process. It's a lot of back and forth, tug and pull, but I think over the years we have, each of us, come more toward the middle." George is hopeful that in time they will be more in sync as a parenting team.

Candace and Jill, by contrast, do not argue more since becoming parents. Candace reasons, "I think the fact that I've been able to be home with him has reduced the stress in my life. I don't feel nearly as much pressure as when I was commuting an hour each way to work."

They do find, however, that they don't have the same freedom to iron out conflicts when they do occur. Candace explains, "You can't discuss it right then and there. If you get really loud or something, he starts crying, so you have to wait until he is in bed. And it's hard to wait when you're upset about something. Now we have to look at each other and say, 'We'll discuss this later.'"

Similarly, Jean feels that she and Evelyn have less conflict in their relationship now, because "there's been greater motivation to talk over our problems and to work things out. We are much more conscious of the way we argue and its impact on Kay. Now we tend to have more quiet disagreements."

Elise finds that the content of her communication with Virginia has changed. She says, "We have lost the way we used to talk, which centered more around political or professional discussions. While we still do that, it's just not as usual." They feel a certain loss of their intellectual rapport but agree that the communication they have around parenting issues is deeply satisfying. Elise goes on, "I think our talking and intimacy has been enhanced because we both really enjoy talking about Todd, and the things he's done and accomplished, and his adorableness, and that this or that might be a problem and what do you think?"

Sex Lives

Sunday afternoon lovemaking is likely to take a hiatus for about eighteen years or so. I have yet to hear from a couple who feels their sex life was improved by having a child. The early months of parenting a newborn usually contain little hope for passionate encounters. After that, some couples manage to recover their lost ardor, while others accept, more and less gracefully, the reality that privacy and energy are going to remain in scarcer supply than they once were.

Candace and Jill noted that their sex life declined for a number of reasons. Candace recalls, "Toward the end of my pregnancy, Jill was afraid to have sex with me, because we'd had a miscarriage last time. Now, since the baby, sex has changed for me. I haven't been nearly as interested as I was before. It's not just the tiredness, but the fact that I get a lot of touching and hugging and physical stuff from the baby. Sex just isn't as important. It was never a really huge part of our relationship, either, so it wasn't like we went from every night to nothing."

Petra and Adrienne are more distressed by the changes. Petra explains, "It's still hard to find a block of time for lovemaking. At night, forget it. It's too exhausting. And in the morning Adrienne is up at six o'clock and off to work by seven, and of course Kim is up too. So that leaves nap time on weekends, when it's very tempting to go and do all the stuff that you haven't had a chance to do. We know it's not going to be forever, but it takes its toll. It's hard to maintain a sense of intimacy emotionally when we're not having sex. We were together a long time before we had Kim, and I think that helps establish some real trust and security and stability, but at the same time we are reminded of how much work has to go into the relationship all the time."

Barry has found that, "In terms of reaching orgasm, we do that a lot. In terms of making love, we don't do that very often. Quantity hasn't suffered but quality has." And Joel feels, "We have to start teaching Martha some boundaries about when to come into our room and when not to come into our room, but she's still too young to understand that."

George, whose son is four years old, admits, "I'm not going to deny it, our sex life is pretty sad. We've made various attempts to improve it, like having Brett have sleep-overs at someone's house on the weekend. But sometimes we're so exhausted that it's nice to just enjoy the peace and quiet and go to sleep early."

Pasqual and Robert now have two children. Pasqual says, "I was complaining about the lack of sex when we had James, and of course having Stephanie made it even worse. You feel like, 'Who wants it?' You are so tired that you just want to go to sleep."

Some couples I spoke with did manage to keep their sex lives active, but it often required conscious effort and planning. Dana relates, "We have to be more deliberate about sex. We have to make sex dates, skip out on work, stuff like that. Sometimes we aren't even doing it at the moment that we feel the passion to do it, but we're doing it to make sure that that part of our relationship doesn't slip away."

Don't give up on your sex life; the physical demands of child rearing ease up after a few years. If lovemaking was an important part of your relationship before, there is no reason why you shouldn't recover it in time. Meanwhile, continue to be affectionate, reminding each other that passion is still alive on the back burner. Steal what intimate moments you can, and accept the limitations with a sense of humor.

Careers and Money

Before we added the physical and emotional challenges of child rearing to our lives, most of us had jobs or careers that mattered to us. Many of us find that our relationship to our careers is one of the things that changes with parenthood, whether we want it to or not. George was working on his doctorate when he and Philip adopted Brett four years ago. Because of Philip's income, George became the full-time homemaker. George laments, "My career has been put on hold. Friends I studied with have graduated. I would have been completely done by now, but it was decided that rather than put Brett in day care right away, I would take care of him. Although I've stayed in school the whole time, I've had to go at a much slower pace."

Pasqual and Robert's children, James and Stephanie, have some special needs due to having been born cocaine-addicted. Because of the extra care they require, it was decided that Pasqual would stay home full-time. He notes, "We cut our income in half, which was never part of our plan. I have never not worked in my life, and it was very difficult to leave my career. But we both decided that the need at this point for our children to have a good start was more important. We put it all on the scale, and we decided it would be better if I stayed home."

Jean and Evelyn were each invested in their careers. Both have cut back somewhat since Kay arrived, but Jean's career is now taking a back seat to Evelyn's. Jean says, "My decision to start cutting back on work really comes out of the fact that even in the best-quality day care, we don't feel Kay is getting the early learning experiences that we want her to have. Evelyn's career is accelerating, and mine is plateaued out a bit, so I will spend the next couple of years giving her the space to do some career advancement. That's going to involve a change from a fifty-fifty situation to giving me more child-care responsibilities, but that's okay."

Even parents who manage to maintain their careers often find that they feel differently about work than they did before. Some compromises are likely to be made. Marcia notes, "It just isn't that important anymore to be the department wunderkind. Not if it means a lot of traveling. I miss Sonia so much when I'm not home that I don't want to work weekends and late nights. So I probably won't get the partnership I was in line for, and I know I'll be upset over it, but right now this is the choice I have to make."

For many parents, career satisfaction is less the issue than just paying the bills. Some are working more than ever to meet the increased expenses of raising a child. Barry echoes a lament of many other parents: "There's never enough money. We're always on the verge of being too much in the red." Maureen and Sherrie always worked full-time, but now that their daughter is four, Maureen has taken on an additional part-time job. She says, "I hate being away for longer hours, but it's a trade-off. We need to get a bigger apartment, and we'd like to be able to afford a family vacation."

Social Lives

Jeff and Peter are one of the few couples who haven't found their social lives significantly altered by becoming parents. Jeff says, "I don't think parenthood has had a great impact on our social circle. We have a large, extended gay family, from coast to coast. I don't think we've lost a single friend. Our social life was always in our home and other people's homes, anyway. It was never the bars. And our gay friends have been wonderfully supportive. They are very good uncles and aunts to Daniel."

Jeff notes that their friends do have to behave a little differently, though. "Since we've had Daniel, they've had to change the things they talk about and the words they use. Someone will start to say something inappropriate and we'll say, 'Hey, there's a child in the room,' and they change their language very quickly."

Jeff and Peter's experience is fairly unusual. Most parents I know find that their social lives undergo changes. Elise's description is more typical of what other parents have felt. "Some of our friends, although they were very much into our having a baby, have found that the reality of the child's existence has not been amenable to their lifestyle, so they just don't come around like they did. I have a couple of women friends who are very career-oriented, and though my career is very important to me, what I want to talk about now is Todd. They are not interested. I mean, they like Todd and they bring him little presents, but basically they find it boring and don't understand. And you can't just sit down and have a conversation—the person has to follow you around while you deal with the baby. So our circle of friends has changed."

Before parenthood, Jean's and Evelyn's primary social circle was a group of somewhat older gay couples in their fifties, none of whom had children. Jean notes, "Our decision to have children was very different from where they were at. Most recently we were invited *not* to go to a Christmas party in a house filled with antiques. So we've moved away some, and toward a social group of gay families and nongay families with children."

Most families find that they eventually gravitate toward social situations where there are other children. One reason is that the other adults in those situations are more child-tolerant. Another reason is that there are shared interests. And a third factor is that the children will amuse each other, which is both good for them and may provide us with a bit of respite.

Jennifer notes, "More and more our social life has tended to be with people who have kids. Even though I don't need to talk about being a parent all the time, I feel a little more comfortable with other parents somehow. It just feels more like home, an understanding of each other's lives."

Even in areas where there are large gay and lesbian parenting groups, socializing with other parents is likely to mean acquiring a lot of new, heterosexual friends. Jennifer adds, "I never had straight friends before Molly. Never. I'll never lose the love of being a lesbian and being with a bunch of lesbians, but I also really like how my life has become more balanced socially. I feel like I've lost a lot of my defensiveness. I have my foot in both worlds, and I've connected up with a lot of wonderful people that if I hadn't had Molly I wouldn't have been as open to."

Dana's perspective is slightly different. She and her partner also have more straight friends now, but she finds that relationships formed on the basis of parenting may not have much else to offer. She explains, "There's one couple we hang out with now, and we aren't even sure if we like them as a couple. We like their daughter, we like the way the kids play together, and we kind of like the way they parent. We'll have good times with them sometimes, but sometimes they'll say or do things that really offend us. I don't think we'd be friends with them if we didn't have kids."

Meanwhile our opportunities for socializing without our children may be few and far between. Though some families are lucky enough to live near supportive extended family members who are willing to care for their children overnight or longer, many of us are limited by babysitting realities to only an occasional evening here and there. George notes that, since parenthood, "We tend to go out a lot less. It's hard to work it out. We've gone on camping trips with the gay and lesbian parenting group, and that's been a lot of fun, but still it's not like Philip and I are there without the children. The focus is still the child."

Dana and Wendy, however, have done very well with their social lives. Dana relates, "We like to dance a lot. That's how we first noticed each other, on the dance floor. So we've kept that as a real priority. We get a babysitter a month in advance when we hear about a dance. And, to my surprise, we've even started teaching swing dance to lesbians, which is great fun. I'm proud that we've managed to take on a project like that with a new baby."

Joel and Glenn also make some good times for themselves. "We don't go out like we used to, but we really do try to have some time together, socially, without her. It's important to us. We try at least once or twice a month to go out, just the two of us, or with other gay couples. Also once a year we leave her with another family, and we've stretched it out every year one or two days longer. This past year it was eight days. Then we also go on a family vacation, to hotels and places that are made for children, all those kinds of things we never thought we would ever be doing."

Single Parenting

Almost everyone who becomes a single parent would have preferred to have a partner to do it with. There is no question that raising a child is easier when there are two parents with a strong, loving, committed relationship. But finding yourself ready and eager to parent when no prospect of a life partnership is in sight may provide the motivation to go it alone. Those who have chosen this route, while acknowledging that there are hardships, also see advantages. Ralph is a gay man who adopted a baby boy, Adam. He says, "Being single, there's no break and no time. But when I hear straight women complain that their husbands are just another burden, I'm glad to be doing it this way." Compared to the potentially troubling interactions of a stormy or difficult relationship, many single parents feel that life, at least in that respect, is easier.

Not all single parents choose the role, however. Some find themselves single when their life partner dies (see Chapter Ten: Crisis and Tragedy). Others embark on parenting in a relationship which later dissolves. The adjustment to being a sole parent is generally harder when it is not the life you would have chosen. However the relationship was lost, you are bound to spend some time grieving before you can embrace your new role as a single parent.

There is an African saying that it takes a whole village to raise a child. Single parents should not try to parent in isolation. Combating the isolation in our society, however, is not always easy. It often requires a lot of effort to coordinate contact with other people, which the sheer workload of single parenting may make difficult. Single parents are not always comfortable in parenting groups where everyone else is coupled. Ralph says, "I belong to a single parents group which is mixed gay and straight. The gay and lesbian parenting group here is not for me. They're all couples and they don't understand." The needs of single parents are not sufficiently addressed in most of our social institutions, including the gay and lesbian community. We can all contribute to getting the word out.

Leslie had not gone into single parenthood by choice. She had planned the pregnancy with her partner, Barbara, but the relationship didn't survive. After the breakup, both women continued to care for Alexander for a while, but Barbara got involved with a woman who was abusive to her and physically threatening to Leslie. To get away from a potentially dangerous situation, Leslie left the Midwest and came to New York. She has found ways to survive single parenthood, but it has not been easy.

By her own admission, Leslie is not someone who would have chosen to parent alone. She is used to leading an ambitious and active life. Leslie has much to say on the hardships of single parenting: "It's having to do everything by myself. I am the one who has to go pick up Alexander. I am the one who has to get up and take him to day care. I am the one who has to deal with him from five o'clock this afternoon until tomorrow morning, and there's no Barbara to get up this time. I knew that single parenting wasn't for me. While Alexander was a very much wanted child, I am not the kind of person who constantly wants to defer her own agenda for a child, or really for anyone. When I took on single parenting I realized that I had to do that."

Leslie feels that Alexander has to do without some things she can't give him. "Even if you do nothing but attend to the child's needs, you always feel that the child is being shortchanged, that he isn't getting half of what he could have. Alexander has had to go to subsidized day schools, and academically they don't offer much. He's a very bright child, and to me this seems like a crime. But because he is not in a two-income household he had to go to the lowest denominator in the preschool system.

"I also think a child benefits from growing up with two personalities. They just learn twice as much and they get twice as much. Two people are going to be different, and so he would get different things from them. There are times when as a single parent I'm not in the mood to deal with anything. And then Alexander is going to fall back on his own resources, one hopes, but that must happen two or three times as often with a single parent."

Like other single parents, Leslie finds that her needs are often in conflict with Alexander's needs, and the job of making compromises is not so easy. She describes, "I love politics. I worked on [a local lesbian candidate's] campaign almost every night and, for me as a person, it was wonderful. As a parent, it was a horrible thing to do. Alexander went with me and his schedule was wrecked. A campaign office night after night is not the kind of place for a three- or four-year-old to eat properly and get rest. At that point in my life I was starved for the company of other lesbians. I was starved for a sense of activism. I was starved for a sense of belonging in a larger group. As a parent I did not balance those things at all.

"After the primary I dropped out but really missed it. There is no way to balance my needs with Alexander's needs. I would hope most of the time the sacrifice is mine."

She goes on: "Right now single parenting has this catch-22. Everybody says, 'You need to network, you need to go here and meet people, and find people who want to be with Alexander. Well, I have very limited time when I can go to meet people. I have recently, however, met one man at work who is wonderful, who decided that he liked Alexander and wanted to be involved with him with some sense of commitment, which is perfect. If there were four or five others like him in my life, it would be great."

Needless to say, dating and having love relationships have also not been easy for Leslie. She relates, "I met someone who I'm still seeing, but, typical of the kind of person I'm attracted to, she's one of these super-independent types, twenty years older than I, who decided long ago not to have any children. She wants me to go to a career night, and to read this and that, and join this political club, and these are all things I want to do, but I don't think she understands that it's not just the time, it's the fact that everything you do makes you feel like you've slighted your child."

On the plus side, however, Leslie admits she feels that single parenting has some advantages. "There's no one around to watch me make my mistakes. There's a sense that parenting is private and it's my own process, and I don't have to answer to anybody but my child."

In general, the parents who seem to have an easier time of single parenting are those with less investment in career and achievement, for whom the loss of freedom and time are well compensated by the pleasure of being home with their child. Everyone agrees that dating is harder as a single parent, but some don't care so much. As Willa put it, "I put out the word to my friends that if they know anyone who's interested in a hot fling every couple of weeks to call me because that's about as much energy as I have to give right now."

Your reward for the hard work of single parenting is the chance to see your child thrive. You can be reassured that the good things you are doing for your child make a difference. And it becomes increasingly easier, as your child matures, to pursue your own needs as well.

Having a Second Child

Rebecca feels, "There are things that I'm learning with Rachel that it would be great to try out on someone else. I definitely want to have another chance." Number two is a big step, however. It can alter your life almost as much as bringing home the first child did.

Mona, in her thirties, would love to have another child. Shana is now five, and Mona would like to provide her with a sibling. At forty-five, her lover, Jamie, has been raising children since she was twenty and is reluctant to take on another one. Mona says, "It's one of the major things that Jamie and I disagree about. She's had enough. To start over again and extend the period of being a primary parent for another five years would be excruciating, and she's very reluctant to get shackled into that lifestyle."

Mona and Jamie are still negotiating, however. "Jamie has agreed that if we don't become legal parents to another baby we will find a way of being in parenting roles to other children. I don't know if that means foster parenting or what, but I feel really good about it."

As thrilled as I was to have our son, Jesse, when Emily was three, there were painful aspects to it. For one thing, I was rarely able to give my total focus and energies to one child. As Pasqual explains, "With James we were so focused on everything we did, making each diaper change a learning experience for him. Having two children has complicated the picture. Now I'm focused on the fact that I need to get things done, so let's do it and get on to the next thing." I remember feeling a level of chronic frustration that I was never giving either child as much attention as they deserved.

The other aspect of having a second child that I found difficult was seeing how hard it was for my first. Some first-born children are more enchanted with a new baby than Emily was, and are more able to enjoy participating in its care. For Emily, however, the new baby had nothing to offer except deprivation, intrusion, noise, and smells. When he became mobile, he invaded her space. Because he adored her, he hounded her constantly. She was angry about it a fair amount of the time. One day the awful realization of what had happened to her life hit her with full force and she fell down in heartbreaking sobs, wailing, "This means I'll have to share *forever.*" For the first few years, I certainly felt like we hadn't given her any gift.

However difficult it may be, it is important to spend time with your first child when the younger sibling is not around. It's particularly helpful to emphasize that there are things you can share that a baby couldn't do. When you are all together, allow your older child to help with the baby's care, if he wants to, and praise him for his competence. The self-esteem your child derives from that will ease some of the pain of loss. Try also to remember that your first-born, even though she may be four or five years old or older, is still a baby in some ways, and needs patience and cuddling as much as the new arrival does.

You may also need to step in, calmly and without shaming, to protect your children against sibling aggression that may be hurtful. It is reassuring to an angry child to see that you will not let his actions get out of hand.

By the time Jesse was four or so, a friendship between my two children began to solidify. Currently, at ages eight and eleven, they get on each other's nerves occasionally, but they have become great playmates, a fabulous comedy duo, and partners in mischief. I now feel sure that both children benefit immensely from having each other, but I would never have predicted it from those early times.

The Joys

The amazing thing about parenting is that at the very same moment you are feeling exhausted, frustrated, guilty, deprived, conflicted, and overwhelmed, you can be feeling happier than you've ever been. We grow as people when we become parents, gaining abilities and self-esteem. Our children's development is a magical process to observe and be a part of. And playing with our kids keeps us young and silly.

Petra finds, "It's more wonderful than I ever thought. I grew up with a 'life is hard and then you die' attitude. It's always been difficult for me to be spontaneous and play, and not care about getting stuff done. The big advantage of having Kim is that we both work a lot less. It's not as important to accomplish things or meet deadlines or jump through hoops. What's more important to me now is making sure that we get to the beach or to the park. It's very difficult to be serious when you have this delightful bundle of joy running around just being amazed at every little leaf that drops. I think that's one reason why I was meant to take this step, to bring that part into my life more."

Pasqual notes that parenting brings "the joy of watching a person become a person, and being a part of it. To help them be all they can be—it's really something very special. And they hug you and love you in a totally open way." Pasqual also feels raising children has added something to his and Robert's life together. "I feel we've gained another dimension to our relationship. Even going through the difficult times makes you appreciate things. Now I know how far we can stretch.

Even when we're angry, I know that this is not going to break our relationship. We're committed. There is more trust. I can rely on him."

Joel agrees that parenting has deepened and enhanced his relationship with Glenn, and adds, "You're building toward eternity, really, in the giving of another life. It has been very moving."

Jean is surprised by what a good time she has. "I never expected it to be this much fun. Kay has the ability to take us away from stress. I work with terminally ill cancer patients, and Evelyn is an emergency room physician working with traumatic injury, so we both see a lot of sadness. When we pick Kay up our eyes just light up. It's like she takes us to a totally different realm. I have become playful for the first time in my life. Kay has a contagious laughter."

Elise notes, "What we get back is waking up every day looking forward to the day, knowing that there's going to be this happy, curious little being wanting to interact with us. It's just the most joyous experience that either of us have ever had. He grounds us in the moment. And his needs, though they are many, are easy to satisfy. I get a real sense of satisfaction at the end of each day that I have taken care of him."

Rebecca has grown a lot through parenthood. "It has really changed my level of self-esteem. It's given me a glimpse of the best parts of myself. It's made me see how strong I am. I never saw how much I could withstand. Being a mother has shifted every internal thing for me, in terms of how I see the world and what it's like to not always think of myself first. It's been wonderful and profound, and very powerful."

Mike, too, has changed. "It's enriched my life tremendously. If we hadn't had children we would still just be trying to get more material things and worrying about our jobs. I don't even care about getting a promotion now. I just want to be able to spend time and be happy with my kids. It's just so special."

Sally's perspective is that "doing it as a single isn't easy, but the rewards are endless. When you have some real strong convictions and you put them into practice with another little being, and you hope to God you're making the right decisions, and everything turns out good, you feel wonderful. The first time they hand something back to you and say, 'Thank you'.... There was a gathering when Anna was three where one child was being very aggressive. He hit Anna a couple of times. I could see on her face that she wanted to wallop this kid. She didn't look for me, and she didn't look for the other parents. She looked straight at him and said, 'I don't like it when you touch me that way.' I felt like '*Yes!*'"

JoAnne, despite having a child who cried a lot in her first year, says, "Before Moira was born I thought infants were boring. They don't do anything. Big deal, they roll over. Well, I didn't realize what a big deal rolling over is. I can't wait until she talks. I'm dying to know what she thinks about things."

Andrew offers his experience: "Initially, you think it's great, but I'll tell you, every day you get more and more attached. You don't know how far your love can go. I mean, it's incredible as time goes on. Every day it gets stronger and stronger. Don said that he is very happy that I pushed him into this. He had tears in his eyes when he told me that it's the best thing that ever happened to him."

9

BREAKING UP

Most of us feel pretty sure, when we plan our families, that our relationships are happy, secure nests. Yet sometimes there are hidden problems in a relationship which surface later, with the demands of child rearing. And sometimes the stress of raising children is enough to create problems that weren't there before.

Family life in our culture is not easy. In addition to sharing the huge workload of providing financial support and caring for child and home, we expect our partners to meet many of our emotional needs as well. In a good relationship, we want communication, understanding, generosity, and compassion. We expect a good mentor, a care-giver in times of illness, a supporter of our personal and career goals, a good playmate, and a passionate lover. This is a lot to ask of one person.

With the sheer burdens of raising a child together, we may have less opportunity to have some of these needs met by friends and family, and feel even more dependent on each other. At the same time, we have less to give each other as our energies are consumed by the needs of our children. The results may leave us with feelings of deprivation and frustration. We may be functioning under conditions of physical fatigue and lack of sleep. There may be money worries. A child's temperamental difficulties or medical problems may tax our resources even more.

These are the struggles of any family, and they are hard enough by themselves. In our lesbian and gay families, however, there is often the additional complication that one parent has no legal rights and no socially recognized role. Often the nonlegal parent is also the one to whom a very young child is less attached, because of nursing or child-care arrangements. This can skew the family dynamics, unless we do a lot of work to reinforce that parent's position in the family. The nonlegal parent may feel left out of the family picture or insecure about his or her relationship to the child.

In addition, some of us have extended families which are unable to come to terms with their homophobia and cannot give us the support we need. The institutions and people we deal with—schools, employers, medical personnel, among others—may also be unfamiliar with or unsupportive of our family structures, requiring that we both educate and endure.

Ideally we can handle the increased strains and weather a certain amount of deprivation because we are compensated by the areas of strength in our relationships, by the joys of having our babies' smiles, and by sources of outside support. Sometimes, though, despite the best intentions, the system collapses and one or both partners simply can't continue trying to make it work.

In some of the families that I have seen break up, the writing was on the wall from the beginning. The partners may have known, on some level, that the relationship wasn't working even before the child came into the picture. Sometimes they wanted a child so badly that they ignored the problem, hoping it would go away. In a few families, the partners simply didn't have the emotional and psychological tools to evaluate the health of a relationship. With hindsight and therapy, they see that it never had a chance.

By contrast, Rebecca and Tina were in a relationship that was working well for them when they decided to have children. I chose their story for this chapter precisely because it could have happened to any of us. In part, it's a cautionary tale. Tina says now that if someone had told them to regard the first two years with a child as an ongoing crisis and insisted that they hang in there until it improved, they might still be together. They didn't understand what was happening to them or how to fix it until it was too late.

Rebecca was thirty and Tina was twenty-two when they got involved. After three happy years together, Rebecca's parenthood clock was ticking loudly. Tina also wanted very much to be a parent but had some concerns about whether this was the right time to go ahead with it. She understood Rebecca's need to do it right away, however, and pledged her commitment to coparenting.

Rebecca recalls, "I was having this intense biological experience. I could not go on with my life until I had a baby. Tina was eight years younger and we were at different places in our lives. There were some things that we were just too afraid to confront head-on."

Tina describes their situation at the time. "Rebecca had quit her job because she was in a pretty bad work situation. About a month later she was pushing the baby idea. I questioned it and wanted to make sure this was not just because she didn't have a job. I said, 'I really want you to think about this.' After a few days she said, 'Yeah, I really want to do this.'"

Part of what made the timing difficult was that Tina was studying for a real estate license and had also just started an outpatient recovery program. Like many people, she had begun using pot and drugs in college but then continued afterward. Concerned about alcoholism in her family and feeling that she wasn't reaching her own potential, she began treatment in February. It was April, just two months later, when they started inseminations and, as luck would have it, Rebecca became pregnant immediately.

Though it was a somewhat stressful time, they both enjoyed the pregnancy. They certainly both had the sense that the relationship was healthy and doing well. Tina says, "We thought we had a really good relationship. It was one of the happiest parts of our lives."

They were both ecstatic at the birth of Rachel. By that time Tina's sobriety was well established, and she had her real estate license. They began parenthood joyfully with their beautiful baby girl. They were not prepared, however, for the strain it would put on their relationship.

Rebecca describes the dynamics as she sees them. "I really fell in love with Rachel. It's as profound as any relationship I've ever been in. I think it was really hard for Tina to take a back seat to that kind of emotional intensity. For me to be so obsessed and absorbed in this gorgeous, wonderful daughter was overwhelming. Rachel was an easy baby, but all babies are demanding. I think Tina was shocked that I wasn't available in the same way."

Tina's perspective on it is that "we were both so in love with the baby that we forgot to take care of and communicate with each other. I can remember our first date when we actually left the baby with a friend to go out and have a cup of coffee. We sat there for the entire two hours talking about Rachel. Rachel was the focus of our lives and very much the most important thing going on for both of us."

Tina agrees with Rebecca, however, that she felt left out of the closeness between Rebecca and Rachel. "I had agreed to support the family completely for a year. I was working a lot, leaving the house at seven in the morning and working straight through until eight or nine at night. I was going to AA meetings, because sobriety was really important. Rebecca was home with the baby, breast-feeding all day. Then I'd get home and want some attention and some physical contact, and that was the last thing she wanted to do."

Real estate can be a demanding business, and when Tina wasn't at work she was often making phone calls. She rarely had days off. "I felt this huge responsibility to make sure that we did okay." She was philo-sophically in support of Rebecca's full-time parenting, but she felt deprived of contact with both Rebecca and Rachel. "I would go crazy if I couldn't spend time with Rachel on a daily basis."

Tina's lack of a defined parenting role was also difficult to handle. Rebecca remembers, "At one point Tina was saying she wanted to go to a group for nonbiological parents because I was going to a mothers' group. Now I look back and see that she wasn't being validated as a parent. She was a mother, but she wasn't really a mother. It was just such an ambiguous role for her."

When they had a bit of time to do something relaxing, Rebecca and Tina had trouble reconciling their different needs. For example, Tina recalls, "We had some friends with a pool in the country, and I thought it was heaven, on my rare days off, to go up there and hang out with the baby. Rebecca got sick of that scene." Rebecca felt, "I wasn't willing to schlep Rachel all over creation visiting friends. I wanted to settle down a bit and be more of a family. It became a big conflict."

Though neither of them wanted things to get worse, they just didn't have the tools at the time to know how to work it out.

Rebecca: "We weren't fighting. We are not fighters. I mean, we should have fought. We both withdrew. Both of us have a very hard time with standing up for ourselves and getting our needs met. And having the baby just brought everything to the forefront."

Tina: "Our communication had broken down. All we talked about was Rachel. I was a big avoider of marital controversy, having grown up in a family where Mom and Dad did a lot of screaming at each other. I did not realize the value of arguing."

Meanwhile, their sex life had deteriorated. Rebecca explains, "The breast-feeding was something very intimate, and I think it pushed Tina's buttons. It seems like such a basic human function, but it's also a sensual function. You don't realize until you're in it what a sensual bonding you have with your child. I am a very sexual person, and Tina and I started out having an incredibly intense sexual relationship. As soon as I had Rachel it was as if my libido did not exist. We became afraid that things between us were getting damaged, and the more we became afraid, the less time we spent together intimately. It really became a cycle."

Rebecca and Tina had seen a counselor when Tina first went into recovery because it was part of the program. It had been a good experience, and they had become comfortable with the idea of counseling. When Rachel was four months old they were back in counseling. Rebecca recalls, "It had started to feel like Tina was moving away from me. I wanted unequivocal emotional support. She was just unavailable. We were both feeling abandoned."

Both women recall that the decisions they made during that time were clouded by sleep deprivation and exhaustion. The discussion about breaking up happened one Wednesday night when Rachel was eighteen months old. They had been together five years at that point.

Rebecca: "She came in and said, 'I just can't do this anymore. I've got to go.' And I just said, 'You know what? I'm really tired of how difficult this has been. Go.' At that moment, I didn't realize the ramifications and I didn't have the energy to fight. I was just willing to let it go."

Feeling emotionally deprived is painful. When someone else comes along who offers us attention and affection, we may be vulnerable to an affair. As a nonbiological mother, feeling left out of the emotional intensity that Rebecca and Rachel shared, Tina found herself getting involved with another woman. In the course of that Wednesday night discussion, Tina confessed that she was seeing someone else.

Rebecca was shocked by Tina's revelation. "It was traumatic. I thought we were in a very committed relationship and we were both putting a lot into working it out."

Tina explains, "I didn't know how to have an affair and come home and say, 'How was your day? Fine, thank you.' So once I slept with someone twice, I couldn't face Rebecca. In hindsight, I would never do that again. That was probably the worst way to leave a relationship."

Rebecca moved out, ending what Dr. Neil Kalter, a specialist in divorcing families and author of *Growing Up with Divorce*, calls the "immediate crisis" stage of a breakup and entering the "short-term aftermath" stage. Kalter has observed that for a couple that has been tense and unhappy, there may be an initial feeling of relief at the decision to separate. In the following months, however, things are likely to become more difficult. The feelings of loss, guilt, failure, and anger will take quite a while to work through. Finding oneself single again is not easy. One or both partners is likely to become depressed. Even if they share parenting equally, each will be a single parent. In addition, each will be dealing with a loss of contact with the child during the other parent's time. Separate homes also mean additional expenses and may require longer work hours.

For Rebecca, life was painful during that period. She started a full-time job, and her mother, who lived downstairs, would pick Rachel up from day care and make dinner. Her friends and family were supportive. But "It was a very difficult and lonely time for me, working and having an eighteen-month-old baby who was stressed out by the separation also. There were nights when I couldn't get her to go to sleep, and the stress level was just ... When I look back at the last two and a half years we've been apart, I still feel like I am recovering from the stress I went through. It pushed me to the edge of all my emotional resources."

For the child, this period is very, very hard. Even babies and toddlers resonate profoundly with the feelings of their parents. They have, most likely, felt the anger and tension even if the couple has not been fighting. At the point of separation, they may face the loss of both parents, on some level, because of the parents' emotional preoccupation, longer work hours, and separate homes. All children will experience stress if their routine is changed. For some babies and toddlers, the adjustment to the changes may be very disruptive. Preschoolers and young school-age children may additionally feel responsible for the breakup and frightened about being abandoned.

This is also the time in which the couple must work out a responsible parenting plan together, despite their anger at each other. They must make many difficult decisions, based on their child's needs, about the nature and quantity of contact each parent will have. Assuming that neither parent is abusive or neglectful of the child, it is important for the child that regular contact be continued with both parents. The parents may find it very painful to work together at this time, but they continue to be partners in parenting even though they dissolve their romantic relationship.

Working out coparenting after a breakup is extremely difficult in any family, but in our lesbian and gay families it is complicated by the legal issues. The legal parent has the right to take the child away, forbid contact, and shut the other parent out of the child's life forever. If the nonlegal parent tries to fight it in court, his or her chances of winning are extremely small. The legal system does not recognize the psychological realities of our families. At a time when communication is strained, when love has turned bitter, and when hearts are broken, one parent may also be tempted to disregard the other parent's importance in the family. In heterosexual divorces, mothers often want to exclude the fathers from the children's lives. In our families, the laws support the exclusion of one parent. The consequences for the child, though, could be disastrous.

Rebecca remembers, "I was very angry at Tina, and she and I had a hard time sorting out what we were doing. At first I was so angry I said, 'You are not going to see Rachel. If you're leaving, that's it.'"

Tina recalls that painful time, "She would go through periods where she'd say, 'It's the right thing to do to let you see Rachel.' But then she'd go through periods where she was so angry that she'd say, 'Fuck you, I don't want you to see Rachel.' Rachel is my daughter, too, but Rebecca had all the power in the relationship."

Dr. Diane Ehrensaft is a psychologist and author in Oakland, California, who does consultation on parenting and developmental issues. She has worked with many lesbian and gay couples who have separated and has been an expert witness in court, advocating for the recognition of lesbian and gay family structures. She has observed that the commitment to parent together often breaks down when the commitment to the relationship falls apart. Parents may feel that their pledge to live together and raise the child in a loving home has been violated, and the sense of betrayal about that is very painful. At that point, the legal parent may say, "It's my football and I'm taking it home." Ehrensaft notes that while some people do this quite intentionally, for others the process may be less conscious. She says, "The legal parent usually has a rationalization as to why they're doing it, which focuses on the best interests of the child." He or she may say something like, "There's a tension between us that wouldn't be good for the child, so I don't think you should see her."[1]

Anger and betrayal may not be the only unconscious motivations, however. According to Ehrensaft, parents have "a lot of anxiety about having this child as one's own, not having to share it." Parents may be afraid of losing the intensity of the bond with the child. They may also find the thought of being separated from the child, while the child is with the other parent, almost unbearable.

It cannot be emphasized enough that any attempt to deprive a child of one of his or her parents is harmful to the child. There is no such thing as a child who is too young to feel a loss. Attachments are made from birth onward. By six months of age, bonds are very intense, and there may be considerable harm done to a child's developing sense of security and basic trust if a parent is lost. If you find yourself feeling too angry to continue coparenting with your ex, get help immediately. If you aren't aware of feeling angry, but find yourself wanting to cut off contact for what seem like good reasons, seek guidance in separating your needs from your child's needs. Help should take the form of someone—a friend or family member, if that is reasonable, or a professional counselor or mediator—who can sit down with both parents and help them focus on the child's needs.

Once there is a basic commitment to continue parenting together, there is a still a lot of very difficult work to do to carry it out. The conflicts between the couple will continue to surface in the negotiations. Here again the lopsided legal picture will influence things. Ehrensaft observes, "When parents are trying to work out a fair arrangement, comments will come up like, 'If you're going to keep doing such and such then you can't have your visit Tuesday.' The other parent, who has no legal rights, says, 'Look what you're doing. Are you trying to say this is more your child than mine?' And the legal parent says, 'No, I'm just trying to say this is not good for our child, so I'm not going to let you have the visit.' The nonlegal parent goes nuts, yelling, 'You're doing exactly what we said we would never do.' And the other parent says, 'No, I'm not. I love your relationship with our child and I'm completely committed to it, it's just that ...'"

The legal parent in that situation is, however, using his or her power to control things. As Tina puts it, "Rebecca feels she's so magnanimous for letting me see Rachel. There's no reason in the world I shouldn't be seeing Rachel. I'm Rachel's other parent, and it doesn't have anything to do with Rebecca's magnanimous self." Yet putting aside your legal power, which offers you complete control over the relationship with your child—the child who matters more to you than anything in the world—is a very hard thing to do. The amount of maturity this requires, at a very difficult time, is a major stretch for the best of us. Yet the children need and deserve it.

Furthermore, the decisions about what coparenting will consist of are not easy to make. A couple may agree to have a 50-50 investment in decision making for the child, but that is not the same as having 50-50 physical custody. This is another area where it is important to distinguish between the child's needs and the needs of the parents. Parents often think in terms of the time they are "entitled to" with their child, but must consider the realities of the child's age, temperament, and circumstances.

Infants and toddlers have not yet matured to the point where they can imagine the future. If a separation from a parent goes on for too long, they cannot envision their absent parent returning for them. Frequency of contact with both parents is important to their sense of basic continuity. For a very young child, one can't even consider, for example, a custody arrangement that leaves the child with each parent alternate weeks, with no contact with the other parent in between. Shorter intervals are likely to be necessary. On the other hand, when parents propose a checkerboard arrangement of one day here and one day there, they may be motivated by their own separation anxiety. It may be the parents who can't handle being away from the child for more than a day. The child may experience all the shuttling back and forth as disorienting and disruptive.

Very young children need continuity and predictability in their schedules. They do best when they have familiar toys, bedding, foods, and routines. They feel safest when their parents, even though separated, get along with each other. If they go back and forth between houses, they may feel most reassured when the other parent can visit in the home of the parent they are with.

Both parents will have to maintain an ongoing willingness to reevaluate the child's needs, which vary from child to child, and with each developmental stage and each environmental change. There are some children who have the innate ability to adapt to new situations easily, managing to sleep anywhere, anytime, and responding to different care-givers easily. Other children fall apart without more structure and sameness in their lives. Either type of child may change as she matures. A somewhat older child may be more able to handle going back and forth between houses, for example. On the other hand, a child who did well with shared custody as a baby may suddenly show signs of distress as maturity increases the tendency to have frightening fantasies or as the demands of school complicate his or her life.

A nonlegal parent who feels defensive about his or her equal status, especially when the child is more evidently attached to the other parent, may find it hard to let go of a claim to a strict 50–50 custody arrangement and accept a more fluid or even unequal schedule instead. Keep in mind that every custody plan is temporary, based on the child's needs at a given moment in time. As long as you continue to be actively involved, your position in your child's life will become strong and irrefutable as time goes on.

The ongoing work of evaluating your child's needs with respect to visitation and custody is, of course, made more difficult by the fact that your child probably can't verbalize his or her experience. You will have to look for signs of distress and figure out what they mean. Seeing a child regress to an earlier level of development—have difficulties eating or sleeping, or become aggressive with other children or teachers, for example—may be indications that your child is suffering. This is an area where you may need help to know what is really best for your child.

Rebecca and Tina, recognizing that the conflicts over Rachel could be harmful to her, decided to consult a child-development specialist, who, in Rebecca's words, was "adamant that even though Rachel was preverbal at that point, she had made an intimate bond with Tina. If Tina disappeared altogether, it would affect her psychologically. If Tina continued a relationship with her she would realize that people might come and go, but they don't disappear, and psychologically that would be better. At that point I was willing to put my own heart on hold and say, 'I don't care how angry I am, I'm putting my child first.'"

Even so, Rebecca was ambivalent about fully acknowledging Tina's status as a parent. When she became angry, she would again revert to using her position of power. Tina remembers that Rebecca "sat in the psychologist's office and said, 'I don't consider you a parent. You can see Rachel, but to be married to you for eighteen years around Rachel—forget it!'"

Their commitment to parenting was challenged to the maximum. Rachel spent time at both houses, and the transitions were hard on her. Nobody fared really well during this time.

Rebecca: "Talk about fighting. All the fighting we didn't do for five years we've done in the last two and a half years. There have been a lot of difficult periods around both of us not being able to let go of Rachel. Rachel would come back after spending a few days with Tina, and I would feel frantic from being separated from her for three or four days. And then she would have a difficult time bonding back with me. I hated to leave my baby off when she was clinging to me, saying, 'No, no, no, I don't want to go' ... or to have her delivered back to me when she was angry at me. A couple of times she came home and hit me, because she was mad at me for having been apart from her. The transitions were horrific. I wasn't able to get her to sleep. Again I got to the point of saying, 'No, you're never going to see her.' We went back to the child-development psychologist for a while, and I said, 'Look, I think Rachel needs to be home with me for a while.'"

It is not at all uncommon for a child to begin to show great distress at having to visit the other parent. Though it may result from the child's anxiety over separation from the primary parent, it may also result from the child's awareness that the contact between the parents becomes an occasion for hostilities. Assuming there is no abuse or neglect going on, a child's refusal to visit the other parent has nothing to do with not loving or being attached to that parent. It may just be the child's way of saying, "I can't handle the stress of this." The rejected parent can be devastated by this. It's hard enough fighting for your rights to be with your own child and arranging your life to make it possible, but it's excruciating when your child cries at the thought of seeing you. At those times, the primary parent will understandably want to calm the child down by refusing visitation. It is the wrong solution, however. It could push the other parent out of the picture entirely, which would have serious long-term consequences for the child.

Tina: "There were points where it was so bad that I said, 'I can't live like this.' At the office I would just sit and cry. And I would wonder, 'Should I just take myself out of this relationship?' One time I got halfway home with Rachel and almost drove back to say to Rebecca, 'It's not worth it anymore.' But I realize that's not an alternative. Nothing is going to come between me and Rachel."

If the parents cannot prevent themselves from being hostile when they pick up and drop the child off, they may have to arrange to avoid each other at those times. If they are able to be with each other amicably, and the child is still showing distress about the transitions, changing the custody and visitation schedules may help. It will require the commitment of both parents to keep the nonlegal parent in the picture. With the help of the child psychologist, Rebecca and Tina agreed that Rachel needed more time in Rebecca's home for a while, to calm down and feel more secure.

This family has now progressed to what psychologist and divorce specialist Kalter calls the "long range period."[2] The chaotic, angry aftermath of the separation has been replaced by an adjustment to the new circumstances. The arguments have died down, and negotiations go more smoothly. At the same time, Rachel has matured.

Rebecca: "In the last several months, those really frantic times have disappeared. Rachel has been much easier-going about the whole thing, which has made a tremendous difference. We try to make up the schedules a few months in advance so that we don't have to struggle on a weekly basis. Then we try to negotiate week by week if things come up that require flexibility."

Some of the issues that occasioned conflict before have disappeared, as both women are more secure with Rachel's bond to each of them. For example, Rebecca had been threatened by Tina's greater financial resources, fearing that Rachel would be seduced by the excitement material things could provide. By now she is able to say, "It means nothing. The ski trips, the waterskiing, it's great and it's fun, but I'm Rachel's mother and there's nothing that's ever going to undermine that. I feel much more confident than I did a year and a half ago."

As with most couples, Rebecca and Tina have different parenting styles. Tina tends to be more the disciplinarian, and Rebecca is somewhat more permissive, but they have a basic respect for each other's contribution to Rachel's development. Ultimately their conflicts with each other have not prevented them from seeing that it is in Rachel's best interests to have the benefit of what both of them have to offer.

The current source of struggle between them is that Tina wants to adopt Rachel legally. Where they live, this is fairly easy to do and has even been done before in a case where the couple no longer lived together. Tina feels that power struggles between them will go on as long as she has no legal rights to Rachel. In addition, if Rebecca were to die and Tina were the legal adoptive parent, Tina would be assured of getting custody. If Tina were to die, as a legal adoptive parent her assets would go to Rachel without any danger that her family would contest it.

Rebecca, however, is not so sure about giving up her power. "I am concerned about what happens if I want to move out of the area. Do I want to stay here another twelve years until Rachel goes to college? As much as I trust Tina to see Rachel on a weekly basis, I don't trust her to have legal rights to Rachel. She's impetuous enough to come to me and say, 'Well, we're going to move to Hawaii for two years and you can come and visit us.' So part of my escape hatch in this whole thing is that I'm not required to do anything. I can come and go if I want. Not that I am going to, but I could, and I want to protect that."

The reality, however, is that even if Tina adopted Rachel, she would not have the legal right to move somewhere that would prevent them from sharing custody. More important, neither woman can realistically consider taking the child away from the other because it would hurt Rachel too much. As Tina says, "It's not like she could pick up and leave and not scar Rachel, whether there are legal rights or not. It's got to be worked out in Rachel's best interests."

The discussion around this issue is in its preliminary stages and will clearly have to go on for some time. The issue has to do with trust, which is likely to be strengthened as they continue to rely on each other to raise their daughter. Rebecca says, "I am really proud that I was able to make the leap and put Rachel first. Rachel didn't sign up for this, I did. And I really feel like I would protect her mental health at any cost."

Tina and Rebecca have been in couples therapy since they broke up, in addition to the consultations with the child-development specialist. Their goal is to work out the painful feelings between the two of them. In the process, there have been times when they've considered getting back together. Tina says, "We've had dinner with Rachel a couple of times. We've gone out by ourselves a couple of times. We're enjoying the time we spend together. I came home to a little note from Rebecca last night: 'Rachel's only four. She's got lots of good years ahead. Want to try it again?' I don't know how realistic it is. I've asked that we table that conversation for a year and learn how to love each other again as primary people in each other's lives. But it is getting better and better."

Whether or not they get back together, and whether or not each of them has other relationships, they have a powerful connection to each other as Rachel's parents. As Tina says, "Basically, there's Rebecca, Rachel, and me. There may be other players and different scenarios going on, but the three of us are stuck with each other for a long time, and I'd really like to see that be a viable family on some level."

None of us wants to endure the anguish of our family breaking up. Prevention, in the form of good communication and professional couples counseling, if necessary, is the ideal solution. But even with the best of help and intentions, relationships will sometimes fall apart. When they do, it is crucial to remember that a child's bond to a parent never breaks up. Unless the child is being abused or neglected, our responsibility is to preserve and protect those bonds. At a difficult time in our lives, we may need professional help to evaluate our child's needs, to make the critical custody and visitation decisions, to understand the impact on our child of the things we say and do in regard to the other parent, and to deal with our own grief and anger. Though a breakup is always disruptive, parents who proceed with compassion and understanding for each other and for the child can go on to restructure the family in a healthy way.

10

CRISIS AND TRAGEDY

When I decided to become a parent, I was still naive enough to believe that I had control over the outcome. It takes so much effort and planning to become a parent as a lesbian or a gay man that I thought I was steering the ship. I supposed that if I did enough research, ate right, saw the doctor regularly, and didn't jaywalk, I could insure that all would go well. Most tragedies, I imagined, could be avoided. In any event, they weren't going to happen to me.

In this age of AIDS, we have all had to wake up to the painful reality that tragedy can happen to anyone. We still have to eat well and not jaywalk, but those are not guarantees. The crises, hard times, illnesses, and deaths that occur in any family can and do happen to lesbian and gay families as well. We sometimes suffer infertility and have miscarriages. On occasion, our children are born with serious birth defects. Some of our children develop diseases or suffer injuries. These things happen no more often in our families than in heterosexual families, but when they do, it may be harder for us to find help. Having to access systems of support which may not be sensitive to our family structures can make the process of coping a great deal more difficult.

There are some tragedies that may happen more often in our families. A few of the gay fathers who contributed to this book have AIDS. Breast and ovarian cancer, which occur more frequently among women who have not been pregnant, have a higher incidence among lesbians than the general population.

In the last decade, the community of gay men and lesbians has done a remarkable job of putting compassion into action. We have established and are continuing to develop systems of support for those among us who are suffering. We have also done a great deal to begin to educate mainstream health-care providers about our existence and our needs. As the number of lesbian and gay parents continues to grow at what appears to be an astounding rate, we are going to have to address the needs of families with children.

The following stories are painful, but they are full of love.

A Miscarriage

After years of talking, planning, and researching, Candace and Jill spent fourteen months doing inseminations. They did everything right, driving many hours to a clinic in Chicago to pick up their frozen sperm because no place in their town in Indiana had been able to offer the kind of loving atmosphere they wanted for the start of their family. Back home, Jill would use the sperm to inseminate Candace. Though it didn't work for a long time, there was never any question of their giving up. When the pregnancy test finally came out positive, they were overjoyed.

Candace remembers, "I was jumping up and down, really excited. I called people that very night, that's how crazy I was. 'I'm pregnant, I'm pregnant,' and here I was only three weeks pregnant. I was really elated.

"The pregnancy seemed very normal. I didn't have morning sickness at all. There was nothing negative or bad about it. I might have felt a little queasy once in a while and certain smells were obnoxious, but I felt great. I worked full-time.

"I started going to a midwife as soon as I found out I was pregnant. We were going to have a home birth. The midwife suggested that I see the HMO doctor simultaneously in case I needed an ultrasound or something. So this baby had double health care. The midwife was experienced, very professional, and very warm and wonderful. The doctor was typically cold.

"I was excited, and telling everybody. Some of our friends had already bought baby gifts for us. It was a really exciting time. I had maternity clothes, everything. I wasn't showing a bit, of course.

"I came home from work one day when I was about thirteen

weeks pregnant and there was just a tiny spot of blood when I wiped. The interesting thing is that this is always how my period starts. I have this twenty-four-hour notice of my period, this little spot of blood, and the next day my period starts. I thought 'Oh, no, this is my period, after thirteen weeks.' I called Jill at work, and she told me to call the midwife. The midwife asked, 'Are you having any cramping? Do you feel bad?' I said 'No. I feel fine. There's no cramping.' She said, 'Well, I wouldn't worry about it. Sometimes that will happen, that a little will bleed through. If that's all there is and there are no other symptoms, then don't worry about it.' She said to take it easy, don't overdo, but it's probably nothing to worry about. So I did. I felt relieved and thought it was no big deal.

"The next day was Saturday. We went into the city to have dinner with some friends, walked around the university campus, and went to see Lily Tomlin. I had a great time but toward the end of it I felt weird. I thought I had cramps. In the car on the way home I told Jill. She asked what I wanted to do. I reclined the seat back in the car and said, 'I don't know. I don't want to go to the bathroom. I don't want to look.' In some way I knew, but I was also trying to deny it. I was bleeding when I got home, and I called the midwives. They suggested that I go to the emergency room, just in case there was a problem, and have an ultrasound done. We had never heard this baby's heartbeat yet, which was strange, though sometimes it doesn't happen until later, especially in first pregnancies.

"The emergency room was a horrible experience. The nurse who helped me was very pregnant. I was on an HMO, and there was a number you were supposed to call from the house, but there had been no answer, so Jill just drove me straight to the hospital. They wouldn't admit me to the emergency room until they had an answer from the HMO. Jill said, 'Just get her in there, we'll pay for it, just get her in there.' And then this very pregnant nurse came in and started asking who my doctor was, and she said, 'Oh, that's my doctor, too,' and she started talking about babies with me. It was just so awful. They wanted to make sure it wasn't a urinary tract infection. I said, 'It's not my urinary tract. I'm bleeding from my vagina.' But they catheterized me to check for a urinary infection. So I was lying on this cold, hard table, with these awful lights, catheterized. They wouldn't let Jill in. They wouldn't do the ultrasound because it was the middle of the night and they didn't have people around the clock to do ultrasounds and they didn't want to wake anybody up. I said, 'I want an ultrasound before I leave.' They said, 'No, you have to come back tomorrow for an ultrasound. Just go home and let nature take its course, and your urine is fine, there's no infection.' The whole experience was like I existed from my waist down. No one ever came up and patted me on the shoulder and asked, 'How are you feeling?' No one said, 'This must be hard.' The pregnant nurse never got the connection of how weird it is to talk about a baby that you might be miscarrying. It was terrible.

"I didn't cry at all. I thought, 'I'm not letting these assholes see me vulnerable. I felt like I had to just lie there for the two or three hours that this was taking place. I also felt that I had to be real strong because they wouldn't let Jill come in and help, so there was no one to speak for me or with me about having an ultrasound or anything. I would sing to myself, not out loud but in my head, songs that were soothing to me, things like Chris Williamson's lullaby song ... 'like a ship on the ocean ...'

"I never really bled very heavily. I was spotting. They suggested I see my HMO doctor the next day, so I did. He did a vaginal exam and said, 'Well, the cervix isn't dilated or anything, and sometimes you spot and it's no big deal.' I had a book on herbs for the childbearing years, so we made herbal teas and I tried to do a lot of imagery. I had taken a psychic training class, and I was trying to go into these trances and go in my body and imagine it being healthy. I imagined going into my uterus, imagining my uterus as a healthy place, but while I was looking at it, I saw cobwebs in the corner of it, and this shriveled-up black thing. I knew at that moment that the baby was dead.

"About twelve hours later I had very heavy bleeding and lots of clotting. It was like I let go of it then. I think that's how I see it, that I was able to let go then. And horrible, horrible cramps. I couldn't sleep because the cramps were so bad. Jill stayed up with me for a while, but I told her to go to bed, there was no point in both of us not sleeping. I was sitting in the rocking chair, thinking about this pregnancy, and what we had gone through to get here, how sad it was that it was all over, and how exciting those first weeks had been, and how wonderful people had been. I didn't mind sitting up at all at that point, because I thought about how I wouldn't be sitting up with the child when it was sick or upset. I thought about all of the things I would be missing with the child, not seeing it go to school and all. It was a real night of grieving for me, and I cried a lot. I was sort of glad Jill was asleep, because I was better able to process it all than if I had been concerned about how she felt. I felt a whole lot better after that night. It was like I said good-bye.

"We performed a sort of ritual—we named it. A few weeks later we did a symbolic burial, just some tissues and stuff, in the backyard of some friends in Indiana who live in the country. It was good for me, I needed to do that."

Often the hardest part of suffering a loss is that very few people around you know how to respond. Most people won't bring the subject up for fear of upsetting you, and many will rush to cheer you up when you may need simply to be listened to.

Candace continues, "One of my friends was real emotional and able to talk about feelings with me. Some of our friends didn't know what to say, so they just pretended like nothing had happened. I needed people to know that this was already a part of our family even though it was never born. I don't know that I would have known that had I not gone through it. I would handle a friend who had a miscarriage very differently now than I would have beforehand.

"The last thing they said in the hospital was to go home and let nature take its course. Well, this is an unusual situation. When gays and lesbians are having children, nature doesn't just take its course. One friend, when I told her how angry I had been about it, told me to keep in mind that they didn't know everything we went through to get there. And it's true, people don't necessarily know all the years of research you've done, and the years of trying to get pregnant, so I had to be a little bit forgiving. That was a good thing for her to say to me.

"The hardest thing was to see all the baby gifts friends had given us, and put them away, and put those hopes away, and just say, 'I don't know, I don't feel like going on.'

"I stayed in the house for several days, first trying not to miscarry and then having the miscarriage. Then one day Jill came home from work and noticed the tire was leaking on the car. She had to go and get it patched and asked me to come out with her for the ride. Physically there was nothing wrong with me; I could certainly go out. When I did, I felt so out of place. All of a sudden I felt like a stranger in a strange land. Life continued while I was in this house trying to save this pregnancy.

"I really knew I would keep trying to get pregnant, but I was changed after that. I didn't trust my body as much. I thought, 'Oh, God, if I get pregnant again will this one be a miscarriage, too? So many people have four and five miscarriages.'

"I bought tons of books. I have three books about miscarriages. It made me sadder to read them. I got so worried when I was reading about people who had lots of miscarriages and SIDS babies, I was almost getting obsessed with it. So I stopped reading about it and went back to reading books about getting pregnant again."

Candace started trying to conceive again a few months after the miscarriage. "The second time I was pregnant was very different for me. It was much more guarded. We didn't tell anybody until I was past the point where I had miscarried the first time. I was just too afraid to get emotionally committed to the child. About a week or so past the thirteen-week mark I started letting myself get a little bit excited about it. It was like holding your breath ... 'Oh, please, please, don't let this one ...' A very different experience."

All went well, and Ethan, robust and healthy, is now eighteen months old. Candace and Jill are the proud, delighted parents they hoped to be.

Michael—A Birth Defect and a Child's Death

Michael George, our first baby, was born on August 13, 1981. I had prepared for the birth with my usual obsessive zeal, none of which helped a bit when real pain set in. Breathing, timing, body-relaxation exercises were all thrown to the winds in the face of breathtaking pain. I remembered the films I had seen of women successfully riding the crests of their contractions with skillful control, sweating and even smiling as people wiped their brows. Those images made me feel like a total failure. It hurt, and I yelled. I was stunned and frightened. Lamaze classes had said I would feel strong discomfort, but this was nightmare pain.

After twelve hours of this, our obstetrician said I needed a Cesarean section. At that point it was a relief, and all I wanted was to have the baby and be done with it. Susan had been with me all through labor, and it had been prearranged that if surgery were necessary she would be in the operating room, too. Susan herself was almost eight months pregnant at the time with our daughter, Emily, and they had trouble finding a surgical gown that would fit over her belly. I was awake for the surgery, so together we watched as they pulled our first-born from my body.

Susan saw him first and held him right away. Needless to say, he was the most beautiful baby we had ever laid eyes on. Then they took him away to be cleaned up and examined while Susan called our families with the good news. They shared our joy and our relief that all had gone well. As Susan and I beamed together in the recovery room, a doctor came in and gave us the devastating news that Michael was born with a condition called achondroplasia, a form of dwarfism.

The surgical anesthesia was just beginning to wear off, and my body had started shaking uncontrollably. The doctor was smiling over me, telling me that my perfect son would never be taller than 4'1" at best, with a proportionately larger head and torso and short arms and legs. Her manner was clinical, bordering on cold, and she had brought a student with her to observe how she broke the news to the parents. Susan clutched my hand. I wanted to throw up. Instead, as I have sometimes done at moments of overwhelming anguish, I took care to thank the doctor for telling us and to praise her for telling us so nicely. There was no sarcasm in what I said—I was just out of my mind. In that state I even consented when she requested permission to take Michael away so the hospital could photograph him for teaching purposes. Only after they hadn't returned him an hour later did the rage rise up in me. In a state of physical and mental agony, I was terrifyingly vulnerable to people who didn't care about us or our baby, and I felt powerless to take any action.

Susan heard the same news I did, but I didn't know what she felt. She often doesn't show what's going on with her, but even if she had, I don't think I would have seen it. I was lost in devastation. I was also ashamed of my reaction. After all, the good news was that his intelligence was fine and his life span would be normal. His condition was in no way life-threatening, and we would have all the joys of seeing him develop and thrive. I tried to remind myself that Michael's dwarfism affected only his appearance, and how little that has to do with a person's soul. It didn't work. I know Susan cares less about appearances in general than I do, and I felt ashamed of my pettiness. I felt ashamed that I could feel anything negative about a baby I already loved so much.

Michael stayed in the room with me during my hospital stay. Susan spent all day there with us, though we were called on to defend her right to be there when only fathers were permitted. Her immediate and unreserved rapture with Michael gave comfort to my sagging spirit. She adored him instantly. She embraced his dwarfism as a part of him, and she was determined that he would be the most loved baby in the world. I tried to follow her example, but I was a weak imitation. I still knew nothing of the kinds of serious orthopedic problems that dwarfs often suffer, but even so I was heartsick at the thought that his life would be so limited. To go through life so visibly different—the word "deformed" was never spoken, though it cast its shadow—what kind of life would he have? I, for whom adolescence had been an unending nightmare of never feeling pretty enough, now found it unbearable to imagine my teenage son, three and a half feet tall, at his high school locker with the other kids.

In retrospect, I have to admit that part of my anguish was a terrible narcissism. I felt ashamed that I had produced a baby so damaged. Though I had done years of work in therapy to repair the withered self-esteem of a painful childhood, at core my feeling was that Michael's defect was my own, to be seen by the world. It was also, somehow, my fault. My rational mind went over and over the care I had taken during the pregnancy. I had read every book, taken every vitamin, gone to every appointment. Still, there must have been something I did wrong. That one cup of caffeinated cola I drank on a hot summer's day. Too many desserts, not enough exercise. None of these made sense, but I tormented myself with them anyway.

As we were later to learn, achondroplasia is only one of many different forms of dwarfism. It has nothing to do with growth hormones, so it cannot be treated. It occurs as a spontaneous mutation in one single gene which impairs the ability of the long bones to grow. No one knows why it happens. Once it occurs, it becomes a dominant trait and can be passed on genetically. Because it is a dominant characteristic, it is not possible to be a carrier of the gene for achondroplasia without being a manifest dwarf. We had wanted to know if it could have come from the donor's genetic background and were relieved to discover that it was not possible. The donor was of normal height and therefore could not have contributed to this happening. Though the result for Michael was the same, it was easier to accept that this was a fluke of nature rather than a medical negligence.

I cried much of every day in the hospital. At the same time, I was utterly and hopelessly in love with him. I held him all night, and nursed him and sang to him. Susan and I talked endlessly and inanely about how wonderful he was. She would wait impatiently for his diaper to be wet, so she could have an excuse to change him. I let her do the diapers, partly because she was missing out on the nursing, but also because I was afraid to really, fully look at him without his swaddlings on. I was so frightened of seeing something wrong with his proportions. His little hands were very broad, a characteristic of achondroplasia, but I imagined they were just the peasant hands of my father's side of the family. His forehead was also a little high, another typical characteristic, but I pretended it wasn't. I wasn't yet able to face the short little arms and legs without crying, so I didn't look. It took many weeks before I would come to delight in his little stocky build, though eventually I felt there could not have been a more perfect child.

My father and his wife, Olga, came to the hospital to see him. We hadn't told them ahead of time about his dwarfism. We wanted them to meet him and fall in love the way we had before they knew anything was wrong. Michael had my father's name (his middle name, George, was Susan's father's), and this was his first grandchild. I could see in his face that Michael looked as perfect to him, at first glance, as he had to us in the delivery room. When I told them the truth, I felt as if I were confessing to having committed a crime. I braced myself for their shock and disbelief, but they responded instead with warmth and encouragement. They said it was going to be all right. I didn't know how it could be, but I was grateful for their optimism. I was even able to make a joke about how his diminutive size would mean we'd have more room in our small apartment. My father went home and set to work right away with plans to build Michael a set of extra-small furniture and riding toys.

Meanwhile, help came from several sources. I can't even remember what led to what in the blur of the first weeks back home. A friend of ours had a friend who is a dwarf. She visited us and was clearly such a remarkable person that we agreed later we'd be delighted if Michael grew up like her. We learned there was an organization, called the Little People of America, for dwarfs and their families. Johns Hopkins hospital in Baltimore hosts an annual convention for dwarfs and their families, with workshops on a variety of social and medical and psychological issues. A wonderful woman whose daughter is a dwarf reached out to us. She came to our home, held Michael, gave us lots of information, and was very understanding. She invited us to her home to meet her family. Her husband, son, and daughter welcomed us and admired Michael. Her daughter, Anna, was seven years old and achondroplastic like Michael. She played the piano for us, showed us her bicycle, and seemed to be absorbed in the usual assortment of birthday parties, friends, and school activities typical of any second-grader. Her life was so hearteningly ordinary that I began to feel better. We learned of dwarfs who were in many of the major professions, and dwarfs with good marriages. I began to believe that all Michael needed to have a rich and satisfying life was to feel good about himself. And he was already the finest baby in the world, so why shouldn't he?

We came to realize that our being lesbians gave us some particular advantages in understanding Michael. Being gay in a predominantly heterosexual world had forced us to grow—to go through a process of learning how to value ourselves independent of society's judgments. It was immensely helpful to understand that Michael would be going through the same process of learning to accept and value his difference, and finding the strength that comes from self-definition. That there would be some painful moments for him no longer seemed so terrible. We could help him use those moments to grow instead of retreat. I don't think I could have ever come to that without the experience of having come to terms with being a lesbian. We eagerly began the networking process that would make us a part of the Little People's community, much as we had pursued connections to the gay and lesbian community years earlier.

Seven weeks after Michael's birth, Emily Carol arrived. Susan's delivery took six hours from start to finish and, unlike me, she never made a whimper. She says it's dreadfully unfair that people refer to her experience as an easy delivery, since it was some of the most impressive pain she's ever known. I remain in awe of how she handled it. As Emily's head was emerging I remember suddenly being seized by an irrational anxiety that perhaps our doctor had no idea what she was doing. I tried to sound casual and conversational, asking her if she'd done many of these before. I was so frightened of something being wrong with Emily that I remained tense and cautious throughout. Even when I saw her, I was afraid to let myself feel the elation I had felt when I first saw Michael.

It was lucky that Susan's delivery was so short, because the logistics of things were difficult. Michael was nursing every hour and a half or so, and would not take a bottle. They would not allow him in the hospital, so a friend held him in the hospital lobby. I ran back and forth from Susan's bedside to care for him, feeling torn both ways. When Susan was settled in her room with Emily, the hospital made it clear that they would not allow Michael in under the sibling visitation policy, because they refused to consider him a real sibling. We bundled Susan and Emily home less than twenty-four hours later.

Now that we were used to Michael, Emily's arms and legs looked amazingly long. It took time to adjust to the proportions of a normal baby.

Life with two babies was certainly intense. My respect for the parents of twins took a quantum leap. We had felt so proud of ourselves for learning how to handle Michael. We'd been parents for seven weeks already and figured we were pros by now. We hadn't counted on how different two babies can be. The things that soothed Michael were intolerable to Emily, and what worked for her would have set him howling. To add to the household chaos, I had to go back to work the week after Emily was born, having already taken two months away from my practice. Susan did a heroic job of caring for both babies while I was seeing patients. She breathed an audible sigh of relief every time I came in on a break from work.

It was very difficult. We were seriously sleep-deprived. But it was also the most wonderful of times. There were the endless minute-to-minute discoveries of what the two of them liked, how they responded to things, how they were different. Susan and I babbled incessantly to each other about the miracles that were unfolding before our eyes. These were the children we had spent years dreaming about. Even so, the reality of how much love we felt was astounding.

Two days after Christmas—Michael and Emily were four and a half months and three months old, respectively—we were in the car on our way to visit my mother and stepfather. The babies fell asleep in their car seats as usual. Emily woke up as soon as we got there. Michael was still asleep. So as not to wake him, we brought the whole car seat, with him sleeping in it, into the house and set it down. We went through about five minutes of exchanging greetings and removing coats. My mother wanted us to see the new carpeting in their den. I said I just wanted to check on Michael first, in my worrywart way, to make sure he was breathing, and then I would join them. With horror, I found him lying dead in his car seat. I picked him up and he was limp in my arms.

I must have screamed. The car was rushed out of the garage. My mother grabbed Michael and started doing mouth-to-mouth resuscitation as we ran with him to the car and raced to the hospital. Susan and I were in the back seat holding Emily while Henning, my stepfather, drove, and my mother continued trying to revive Michael in the front seat. Some awful, primitive moan came from deep within me and the word it formed was "Mommy"—the only thing I could think of that meant help.

In seconds we were at the local hospital where they rushed him away and herded us into a room to wait. I overheard one doctor refer to him as a SIDS—sudden infant death syndrome—but I thought, no, that can't be right, he isn't dead. When a priest walked into our room I screamed. Not wanting to upset us, he turned and left, and I thought, good, that means Michael's not dead. Eventually, who knows how long, someone came and told us that his heartbeat had been revived, but they didn't know what the outcome would be. There might be brain damage.

More hours of waiting and more not knowing, until they said they wanted Michael to be transferred to a major hospital in the city where there were experts in pediatric neurology. I remember the three of us, Susan, me and Emily, alone in our own car. Susan was driving, heading for the downtown hospital in the pouring rain at night. It was a surreal, nightmare drive. By that time we knew that he was possibly so brain-damaged that there was nothing left of the Michael we knew. My breasts were hurting from being swollen with milk.

The hospital staff confirmed our worst fears. We repeatedly had to make explanations when someone new came into the room and asked which of us was the mother, but they treated us kindly. My father and Olga came to meet us and wait with us for a while. It helped that they were there. Susan and I made the decision that we wanted no heroic measures taken. They let us know that his neurological signs were virtually absent, at a level where it was legal and advisable to remove him from the respirator and allow him to die. What cruelty had we inflicted on him that the poor baby now had to die a second time?

The night was endless. We'd go in and talk to him, touching his little body, telling him we loved him and that he would be all right. When we could not stand it anymore we'd go back to the waiting room to sob. Back and forth like that, all night long. We kissed him good-bye and told him not to be afraid to leave us. At some point later in the morning a quietness overcame us both. Maybe it was just exhaustion. The hospital staff, which had kept a respectful and gentle distance the whole time, suggested we go home and get some sleep. No one knew how long this would take. It felt right to us to leave. Almost as soon as we got home the call came that he had died, and we turned around and went back to officially identify him. We did not feel bad that we hadn't been with him. For whatever it was worth, we imagined that our leaving gave him more freedom to let go.

Friends and family poured in over the next few days. I never would have believed how much it helps to have people come. Susan and I continue to be grateful to every person who came to the funeral home, and to our house, and to the funeral itself, even though it was quite a distance away. In fact, the world seems to have permanently divided at that time into those who were there and those few who weren't. There were only a couple of people who didn't extend themselves to us, and we haven't been able to bear their company since. Even knowing that so many people are uncomfortable around loss has not restored my generosity toward them. The people who came to see us brought love and sympathy, at a time when life had inflicted the worst pain it has to offer.

Most people did not understand that Susan had just lost her son. The expressions of sympathy were much louder and more prolonged for me. She often received an afterthought. When I noticed it I would make gentle efforts to bring her presence into more central focus. I didn't always notice it and she didn't complain about it. Sometimes she just withdrew a little when it hurt. One old friend of mine, who didn't really know Susan, paid a sympathy call at our home and completely ignored her. On his way out he barely said good-bye to her. I had to stop him from unwittingly dealing her such a blow, so I took him aside to say that Michael was just as much Susan's son as mine. He was startled, though he had known all along that we created this family together. He managed an expression of sympathy for her before he left. Later he told me that he had avoided Susan because he assumed her presence was painful to me, given that she still had "her" child and I had lost "mine." Even our gay pediatrician, who had met us when we were both pregnant and brimming with joy about our plans, told me how sorry he was and encouraged Susan to take good care of me.

We were luckier than people who lose their only child. We didn't also lose our roles as parents. But that brighter side to our suffering is something we can appreciate only in retrospect. In the months of anguish that follow losing a child, there is no way to feel lucky about anything. It only hurt when people would say, "At least you still have Emily." Of course we were overjoyed to have Emily, but it didn't lessen one bit the pain of losing Michael.

We cried every day, often many times a day. Pain that would just rip me open would come out of nowhere, in the middle of scrambling an egg. Then just as mysteriously it would leave, and I would go back to being numb and gray. It seemed the pain would arrive when I couldn't stand the mute, lifeless numbness anymore. Then the numbness was a blessed relief when I could not bear any more pain. Susan was unfailingly there to hold me when I needed it.

Wanting Emily not to be hurt by our grieving, we made special efforts to give her attention that was cheerful, playful, and loving. I found I could manage it only for a little while until thoughts of Michael would make me need time alone to cry. Then Susan would take over with Emily until she needed time for her own tears, by which time I would have recovered.

I went back to work a week after the funeral. It was at least a distraction. It is amazing to me to see in retrospect that I actually did some work of value in that time, though I also see that I could not bring any joy to my work. When patients were dealing with issues of loss, in particular, it took a monumental effort of will to suppress my own sobs and keep the focus on them. I always knew I would recover at some point. I knew the pain would last a long time, but that it would someday get better. Still, it was only my bonds with Emily and Susan that gave me any will to live. If not for them my preference would have been to die.

There was an added dimension to our loss that came from being a lesbian family. We were conscious of the eyes upon us. We had spent years reassuring people of our ability to parent, of the resources we could offer a child, of the viability of a nontraditional family. I often experienced the stress of trying to be a model family, to present an unassailable picture to doubting onlookers. I did not want to be seen now as a family of tragedy. I knew that when people talked about what happened to us, the sympathy for our loss was going to be mixed with their reservations about our doing this in the first place. In that state of vulnerability, the thought of someone being critical of our parenting felt like violence.

There is support available for families who have lost a child, but we could never make use of it. We agreed repeatedly that we needed to talk to other people about it, but as a lesbian family in 1981 we found it difficult. The New York chapter of the Sudden Infant Death Syndrome Foundation offers support groups, but they treated us very badly. We never knew for certain if it had anything to do with our being lesbians. They told us on the phone that they could not accept us unless we had the official autopsy report confirming that Michael's death was, in fact, a SIDS. In New York an autopsy takes many months. We did not need the help six months from now, we needed it now; given that our baby had died suddenly in his sleep, what did it matter what the official document said? They were rigid and adamant. Months later I wrote to them about how painful their response had been, but they never responded.

There was another group, called Compassionate Friends, for parents who had lost a child through any means. It met on an evening that conflicted with my work schedule. Looking back, I see that I could have rearranged my patients to make it possible, but at the time I just lamented that we couldn't make it. I know that part of the problem was that I couldn't bear to deal with coming out in a group of heterosexual parents when I was already so vulnerable. Conscious of society's disapproval of a lesbian trying to become a parent, I expected rejection when I most needed sympathy. I'm sorry now that I let my timidity make that decision. I have since learned that most people who share a tragedy with you don't judge. They may not always understand at first what your loss means to you, but they generally open their hearts to you with a generosity that is some of the best of what humanity has to offer.

A wonderful, giving woman reached out to us. I don't even know how I found her. To this day I have never met her, but our phone conversations were of enormous help to me. She had lost a child also, and was willing to listen to me cry and to give me a road map of the grieving process, cautioning me that it takes much longer than one ever imagines. In general, people who hadn't been through this kind of loss didn't really know how to help. With a few exceptions, most friends and family expected things to be fine within a month or two. It was hard to pretend that things were okay, but they clearly had little tolerance for continued suffering. Often, if I didn't move right on to cheerier topics, they would suddenly have to get off the phone.

Susan and I had our worst times as a couple during the next year. We held each other and cried together often, but our characteristically different ways of handling the grief also caused tension between us. My need for affirmation of our love and commitment became intense, just as she needed to withdraw, emotionally and sexually, to heal herself. We each struggled with feeling misunderstood, without comprehending the real problem. Just a few months after Michael died, we went to see a therapist, ostensibly to address our failing sex life. Unfortunately, the therapist also did not understand. She should have reminded us that we were in an acute state of grieving and offered us the support as a couple that we desperately needed. Instead, she joined us in obscuring the real problem. Though we only saw her for a couple of months, the effect of it was destructive. It polarized us further. It took years for us to really understand what happened there and repair the damage. Many couples are not so lucky. The divorce and separation rates are very high after the loss of a child.

I started trying to get pregnant again and went through two years of miserable infertility (see Chapter Two: Lesbians Choosing Pregnancy). My obsessive and frustrating pursuit of pregnancy added yet another measure of stress to our lives. During that time, between Michael's death and Jesse's birth two and a half years later, Susan got seriously shortchanged. Not only was her grief often invisible to the people who were comforting me, but she herself accepted the idea that she had to be the strong one. While we held and supported each other, she still gave more to me. In my neediness I took advantage of her willingness to be my rock. In short, we both gave *me* the opportunity to grieve loudly and openly for many, many months. She gave me comfort whenever I was in pain, and that gave me the strength to work, and to live, and to help care for Emily. She was patient and loving through my insufferable crankiness during the infertility. Together we held our breath through my pregnancy until Jesse was born. At that point, when I became able to feel truly hopeful again, all Susan's unacknowledged pain caught up with her.

Jesse's presence was painful at times to Susan because it brought back so many memories of Michael. It was frightening to begin to love him because we feared he might never wake up from his next nap. He was born in August, like Michael, so he went through each little developmental advance at the same time of year Michael did. We stayed awake at night listening to him breathe. Christmas found us both frightened, exhausted. Susan was irritable a lot. I tried to be understanding but also felt overwhelmed. We fought, we cried, and we muddled through.

Things got easier with the new year. Jesse not only survived past the critical age for most SIDS deaths, he grew to such strapping abundance that we all relaxed. Emily, who had undoubtedly felt the strain on the family and had become a rather cautious child, began to blossom. She became willing to get on with her somewhat delayed toilet training, and this coincided with her becoming much more willing to take risks in general. Though she has always been a very special, joyful, uniquely imaginative child, she now became freer to be difficult and obstinate at times—signs to us that she was feeling the confidence to become more independent.

Michael's photograph hangs on the wall along with numerous pictures of Emily and Jesse and other family members. We talk about him occasionally. Seeing a dwarf in the movies or on the street sometimes prompts a discussion about Michael. The children ask how tall he would have been by now. We could not feel more blessed than to have the two wonderful, special children we have, but Michael will always be remembered as our first.

Death of a Parent

Susan Hester is forty-two. Her lover, Mary-Helen Mautner, died of breast cancer two and a half years ago, at the age of forty-four. Susan continues to raise their daughter, Jessica, who is now seven and a half.[1]

Mary-Helen and Susan met twelve years ago, at a party at Mary-Helen's house in Washington, DC. Susan was new in town and was invited to the party as an introduction to the community. She recalls, "I was completely, completely taken with her. As soon as we started seeing one another, neither one of us ever saw anyone else." They began dating in January, spending most nights together in one or the other's apartment. Mary-Helen was a wonderful vacation planner, and that August they went hiking in the White Mountains of New Hampshire. While they were on vacation, Susan discovered a lump in Mary-Helen's breast. She remembers, "I was terrified."

Mary-Helen had had lumps before. They had always turned out to be cysts. So they continued to enjoy their trip and dealt with it when they got home. They were referred to a breast surgeon, reputed to be one of the best, who told them not to worry. Despite the fact that Mary-Helen's mother had had breast cancer, he didn't want to do a biopsy or even order a mammogram and said he preferred just to watch it over time instead. Mary-Helen went back to the breast surgeon for checkups every three months, and all seemed fine. Her regular gynecologist saw her about nine months later, however, and was very distressed by the size of the lump. He said, "What in the world is going on here? I want you to go back to the breast surgeon immediately." The breast surgeon again affirmed that it was not a problem. Though he deserves a reputation as a masterful surgeon, his diagnostic errors were tragic. This was the first of four separate misdiagnoses in Mary-Helen's case.

Their second summer vacation was a bicycle trip to Vermont for a week, followed by a week in a house in West Virginia. They decided during that week that if things continued to go so well between them, they would live together after the new year. When they returned from vacation, the surgeon said, "This thing has gotten too big. It's got to come out. It's not a problem, it just ought to come out." The day after the biopsy they got the news that it was malignant.

Two weeks later Mary-Helen had a mastectomy. She considered changing doctors, but, faced with the need for surgery, decided to stay with the breast surgeon who had misdiagnosed her. Right now, she reasoned, she needed someone who could cut, and he was the best. Susan remembers, "I just went into a coping mode." That hospital stay was the first of many, and the beginning of Susan's education about dealing with the medical establishment. She recalls, "I was young, and I didn't know that the rules are for their convenience. Over the course of the years I learned how to get around all that stuff." They were always completely open about the nature of their relationship. Susan continues, "We never had a problem, because we never made any issue about it. We were a couple. I was her partner. I was the primary decision maker with her. And I have to say, other than maybe two times when there were nurses who were uncomfortable, we literally never had a problem. I think it had to do with being assertive and self-confident. We presented ourselves as not at anybody else's mercy. We asked a lot of questions, and we were nice. Not nice like cooperative, but friendly, warm. Together we agreed that would be our style. We would make people comfortable with us in a way that they would let us do what we wanted."

They waited for several interminable days after the mastectomy for word about whether cancer was found in the lymph nodes. When the doctor stuck his head in the door to say that the lymph nodes were clear, Susan remembers that she "literally let out this whoop. I just yelled, I was so relieved." Mary-Helen's prognosis was good. She had an 80 percent chance of never having a recurrence. They felt free now to just go about their lives. Susan knows now that they should immediately have gone to an oncologist for further care, but the surgeon said he would handle the follow-up, and they let it stay in his hands. At any rate, it looked to them as if the cancer was behind them forever.

They moved in together that fall, and by winter they were talking about having a child. It was Mary-Helen's idea, and she wanted it very much. Susan was not negative about it but felt more cautious. She had lost her father to cancer when she was a child. Her mother now had cancer. She recalls feeling, "Why would I want to put another person in my life? It was like one more person to lose." She now feels it was the best idea Mary-Helen ever had, but at the time she let Mary-Helen take the initiative about it.

Mary-Helen was the type of person who researched everything. She explored the possibilities for getting pregnant. Some cancers are thought to be stimulated hormonally, so she explored the question of whether pregnancy would put her at greater risk for a recurrence. While the conflicting opinions about it were coming in, Mary-Helen attended a conference on adoption. It seemed there were routes through which a single woman, even with a history of breast cancer, could become a mother by adoption. All they needed was a note from the doctor attesting that she was free of cancer and that it was not likely to return. By this time Susan was into the process wholeheartedly.

The adoption application was in the works, and while they waited for their agency to find a child for them, they took another fabulous summer vacation. This time they went hiking in Switzerland, and then to London and Paris. It was Mary-Helen's way of saying, "We're going to keep on living. So I had this mastectomy, big deal."

Their adoption story is full of the tumultuous ups and downs of so many similar stories. There were several rounds of false hopes, crashing disappointments, and cautious hopes again. Finally they met their little baby girl and took her home. Mary-Helen became the legal mother in the adoption proceeding. Susan had been listed as another adult in the home who would share in the child care. Once the adoption was complete, they told their agency that they were lesbians. The agency worker appreciated their openness and wished them well.

Susan remembers, "Jessie was a wonderful baby. Our coparenting was actually one of the very best pieces of the relationship. It was the piece that we did the best. So, now, though I miss Mary-Helen for me, I miss her most in the comothering. And I miss her for Jessie. I thought three as a family unit was just the best thing. It was wonderful."

When Jessie was a year and a half old, four years after the mastectomy, Mary-Helen was officially diagnosed with a recurrence of breast cancer. She had found a lump in her remaining breast in January of that year but again the surgeon had said there was no need for a biopsy. In the spring, she found a couple of subcutaneous lumps on her body but didn't tell Susan. They were at Mary-Helen's sister's house for Passover when Mary-Helen casually asked her brother-in-law, a physician, what he thought of a lump on her eye. Susan remembers, "I went berserk. I immediately got her in another room and said, 'What in the world is going on and why haven't you told me about it?' I went into total catastrophic thinking."

The ophthalmologist was concerned and said it had to come out. That was Memorial Day weekend. They spent the weekend away with friends, and Susan describes it as "a really grave weekend. I remember swinging Jessie on the swing at this cabin and thinking, 'I can't do this. I can't raise this child by myself.' I was really devastated and totally terrified."

The breast surgeon continued to say it was not a problem, that it couldn't possibly be a metastasis of the breast cancer. The biopsy, however, revealed that the lump on her eye and the several lumps on her body were all malignant. There was also bone involvement—the breast cancer had located in several places on her spine and hip. Some of it had also spread to her lung. Susan recalls, "On the one hand, it was this terrible picture. On the other hand, it was this wonderful picture because her liver and her brain weren't involved. That was my first lesson in learning that bad news can be good news, because of all the bad news that you didn't get."

Mary-Helen was adamant that they were going to live positively and that their lives were going to change as little as possible. She finally chose a good oncologist and set about her treatment aggressively. The cancer clinic knew from the beginning that they were a lesbian family. Susan usually accompanied Mary-Helen to treatment. Sometimes Jessie came, too. Mary-Helen lost her hair but had little patience for wearing wigs. She also got fed up with wearing a breast prosthesis. In a declaration of freedom she threw it away and went braless. She wore a bathing suit unselfconsciously at the public pool.

Parenting was Mary-Helen's favorite thing in life. Jessie always knew that Mommy had a disease. That was why Mommy had only one breast, and why she spent many hours every week at doctors' offices and emergency rooms. They told Jessie that Mary-Helen had some confused cells that didn't know how to act right, and the doctors were trying to get them out of her body. Chemotherapy compromises the immune system, so the whole family had to be especially careful about washing hands and not sharing food. To this day Jessie is phobic about germs.

Susan says of that period, "We spent every minute together. We sort of bunkered in. We spent a lot of time reading. Mary-Helen was doing a lot of reading about breast cancer and survivorship, and using relaxation tapes and biofeedback. The parenting had already put some strain on our relationship, then the cancer on top was really a strain. On the one hand, we were totally connected to each other and had this very loving relationship, but it was strained to the max by the fact that I was working, I was terrified, we had this young child, and all this medical stuff. Mary-Helen would distance herself emotionally. I would pull at her all the time, asking, 'What are you thinking? What's the matter? What's going on?'"

Worried about the tension between them, they saw a therapist who specialized in chronic illness. The therapist told them they were crowding the hell out of one another. She said they were so busy coping that they had barely acknowledged the enormity of the cancer's impact on their lives. Susan's very stressful job looked like one of the burdens they could jettison, so she quit work and began to free-lance at home instead. The resulting flexibility in her schedule was essential for managing the medical appointments as well as Jessie's care.

Susan reflects, "We were incredibly privileged. We did not have any economic difficulty because Mary-Helen had extremely good insurance and a good salary. We have a really nice house. We're white, middle-class, well educated, and we had only one child. I don't know how other people do it. Both of our families were totally supportive. Both of our sisters were completely involved with us. We had a wonderful network."

Mary-Helen continued to work every day and to be involved with Jessie. That first summer on chemotherapy they took a very relaxed vacation, but the following year they arranged to go hiking again. Despite the chemotherapy, Mary-Helen was in great shape and managed a ten-mile hike that was too much for Susan.

In the fall the chemotherapy stopped working. They began trying other things—hormone therapies, radiation. Mary-Helen got internal radiation burns which scrambled her digestive tract. Her eye could no longer produce tears and had to be lubricated every thirty minutes or so. By the spring, when Jessie was three and a half, Mary-Helen had trouble getting around because of the cancer in her bones. The cancer in her lungs made it hard to breathe. She could walk across the room, but she'd have to sit down and regroup. Colleagues would pick her up and take her to work, and get her lunch for her while she stayed in her office. Even so, she planned another wonderful vacation in Vermont for that summer.

Up until this point, Susan and Mary-Helen had handled everything themselves. Now it became clear that they needed help. They put the word out in their lesbian mother's group and got immediate response. People they didn't necessarily have close relationships with pitched in like family. They ran errands, picked up X rays, brought food. Susan realized she couldn't handle a vacation without help, so they lined up Mary-Helen's sister, and their friends from California also came to spend time in Vermont with them. Mary-Helen started on a new chemotherapy shortly before going, and rallied impressively. She was able to walk a mile in Vermont and started swimming again when they returned home. She gained weight, her hair looked good, and she delighted in Jessie's preschool experience.

The treatment stopped working by winter. In the spring Mary-Helen's bones were so weak that she fractured her hip. She went to the abortion-rights rally in a wheelchair, and immediately afterward they checked her into the hospital for hip replacement surgery. The doctor tried to tell her that the situation was grave. In his clumsy style, he asked if her papers were in order. Mary-Helen was angry and adamant that she was not going to have this conversation. She refused to think about dying, even up to the minute of her death. Susan also remembers that "I didn't want her to die. I didn't accept that she was going to die." They never discussed the doctor's words. After the surgery Mary-Helen was on crutches and in physical pain but resumed working as soon as she could.

Four-year-old Jessie understood what was going on, but life was still happy for her. She would ride up and down the stair-lift they had installed in the house. Every morning, Jessie climbed into bed with Mary-Helen and Susan brought them breakfast. While Susan stole a private hour to take a walk, Jessie and Mary-Helen would play together. Susan remembers, "Mary-Helen did everything you can do sitting down." The bulk of the child care, and everything else, fell to Susan, who says, "I only know now how exhausted I was then. At the time I didn't have a clue."

Mary-Helen was deteriorating. Even so, planning yet another vacation for August became her single-minded focus. By now she was on oxygen and an infusion pump. Their network of family and friends helped them find an airline willing to fly her and all her equipment to the house they rented in Vermont. They helped to arrange for medical care once they got there. Susan asked Mary-Helen's niece, Rebecca, to meet them at the house so she wouldn't be alone in an emergency. Their first night there, when they tried to get Mary-Helen to bed, she had a major respiratory spasm. She began choking, coughing, and gasping for breath. Susan was terrified, holding her in her arms. Jessie woke up and demanded, "Is Mommy dying? Is she dying?" Susan told her to "stop asking questions" and told Rebecca to sit with Jessie to quiet her down. Susan says, "I just totally panicked. I was asking Mary-Helen questions and she motioned me to be quiet. She just really concentrated and finally got her breath back. I had a major anxiety attack that night. I thought, 'I just can't do this.'"

That was Saturday. Mary-Helen's sister came up the next day and they called the doctors, who advised getting her back home at once. Mary-Helen refused. She had no intention of dying, or of going to a hospital, or even of cutting her vacation short. Susan relates, "I sat down beside her and said, 'I'm really scared,' and she said, 'I'm not.' And it knocked it out of me. There was no way I could say, 'We have to go home.'" The next several days were an absurdity of crisis after crisis, with everyone working to keep Mary-Helen breathing. Susan was beside herself, and the doctors accused her of being a maniac for allowing Mary-Helen to remain there. By the weekend, they found a way to transport her back home, and Mary-Helen finally allowed them to take her.

Even so, neither Susan nor Mary-Helen imagined that she was dying when they admitted her to the hospital. A nurse said she would probably not make it through the night, but they didn't believe it. Mary-Helen kept fighting for days. By Wednesday Mary-Helen told Susan weakly, "I don't think I can make it." Still, when an insensitive intern offered to increase her morphine and "snow you out," Mary-Helen pulled the mask off her face and answered angrily, "If you're asking me if I'm ready to kick the bucket, the answer is NO!" Jessie got to visit her once more that day, and Mary-Helen died the next morning. The obituary listed her as "Mary-Helen Mautner, 44, a lawyer at the Department of Labor who was active in feminist organizations. Mautner was a past editor of Quest: A Feminist Quarterly. She also was founder of the Women's Legal Defense Fund and was active on the DC Council task force that amended the District's rape law. Survivors include her companion of 10 years, Susan Hester, and their daughter, Jessica Hester-Mautner."[2]

Susan remembers, "It was like going into a numb place. I mostly just sat. Things happened around me. People would come and say so-and-so is on the phone, do you want to talk? At one point I realized I was sort of embarrassed because I didn't feel like I had any emotion about the whole thing. I was just this person that this thing had happened to, and, yes, I was describing how we'd gotten her back from Vermont. Some people were mad that they hadn't gotten to say good-bye, but nobody had said good-bye because Mary-Helen wasn't going anywhere." The mother's group arranged for them to sit shiva for three days, while family and friends came to visit. A photographer friend helped Susan go through thousands of family pictures to put together a collection for the memorial service. Susan recalls, "I don't know why, but the group I broke down with was her work colleagues. They all came together on Friday. They weren't lesbians, but they had been so completely supportive and so totally acknowledging of us as a family for the whole ten years we had been together."

Jessie, meanwhile, went uncharacteristically berserk. She was enraged, kicking and throwing things. She was hitting and screaming, totally out of control.

Susan panicked about cremating Mary-Helen's body because she could not imagine having to explain it to Jessie. A friend cautioned her that not carrying out Mary-Helen's wishes would be a serious mistake.

They called a child specialist who helped them come up with an explanation: "Mommy wanted her body to be turned to ashes. They put the body in a place where there is a lot of heat, which turns it to ashes. Mommy doesn't need her body anymore because she's a spirit now. Her body was diseased, so to be done with it was okay." For three months, Jessie asked questions constantly, repetitively, about why Mary-Helen had died, how she died, why she had had cancer, and how she'd gotten it. She seemed never to be sad, only thoughtful and angry.

Susan describes, "Jessie is not a yackety-yack kid. Her school could burn down and she wouldn't tell me. She didn't say a lot of what she thought." Recently, two years after Mary-Helen's death, Jessie revived the questions about how you get cancer. Out of nowhere she suddenly offered the explanation that she had been harboring: "Maybe you get it from adopting a baby." Susan was able to tell her that adopting a baby was the very best thing that had ever happened in Mary-Helen's life. Mary-Helen had started a letter to Jessie which she never finished. It begins, "The saddest thing in my life is to know that I will die before you grow up." It goes on to say how she will miss seeing Jessie learn to read and write and ride a bike. Jessie has heard the letter, and knows it is being saved for her.

In one unusual confrontation with the reality that she was going to die, Mary-Helen had told Susan she wanted people to write letters, anecdotes—"snippets," as she called them—about her for Jessie to have. She had said, "I don't want them to make me out a saint. I just want them to write about some experience with me." The pieces that people wrote form a wonderful collection that is being kept for Jessie.

Susan's focus revolved around Jessie for the first three months after Mary-Helen's death. "She provided structure for me—getting her to school, getting her dinner." As a lesbian nonlegal mother, Susan had no parental rights to Jessie. The lawyer advised her to immediately begin adoption proceedings. Susan recalls, "I got very resistant about it. I said, 'She's my daughter. I'm just not going to do it.'" The lawyer responded, "If something happens to you, Jessie could become a ward of the state because she doesn't belong to anybody." Susan consented, "All right, I'll do it, but you have to understand how horrible this is to me, to have to adopt my own daughter, and I don't want Jessie to know about it." Jessie had always assumed that both her mothers were just that. The worker who did the home study was sensitive, presenting herself to Jessie as someone who comes to see how things are going when one of your mothers dies. The lawyer also was very supportive and helped speed up the process of finalization.

Jessie never admitted to being sad at all. Susan says, "I think it was because I was sad so much of the time and she resented it. Instead, she would cry about things she wouldn't normally cry about. Something would get broken and she would cry like it was the end of the world." About a year after Mary-Helen died, Jessie came over to Susan one night and said, "I know you're crying about Mommy. Some people don't cry when they're sad." Susan said, "That's right. Some people cry and some people don't." Jessie talks about Mary-Helen all the time, "If Mommy were alive she would love to go to outer space," and so on.

It was discouraging to try to locate a grieving group for children. Susan says, "Everywhere I called I would say, 'I have a child, she had another mother, her mother died. I'm looking for a grieving group for her.'" Word of mouth located the only two groups within a reasonable distance. Susan remembers, "One of them had come really highly recommended. This person was sort of the 'it' for dealing with grieving children. When I called, she was totally hostile about the fact that I was a lesbian. She didn't think Jessie would 'fit' in their group because how would she explain to the other children that this child had two mothers? I was welcome to bring her, but she didn't think it would work. I said thanks. I wouldn't have dreamed of taking Jessie there." The other group, run through a Virginia hospice, was ideal for Jessie. The woman who ran it was warm and accepting. She came to their house to do an individual assessment, and was immensely reassuring to Susan. She said, "Jessie's not in trouble. She's where she ought to be with this." Jessie didn't talk much in the group but got involved in the art projects, and it was good for her.

Susan remembers, "By January I realized I wanted to be in a grieving group. I called around, but there was nothing for lesbians. Absolutely nothing. I found a straight group, which actually had to vote as to whether a lesbian could join them." It was a good group, however, because all the people in it were close to Susan's age and had lost a partner within two years. Susan relates, "I went to the group knowing that the politics was just not that important, that the bond I was going to have over losing a partner was so clear." The group was highly structured, with readings and discussion every week. "It worked for me for about the first four months. Then there came a point where I really began to have more trouble with the fact that they didn't have any political consciousness. Once the word 'widow' came up, and someone said to me, 'You're not really a widow.' I think they got it about sixty percent of the time."

One of the major spurs to Susan's healing came from Mary-Helen herself. Shortly before she died, she was in the hospital for a bone scan. Susan left to take Jessie to school and describes that when she returned, "Mary-Helen's face was radiant, in a way that it had not been for a year, and was not to be again. She was calm and happy. She said, 'I've got this idea. We have to start a project. I was sitting in there imagining if I were alone. I knew you were coming back, but I imagined what it would be like for someone to have the test with nobody to be there when they got out. We have to start a project for lesbians because not everybody has the support network or the friendships that we have.'" Mary-Helen had made a page of notes about a project for lesbians with life-threatening illness, suggesting it be modeled after the AIDS buddy programs, with recommendations about lawyers and who should be included. After she died, people were told they could contribute money to the "Lesbian Health Care Project." About $4,000 came in to a post office box, and it sat in an account until January. At that point, Susan realized she was ready to go ahead with it. Word went out, and an incredible amount of energy poured forth from the lesbian community to launch the program. A support group started immediately. Meeting space was donated. Over the next few months, a mission statement was drawn up, and the program was officially named "The Mary-Helen Mautner Project for Lesbians with Cancer." Its objective is to provide direct services to lesbians and their families and partners, to do education to the lesbian community about cancer, and to educate the health-care establishment about the needs of lesbians with cancer. Two years later, the project has recruited more than 200 volunteers and mails information to more than 700 individuals and thousands of organizations. It provides direct care, workshops, educational programs, outreach, and public forums about the needs of lesbians with cancer. Susan Hester has been honored by gay and women's organizations for her wonderful work in the creation of the Mautner Project.[3]

Meanwhile, the grieving goes on, and two and a half years later it's still painful. Susan relates, "I had a really terrible slump after the first anniversary. Everybody had said after a year things would be different. I felt like people misled me. Anything around Jessie continues to be hard. I had my parent-teacher conference last Monday, and I stayed on the edge of tears throughout a good deal of the thirty minutes. The teacher asked, 'Do you take her to the library?' and I said, 'No, I don't.' She said, 'Well, you should,' just like that, and I said, 'I know,' but I immediately filled up with tears. All I could say was, 'That was what her other mother did with her.' I will never share a parent-teacher conference with another parent. Nobody else will ever be Jessie's mother.

That's the hardest thing, that I'm never going to have that family again."

Susan also struggles with a deathly fear of losing Jessie. She says, "I have to fight this all the time in terms of letting her go and do things. She has some of those same fears, which she expresses occasionally. I think when you go through something like this together you have a bond that is really different and very strong."

Susan feels that being in a lesbian community has made a difference. She says, "Maybe I'm wrong. Maybe a straight community pulls together. But if I just take the people I was in the grieving group with, none of them had the kind of support that we had. Even those who had their church groups or their friends, none of them ever talked about having the kind of stay-with-it community that we had."

Those of us who have survived crises and losses have learned that, as with everything else in life, there is no perfect way to do it and it cannot be done alone. If you are dealing with a serious medical condition you may need people to provide information, referrals, help with child care, home care, or nursing needs. People who understand can also help you make the numerous difficult decisions that a health crisis will require, and may offer shoulders to cry on.

If you have experienced a loss, remember that grief and healing take time, usually much more than you expect. You can't speed up the process, but you can help it along by accepting whatever you feel, and by talking the feelings over, frequently, with people you trust.

The people we find to help us through hard times may come from many different places. Sometimes it is our gay and lesbian friends, or people in the gay and lesbian communities, who can best understand what we are going through. Sometimes we need people who have been through the same kind of crisis as the one we are experiencing. If they are heterosexual, we may have to decide whether to overcome our reticence and disclose our identities, or to stay hidden and accept a more limited contact. Often the people we need to help us are professionals—physicians and psychotherapists—and it may take hard work to find the right combination of expertise and gay-affirmative sensibility. It may be even harder to find professionals who understand gay and lesbian families with children.

Don't overlook any avenue of support; take the initiative to go looking for it. Talk to your friends and the family members you trust. Try getting in touch with your local gay and lesbian parenting group, for example, and let them know what you are going through. If there is a foundation or organization devoted to your particular medical condition or situation, contact your local chapter. Find out about possible support groups or sources of information.

Finally, if possible, seek some spiritual nourishment through whatever path appeals to you. Times of great emotional and physical hardship intensify our need to feel a part of something larger in the universe, and to maintain our sense of purpose in life.

11

OUR FAMILIES OF ORIGIN

Breaking the News

At the time we planned to have children, my father, who was Italian-American, was living with his wife Olga. He was raised as a Catholic, and his politics were somewhere to the right of the NRA. For him, sexuality was something you only talked about in a dirty joke. A woman who dared to be openly sexual was an object of scorn and shame. It had not been easy for him to come to terms with the fact that his first daughter reached maturity during the sexual revolution. When I was seventeen, my parents found evidence of my having a (heterosexual) sex life and all hell broke loose. Though I moved out right away, there followed two very painful, stormy years. It was a struggle for me to uphold my own sense of worth as a human being and a sexual being, in the face of so much rage and shame coming from my father. By the time I was twenty, however, things had improved. Seeing that I wasn't going to change, he adapted to my having my own apartment, though it was a stretch for him. We had never really talked things out—that simply wasn't my father's style. If there was a problem, my father stormed. Or maybe he lectured. If he couldn't win, he sulked. But what he never did was talk about an internal conflict he was having or a struggle to resolve it. Instead, what made the difference was the passage of time, and my unspoken ultimatum, as hard as it was for me, that I was who I was and he would have to take it or leave it. He basically wanted a tie to me, and he wanted it enough to change himself, if necessary. When I was twenty-one, he came through for me again and wished me well when I moved in with a boyfriend.

When Susan and I fell in love I told him right away. I have never been comfortable keeping secrets about important things. We were supposed to have a lunch date the following day, and I thought it would be kinder to us both to tell him over the phone. I figured that once he knew, he might not want to keep our date. The phone would also allow us both a measure of privacy for our reactions, avoid a prolonged and difficult contact, and prevent a scene at a restaurant. I called and asked if he were sitting down, that I had something important to say. He assured me apprehensively that he was ready, and I announced, "Dad, I'm in love." There was a very long pause on his end, until he finally asked, "Is he white?" Several responses flashed through my thoughts, including chiding him for his racism, but what finally came out was, "Yes, *she* is."

He was flustered and angry, though he denied it. In a very hostile tone of voice, he said, "No, I'm not upset. Why should I be upset? It's none of my business. If you want to have a liaison with this type of a person, that's up to you. I mean, it's not as if you've become a thief or a prostitute or anything. So why should I be upset?" I gently suggested we postpone our lunch date for the following week to give us both time to sort out our feelings.

To his remarkable credit, he came through for me again (as I also know he would have if she had not been white). It wasn't immediate. There was cool tolerance at first, but he continued to get to know Susan. He saw that I was happy. Over the course of several months he came to realize that she was the best thing that had ever happened to me. Within a few more months, he came to love her for herself. Eventually he began to introduce her as his daughter.

Needless to say, however, telling him that we were planning to bear children placed additional demands on his flexibility. His wife, Olga, was a major ally. We broke the news at a Chinese restaurant on Mother's Day, months before we started trying to conceive. Olga kept making unsubtle attempts to steer the conversation around to babies. "You know," she started, "I never had children of my own, and I regret it." He ignored her and lit a cigarette. "In those days," she went on, "you wouldn't think of having a baby if you weren't married." He clearly had some sense of what was going on and buried his face in the menu. Olga pressed, "But now lots of single women are having babies."

Susan and I thought it best to cool it for a while as he signaled the waiter and the food was brought. Undaunted, Olga continued to champion our cause. "I think it would be wonderful if we could have grandchildren." He nearly choked on his sweet and sour pork, but at least the cat was out of the bag. By that time, we had the confidence to know that this, too, was going to be a process. We knew from experience that he would just have to see it work. In time, he would accept the situation because he had to. Ultimately, he would do even better than that. He would see our joy and meet his grandchildren, and his basic love for us would eventually overcome his difficulties.

Fortunately, my mother had never suffered from some of the dependence upon tradition that characterized my father. An extremely independent woman, a professor and scientist at the top of her field, she had long ago broken with the confines of her conservative Jewish upbringing. She felt people should do what they want with their lives as long as it didn't impinge on hers. She had accepted my initial coming out as a lesbian with graceful good wishes. I think she thought I was stark, staring mad to try to get pregnant when I didn't have to, as her own experiences with pregnancy and motherhood had been complicated and difficult. She was, however, more than willing to acknowledge that we are of very different temperaments, and that if this was truly what I wanted she would support it.

Breaking the news to our parents that we are planning to provide them with a grandchild should be one of life's truly joyful moments. Whatever conflicts we may have had with them before, whatever growing pains childhood contained, the news of our impending parenthood should bring whoops and hugs and tears to the eyes for everyone. At the threshold of taking the most momentous step of our lives—committing ourselves to a new generation—we look for the love and support of the generation that spawned us.

Some of us do, indeed, find that our parents respond with immediate excitement, congratulations, and offers of help. Some parents are able to feel instantly, without reservation, that our decision to have a child is a wonderful event in the family. Even parents whose initial reactions to our sexual orientation were hostile and troubled have often progressed, by the time we plan to raise children, to the point where the news comes as no big deal and elicits lots of good wishes.

Most often, though, the initial reactions of our parents fall short of unbridled enthusiasm. Mixed with some positive desire to become grandparents through us, our parents' responses may also range from reserved to apprehensive to downright negative, including shock, shame, anger, even horror. If they made only limited progress accepting our sexual orientation when we first came out to them, the news that we are planning to parent will again make them confront the painful necessity to change. For many, this is difficult and taxing. For those few parents who found the task of accepting our homosexuality insurmountably painful, hearing that we want to raise a family may be salt in a bitter wound. Their reactions, at a time of major transition in our lives, may cause us pain. It can hurt even more to contrast such negative responses with the jubilant receptions our heterosexual siblings receive when they have children.

We need our parents. Even though we may be mature adults, life is easier when they are behind us. The process of raising a child, in particular, intensifies the need for continuity among the generations. Sharon says, "It's not that I need their acceptance to do things that I do, but it's very nice to have their acceptance. It would be very lonely for me not to have a good relationship with them. They're like all parents, they drive me nuts sometimes, but it's very important to me that they be a part of my life." Pasqual explains, "I need to be open with my family. I owe it to them. I owe it to my children. Our families give us advice, and they support us, and that helps us be a family, stay together. It helps to have our families behind us supporting us emotionally."

Our parents also need us. It is safe to assume that all parents want to love and approve of their children. No parent wishes to be in the awful position of feeling ashamed or angry about how her child chooses to live. Our parenthood often provides our own parents with another opportunity to grow. And even hard-core holdouts have been known to find the sweetness of a grandchild motivation enough to attempt to change. The awareness of our mutual needs can help to keep the struggle for acceptance from becoming adversarial. Though we may see things in different ways, we are not on different sides. Our parents have the difficult task of changing their attitudes and behavior to embrace a reality that may be frightening or unfamiliar to them, while we have the work of providing compassion and support for their struggle, in the service of our mutually loving goal.

Coming Out

Most of our parents have to go through a process toward acceptance of our sexual orientations. It may take time for our parents to understand that the problem resides in society's bigotry and not in our lives or our desires. It further may take them time to be reassured that our confidence and pride can overcome the effects of homophobia, and that our children can be healthy and happy. Even more time may be needed for our parents to muster the courage necessary to break with tradition themselves and openly support us among their friends and relatives.

The process our parents have to go through is akin to our own coming-out process. It took most of us some time to get used to our own sexual orientations, and to feel at ease with the idea of becoming gay or lesbian parents. Many of us feel that coming out continues, throughout our lifetimes, as we expand our awareness of what our sexual orientations mean to us in the context of our different life stages and the world's changing attitudes. For our parents, also, there are many layers of consciousness to pass through, leading to deeper levels of understanding.

How fast our parents proceed with their process of acceptance, and how far they go with it, will depend on three major factors:

Their individual psychologies. This includes their personal strengths and weaknesses, rigidities and flexibilities, their ability to love, to empathize, to be intimate and talk about feelings, their innate personal courage, and the sum total of all of their life experiences. We have no control over who our parents are in this regard, though by now we probably have a good idea of their capabilities. We can and should demand that our parents come through for us with the best they have to offer, but we cannot reasonably expect them to give us things that they have never been able to give themselves or anyone else. We have to have some understanding of their limitations. For example, we can insist that our parents overcome their prejudices to treat us as lovingly and respectfully as they would treat their heterosexual children. However, if they have never been very close to any of their children or grandchildren, they are not likely to be much different with us.

Their external environment, including friends, neighbors, relatives, and religious affiliations. The responses our parents anticipate and get when they tell people what we are doing with our lives will impact greatly on how far their consciousness-raising can go. When people in their social circles are positive and supportive, fear is dispelled and courage renewed. Parents who generally travel in liberal circles, and whose extended family tends to be open-minded, are more likely to risk revealing the news, which is in and of itself an affirming experience. If, however, they belong to conservative churches or synagogues, come from narrowly judgmental family systems, and have bigoted friends, their anticipation of rejection may reinforce secrecy and retard the process of acceptance. Coming to a joyfully welcoming attitude about our impending lesbian or gay parenthood may require that they challenge those close to them, and even break with some who do not approve. This is a hard thing to do. Our understanding of the difficulties involved can be helpful to them.

The degree to which our parents *have* friends they confide in will also make a difference. If they keep to themselves, generally having few friends and affiliations, they will not be as challenged to come out about their lesbian daughter's pregnancy, for example. They may miss out on the further development that telling people can foster. Parents who actively maintain personal friendships may feel more of a struggle about how to handle the situation but will also therefore have more opportunity and motivation to work on their homophobic attitudes and fears.

The help we give to them. A lot of this is up to us. Our continued efforts at communication, our hard work at trying to understand and empathize with their concerns, and our commitment to set clear standards for how we and our children will be treated will help to further the process of acceptance. In addition, our ability to supply our parents with information, reading material, and exposure to other lesbian and gay parents and their children, as well as to other parents of lesbians and gays, will be a useful adjunct to love and contact.

Our Parents' Journey

Though there are some families that feel at ease with our sexual orientations when we first come out to them, for most the process of acceptance is painful. Carolyn Griffin, Marian Wirth, and Arthur Wirth, the authors of *Beyond Acceptance,* a book for the parents of lesbians and gay men, note, "For most, there was a sense of tragedy, of loss, and for a time, an all-consuming pain. The very foundation on which their daily lives was built felt shaky and insecure."[1] Parents will feel grief and anger about the loss of their dreams for their child. They may direct guilt and blame at themselves and each other about what could have caused this. The sense of shame may be excruciating. Their images of homosexuality may be limited to negative stereotypes in the media. Fears of being rejected by their own extended families, friends, or religious groups may be profound. They may direct anger at us for putting them through all this pain, or they may withdraw in tears and silence. However, the authors write, "Early reactions are not a reliable indication of whether parents will move towards and beyond acceptance. A much better indicator is willingness to open themselves to new information and to maintain contact with their child."[2]

The news that we are planning to bring a child into our lesbian or gay household may force the original coming-out issues to the fore again. Concerns that were swept under the rug may resurface. Parents who accommodated to our sexual orientation by being privately accepting of us while remaining in the closet with regard to the rest of the world, for example, may be threatened by how public a grandchild is likely to be. They realize that people will ask questions, and they will have to confront their fears when they answer.

Parents may have additional concerns about the welfare of our children. They will worry about social stigma hurting the child. They may worry about the psychological health of a child raised with parents of only one gender. Where there has been a nontraditional conception, through alternative insemination or surrogacy, they may worry about how the child will deal with being different in that way. If their family is about to become interracial through adoption, they may have to deal with their own racism and be educated about racial issues. They will once again have to work on the prospect of presenting the situation to their extended family and friends. We can reasonably expect that if our parents made progress in dealing with our sexual orientation, then they will make similar progress in dealing with our becoming parents.

How We Can Help

Communicating: Ideally, we need to be able to come up with a genuinely empathic understanding of the nature of their difficulties, without wavering an inch in our belief that we deserve support for the family we are creating. From that perspective, our first job will be to keep the lines of communication open. Of course, most families want to avoid painful topics, and we have to overcome our own reluctance to raise difficult questions.

It will be important for our parents that we hear their concerns, even if they are expressed in anger or criticism. Instead of rebutting and arguing, it is more helpful if we can genuinely listen to what worries them. Our parents may not be aware that much of their anger is coming from shame, or from fear. We should let them know that we can truly imagine why they feel the way they do. The more our position can be one of understanding, without criticism of their feelings, the faster they are likely to be able to work on their own conflicts.

Educating: Our parents may be operating under stereotypes and lack of experience. They probably won't have any precedents for gay and lesbian couples raising healthy, happy children, and they may need input from sources other than us. Reading material is a very useful place to start. Books that deal with having a gay son or lesbian daughter can be very supportive. In addition, books that deal with lesbian or gay parenting are helpful.

Other parents of lesbians and gays may also provide a great deal of help and support. The Federation of Parents and Friends of Lesbians and Gays, called Parents FLAG or P-FLAG, has more than three hundred chapters throughout the United States and eleven other countries with contacts in many other cities which do not yet have official groups (see the Resources section). The atmosphere at meetings is warm and welcoming, as parents who've been through the difficult process of acceptance share their perspective and experience with parents courageous enough to attend for the first time.

Because the process of acceptance is fostered every time our parents speak to someone about their concerns, it is a good idea to encourage them to talk to friends, family, and clergy. Even if some of those people do not hold particularly evolved attitudes toward lesbians and gay men, the mere act of discussing the issues can be affirming.

If you live near your parents, you can invite them to attend a meeting of your local lesbian and gay parenting group. The reality of beautiful, happy children is one of the best antidotes to homophobic fears there is. The opportunity to meet lesbian and gay parents also contributes to giving the whole idea a sense of the familiar.

Setting limits and providing guidelines: An important factor in our parents' progress on these issues is a very clear explanation of our expectations. While they struggle with their feelings, and we sympathize with the fact that shame and disappointment may be present for a long time, we can insist on certain standards of behavior from them. For example, a parent may wish to ignore our lover in an attempt to blot out the reality of our being gay or lesbian. It is our job, however, to insist that our relationships be treated with the same respect they would show to a heterosexual relationship. This includes extending to our partners all the acknowledgment and courtesy they would extend to our straight siblings' husbands and wives, for example. Being forced to give full "in-law" status to our lovers can help our parents to break through denial; it can provide the impetus for them to truly look at our loving relationships for what they are.

We also need to let our parents know how we expect them to behave with regard to our children. You may need to spell out that the child born to or legally adopted by your lover, though not legally your own, is still *your* child and consequently their grandchild. This means that you will expect them to treat the child the same way they may treat other grandchildren who might be biologically and legally related to them. You will want to make clear what your expectations are about the role of the extended family. You can brainstorm with them about how to describe the child to other family members and outsiders. The details of alternative insemination, sperm donors, surrogate mothers, and other matters may be difficult for them to talk about. They may worry that if they mention their grandchild, they will be asked embarrassing questions. Together you may be able to come up with ways of presenting their grandchild to their family and friends that feel both respectful of you and comfortable for them.

Finally, if your parents' criticisms feel abusive to you or to your lover, or potentially to your child, you will need to tell them that attacking, shaming, or threatening you verbally is unproductive and painful, and you will not continue any conversation in which that takes place. You can let them know that you will resume discussing their concerns with them when they can present them in a less hurtful way. Similarly, if they want to have contact with their grandchild, they will have to refrain from making negative or insulting comments about lesbians and gay men which could be damaging to your child.

Timing: Since time is a major factor in the process of acceptance, it is a good idea to give your parents plenty of it before the actual arrival of your child. Ideally, coming out about being gay or lesbian should precede by a few years the news that you are planning to parent. That allows them a chance to make progress with those issues before you up the ante. Then, again ideally, you should let them know of your plans to have children well in advance of your actually doing so, to provide time for them to get used to the changes. In general, the families I know who told their parents early in the decision-making process found that by the time the child arrived, much of the work had been done already. By contrast, those lesbian and gay parents who don't tell their families until it is a fait accompli have to deal with a more complicated set of responses. For one thing, parents feel bruised by not having been told from the beginning. For another thing, once you are changing diapers you may not have the energy to patiently deal with your parents' concerns. Negative attitudes, expressed when you already have or are expecting a child, are likely to hurt more. Don't be tempted to "trap" them into acceptance by presenting them with an irresistible grandchild, since it may force them to suppress negative feelings that they would be better off dealing with.

Keep in mind with all of this, however, that each family has its unique way of growing and accommodating to the individualities of its members. There is no perfect way to do this, and what may be ideal for one family wouldn't work for another. Your own considered hunches about what your family needs will probably be your best guide for how to proceed. The likelihood is that everyone will end up gaining something from the experience.

If your parents are truly unable, over time, to embrace the loving family you have created with your beautiful children, you may have to recognize that they are limited by fears and rigidities that they simply can't let go of. They may not possess the flexibility necessary for change, or they may not have the strength to get past their own internal shame, or, even worse, they may not be able to tolerate the intimacy of a loving relationship with their adult children. These are all dreadful situations, for us and for them. They happen only when parents are quite damaged psychologically. And though knowing that doesn't lessen the pain for us at a time when we need parents, it does make clear that it is not about us. If your parents have this much difficulty, by now you probably will have learned to find your support from other sources.

How It Works

Some parents make it easy for us. If you are blessed with parents who are secure about themselves, open-minded, and loving, a baby's impending arrival is an occasion for family celebration. Pasqual describes his lover Robert's mother's reaction. "When we told Robert's mom that we were thinking of adoption, Robert was absolutely falling apart, nervous that his mother would have an adverse reaction. She said, 'Oh, gosh. I've been meaning to tell you for years that I thought you should adopt kids!"

Similarly, Jeff and Peter got immediate family congratulations. Jeff says, "When we told them what we were doing, they thought it was great." Jeff's mother has also provided concrete help. Jeff describes, "She provided technical support at the beginning, you know, this is how you burp a child, and this is how you do this and that. And of course every time we've needed a babysitter, she's available. It's been great."

Kathleen is an example of a parent who did a great deal of work on her homophobia long before she learned she was to become a grandmother through her daughter, Mindy, and Mindy's lover, Jennifer. Kathleen is almost sixty-eight, a retired secretary from an Irish Catholic background. She describes herself today as a "recovering Roman Catholic," meaning that she has come to feel that for her, the Catholic Church put too much emphasis on guilt, ritual, and duty, and not enough on love and tolerance. Since moving to a small New England town, she has become involved with a congregationalist church whose minister preaches love and acceptance, and it has helped her do a lot of personal growing. It is clear, however, that she was always a person who was willing to listen to her heart first.

She recounts, "Mindy came to me one day and said that she was a lesbian, and I cried, like any mother does. I can remember talking about it with people who were close to me and saying I didn't really know whether I was crying for myself, whether I was crying for the difficult task she had in front of her, or for the way society reacts to this kind of orientation. I decided it was probably a little of all three. But my first reaction to Mindy was that it didn't change who she was and it didn't change the way I loved her. I knew that if this was the conclusion she had come to, that it was very legitimate. She would never have done this without a lot of soul-searching, so that was the way it was and that was okay."

As soon as Mindy came out to her mother, Kathleen began educating herself about lesbians and gay men. "I never knew anyone who was involved in lesbian or gay relationships. Mindy gave me some reading material, which was very helpful. I was surprised one day to realize that I couldn't care less about what people think. What's important to me is the love that we share in this family.

"When Mindy and Jennifer told me they were planning to have a child, Jennifer had truly become a fourth daughter in our family. We just love her, and I had a whole lot of faith in their relationship. My first concerns about their having a child were financial, because their economic situation was not good at that time. But they talked about the fact that they were getting older, and it was very obvious that this was something they really wanted to do. And I don't really believe that you have to have money to be good parents. I had no question that they would be good parents.

"I did have some question about how they would explain their relationship to their child, but at the same time I knew that whatever happened this child would grow up feeling secure."

Kathleen is also able to mobilize support from other people. She tells people openly and proudly about the situation, and gets back warmth and enthusiasm from her community. "I tell them that this is a lesbian relationship. I don't cover that up in any way. And I tell them how much I love them, and how I feel they are entitled to have a child if this is what they choose to do as a family."

Kathleen, now the proud grandmother of four-year-old Molly, believes that lesbian and gay families are at least as good as heterosexual families at caring for children. "I don't know how many [heterosexual] dads would do what these girls do for each other. These are two very distinct personalities who work very well together. If one is testy or tired, the other one slides right in and takes over. I think what Molly has is equal to, if not better than, what she might have had in another family."

Unfortunately, not all of our parents adapt so readily. Sharon did not get a wonderful reception when she came out to her parents. The family went through years of difficult feelings around it. Sharon recalls, "I remember going to my mother's house alone and in tears, saying, 'You can't expect me to stick around if you're going to be this cruel to me.'" By the time they heard that Sharon and her lover, Kathy, were planning for Kathy's pregnancy, they had done a lot of growing. Still, the news was not easy for them. Much of the difficulty for Sharon's mother centered around having to face people with the truth. Sharon recalls, "She said to us, 'You've chosen to be different, you've chosen to come out when you want to come out, but I never had to come out.' My mother is uncomfortable being different, and suddenly she had to come out as the mother of a gay daughter. Now, also, [because of a grandchild] it was not just friends. It was the doormen in her building, the women in the beauty parlor."

With Sharon and Kathy making clear what they expected of Sharon's mother, she became able to talk with her friends. As Sharon recalls, "Kathy was having the first baby, and my parents weren't sure how to acknowledge it, and their friends didn't know what to say. When my mother called her best friend to tell her that Kathy had had the baby, her friend said, 'Now, Sylvia, don't get mad at me, but what are we supposed to say? How are we supposed to take this?' My mother said, 'You're supposed to congratulate me, I'm a grandmother.' And her friend then said *Congratulations!* and the gifts came in from all the friends in the group. It just took my mother saying it, but it was hard for her."

When Andrew and Don adopted Chad, Andrew's mother accompanied Andrew to Peru to pick up the baby. Though this was clearly energetic support, all was not peaceful. Andrew had to do some firm limit-setting to make it work. "Even on the plane there she said, 'I don't know why you're doing this.' I said, 'If you start now I'm going to throw you right off the plane.'"

Andrew's mother made wonderful progress overcoming some conventional viewpoints. "She just couldn't understand why I wanted this. She understood that a [heterosexually] married couple wants to make something out of the two of them, or they want to have children because it's the right thing to do. But I'm not married, and Don and I could enjoy ourselves and not have any of that responsibility, so why was I doing this? She has now come around completely, to the point where she won't hesitate to tell anyone that Chad has two daddies, anywhere, anytime." Andrew's father has also come a long way, and is even closer to Andrew and Don now because of Chad. "My father, who used to be just like Archie Bunker, is the most loving grandfather. This man calls me and talks to me for great lengths of time about Chad. He loves this kid to death, and he has two other grandsons. We had a good relationship, but now it's even better."

George and Philip also had to make their expectations of George's mother very clear. Their son, Brett, was four months old, and George was about to take his first trip East to see his family. George describes, "My mother asked if I would leave Brett home and come by myself. It wasn't that she didn't want to meet him, it was just that she didn't want to have to deal with all her friends. I was very upset and said, 'Well, then I won't come home at all. Would you ever dare to ask my sister not to bring her son home?'" Once they got there, things were fine. "They were able to relate to this specific little baby, whereas when I was still in San Francisco, they had trouble with the whole idea of two men raising a child. Now they are all very bonded to him, and miss him a lot."

JoAnne and Gwen are the mothers of fifteen-month-old Moira. They have been together for seven years, since they were twenty-eight and twenty-six. They describe the years of work that went into

JoAnne's parents becoming comfortable with their having a child.

JoAnne recalls, "When I told them that we were having a child, they tried to convince me not to. They made a special trip down here [they live hundreds of miles away] to have a serious conversation with us. They didn't understand at all why we would want to have children, why we would do that to ourselves, and especially why we would do that to an innocent child."

JoAnne's parents hold politically liberal attitudes, but things are harder when it's in your own home. JoAnne describes, "Their gut response to it is much more negative than their intellectual response. That's also true of all the people they know who are older, and suburban, and upper middle class. Their expectations were that a child's life in this situation would be very painful. They felt it would mean that our lives would also be very painful, and they just thought this was a terrible decision. And my father, in particular, is not one to tell somebody else what to do, so this was a pretty big thing for him."

JoAnne's parents were struggling with the shame of what people might think. "I think the biggest problem for them was that it put them in a position where they had to come out to everybody they knew in order to have this grandchild. They didn't think that I recognized how difficult this was for them. The way my mother's friends all judge each other is by how 'well' their children turned out. My mother's self-esteem was at stake, because my choice was a reflection on how well she had done as a mother."

JoAnne and Gwen let JoAnne's parents know what kind of behavior they expected from them. "We said that we were not ashamed of who we were, and we did not want our child to be exposed to close members of the family who were ashamed of who we were. When I spoke to them I made it very clear that I was an adult and this was my life and this was the way things were going to be. They absolutely understood. They admitted in later discussions that they didn't know how to deal with being ashamed of their own child for a reason like homosexuality. I think when we clarified our response to their feelings of shame, it lit a fire underneath them."

JoAnne's parents were now motivated to make use of outside support. "I was able to convince them to go to P-FLAG meetings. They went for about six months, driving to meetings in a town forty-five miles away from them so that they didn't have to worry about running into anybody they knew. After a meeting, though, my mother would get on the phone and tell me about it in detail. I think she was really excited with the response she got there. They went into the first meeting and said, 'Our daughter is a lesbian and she's just told us that she's planning on having a child.' Instead of the response being, 'Oh, isn't that lovely,' which would have turned my mother right off, the response was, 'Oh, wow, that's really an extra thing to have to deal with.' They really validated her fears and concerns about it, but they also helped her work through them."

Acceptance takes time, however, and there are ups and downs in the process. JoAnne recalls, "It was very shaky for a while. In some ways it was worse than when I came out to them. I was very angry that they seemed to want to place blame. They said, 'We don't know if it was because you had a bad childhood or what it is you're trying to make up for.' They just decided that we felt the need to have a child in order to prove a point."

Although JoAnne had come out to her parents long before, until JoAnne became pregnant no one in the extended family was told that Gwen and JoAnne were a lesbian couple, though many probably suspected. "The six months of P-FLAG meetings had been helpful to my parents, but the actual pregnancy was a real crisis for them. Within a week of my telling them I was pregnant my mother got on the phone to all of her family and came out to them. My father was in shock. He did not expect my mother to do it. He realized that he had to do it, too."

JoAnne's father had more difficulty with it than her mother. The P-FLAG meetings had been less helpful to him. He was struggling with shame about his daughter's lesbianism, as well as shame about being ashamed, because it was inconsistent with his ideals. JoAnne remembers, "He ended up in therapy. My parents were having marital problems, and although my mother was not quite coming right out and accusing me of ruining their marriage, she did suggest that this was the catalyst for it all."

The response that JoAnne's parents got from the family was only positive. JoAnne recalls, "That was the thing that was most astounding to them. Over the course of the next week or two, we received several letters from different family members just telling us how wonderful and brave we were, and that they were looking forward to the baby. It made it somewhat easier for my parents. It made them realize that the sky was not going to fall. Given my parents' expectations, what they did was very brave."

JoAnne and Gwen did a number of things in this process that helped the situation. They presented the situation openly and honestly. They were very clear and unwavering about their own pride in their decision and their intended family. It was stated in no uncertain terms that JoAnne's parents would have to be able to overcome their shame if they wanted contact with their grandchild.

At the same time, JoAnne felt sympathy for her parents' struggle, and respect for the courage it took them to face it. Both women took pains to understand what this meant to JoAnne's parents, how their backgrounds, friends, social circle, and psychological makeup contributed to their shame. In addition, JoAnne and Gwen talked with each other about their anger and worked together, as a team, deciding what responses to make to the things JoAnne's parents did and said that angered them.

JoAnne's parents, for their part, are really to be commended for what they did. They were faced with a challenge to grow. Though they balked and complained at having been put in that situation, they rose to the challenge. They could have withdrawn in silence, refusing to deal with their own conflicts about it. Instead, they did the thing that is hardest to do when one is feeling ashamed: They talked to people about it. Their motivation was their love of their daughter and their desire for a relationship with their grandchild. It was also their desire to improve themselves, to raise their behavior up to the level of their ideals, that motivated them to come out. Seeing their willingness to struggle was a tremendous help to JoAnne and Gwen.

JoAnne says, "The fact that they went to P-FLAG meetings made me much more patient, because they were really trying to work it out. Though I got frustrated at times, I don't think I got angry because I realized they were doing the most positive thing they could be doing. Certainly getting angry with them was not going to help."

Gwen adds, "What also helped was that at no point in time was there a threat that they would cut us off. Although we weren't sure of that when we first told them, after the first conversation we felt secure about that. And for all the problems that they caused, they were still very warm, and very friendly, and very nice. They were just trying very hard to understand."

JoAnne's parents are now very involved with their granddaughter, Moira, JoAnne's father is no longer in therapy, the tensions in their marriage have eased up, and they have come to treat Gwen as a daughter-in-law. Their involvement is extremely important to JoAnne and Gwen.

The willingness of everyone in JoAnne's family to communicate helped them work through their conflicts. In many families, however, people do not discuss upsetting things. You may have to be very assertive to bring up the important issues. In Iowa City, Petra and

Adrienne, the mothers of three-year-old Kim, found that dealing with Adrienne's parents meant cutting through generations of midwestern reserve. Adrienne's family is not accustomed to discussing personal matters, and Adrienne put off mentioning their plans to have a child. Throughout the entire year and a half that they were inseminating not a word was hinted. Petra got pregnant and still nothing was said. Adrienne's family would visit them frequently during the football season, when they came in to Iowa City to attend games, while Petra was getting progressively more pregnant. Finally, they felt they had better say something. Petra recalls, "We sat down at lunch and told them that I was going to have a baby. They just looked at us. You could sort of see the wheels turning in their heads and they didn't know what to think about it. All they said was, 'Huh!' and that was it. They never asked a question. They did not express any other feeling about it. The next day, when they had Adrienne alone, they asked for a few details, but I honestly think that they thought that I had gone out and slept with some man or that something bizarre had happened. They couldn't figure out how two lesbians could make themselves pregnant."

The news had been accompanied by very few details, and a lot was left unsaid. Petra's perspective was, "I felt it was Adrienne's responsibility. I was really trying to back off and let her resolve her own family relationships. In her typical style she was just as vague and minimal as her family, and we paid for that later. We never clearly communicated what we wanted their role to be as grandparents."

Based on the family's ignorance of the situation, mistakes were made. Every year Adrienne's parents send out a Christmas letter to friends and family all over the country, saying what the kids are doing. Petra's name would sometimes be mentioned, but that next year, while she was pregnant, it was omitted.

The following year, the couple's daughter, Kim, had been born and was almost a year old. Adrienne's parents had been very loving and attentive with Kim and obviously adored her, but they clearly didn't know what place she had in the family. Petra recalls, "We got the Christmas letter and went down the list of kids, and they announced that another granddaughter had been born [to one of Adrienne's siblings] and that was the highlight of their year. Then we got to the part about Adrienne, and it said that she was still teaching at the university. They skipped Kim completely."

Petra and Adrienne were devastated. Petra decided it was time to take action. "I said, 'I don't know what you want to do about this, but we have got to do something for Kim's sake. That's going to be our role forever, to educate and protect her, and I can't let this go by. If you're not going to talk to them, I'm going to.'"

Adrienne agreed. She sat down and wrote her parents a letter. Petra remembers, "She said how hurt and disappointed she was, and that although we hadn't really done a very good job of telling them what we hoped and wanted from them in terms of their being grandparents, they were going to have to figure out a way to talk about Kim, to explain her."

This all took place in December, and Adrienne's parents got the letter before Petra, Adrienne, and Kim arrived at their house for Christmas. Petra describes, "When we got there, her father came running out of the house with Adrienne's letter in his hand, saying, 'I'm sorry. We just didn't know how to handle it. We didn't know what you wanted.'"

True to this family's style, it was never discussed again, but the action Petra and Adrienne took was essential to the family unity. Petra adds, "The next year I was mentioned in the letter, and Kim was described as 'almost two years old and keeps things humming.' Since then they call themselves Grandma and Grandpa, so it really was a turning point. The fact that Adrienne was able to take action for herself and for us really brought us together and cemented our commitment to Kim and to our family."

Petra's family, in contrast to Adrienne's, is Italian, reactive, emotional, and dramatic. Coming out had been very stormy but had been resolved long before Petra became pregnant. Petra describes, "My mother threw me out of the house twenty years ago when I told her I was a lesbian. She just threw me out, didn't want anything to do with me. Two years after that she came around and we've been very cordial ever since. So she had plenty of time to get used to this—she knows it's not just a phase. And she really likes Adrienne and always has, so it's no longer an issue that we're lesbians."

When Petra got pregnant she got a lot of welcome attention from her mother but found she also had mixed feelings about it. "I felt a little resentful about it. Now that I was acting like a heterosexual and producing offspring, I got attention. I'd lived in Iowa for ten years and she never visited me until I got pregnant, and that hurt. Now she wants to come and visit as Grandma, and she's been here several times since then. I felt like suddenly I was in the fold of the rest of the family. Kim was something she could brag about."

It may feel painful that our parents can come around for the sake of a grandchild, when they couldn't support us as their adult children.

On the other hand, the fact that our parents are drawn to their grand-children often provides a means by which they can come to know and appreciate us in a different context. Seeing us in our roles as parents promotes an identification with us in a new way. By the same token, raising a child also gives us a greater sensitivity to our parents' experi-ence. No matter how different from theirs we intend our parenting to be, our empathy for our parents will be increased when we are in the role ourselves.

Siblings and Other Extended Family

Our siblings often have less trouble dealing with our parenthood than our parents do, and may be a valuable source of support, espe-cially while our parents are going through their process of growing into the idea. Siblings are less likely to have the same ego investment in our behavior that our parents have, and since they usually haven't spent decades feeling protective of us and responsible for our health and hap-piness, they are less likely to worry about our well-being in quite the same way as parents. In short, our siblings are often better able than our parents to see us as separate people and to respect our choices.

Pasqual describes the family of his lover, Robert. "His older brother is a born-again Christian, ultra right wing, and yet they were wonderful. They had us over for dinner. We played with their kids. We were expecting the worst, a really difficult situation, that it would be embarrassing, that they would be sort of quiet. But they were very sup-portive and friendly. I have not one bit of complaint. Robert's other brothers have been very supportive as well. We spend Christmas with them, and receive presents for both of us and the kids. They call us, and we call them." Many lesbian and gay parents find that the support and acceptance they get from their siblings is truly sustaining to them. Sib-lings are often there in crisis, to help with child care, to intercede in conflicts with extended family, and to share in the experience of parent-hood.

However, siblings have their concerns, too. If there are long-standing rivalries in the family, the news of our parenthood may pro-vide an opportunity for them to express their disapproval of us. If they are significantly homophobic, their attitudes may be very judgmental. Our parenthood may embarrass them. Unfortunately, because they do not need us and our children in quite the same way our parents do, they may have less motivation to struggle with their own conflicts. If a relationship with a sibling has never been good, our parenthood is not often going to be a catalyst for change.

Some siblings, however, do want to struggle with their conflicts. Mona describes, "My older brother had a lot of trouble accepting my becoming a mother. It was okay that Jamie and I were lesbians and were raising Jamie's sons, because Thomas and Luke still had a father that they lived with half the time. But when we adopted Shana he felt really threatened and negated by our intention to raise a child without a father. He felt very rejected by me, and thought that maybe he was worth less in my life because men had no role in the family I created. It was very painful to him, and it took him a really long time to get used to. I know that now he doesn't feel that way at all, but we had many painful conversations until Shana was between two and three years old." Mona's brother's willingness to admit to his conflicts, out of his basic love for his sister and wish to resolve things, was what made the difference.

Sometimes our siblings are married to people who have major problems with homophobia. Our siblings may feel caught in the middle, and their loyalties will often go to their spouses instead of us. Pasqual and Robert took their first child to Panama to meet Pasqual's family. Pasqual remembers, "Although my immediate family was very responsive, my younger sister, who I thought would be very supportive, was very weird about the whole thing. Her husband forbade her kids to come and see us. That was very painful for us, because we've had such wonderful reactions everywhere. For the first time we felt what discrimination is all about. I was surprised because my sister is not the very submissive type of wife who obeys whatever the husband says. I thought if I were her, I would just put my kids in the car and not care what my husband says. My mother, said, 'Well, she has to protect her marriage.' I said, 'Mother, if that's all it takes to break her marriage then we are not the problem,' but I was very hurt. I've written her a letter telling her how I feel about what happened. I don't expect a response to it, but I wanted her to know how her actions made me feel." These are losses we may just have to accept, and hope that time and communication will effect some change.

It is often anticipated that our grandparents, coming from a time when the world was very different, will have the most difficulty with our lesbian or gay parenthood. Our grandparents should not be underestimated, however. Many lesbian and gay parents find that their grandparents are able to support them, even when their parents or other relatives can't.

John, who parents Sara with his lover, Brendon, says "My grandmother is in her late eighties, and she's great." John's uncle is a minister, with rather conservative viewpoints. John's grandmother set him and his wife straight. "My aunt started giving her some flak about how she doesn't approve of this, and my grandmother stood up and said, 'I'm not the judge and jury. I'm just the loving grandmother,' and walked out of the room, which I thought was terrific."

John's grandmother also helped by pushing the issue with John's mother. Though John's mother adores Sara, she has been unwilling to let anyone in her life know that she has a grandchild, for fear of their reactions. John's grandmother, however, put Sara in the stroller and walked her around the neighborhood. John describes, "A neighbor woman who is a good friend of my mother's came out of her house because she saw my grandmother pushing a stroller, and she asked, 'Who's the baby?' My grandmother said, 'Oh, this is John's daughter, Sara,' and the woman's jaw dropped because in fifteen months her friend, my mother, hadn't told her she was a grandmother." John's mother has not yet resolved her difficulties with the situation, but John's grandmother continues to nudge things toward acceptance.

Our parents may urge us not to tell our grandparents because their health is poor, and we have to evaluate the degree to which their concerns are realistic. We obviously don't want to endanger our grandparents, and there are some situations in which the news of our lesbian or gay parenthood might inflict serious distress on them. But our parents may also be projecting their own anxiety or shame onto their parents. If you sense that your grandparents are more resilient than your parents give them credit for, talk it over with your parents and with other relatives. Let them know why it matters to have everyone in your extended family understand the family you are creating. Not all grandparents will become champions of our families, but they may not fall apart at the news either.

12

OUT IN THE WORLD

Going Public

My lover, Susan, used to take our son, Jesse, into the bakery a few times a week when he was still in his stroller. Dimpled and curly-haired, he always engaged the attention of the clerk behind the counter. She spoke very little English but would smile at him and offer him his favorite cookie. One day I went in with him instead. The clerk, noting Susan's absence, asked Jesse in her heavy accent where his mommy was. He turned and pointed up at me. She looked confused and asked me, "Other lady?" meaning who is the other woman she thought was Mommy. I mentally ran through my possibilities, suspecting that the word "lesbian" might not be familiar to her, and not really wanting to get into a lengthy, awkward interaction in the crowded shop. I felt strongly, however, that I wanted to be truthful, knowing that my son was learning from everything he heard. So I went for it, and said, "He has two mommies," holding up two fingers. She looked bewildered. With accompanying gestures, I added, "Two women. We raise him together. He is both of ours. We all love each other. We are a different kind of family." I did not look to see how the other customers, within earshot, were taking this. The clerk continued to look very confused for about another twenty seconds, while I stood at a loss to explain it any better. Suddenly her face brightened, with what was either understanding or just sweetness. She smiled and said, "Oh!" and gave Jesse his cookie.

Before we become parents, many of us have the luxury of coming out only when it feels comfortable to us. If our lives have something of a routine, we may only occasionally be confronted with new situations requiring that we decide whether or not to reveal our sexuality. The circles we move in, our jobs, our friends, and the gay and lesbian community may already be places where we are known. Beyond those spheres, we may volunteer what we wish, depending on our comfort level, our safety, our political commitment to visibility, and our wish for privacy.

Parenthood changes the picture. For one thing, children engage people's attention, and it is completely ordinary, acceptable conversation for someone to ask, "Which one of you is her mother?" or "What does your husband/wife do?" As lesbian and gay parents, we find ourselves in heterosexual territory at the playground, the pediatrician's office, in the schools, etc., where friendly and interested people will casually ask the questions that may make us cringe. Many of the people who ask are strangers to whom one might ordinarily never say anything personal, yet suddenly we are put on the spot about revealing our sexual orientation.

Furthermore, the consequences of our decisions to come out or not are no longer ours alone. Our children are now listening to what we say, drawing conclusions about how we feel about our family, about gay people in general, and about telling the truth. Our desire to model openness, honesty, and pride for our children may put us in the difficult position of having to override our personal preferences for privacy.

As lesbian and gay parents, we are all under the stress of knowing that some people harbor violently negative feelings about our families. It is an awareness that may remain a mere whisper in the dim recesses of our consciousness or move to the foreground with frightening clarity, but it is an ongoing part of our lives. Furthermore, among the people who are not actively hostile to lesbians and gay men are those who are merely skeptical about our ability to be decent parents. With exposure to us and our children over time they may come around, but not before they have had a chance to express their misgivings. Finally, there are legions of the simply curious, who are neither hostile nor necessarily skeptical but merely unfamiliar with us, who want to look and learn. Benign though their interest is, we endure the stress of being observed and sometimes feeling on display.

All of us who have children, however, have discovered that there is no shortage of people out there who will welcome, support, help, and love us. We have allies among other gay and lesbian parents, of course, but most of us have also found wonderful acceptance from co-workers, neighbors, the heterosexual parents of our children's friends, our children's teachers, and our religious institutions.

In approaching each new situation, we mentally calculate the possible consequences of revealing or hiding who we are. Each time we address the issue of our visibility we balance our ideals, our politics, our hope for support, and our parenting goals against our caution, our need for privacy, and our fatigue. What comes out of our mouths may differ from family to family, with the situation at hand, the geographic location, and the energy level of the moment. While we all look forward to the day when societal homophobia will have dwindled to nothing and we can be completely relaxed about being openly gay and lesbian families, for now we do the best we can. There is no point in weakening our reserves by imposing perfectionistic standards on ourselves. We have earned our pride and self-respect just by the courage it takes to do what we are doing.

Despite the overwhelming support most lesbian and gay parents I know manage to find, many describe a certain toll that being different takes on them. Pasqual puts it this way: "I feel sometimes that we are being watched. Not only by other gay people but by people at large, and by our families as well, because I guess in the back of their minds people think we can't do this."

Dana adds, "I'm afraid of judgment anyway, so this is another area to feel vulnerable in. I feel like I have to prove that I'm really a good parent, that there's nothing wrong with lesbians having babies. I feel anxious sometimes, and inadequate. Sometimes I'm afraid that somebody is going to be mean to me or to Amanda. I have to work extra hard to do reality checks, to validate myself, to say, 'I'm okay. I'm a good mother. It's their problem, not mine.' The other stress is feeling like I have to think so hard, anticipating what I'm going to do in this or that situation. I think straight people don't ever have to think about it. Who do we come out to? How do we describe this relationship? What are they going to think? Are they going to give Amanda inferior care if they know that we're lesbians?"

Jean remarks, "Sometimes I step back and put myself in the role of the facilitator or the therapist, and that makes it a little easier. Sometimes it's very painful because you have to do it over and over again, each time you're in a new situation. Straight couples walk in and there's no issue of acceptability. Evelyn and I walk in together, introducing Kay into a new environment, and many questions get asked and many assumptions get made that have to be broken. You always have to do that education."

Petra adds, "It makes me uncomfortable, because I tend to be somewhat reserved in who I want to reveal my sexuality to. I haven't gotten real casual about it yet, and I don't know if I ever will. There are going to be those awkward moments; it comes with the territory."

On occasion, we may manifest the strain of being different or feeling on display without knowing why we are angry or depressed. It is very helpful to be able to recognize the cause of the problem. Millie and Jeannette are raising their son, Kyle, in New England. Jeannette observes, "The whole time I was pregnant with Kyle and going to the maternity center I'd leave those appointments and feel really irritable and cross. It finally dawned on me that it was because I felt weird about us not being out about our family situation." Jeannette also noticed that she was angry when they were preparing to go to the Gay and Lesbian Pride Day march. "I'm just angry that gay people even have to march. And I got irritated with Millie because she was really excited about it. I had to stop and think, 'Why am I feeling this way?'" Realizing that the problem is out there, and not in our homes, can keep us from getting into unnecessary conflicts.

Jeannette's feelings echo an experience we often have, namely that it is utterly absurd to be regarded so strangely for doing something so completely human and ordinary. Barry, who is an open and active advocate for gay and lesbian parenting, puts it this way: "I wish Phil Donahue would stop calling. And Geraldo, and Sally Jessy Raphael. I understand there's a reason to be public, and in fact we are very visible, but the other side of it is the loss of privacy. I would like to be accepted as just another part of the lesbian and gay community. I don't want to be thought of as something tremendously out of the ordinary. It's not. It's a very normal experience for those who choose it."

Different Arenas

Our approach to identifying our family is likely to vary with the nature of the circumstances. Casual encounters with strangers will challenge us on the spot to come up with our own standards of openness, and to exercise them on a case-by-case basis. Your personal style and the political climate of your surroundings will greatly impact on what you decide to do, but preparing ahead of time can help you avoid being at a loss for words.

Situations which involve ongoing contact, such as our neighborhoods and religious groups, will often motivate us to be as honest as we can be. Misinformation conveyed today will be questioned tomorrow, so it makes sense to plan a consistent and truthful presentation from the beginning.

In day care and school situations, where our child is present when we are not and family structures are likely to be discussed, we may want to go one step further and do active advocacy and education. Our efforts to instruct our children's teachers will help insure that they represent our families the way we want them to.

Our children will also need medical care. In their ongoing relationships with medical personnel, such as the family pediatrician, it is generally in our children's best interests for us to be completely open about the nature of our families. Emergency medical situations, where there are no ongoing relationships, may also work best when you are open, but it may feel more difficult to come out under those circumstances.

Meanwhile, our ability to be open in our places of employment will vary, depending on the risks of disclosure as we calculate them. Some lesbian and gay parents who make a point of being completely open with strangers and neighbors find themselves having to maintain some secrecy about the nature of their families in their workplaces. Being in the closet is never easy, and it's even more difficult when a child is involved, so this is a decision you must make carefully.

Finally, our relationships to the lesbian and gay communities will be altered by our parenthood. Though revealing our sexuality is not the issue in this arena, integrating our sexual orientations and cultures with a community largely unprepared for children may raise conflicts.

On the Spot with Strangers

In general, people's tendency to presume we are heterosexual will be magnified by seeing us with a child. If we are alone with our child, they will envision a parent of the opposite gender waiting in the wings:

The absent daddy is at the office or the missing mommy is home cooking dinner. If our partner is with us, one of us will be presumed to be a family friend or relative.

The heterosexual strangers we encounter in brief conversations drop numerous references to their sexuality in the course of their normal speech. The woman you are chatting with at the bus stop mentions that her husband left home without his umbrella today. A man on the commuter train notices that you are reading the same book his wife just read. If we are not asked directly, we have the option of allowing their presumption that we are heterosexual to go unchallenged, without actively lying. We all do this some of the time. We must be aware, however, that there are emotional consequences to us of omitting the reality of our lives. Though we may be under no social pressure to volunteer our partner's gender, for example, we live with the internal awareness that we choose to avoid it because we are uncomfortable with people's potential reactions. The fallout from that choice often includes feelings of isolation and diminished self-esteem.

In addition, if our children happen to be present, we must remember that they learn as much from what they don't hear as from what they do. The fact that you regularly do not mention your child's other mother, for example, becomes part of his understanding of what his family is about.

Because of the potentially negative effects, both on us and on our children, of being less visible than traditional families, many lesbian and gay parents strive to be actively open at almost every opportunity. One lesbian with a talkative and outgoing personality was asked by the supermarket checkout clerk if the tomato sauce she was buying was any good. Aware that she would never hesitate if she were heterosexual, she replied, "Well, my lover thinks it's delicious. She adds a little basil and garlic and cooks it for about fifteen minutes." She could obviously have just said, "Yes, it's pretty good" and left it at that. In fact, on this occasion her children weren't even with her. But she has strong political feelings about the visibility of lesbians and gay men, she lives in a liberal part of town, and she feels quite secure about her sexuality. Every one of her self-revelations is a gift to the rest of us, and we have to applaud her for it.

Similarly, Barry and Tony, though they live in a more conservative area, have strong feelings about being open. Barry asserts, "We are out under all circumstances. No mixed messages. If Carla is going to catch us someplace that we're hedging, what message is that going to give her? We had just moved to our neighborhood when Carla was two and still in diapers. So there I was at the supermarket with the kiddie food and the diapers and the A & D Ointment. The checkout lady said, 'Oh, your wife is so lucky to have a husband like you doing the shopping.' I could have ignored this. I could have said lots of things. But I said, 'No, I'm not married. In fact, I'm gay, and I'm in a long-term relationship, and my lover and I have adopted a child, and that's why you see all this stuff.' Why? I need to be able to talk about this under every circumstance without any hedging. And there are times when I want to hedge. You don't want to put yourself in a dangerous situation where you'll be fag-bashed, but I have found that throughout my life, whether as a parent or not, by dealing with being gay up front it becomes a nonissue. I've worked in some very conservative places, in banking, and Tony's picture was always on my desk. Being public about it, people give you respect for standing up for what is right. I think that sets a good example. I suspect Carla will experience discrimination here and there, and I expect Tony and I will be able to give her the strength to accept whatever is thrown at her and move forward. If someone comes up to her in school and says, 'Your daddy's a faggot,' she can say 'Yeah,' and move on. It should be a nonissue. So what."

Barry is speaking for all of us when he says there are times when he wants to hedge. Risking other people's rejection, ridicule, or disapproval is anxiety-provoking for the most secure among us. It is clear, however, that how we present ourselves has a great impact on the kind of response we get. When we speak about our families without hesitation, with a cheerful, confident attitude that presumes we will be respected and liked we make it almost impossible for other people to respond negatively. I know from my own experience that this sometimes requires a creditable acting performance. I sometimes work hard at keeping my private experience—complete with sweaty palms and upset stomach—out of view, and presenting instead a relaxed and easy self-acceptance. My aim is to convey the unspoken message that anyone worthy of my respect and friendship will simply not have a problem with lesbian and gay parents.

The effect has been consistently positive. Susan, my children, and I have never once had to suffer a negative comment from a stranger. I have no doubt that people have had critical thoughts about us, but as long as they keep them to themselves I'm happy. What they think, or what they go home and say to their spouses, is their own business.

Sharon describes the way she and her lover, Kathy, have handled coming out since they became parents. "It wasn't always like this, but

Kathy and I developed a very strong attitude about who we are. We don't give people a lot of room to question or comment. We're not cryptic. We don't hold back. And we don't really invite their opinions. What Kathy and I have learned is that Jake is watching us. I think it's very important for Jake to see how strongly we feel about being a family. We're not letting the fact that we're both women justify anybody's bad responses. We're very careful to answer these questions exactly the way Jake is going to answer them when another kid asks him. We say Jake has two mothers. We let people know what our story is. We don't kiss on the playground or anything, but it's clear when Jake is calling me Mommy and her Momma that he's got two mothers."

Their efforts have paid off, because they have never had a bad response. "If people are uncomfortable, they say nothing. One woman said, 'Oh,' then a long pause, then, '*Ooooohhhh!* That's *great!*' It was funny because she was sort of a proper person, the kind you wouldn't expect to let her hair down. She said, 'Now that's the way to do it!' and she thought it was terrific."

Pasqual and Robert also work hard to be as open as possible in every situation. "The response we've had has been so great. Coming through airport customs back to the States the guy at the gate looked at Robert, who was holding James, and asked, 'Are you the father?' We both answered, in unison, 'No, we're both the fathers.' He looked at us and said, 'Oh, okay, I believe you.'" On another occasion at the same airport, Pasqual was stopped by FBI agents. As a Latino man, coming through Miami on his way back from South America, he fit their profile of a drug smuggler, but Pasqual relates that, "When he saw I was a gay dad, he let me go."

John and Brendon also travel a lot with their daughter, Sara. John notes that travel agents, flight attendants, and rent-a-car people are forever commenting to them, "Oh, it's Mother's weekend off and Father has the baby. Which one of yours is it?" John describes their response, "We instantly say she has two fathers, and you see their wheels spinning while they're trying to figure this out. They say, 'Oh, she's so lucky.' Or, 'I can see how happy she is.'"

Like many parents living in a variety of different states and settings, Mona was hard-pressed to think of any negative responses they've gotten to being a lesbian family. "I know it sounds crazy, but I haven't had any. People have been really wonderful. I think it has a lot to do with our attitudes. I mean, if we feel totally and completely prepared to parent our children, there's no way that doesn't come across."

Similarly, Roberta, who has raised her son to adulthood with her lover, Elizabeth, and her friend Shirley, says "This was not a trial by fire for me in any way. I was always met with great support."

JoAnne echoes, "There has not been one negative experience. We have been astonished. We keep expecting it, but it's been quite the opposite."

Of course, not everyone is invested in a mission of advocacy. Some of us are more private in our personal styles and would rather not volunteer information about our situations if we don't have to. Petra noted that living in the Midwest makes that easy, because "people in Iowa don't ask questions. They may be curious but they just don't ask." And even the most politically active among us have days where we are simply not in the mood to be public if we can avoid it. Marty remembers when his daughter, Joy, was a baby. "There were times when I was exhausted, Joy was getting crabby, I was in the supermarket, and I just thought you know what? I'm not going to enlighten yet another soul today. I just want to get home and get this stuff put away. So, when they'd ask about her mother, I'd just avoid the issue." But Marty notes that now that Joy is older and listening, he no longer allows himself that luxury. "Everything I say goes directly into Joy's sense of herself and her sense of security, so now I say, 'Joy has two daddies,' or 'I live with a man and we're both her parents.'"

Rather than attempting to be universally open, Mona bases her decision on what she feels about the other person. She says, "I don't feel it's my responsibility to educate everyone who asks me an ignorant question, though I do try to set them straight. If it feels like there's some openness or receptivity on their part then I'll go a little further."

Andrew, coparent with Don of Chad, will also correct people's misconceptions but is inclined not to volunteer information unless he feels some reason to. "I wait and evaluate each situation as it comes up. I don't lie to anybody, but I don't need to share my life with a stranger. I say, 'This is my son.' They say, 'Oh, really, your wife must be very happy.' I say, 'Actually, I'm not married.' I don't need to say that I have a male lover."

There isn't any perfect way to do this, and even though we attempt to be consistent there will be times when we deviate. While I was watching my children at the skating rink one day, the woman next to me started up a conversation. Not at my best that day, I didn't particularly welcome the social contact. Amazed to learn that my giant son was only seven, she asked, "Is his father very tall?" On a good day I would have explained that my lover and I had him via alternative

316 THE LESBIAN AND GAY PARENTING HANDBOOK

insemination so we have never met his biological father. On a less good day I might have simply said, "No, his father is only medium height," which is what we know about the donor. In my mood of irritation, however, I answered bluntly, "I don't know," leaving her gaping and no doubt wondering how many men I must have slept with.

Despite the fact that in the overwhelming majority of encounters lesbian and gay parents are met with respectful and accepting responses, there are occasions when people are rude or hostile. Gay fathers whose children are still very young seem somewhat more likely to be singled out for criticism. Men with infants are unusual enough in our society that people are more likely to be distressed by it. A father with an older child will not often evoke the same sort of inquiry. George affirms, "Now that Brett is older no one bothers to ask, but there was always this underlying assumption that fathers can't handle infants."

George reports that the questions strangers would ask when Brett was a baby sometimes did not feel like benign or friendly conversation. He describes, "Often it felt like we were being grilled. 'Where's the mother? Why isn't the mother with the baby?'"

George remembers one particularly difficult incident on a plane when Brett was six months old. "On this one ride, people around us just stared. Finally, this one woman got up, and as she was coming back to her seat she said, 'I just have to ask, who is the father? Where is the mother?' We had never agreed ahead of time on how to deal with each and every situation, so we never were sure what the other one would say. But this time we both said, in front of all the other people in the plane who wanted to know, too, 'Well, we're both the fathers. We're raising this child together.' She was shocked. She didn't say anything. When she got to her seat, right behind us, she said loudly, 'I think that's horrible. That poor child. I feel so sorry for it.'"

Barry and Tony had an experience while traveling with their five-year-old daughter, Carla. They were driving through Richmond, Virginia, on their way to Disneyworld. A civic-minded truck driver on the road, seeing two men and a little girl in a car, became suspicious and started following them. He drove up along one side of them, then changed lanes and pulled up along the other side, trying to get a good look at them. When Barry and Tony pulled off the highway for lunch, the truck pulled into the gas station. Unbeknownst to Barry, Tony, and Carla, the truck driver alerted the highway police, who instructed the restaurant manager to detain the three until they could get there. Carla's chicken leg kept taking "just a little longer, sorry" to arrive. The police watched them from a distance for a while. When Carla had to go to the bathroom, Tony took her to the men's room, as he always does. (A five-year-old still needs help sometimes.) The police followed and very politely asked if everything was all right. They asked what Tony's relationship to Carla was. Barry recalls, "They treated us quite respectfully throughout, and eventually believed us. We told them we were her fathers, that she had no mother." Barry and Tony felt quite insecure realizing that they carried no proof of their relationship to Carla. Barry says, "I didn't know I'd have to travel with adoption papers." Ultimately, their verbal skills prevailed, along with the fact that Carla clearly related to both men as her parents. After what was probably about an hour's interlude, Carla's lunch was served and they continued on to Disneyworld without further incident. Presumably, however, the Virginia highway patrol, and maybe even the truck driver, had their consciousness raised a bit. Hopefully, there will come a time when our family constellations are familiar enough to people that this kind of thing won't happen.

Because so many of our lesbian and gay families are formed by adoption, we often have to respond to the questions of strangers regarding what our relationships are to our children. Correcting people's language and assumptions regarding adoption is part of what we often find ourselves doing. "Is she yours or did you adopt her?" is the kind of misinformed question that requires some firm but polite education: "She's mine, *and* I adopted her" (for more on the language of adoption, see Chapter Seven: Raising Our Children).

Mona finds she also has to correct the racist assumptions people make when they see a white mother with a black daughter. "I've been in the supermarket with Shana and her best friend, who's Guatemalan. The kids look very different from each other and very different from Caucasians. People came up to me on two occasions and talked to me about being a foster mother, and how wonderful it was that I took these kids in. I looked at them and said, 'I am not a foster mother. This is my child, and this is my child's best friend.' It was like the only reason we would be together, being racially different, was if it wasn't a permanent relationship. I was very taken aback by it both times."

A fringe benefit some parents have found, however, is that looking very different from their child helps with their identity as a gay or lesbian family. One mother said, "They never ask which of us is the real mother. I think they have an easier time getting it—that we are both raising her."

Neighbors and Communities

Unlike strangers in the supermarket, neighbors are people with whom you have an ongoing contact, although not necessarily a relationship of any intimacy. Because neighbors know you over time and talk to each other, life is easier if there are no deceptions to maintain. Though gay parents in liberal areas tend to feel that life is easier for them, those in rural and suburban settings report that they get generally excellent responses from their neighbors. Parenting seems to be a great equalizer. Heterosexual parents with whom we might otherwise have little in common can identify with our concerns for our children and the hard work we put in to raise them properly. Neighbors who are not parents respond to the fact that we, too, care about how our houses and property are maintained. And, as Sally reports from a small town in Ohio, "Some people just respect the hell out of you for having enough guts to stand up and be who you are."

Jeff and Peter live in a pretty, rather conservative, community by a bay. They have been met with completely loving acceptance. Jeff says, "We have the same experience with neighbor after neighbor. Children play with Daniel. Children help watch him. Children come to his birthday parties and he goes to theirs. I have never heard a negative word."

Peter adds, "It just sounds too sickeningly sweet to be real, but in this town here ... I mean, where is all the oppression? We thank God we haven't experienced it."

Sophie says of her community, "I live in a mountain town where everybody knows everybody, and it seems at times like everybody is everybody's ex. I am an open lesbian and it's okay. I don't feel discrimination. I don't know if I'm just being blind to it, but I don't feel like I've been shunned by people I care about or want to know better."

Sophie lets people know who she is by simply "assuming they know that I'm gay and working from there, correcting their assumptions when necessary. People will assume that I have a husband when I talk about my daughter. So I say, 'Oh, no, we're a lesbian family. I had a partner when Aria was born.' It's a gentle way to do it. I think a lot of times I might be the only person that they've ever met who's gay."

Joel, also living in a rural area, says, "We have experienced absolutely no homophobia at all. Both neighbors have been over for socializing and have invited us over. The neighbors next door have two adopted children, and one of their little boys talks about Martha having two daddies."

For many of us, an important segment of our communities is our religious affiliations. Though some religious institutions are well known for their anti-gay hate campaigns, there are spiritual communities which do indeed believe in love. Some of them may even welcome the opportunity to expand their understanding of lesbian and gay families. JoAnne describes what happened when she and Gwen went looking for a synagogue. "I felt like we were in a bidding war between two rabbis. Nobody had a lesbian couple, especially not with a child, so this was like a big deal for the local synagogues. One of the rabbis wanted to use us as a teaching tool."

Joel and Glenn, the parents of two and a half year old Martha, find that their church is their main source of community nourishment. They live in a largely rural area, away from any organized gay groups. Joel explains, "I'm very involved in my church. When we first got Martha, Glenn and I weren't living together and I didn't know how much a part of this he was going to be, so I was a single father. The women at the church thought that was wonderful."

As time went by, the three of them became a family. Joel describes, "When Martha began walking she started insisting that when we go to church she walk in the middle of us, holding each of our hands. So every Sunday morning you see the three of us going in and out of church together, and a lot of people who may never have thought about who we were began to put together that this is a family here. We've also just finished up a parenting class that the church gives, with about seven other couples, and not one person in that room has shown even the slightest indication that it's strange or anything. They are just wonderful, wonderful people. It's been a very important part of our family."

The positive response these parents describe does not mean that absolutely everyone in their towns feels supportive of gay and lesbian families. In fact, the likelihood is that few of their neighbors would vote for a gay rights candidate. On a personal level, however, they find that no one responds in an overtly negative way, and many people are delighted to be their friends. The fears we may have that we or our children will be shunned because we are gay parents do not seem to materialize.

For those parents living close to urban areas with large gay and lesbian populations, however, there are some advantages. Primary among them is access to other lesbian and gay parents, and to ongoing social and support groups. For many people, the lesbian and gay community alone is enough to keep them living in the city. As Elise says, "We've been considering moving to a beautiful place where the air smells good and the streets are relatively safe and the schools are good, but what's holding us back is that we'd rather have Todd grow up in an environment where there are other children of lesbians and gay men around. Not that he necessarily needs to be great friends with them or anything, but just so that he knows they're there and he doesn't feel like he's different."

The thing to remember about coming out in a context where you have ongoing contact is that it generally takes people time to get used to it. They are usually shy about asking the questions that might deepen their understanding. We often have to do the work of volunteering information and inviting questions if we want them to make progress with this. Candace had just started a graduate program in family therapy in their home state of Texas. Traditionally, students of family therapy spend a great deal of class time discussing the dynamics and structures of their own families. Candace reports, "I came out in my 'Life Cycles' class. I said I'm a lesbian and have been with my partner for eight years, and we have a son who was conceived through artificial insemination. I didn't say 'alternative' because I figured they wouldn't know what that was. I was very disappointed in the response because these were supposed to be caring, empathic people. No one said anything. As they were leaving class, whereas usually they are all talkative and we walk out in a group saying, 'Oh, what did you think of such and such?' no one spoke to me. People went around me, out of their way to go out the door without going by me. It really threw me, especially because I've never gotten a reaction like this before. I told myself that I will not go through a graduate program and not talk about my family, because in order to get what I need from this program I have to be able to share what's going on in my life, too."

Despite this initial disappointment, however, by the following week there were some signs of progress. "I saw some of them the following Saturday at a meeting, and one woman asked, 'Is your partner able to take care of your baby today?'"

Our babysitters often come from among our neighbors and the people in our communities. Petra reports that her experiences in Iowa have been good. "I have hired two babysitters who both know that we're lesbians. They're the most mainstream, straight college kids that you could imagine, and both have had absolutely no problem with it. It's another example of how far people are willing to go when it comes to love."

I have personally felt a little awkward with new babysitters. Having someone come into my home to care for my children feels fairly intrusive anyway, and I don't enjoy having to deal with coming out at the same time. On occasion I have sought babysitters through lesbian and gay channels just to avoid the problem. At other times, though, we have simply toughed it out, sometimes more gracefully than others. One young woman who came to babysit was the daughter of an employee of two heterosexual friends of ours. We introduced her to our baby daughter, made her comfortable, and went about our business without explaining a great deal. Our married friends received a very distressed call from the girl's mother that night, reporting that there were lesbian titles on our bookshelves and wanting to know what our story was. Our friends told her that, yes, we are lesbians, and they have known us for many years and we are lovely, respectable people. Her daughter returned to work for us the next day, and stayed for five years. We felt we'd handled it a little clumsily, leaving it up to our friends to come out for us. On the other hand, we weren't sure how to do it better.

Candace, in Texas, also feels this can be a tough issue. "Right now when I go to class, I take Ethan to a woman's house for day care. I haven't told her about his other parent. If he were older I would have, because he would be talking about her. Since he's not verbal yet, I don't. I think that's sort of a cop-out, but I looked and looked and looked for this woman I really like, and I don't want to jeopardize it by coming out to her and having her say she didn't want to take him. But we're going to have to come out soon. I'm serious about it."

One of the things we naively overlooked when we became parents was that anyone caring for our children would also have to grapple with coming out. Five years ago we were blessed with a truly special babysitter who raised our consciousness, along with her own. Chinazo grew up in Nigeria, in a strongly Christian and anti-gay environment. She had never met an avowed lesbian before responding to our ad, and did not know what to make of us. She decided she would try it, though, despite the letter from her mother in Nigeria warning her not to work for us. It never occurred to us to help her deal with people's questions about our family. Making conversation in the park confronted her with all the difficulties we encounter in such situations, without the benefit of our years of practice or our personal stake in it. Chinazo recalls that she was embarrassed at first. "I would say their father is a psychologist." On her own, she decided she would try to be more truthful. "I started saying they have two moms." With remarkable initiative, she went on to read books about gay men and lesbians and ask us questions. Chinazo has since become an advocate for lesbian and gay parenting, as well as our cherished and respected family friend. (Even her mother now champions gay and lesbian families.) In her nursing courses at school she talks about our family, and she has become quite an ambassador. She reports that people are genuinely open to what she has to say.

Schools

This year my daughter will start junior high school. Though we will continue to fill out all the relevant forms indicating that Susan and I are both her mothers, and we will both show up for all school events and conferences, this marks the first time we won't go in to actively educate people about our lesbian family. At eleven, my daughter has the skills to do her own advocacy work. She will choose how and with whom she wants to discuss her family, deciding where she feels comfortable and where it seems relevant.

Up until now, however, we have felt it was our responsibility to intercede for our children in their school and day-care environments, and we will continue to do so when Jesse starts third grade this year. School (including organized day care and preschool) is the first institutional setting our children have to negotiate without us. In addition, schools are the strongest, most active purveyors of mainstream culture, with all its heterosexist assumptions. If we are not involved in helping to shape that curriculum, there is a danger that our children's nontraditional families may be left out of or, worse, demeaned by the school's teachings. It is therefore important that in our children's early school years we try to select supportive educational institutions, and then offer them information about how to talk about our families in class.

Lesbian and gay parents I've spoken with regard openness to nontraditional families as one of their primary criteria for selecting a school. Many of our children are sent to alternative public schools, which are known for their liberal views of education. Schools are interviewed ahead of time, and asked about their familiarity with lesbian and gay families, their attitudes, and their curriculum on family issues. Some families are willing to go to great lengths to find the right school environment. Candace and Jill, in a small town south of Houston, have very strong feelings about the conservative attitudes of their local schools. Candace reports, "I'm not sure they would be very supportive of who he is and the family he has. I'm not going to spend three years telling him how great our family is, and then say, 'Well, now you can't tell anybody else about it.' If I have to drive all the way to Houston to get him in somewhere that he can be okay with, I will." One reassurance is that not only are *we* everywhere, but those who will support us are almost everywhere as well. It is worth some aggressive searching to find an atmosphere in which you can all relax.

My own children go to public school, and went to private nursery school before that. With every new teacher and school administrator we have made a point of arranging a conference and describing our family. We ask if they are comfortable with the situation, and offer to answer any questions they might have. We ask that in class discussions they try to be conscious of the fact that families are not just Mommy-and-Daddy. We let them know that there are children's books available which feature or describe nontraditional families. In the course of the school year, we have sometimes had to correct teachers who had a hard time referring to us both as Mommy. Once, a nursery school teacher seemed stubbornly committed to calling only one of us Mommy, and needed some firm but friendly correction to eventually come around. It has helped that we never directly answer the question of which of us is the biological mother.

The most frequent reaction we get reads something like, "It's fine with me, I have no problem with it, and please don't tell me anything about it." School personnel almost never ask questions, and they change the subject as soon as possible. My guess is that they are somewhat embarrassed by the subject of homosexuality in general, and also by having to admit to ignorance. It is a rare person who can say, "How interesting! I don't know much about it, but I'd love to learn." Though their reticence is less than satisfying, we have generally tried to leave it there and not intrude, except to make it clear that we are available should questions arise later.

There has been one notable and remarkable exception to this. Jesse's kindergarten teacher called up one day to say, "The children are asking about where Jesse's daddy is and whether it's true that he has two mommies. I want to explain it the same way you would, so what should I tell them?" We were so delighted to be asked. Surely these questions had come up before in other classes, but no one had ever cared enough or been comfortable enough to come to us about it, despite our invitations. We told her how we talk about two-mom families, and about two-dad families, and about donors and alternative insemination. We also told her that Jesse himself could explain about his family, and she could feel free to encourage him to discuss it. She was interested in reading more on gay families, and asked our opinions of the children's books on the subject. She went on to use the books in the classroom.

The needs of lesbian and gay families in the schools are just beginning to be addressed. Three educational researchers, Virginia Caspar, Steven Schultz, and Elaine Wickens, recently conducted a study of parents, teachers, and school administrators about the experience of lesbian and gay families.[1] The authors conclude that "the work of administrators can encourage frank discussions which can support gay parenting by grappling with such questions as: How can the administration help both teachers and parents? What kinds of parent meetings can support the work of teachers in building a more inclusive curriculum? ... How difficult would it be to alter the 'mother' and 'father' line on school applications to a more generic 'parent' line or simply ask for a listing of family members?" Our increasing visibility in the school system is going to effect changes, slowly, over the coming years.

The first hurdle many of us face is the information card which asks for the name of the parents. I am looking forward to the day when the options on such cards reflect our family structures, but currently they all seem to ask for "Mother's name" and "Father's name." Joel struggled with this problem when his daughter, Martha, first went to day care. "What was I going to write? I wanted them to know that she has two parents. So I put down me as the father, and crossed out "Mother," and put "Uncle Glenn." I went to the woman and said, "Now, look. This is very unusual, I know, but I want you to know that we are her parents, and if there's an emergency we both have all the medical information." Dr. Caspar and her coauthors noted that many families in their study listed "co-mother," or something similar, on the information card without ever explaining it to school personnel. The result was often that teachers and administrators were baffled and didn't know how to regard the family. As difficult as it may be to do, in the long run it is easier for us and for our children if we can approach the school personnel directly and explain the family to them.

Jean is white and Evelyn is African-American. Their daughter, Kay, who was adopted, is also African-American. People tend to assume that Kay is biologically related to Evelyn. As the only white member of this family, Jean feels she has a harder time getting recognition as Kay's other mother. Jean describes her struggles with educating their daughter's day-care center about lesbian families. "Initially I felt the older black staff of the day-care center treated me with tremendous hostility as a coparent to this child. I would cry when I came home from dropping Kay off, because one worker wouldn't even use my name. Evelyn has pointed out something to me that I tend to forget— that we've had a long time to adjust to our being different, but her day-care center has never seen a gay family. We are very different from what they are used to, and we have some obligation to move people along, not to expect to be accepted without helping them. They don't necessarily see two women loving each other as a strength. So I have to be conscious that this is still new to a lot of people, even though it's not new to us."

Even when parents are willing to do the pioneering work of educating the schools, it may still be hard to be the first lesbian or gay family in a school. Sophie, living in her rural mountain town with her daughter, finds that she is forever having to combat traditionalist notions of family. She describes, "In the school recently they had a father-daughter dance and a mother-son dance. Which one do I go to? I called the school and asked, 'What about single moms with daughters?' Their solution was to get a male friend, but I don't have a male friend. I felt like I was being shut out. It seems the healthy way to handle it would be to have a family dance, but just limiting it that way plays into the stereotypical nuclear family assumptions."

Some other families, however, have not found it as difficult. Jeff and Peter, who report getting nothing but support everywhere, have also had good experiences with Daniel's preschool. Jeff says, "The women who run the preschool are totally accepting. On Father's Day they helped him make two Father's Day presents. On Mother's Day they went out of their way to talk about how some people don't have mothers and some people don't have fathers. They call us Daddy Jeff and Daddy Peter, and it's been wonderful."

Families whose children attend schools where there are other openly lesbian and gay parents find that the road has been paved for them. Mona, whose daughter, Shana, is in a school with other lesbian families, reports, "It's very easy. It's been so natural as to be a nonissue."

Aside from being educational institutions, schools are also communities. We are likely to find ourselves involved with the other families in our children's schools. I never imagined, in my preparenting lesbian life, that my major support system would come from heterosexual parents, but it does. It often feels like the other parents at our school are the people we have the most in common with, and we have felt completely accepted. My lover, Susan, was elected president of our school's PTA for two years.

Getting started is not always so easy, however. Mona recalls feeling self-conscious attending the school's open house with her lover, Jamie. "Everybody had name tags. If I had been alone, I would have written, 'Mona, Shana's Mom,' but Jamie was there and I just wrote 'Mona.' I thought, 'Oh boy, this is really screwed up. Why did you do that?' and I realized it was a form of internalized oppression. I was not feeling safe and comfortable at the first meeting of this group of people." Time has nurtured their feeling of belonging, however, and Mona reports, "Now I would have no problem going in and writing it down with Jamie there too."

Jennifer and Mindy got some unexpected help from a heterosexual family in overcoming their initial awkwardness. Jennifer explains, "There were some meetings with parents before school started and we were pretty shy. Usually I see myself as outgoing and talkative, but neither of us were really connecting with the other parents. Then one of Molly's friends said to her dad, 'Molly says she has two moms.' And her dad said, 'Well, she does, and isn't that wonderful?' Then the kids were the ones who started to talk about it. They'd say, 'Are you really Molly's mom?' and that sort of thing. I love it when people ask, so I can tell them who we are and that it's really okay."

Though adults may require time to get used to lesbian and gay families, the children catch on pretty quickly. Homophobia is a learned disease, and fortunately the children our kids meet in the early years of school don't yet suffer from it. Most children just seem to accept it in a matter-of-fact way. On one occasion when my daughter, Emily, was new to the school I called the parents of a school chum of hers about PTA business. The phone was answered by Emily's friend, and we exchanged a few words. As she passed the receiver to her mother, I heard her say in a tone so casual as to approach boredom, "It's Emily's mom. Well, it's one of them—she's got two."

Indeed, some children in more traditional families are utterly delighted with the idea of two moms. One young friend of my son's said, "Wow! Two moms! If you lose one you've always got another." And a lesbian mother reported that her daughter was the envy of the neighborhood when she chanted, "I've got two moms and you only have one."

Medical Settings

Our children will have ongoing relationships with their pediatricians, dentists, and their staff members. It makes sense, therefore, to interview ahead of time the people you will be dealing with for your child's medical care. Because it is important to your child's well-being that they understand and completely support your family structure, if you don't like the response you're getting, go elsewhere. On the other hand, keep in mind that they may not know what you expect of them until you teach them. If yours is the first lesbian or gay family they have encountered, you may have to spend some time emphasizing that you are both equal parents, equally entitled to receive information and make decisions.

Ideally all the negotiating and educating can go on before you ever have to depend on medical people for services, but it doesn't always work that way. Petra describes, "The first time we went to the dentist I filled out all the forms and crossed out 'father' and put in 'coparent' and Adrienne's name. The nurse called all the other secretaries and nurses to look at our form. They were all huddling over it, reading it and whispering among each other, looking back over at us, whispering some more, and looking totally confused. Finally the nurse came over to us and said, 'Now, is there any particular reason why you brought her in today?' And I just said, 'Well, no, it's just time for Kim's first dental exam.' She said, 'Oh, okay.'" Petra and Adrienne, out of their own discomfort, did not offer the dentist's staff any help in dealing with this. Inside the dentist's office, more confusion resulted. Petra recounts, "When we went in, the dentist hadn't read the form, apparently, because he kept saying 'When you get home and Mommy and Daddy tell you to ...' Kim just looked at him and said, 'I don't have a daddy.' The nurse was squirming, trying to figure out how she was going to bail the doctor out of this awkward situation." This interaction eventually worked out well but would have been made a little easier with some frank discussion up front.

Sometimes we have to deal with medical personnel with whom we don't have an ongoing relationship. In an emergency room, for example, or if your child has to spend time in the hospital, you may have to decide quickly what is best for your family at the moment. My son, Jesse, had to be hospitalized for asthma once, and we have been to the emergency room since on several occasions. Those have sometimes felt to me like the most difficult arenas in which to deal with coming out.

For one thing, harried medical personnel in an emergency situation are not likely to take the time to be won over by my warm and friendly personality. Moreover, I am dependent upon them for the care my child receives, at a time when I am likely to be anxious or frightened. On several occasions we have had to insist that we are both the mothers and were therefore both going to be present during the examination or procedure. Raised eyebrows make me acutely uncomfortable, given how vulnerable we are under those circumstances.

In fact, the only truly awful treatment we have ever received because of being a lesbian family occurred in a medical setting, during a serious emergency, though it was actually the fault of a physician who already knew us well. Jesse was two years old; he was having his first and most severe asthma attack, and at the time we had no idea what it was. He wasn't audibly wheezing, only breathing very rapidly and looking very, very sick. Our regular pediatrician, a wonderfully supportive man, was out of town and his backup physician, I'll call her Dr. Shannon, was supervising the emergency room staff. Shannon had been present when our first son, Michael, was born and diagnosed with achondroplasia. She had also been maddeningly unhelpful when our daughter had problems with nursing. With Jesse panting for breath and losing his color, no one was giving us any information we could understand. They told us his blood gases were dropping, that he was in danger of not getting oxygen to his brain. They said they didn't know if it was pneumonia or not, but gave us no indication of what it was. Having watched our son Michael die five years earlier, we felt plunged into a terrifying time warp. Throughout a horrible night of tests and panic we kept trying to find out why our baby was laboring for every breath. Dr. Shannon announced that we had better agree to hospitalize him but wouldn't tell us why. We asked what his diagnosis was and how she was planning to treat him. She wouldn't tell us. She became very provocative with us, saying, 'This is your decision. If he dies, it's your responsibility,' but refusing to offer any useful basis on which we could make that decision. We were frightened that Jesse might die if we didn't hospitalize him, but equally scared that hospital personnel who didn't even seem to know what was wrong with him could make him worse. We insisted that we could not make this decision without speaking to our own pediatrician. Somewhere around 5:00 A.M. he was located, and we were called to the phone. He told us simply that Jesse was suffering from an asthma attack, that he was not going to die, but that he needed intravenous medication and would be fine in a few days. I will never be more grateful than I was at that moment.

Later on, we came to know that Dr. Shannon is a closeted lesbian who feels extremely hostile to our lesbian parenthood. Our pediatrician acknowledged that Shannon's actions were unprofessional and arranged that we would never to have to deal with her again. Shannon's behavior remains the one and only incident of active hostility we have ever encountered in the course of being a lesbian family.

Other dealings with hospital staff may be more humorous than painful. JoAnne and Gwen had to deal with a physician's well-intentioned but misguided attempts at political correctness when JoAnne gave birth to their daughter, Moira. Gwen recounts, "This resident came in and started asking us questions. He was completely and totally confused by the situation. We answered the question of who the father was by saying, 'There is no father. We are the parents.' So then he started taking *my* medical history. I mean, the guy was just lost in the sauce somewhere. I finally stopped and said, 'You don't want *my* medical history. What is that going to do for you?' My mother was there, and had buried her face in her hands. I could see her thinking, 'Oh, god, this is just the beginning.'"

Employers

There is no question that lesbian and gay parents who are open about their sexuality at work find life easier than parents who are not. It just helps to know that people understand your relationship to your child and your partner, and can share the good times and lend support in the crises. Many parents who start out closeted at work find parenthood provides the incentive to come out. Two lesbian mothers I know who are both police officers find that the difficulties of being open lesbians in a very sexist and homophobic work environment are outweighed by the peace of mind they get from not having to hide who they are. Parents who opt to remain closeted in their employment settings rarely do so merely out of a sense of privacy. For most, it is a difficult decision, with painful consequences of isolation and lack of support. It is a choice based on the genuine probability that their careers would not survive the revelation of a lesbian or gay identity. So far, lesbians and gay men are not protected from employment discrimination except where local law has passed gay rights legislation. None of the parents I know, however, attempt to hide the existence of a child in their lives. The information they choose to conceal is that they have a partner with whom they share parenting. Instead, they present themselves as single parents, with their partners sometimes represented as live-in child-care help.

Pearl has a high-level job where she does not feel safe being open about being a lesbian. Her lover, Lynne, describes how they have arranged parenthood around Pearl's need for secrecy at work. "The one thing I insisted on was that the people at work know she's a mother. 'You don't have to come out, but tell them you're adopting a child.' She didn't tell them until after Rosa came home, and subsequently her co-workers gave her a shower. They think she's a single parent who has full-time help. One time I had to call her from the emergency room when Rosa broke her leg. I was calling from a pay phone and said, 'I'm with her daughter who I'm taking care of and there's an emergency.' Now she carries a beeper and we have a whole series of codes, so she knows when it's a real emergency, when it's urgent but not an emergency, and when it's 'Call if you have the chance.'"

The crisis Lynne and Pearl are facing now is that Pearl is unhappy with her job and would love to relocate. Since hers is the family's primary income, Pearl will find a job she likes first. Later Lynne will see what work is available for her. Lynne explains, "The first problem we would face is that the kids are legally mine. Would Pearl, who is very closeted at work, feel that she could come out and ask for health-care benefits for Rosa, Teresa, and me as family members?"

The problem of health-care coverage, which for most people comes through employee benefits, is a serious one for lesbian and gay families. (For more discussion of health insurance and other legal concerns, see Chapter Six: The Legal Issues.) Very few policies will cover a nonmarital spouse or partner, or the children of that partner. In general, only the legal parent will get coverage for the child. Fortunately, this seems to be changing. More and more employers are responding to our visibility and our political activism, demanding that insurance companies catch up with the times. Some sympathetic employers, even though their insurance carriers won't cover our families, are willing to make arrangements that circumvent the official policies.

The Gay and Lesbian Communities

Most lesbians and gay men find that when they become parents, their relationship to the gay community changes. For some, this has meant drifting away from the gay community to affiliate with heterosexual parents. For others, it has meant finding support among lesbian and gay parents, and letting go of active participation with the rest of the gay and lesbian world. For many of us, there have been some inevitable losses involved. Mona reports that the gay community was a much more vital part of her life before she became a parent. Adopting Shana made her feel more like an outsider. "I felt many people drop away, because I think parenting was just not in their experience. Most of the friends I have now in the gay community are parents, too."

The lesbian and gay communities are just beginning to accept that there are children in our midst. Barry laments the fact that our children are not yet welcomed as part of lesbian and gay culture. He says, "I wish the gay community would recognize that there are open lesbians and gay men who are parenting, and that sometimes we want to bring our kids to meetings, and sometimes we want child care at events, and sometimes we would like not to be looked on as something out of the ordinary."

Linda and Lisa raise their five children on a farm in Vermont. As the parents of three boys, they find some parts of the lesbian community off-limits to them. Linda explains, "If we wanted to go to some of the women's music festivals we couldn't take the boys. I hate not being able to go. I respect the women-only space because I really liked it when I could go, but I don't like not being able to expose the boys to our culture. I don't think we should ever take away women-only space, but I would like to see the women's community not condemn our boys, and instead give them good role models and expect responsible behavior from them. Our boys know all the songs. They grew up on Alix Dobkin. They are not ashamed of us, but they need to know we are not isolated."

In Ohio, Sally is painfully aware of losing touch with the lesbian community because of being a parent. She reports, "The gay people here are very homophobic. They stay pretty much to themselves. Sometimes they don't even let each other know they're gay. So before Anna gets too far along in grade school I'm going to leave this town, so I can find a supportive community for both of us. I know it's hard for lesbians who don't have children to understand, but she's my priority."

Even a supportive gay and lesbian parenting group may not be enough. Living in a family that is interracial by adoption, Mona feels the lack of families of color in the gay community. She complains, "I find ignorance even among other gay parents. The gay parents' group is fairly homogeneous, in terms of it being children born into families biologically and everybody being white. And at this point in my life I have fairly low tolerance for all-white groups of any kind. My view of balance in the world has shifted since I became Shana's mother. I don't want to spend my life on a soapbox educating people. I want places where I can assume that other people have some of the knowledge and experiences that I do."

The upshot is that Mona and Jamie, like many families of color, find they can't get all their support in any one place. The lesbian and gay community, other parents both gay and straight, the adoption community, and the African-American community are their sources of support. Personal friends come from each or several of those groups, forming a patchwork network.

Barry and Tony, also an interracial family through adoption, live in New York City, with access to Center Kids, the parenting project of the Lesbian and Gay Community Center. They have found the support they get from other lesbian and gay parents to be nourishing and essential. In particular, Barry loves the fact that parenthood brings lesbians and gay men in contact with each other. "It's wonderful, because very frequently the intermingling of lesbians and gay men is missing. With Center Kids so heavily weighted toward women, about seventy-five percent to twenty-five percent, the women are comfortable and don't feel threatened by the men. The men tend to be very feminist-oriented by virtue of their parenting. Parenting brings us together, and it's great!"

It does not require an urban gay community to provide a supportive environment, however. In Iowa, Petra and Adrienne received a tremendous welcome from the gay and lesbian community when their daughter, Kim, was born. Petra describes, "There were lots of lesbian mothers around who had been married, but no other parents 'by choice' nearby. We were quite aware that we were forging new ground. Plus we were both pretty public figures in the professional community. All the lesbians in town go to Adrienne for their gynecologic care, and many of my clients are lesbians, so it became a community event. It's like Kim is the community's baby. That was a little hard at times, but it was also very comforting and supportive. People had a lot invested in our doing it, because we were pioneers. When Kim was born we got presents and cards and well-wishes and flowers from people that we do not even know, and from all over the country. It was just astonishing. People seemed to lock onto this as some affirmation of their existence and a validation of life, and it was just overwhelming."

Meanwhile, Jean expresses the feeling that while the lesbian and gay community has provided necessary support, it is unfortunate that societal homophobia encourages a segregated grouping. She says, "I would love to see a time when we see ourselves just as families, and come together with nongay families, so Kay can see both, side by side."

Politics

There is no question that the personal is political. The simple act of pushing a child in a stroller, repeated by tens of thousands of lesbian and gay parents across the country every day, is an event that increases visibility for lesbians and gay men everywhere. The impact we have on those who come to know and respect us is profound. Simultaneously, our pioneering efforts are blazing a trail for the generations of lesbians and gays following us, so that they can grow up knowing that all the options of being human are open to them. Finally, the beautiful children we are raising are going forth into the world as ambassadors of tolerance and understanding.

Sophie, Aria's mom, works for a preschool in a rural area. She gives an example of the small, daily way in which we are changing the world. "The woman I work for is pretty conservative. Her gay daughter told me that her mother said, 'Now that I see Sophie, I can totally accept who you are. I can see that you can be a regular person and you can be a parent and you can hold a job.' That was a nice little bonus from being out in a small-town community."

Sophie recognizes the political import of what her efforts are accomplishing. She says, "I sometimes feel bad because I'm not on the coalition for the betterment of Guatemalan weavers, or whatever is going down most currently. I feel like politically I'm a slug. But then I think about it and realize that being out every day as a lesbian parent, in a small town where there are a lot of born-again Christians and mountain people, is a very big way to be political."

It is our sense of responsibility to our children that brings out our most courageous, political selves. Joel, one of Martha's dads, has become more radicalized with parenthood. "I was more in the closet when I got her, but I said to people then that I do not want her growing up conflicted about this. As she gets older I want to be more and more out of the closet with more and more people, because I don't want her to be uncomfortable."

Ron, one of Joshua's dads, finds that parenthood moves him to take a stand. He recounts, "One day the people in the deli section were making jokes with each other about the Gay Pride march. They were saying, 'Oh, yeah, I saw you in the parade the other day, hah hah hah.' So I said, 'You know, some of your customers *were* in the parade the other day, like me.' And I went on and got my hamburger meat. I'm sure that I opened their eyes, at least, and, who knows, maybe they'll shut up next time."

Our children keep us honest and make us brave. In turn, we teach them that love and pride in yourself can accomplish wonders.

Pasqual, who with his partner Robert is parenting their two children, says, "I feel very political about it. Here we are and we can do it. It's no longer mom and dad and the picket fence. We're queer, we're here, and get used to it. We're not the odd couple anymore. We have support in the community. As gay people, we are a part of something larger that they never thought of at Stonewall. Who knows how we're going to project ourselves in the future?"

RESOURCES

Organizations

Support for Gay and Lesbian Families

Center Kids
208 West 13th Street
New York, NY 10011
(212) 620-7310
Family Project of the Lesbian and Gay Community Services Center. Provides information packets, workshops, support groups and advocacy for lesbian and gay parents and their children.

Gay and Lesbian Parents Coalition International (GLPCI)
P.O. Box 50360
Washington, DC 20091
Coalition of lesbian and gay parenting groups nationwide. Sponsors annual national conference of lesbian and gay parents and their children. Publishes newsletter for parents and a publication for children. Offers information, education and support. Has bibliographies of relevant books for gay and lesbian families.

Lesbian Mothers' National Defense Fund
Mom's Apple Pie
P.O. Box 21567
Seattle, WA 98111
(206) 325-2643
Provides information and referrals to lesbians currently fighting for their rights as mothers. Also provides a list of support groups and newsletter.

The Lyon-Martin Women's Health Clinic
Suite 201
1748 Market Street
San Francisco, CA 94102
(415) 565-7674
Sponsors a lesbian and gay parenting program, including seminars and workshops for lesbian and gay parents and prospective parents. Provides information, education, and support.

Alternative Insemination Programs and Support

Fenway Community Health Center
Lesbian-Gay Family and Parenting Services
7 Haviland Street
Boston, MA 02115
(617) 267-0900, ext. 282
Alternative insemination program since 1983. Provides education, support, and advocacy for gay and lesbian families. Publishes a newsletter and holds support groups for gay and lesbian parents and their children.

The Sperm Bank of California
Telegraph Hill Medical Plaza
Suite 2
3007 Telegraph Avenue
Oakland, CA 94609
(415) 444-2014
Alternative insemination program with lesbian-supportive orientation. Will provide frozen sperm samples anywhere in the country. Maintains roster of "YES" donors who agree to disclosure of identity to adult offspring. Does education and fertility awareness.

Surrogate Motherhood

Infertility Center of America

Locations in three states:
Noel Keane, J.D.
Suite 309
14 East 60th Street
New York, NY 10022
(212) 371-0811

2601 Fortune Circle East
Suite 102 B
Indianapolis, IN 46241
(317) 243-8793

101 Larkspur Landing Circle
Suite 318
Larkspur, CA 94939
(415) 925-9020
Surrogate mother matching service. Has successfully worked with gay applicants.

Surrogate Mothers, Inc.
Steven Litz, J.D.
P.O. Box 216
Monrovia, IN 46157
(317) 996-2000
Surrogate mother matching service. Has successfully worked with gay applicants.

Center for Reproductive Alternatives—Southern California
Kathryn Wyckoff
727 Via Otono
San Clemente, CA 92672
(714) 492-2161
Surrogate mother matching service. Has successfully worked with gay applicants.

Support for Offspring of Nontraditional Conception

Donors' Offspring
P.O. Box 33
Sarcoxie, MO 64862
(417) 548-3679
Education and support for people conceived via donor insemination and surrogacy.

Support for Parents of Lesbians and Gays

Federation of Parents and Friends of Lesbians and Gays, Inc. (P-FLAG or PARENTS FLAG)
P.O. Box 27605
Washington, DC 20038-7605
(202) 638-4200
(800) 4-FAMILY

Adoption Information and Support

Adoption Information Services
901-B East Willow Grove Avenue
Wyndmoor, PA 19118
(215) 233-1380
A counseling and educational service providing comprehensive information about current adoption possibilities. Services offered are specifically helpful to gays and lesbians, including how to locate and work with resources supportive of nontraditional families.

Committee for Single Adoptive Parents
P.O. Box 15084
Chevy Chase, MD 20815
Provides information for U.S. and Canadian singles interested in domestic and international adoption.

National Adoption Information Clearinghouse
Suite 600
1400 I Street, N.W.
Washington, DC 20005
(202) 842-1919

Provides information and referrals. Also publishes an annual directory of adoption agencies and adoptive-parent support groups.

Resolve, Inc.
5 Water Street
Arlington, MA 02174
(617) 643-2424
Provides education and support for infertility, and offers adoption information and resources.

Adoptive Families of America, Inc.
Ours Magazine
Suite 203
2207 Highway 100 North
Minneapolis, MN 55422
(612) 535-4829
A national support, advocacy, and educational organization for adoptive and preadoptive parents.

North American Council on Adoptable Children
Suite S-275
1821 University Avenue
St. Paul, MN 55104
(612) 644-3036
Membership of 5,000 groups, agencies, and individuals focusing on the needs of waiting U.S. and Canadian children.

American Adoption Congress
Suite 9
1000 Connecticut Avenue, N.W.
Washington, DC 20035
An umbrella organization for several hundred local search and support organizations accross the United States. Most of its members are searching adult adoptees and birthparents; however a significant number of members are adoptive parents.

International Concerns Committee for Children
Report on Foreign Adoption
911 Cypress Drive
Boulder, CO 80303
(303) 494-8333
Publishes annual listing of U.S. agencies making international placements.

Lesbian and Gay Parenting Groups

There are hundreds of lesbian and gay parenting groups across the country, formal and informal. The following is a list of those who agreed to appear in this book. You might hear of others in your community through word of mouth, or call Gay and Lesbian Parents Coalition International (GLPCI) for more information.

International

Gay and Lesbian Parents Coalition International
P.O. Box 50360
Washington, DC 20091
(202) 583-8029

United States

ARIZONA

Gay and Lesbian Parent Support Network
P.O. Box 66823
Phoenix, AZ 85082-6823
(602) 256-9173

CALIFORNIA

Gay Fathers of Long Beach
c/o The Center
2017 East Fourth Street
Long Beach, CA 90814

Lesbian Mothers Group of Long Beach
2017 East Fourth Street
Long Beach, CA 90814
(310) 434-4455

The Lyon-Martin Women's Health Clinic
1748 Market Street, Suite 201
San Francisco, CA 94102
(415) 565-7674

Outreach for Couples
405 West Washington Street, #86
San Diego, CA 92103

Gay and Lesbian Parents of Los Angeles
Suite 109-346
7985 Santa Monica
West Hollywood, CA 90046
(213) 654-0307

COLORADO

Gay and Lesbian Parents—Denver
P.O. Box Drawer E
Denver, CO 80218
(303) 937-3625

FLORIDA

GLPCI Central Florida Chapter
P.O. Box 561504
Orlando, FL 32856-1504
ATTN: Chris Alexander
(407) 420-2191

INDIANA

Evansville GLPC
P.O. Box 8341
Evansville, IN 47716

Gay and Lesbian Parents—Indiana
P.O. Box 831
Indianapolis, IN 46206
(317) 926-9741 (Craig and Terry)

MARYLAND

Gay and Lesbian Parenting Coalition of Metropolitan Washington
14908 Piney Grove Court
North Potomac, MD 20878
(301) 762-4828

MASSACHUSETTS

Lesbians Choosing Children Network
P.O. Box 393
Arlington, MA 02174
(508) 458-0740

Lesbian/Gay Family and Parenting Services
Fenway Community Health Center
7 Haviland Street
Boston, MA 02115
(617) 267-0900, ext. 282

Gay Fathers of Greater Boston
P.O. Box 1373
Boston, MA 02205

MICHIGAN

Gay and Lesbian Parents Association—Detroit
P.O. Box 2694
Southfield, MI 48037-2694
(313) 891-7292 or (313) 790-2440

NEW HAMPSHIRE

New Hampshire Gay Parents
P.O. Box 5981
Manchester, NH 03108
(603) 527-1082

NEW YORK

Center Kids
208 West 13th Street
New York, NY 10011
(212) 620-7310

Gay Fathers Coalition of Buffalo
Westside Station
P.O. Box 404
Buffalo, NY 14213
(716) 633-2692

Gay Fathers N.Y.
Church Street Station
P.O. Box 2553
New York, NY 10008-7727
(212) 874-7727

Gay Fathers Forum of Greater New York
Midtown Station
P.O. Box 1321
New York, NY 10018-0725
(212) 721-4216

Gay Fathers of Long Island
P.O. Box 2483
Patchogue, NY 11772-0879

Gay Fathers Group
P.O. Box 25525
Rochester, NY 14625

Lesmos
W.A.C.C.
669 Woodfield Road
West Hempstead, NY 11552

NORTH CAROLINA

GLP/Queen City—Charlotte
4417-F Sharon Chase Drive
Charlotte, NC 28215

OHIO

Gay and Lesbian Parenting Group of Central Ohio
P.O. Box 16235
Columbus, OH 43216

PENNSYLVANIA

CALM, Inc. (Custody Action for Lesbian Mothers)
P.O. Box 281
Narbeth, PA 19072
(215) 667-7508

TEXAS

Gay Fathers of Austin
c/o Robert H. Havican
P.O. Box 16181
Austin, TX 78761-6181

Gay Fathers/Fathers First of Houston
P.O. Box 981053
Houston, TX 77098-1053
(713) 782-5414

Houston Gay and Lesbian Parents Support
1301 Richmond, #T10
Houston, TX 77006
(713) 522-6766

SAGL Parents
P.O. Box 15094
San Antonio, TX 78212
Contact: Rob O. Blanch
(512) 828-4092

WASHINGTON, D.C.

Gay Fathers Coalition of Washington, D.C.
P.O. Box 19891
Washington, DC 20036
(202) 583-8029

WISCONSIN

Gay and Lesbian Parents Coalition of Milwaukee
P.O. Box 93503
Milwaukee, WI 53203

Canada

Gay Fathers of Winnipeg
Box 2221
Winnipeg
Manitoba, Canada R3C 3R5

Gay Fathers of Toronto
P.O. Box 187, Station F
Toronto
Ontario, Canada M4Y 2L5

Recommended Reading and Viewing

These are by no means the only good books and resources available on parenthood in general or on lesbian and gay families. An annotated bibliography of 68 picture books for children of gay and lesbian families can be obtained by sending $1 to GLPCI, P.O. Box 50360, Washington, DC 20091. Also available from GLPCI (send $5) is a bibliography of books for lesbian and gay parents.

Books for Children

Bosche, Susanne. *Jenny Lives with Eric and Martin.* Gay Men's Press, London, 1981.

Elwin, Rosamund, and Paulse, Michele. *Asha's Mums.* Women's Press, Toronto, 1990.

Heron, Ann, and Meredith, Maran. *How Would You Feel If Your Dad Was Gay?* Alyson Publications, Boston, 1991.

Krementz, Jill. *How It Feels to be Adopted.* Alfred A. Knopf, New York, 1982. Not specifically lesbian or gay, but includes diverse family constellations.

Newman, Leslea. *Heather Has Two Mommies.* Alyson Publications, Boston, 1989.

———. *Gloria Goes to Gay Pride.* Alyson Publications, Boston, 1991.

Schaffer, Patricia. *How Babies and Families Are Made: There Is More Than One Way!* Tabor Sarah Books, Berkeley, CA, 1988. Includes discussion of alternative insemination.

Skofield, James. *'Round and Around.* HarperCollins, 1993. Not specifically a gay theme but a loving interaction between a father and son with no heterosexual overtones.

Willhoite, Michael. *Daddy's Roommate.* Alyson Publications, Boston, 1990.

———. *Families: A Coloring Book.* Alyson Publications, Boston, 1991.

Books for Gay and Lesbian Parents

Barret, Robert L., and Robinson, Bryan E. *Gay Fathers.* Lexington Books, Lexington, MA, 1990.

Bozett, Frederick W., ed. *Gay and Lesbian Parents.* Praeger, New York, 1987.

Corley, Rip. *The Final Closet: The Gay Parents' Guide for Coming Out to Their Children.* Editech Press, Miami, 1990.

Curry, Hayden, and Clifford, Denis. *A Legal Guide for Lesbian and Gay Couples.* Nolo Press, Berkeley, 1991.

Gil de Lamadrid, Maria, ed. *Lesbians Choosing Motherhood: Legal Implications of Donor Insemination and Co-Parenting.* National Center for Lesbian Rights, San Francisco, 1991.

Hanscombe, Gillian E., and Forster, Jackie. *Rocking the Cradle.* Alyson Publications, Boston, 1981.

Noble, Elizabeth. *Having Your Baby by Donor Insemination.* Houghton Mifflin, Boston, 1987.

Pies, Cheri. *Considering Parenthood: A Workbook for Lesbians.* Spinsters/Aunt Lute, San Francisco, 1985.

Pollack, Sandra, and Vaughn, Jean, eds. *Politics of the Heart: A Lesbian Parenting Anthology.* Firebrand Books, Ithaca, NY, 1987.

Rafkin, Louise, ed. *Different Mothers: Sons and Daughters of Lesbians Talk About Their Lives.* Cleis Press, San Francisco, 1990.

Rafkin, Louise, ed. *Different Daughters: A Book by Mothers of Lesbians.* Cleis Press, San Francisco, 1987.

Schulenberg, Joy. *Gay Parenting: A Complete Guide for Gay Men and Lesbians with Children.* Doubleday, New York, 1985.

Books for Our Extended Families

Fairchild, Betty, and Hayward, Nancy. *Now That You Know: What Every Parent Should Know About Homosexuality.* Harcourt Brace Jovanovich, San Diego, 1989.

Griffin, Carolyn Welch, et al. *Beyond Acceptance: Parents of Lesbians and Gays Talk About Their Experiences.* St. Martin's Press, New York, 1986.

Books on Adoption

On the mechanics of adoption:
Gilman, Lois. *The Adoption Resource Book.* Third ed., Harper Perennial, New York, 1992.

Plumez, Jacqueline Horner. *Successful Adoption.* Harmony Books, New York, 1987.

Sullivan, Michael R. *Adopt the Baby You Want.* Simon and Schuster, New York, 1990.

For sensitive treatments of the psychological issues of adoption for all concerned:

Arms, Suzanne. *Adoption: A Handful of Hope.* Celestial Arts, Berkeley, 1990.

Lifton, Betty Jean. *Lost and Found: The Adoption Experience.* Harper Perennial, New York, 1979.

Melina, Lois Ruskai. *Raising Adopted Children: A Manual for Adoptive Parents.* Harper Perennial, New York, 1987.

Melina, Lois Ruskai. *Making Sense of Adoption: A Parent's Guide.* Harper Perennial, New York, 1989.

Register, Cheri. *"Are Those Kids Yours?"* Free Press, New York, 1991.

Books on Becoming a Mother

Barrett, Nina. *I Wish Someone Had Told Me.* Simon & Schuster, New York, 1990.

Genevie, Louis, and Margolies, Eva. *The Motherhood Report: How Women Feel About Being Mothers.* Macmillan, New York, 1987.

Books on Infertility

Berger, Gary S., et al. *The Couples Guide to Infertility: How New Medical Advances Can Help You Have a Baby.* Doubleday, New York, 1989. Information on the medical options.

Salzer, Linda. *Surviving Infertility: A Compassionate Guide Through the Emotional Crisis of Infertility.* Harper Perennial, New York, 1990. Sensitive and useful information and support.

Books on Pregnancy

Borg, Susan, and Lasker, Judith. *When Pregnancy Fails.* Bantam, New York, 1981. A guide through the crisis of neonatal death.

Eisenberg, Arlene, at al. *What to Expect When You're Expecting.* Workman Publishing, New York, 1984. Just one of many good books available in paperback to describe the experience of pregnancy, including much useful information on diet, exercise, and medical care. It is always a good idea to inform yourself as much as possible, and not to rely solely on your physician.

Videotapes for Lesbian & Gay Parents & Families

Alternative Conceptions, by Christina Sunley and Vicky Funari
Lesbian motherhood through donor insemination, profiling two families.
1985. Video, color. 36 minutes.
Available from:
Women Make Movies
225 Lafayette Street
New York, NY 10012
(212) 925-0606

A Question of Love
A fictional, made-for-TV movie starring Jane Alexander and Gena Rowlands as lesbians battling for child custody.
1978.
Available from:
Lambda Rising
1625 Connecticut Avenue N.W.
Washington, DC 20009
(202) 462-6969

Choosing Children, by Debra Chasnoff and Kim Klausner
An outstanding film about lesbians becoming parents.
1984. 16mm color. 45 minutes.
Available from:
Cambridge Documentary Films
P.O. Box 385
Cambridge, MA 02139
(617) 354-3677

In the Best Interests of the Children, by Frances Reid, Elizabeth Stevens, and Cathy Zheutlin
Film by and about lesbian mothers.
16mm color. 53 minutes.
Available from:
Women Make Movies
225 Lafayette Street
New York, NY 10012
(212) 925-0606

Labor More Than Once, by Liz Mersky
A lesbian mother's legal battle to regain custody of her child.
1983. Video. 52 minutes.
Available from:
Women Make Movies
225 Lafayette Street
New York, NY 10012
(212) 925-0606

Not All Parents Are Straight, by Kevin White
Profile of families in which children are being raised by gay and
lesbian parents.
1987. 16mm or video, color. 58 minutes.
Available from:
Cinema Guild
Suite 802
1697 Broadway
New York, NY 10019
(212) 246-5522

Sandy and Madeleine's Family, by Sharrie Farrell
A lesbian family.
1974. 16mm. 30 minutes.
Available from:
Multi-Focus, Inc.
1525 Franklin Street
San Francisco, CA 94109
415-673-5100

We Are Family, produced by Amee Sands, directed by Dasal
Banks
Explores the legal and social implications of gay and lesbian par-
enting through the lives of three families.
1987. 3/4" video, color.
Available from:
WGBH-TV
125 Western Avenue
Allston, MA 02134
(617) 492-2777

Legal Resources for Lesbian and Gay Families

(Reprinted with permission from "A Lesbian and Gay Parents' Legal Guide to Child Custody," courtesy of the National Center for Lesbian Rights.)

The organizations listed may provide information and/or referrals, services, education, and financial assistance to gay and lesbian parents on legal matters:

Bar Association for Human Rights of Greater New York (BAHRGNY)
P.O. Box 1899 Grand Central Station
New York, NY 10163
(212) 628-8532 (office)
(212) 505-2645 (Information Referral Service)

Bay Area Lawyers for Individual Freedom (BALIF)
P.O. Box 1983
San Francisco, CA 94101
(415) 431-1444

Community Law Office
Suite 1410
621 S.W. Morrison
Portland, OR 97205
(503) 241-4708

Custody Action for Lesbian Mothers (CALM)
P.O. Box 281
Narbeth, PA 19072
(215) 667-7508

Fund for Human Dignity
Suite 410
666 Broadway
New York, NY 10012
(212) 529-1600

Gay Alliance for Genesee Valley, Inc.
713 Monroe Avenue
Rochester, NY 14607
(716) 244-8640

Gay and Lesbian Advocates and Defenders (GLAD)
P.O. Box 218
Boston, MA 02112
(617) 426-1350

Lambda Legal Defense and Education Fund
666 Broadway
New York, NY 10012
(212) 995-8585

Lawyers for Human Rights
P.O. Box 480318
Los Angeles, CA 90048
(213) 659-2800

Lesbian Mothers' National Defense Fund
P.O. Box 21567
Seattle, WA 98111
(206) 325-2643

National Center for Lesbian Rights (NCLR)
(formerly the Lesbian Rights Project)
1663 Mission Street, 5th Floor
San Francisco, CA 94103
(415) 621-0674

National Gay Rights Advocates (NGRA)
540 Castro Street
San Francisco, CA 94114
(415) 863-3624

National NOW Action Center
(National Organization for Women)
Suite 800
1401 New York Avenue, N.W.
Washington, DC 20005-2102
(202) 347-2279

Texas Human Rights Foundation
1519 Maryland
Houston, TX 77006
(713) 526-9139

APPENDIX I: SAMPLE DONOR-RECIPIENT AGREEMENT

(Reprinted with permission, courtesy of the National Center for Lesbian Rights, 1663 Mission Street, 5th Floor, San Francisco, CA 94103.)

Note: This document is not a legally binding contract and therefore does not guarantee the legal outcome of a dispute. Its purpose is to demonstrate the intent of the parties involved. In addition, the provisions contained in this sample may or may not be specifically applicable to your situation. This sample is offered as a guide only and is not a substitute for the advice of an attorney. You should have a lawyer review your own agreement before signing.

This AGREEMENT is made this_____ day of_____ by and between_____, hereafter DONOR, and_____, hereafter RECIPIENT, who may also be referred to as the "parties."

NOW THEREFORE, in consideration of the promises of each other, DONOR and RECIPIENT agree as follows:

      1)   Each clause of this AGREEMENT is separate and divisible from the others and, should a court refuse to enforce one or more clauses of this AGREEMENT, the others are still valid and in full force.

      2)   DONOR has agreed to provide his semen to RECIPIENT for the purpose of artificial insemination. The parties have further agreed that DONOR'S semen may be frozen at the time of donation and may be used by RECIPIENT at a subsequent time.

3)   In exchange, RECIPIENT has agreed to pay the sum of $_____ dollars to DONOR each and every time he makes a semen donation.

4)   Each party is a single person who has never married.

5)   Each party acknowledges and agrees that, during the calendar year _____, RECIPIENT is attempting to become pregnant through the procedure of artificial insemination, and that such inseminations will continue until conception occurs.

6)   Each party acknowledges and agrees that DONOR is providing his semen for the purposes of said artificial inseminations, and does so with clear understanding that he will not demand, request, or compel any guardianship, custody, or visitation rights with any child(ren) resulting from the artificial insemination procedure. Further, DONOR acknowledges that he fully understood that he would have no parental rights whatsoever with said child(ren).

7)   Each party acknowledges and agrees that RECIPIENT, through this AGREEMENT, has relinquished any and all rights that she might otherwise have to hold DONOR legally, financially, or emotionally responsible for any child(ren) that results from the artificial insemination procedure.

8)   Each party acknowledges and agrees that the sole authority to name any child(ren) resulting from the artificial insemination procedure shall rest with RECIPIENT.

9)   Each party acknowledges and agrees that there shall be no father named on the birth certificate of any child(ren) born from the artificial insemination procedure.

10)   Each party acknowledges and agrees that the use of a licensed physician to receive the semen donations, as well as the execution of this AGREEMENT, were specifically chosen to avoid any finding that the DONOR is the legal father of the child(ren) pursuant to *(name and section number of state statute if applicable)*. Consistent with that purpose, each party has executed this AGREEMENT with the purpose of clarifying her or his intent to release and relinquish any and all rights she or he may have to bring a suit to establish the paternity of any child(ren) conceived through the procedure of artificial insemination.

11)   Each party covenants and agrees that, in light of the expectations of each party as stated above, RECIPIENT shall have absolute authority and power to appoint a guardian for her child(ren), and that the RECIPIENT and such guardian may act with sole discretion as to all legal, financial, medical, and emotional needs of said child(ren) without any involvement with or demands of authority from DONOR.

12)   Each party covenants and agrees that neither of them will identify the DONOR as the parent of the child(ren), nor will either of them reveal the identity of the DONOR to their respective relatives or to any individual without the express written consent of the other party.

13)   Each party agrees and acknowledges that the relinquishment of all rights, as stated above, is final and irrevocable. DONOR further understands that his waivers shall prohibit action on his part for custody, guardianship, or visitation in any future situation, including the event of the RECIPIENT'S disability or death.

14)   Each party acknowledges and agrees that any future contact the DONOR may have with any child(ren) that result(s) from the artificial insemination procedure in no way alters the effect of this agreement. Any such contact will be at the discretion of the RECIPIENT and will be consistent with the intent of both parties to sever any and all parental rights and responsibilities of the DONOR.

15)   Each party acknowledges and understands that there may be legal questions which have not been settled by statute or prior court decisions. Notwithstanding the knowledge that certain of the clauses stated herein may not be enforced by a court of law, the parties choose to enter into this agreement.

16)   Each party acknowledges and agrees that she or he signed this AGREEMENT voluntarily and freely, of his or her own choice, without any duress of any kind whatsoever. It is further acknowledged that each party has been advised to secure the advice and consent of an attorney of her or his own choosing, and that each party understands the meaning and significance of each provision of this AGREEMENT.

17)   Each party acknowledges and agrees that any changes made in the terms and conditions of this AGREEMENT shall be made in writing and signed by both parties.

18)   This AGREEMENT contains the entire understanding of the parties. There are no promises, understandings, agreements or representations between the parties other than those expressly stated in this AGREEMENT.

IN WITNESS THEREOF, the parties hereunto have executed this AGREEMENT, consisting of _____ typewritten pages, in the City of _____, County of _____, State of _____, on the date and year first written above.

_____   _____
DONOR   RECIPIENT

APPENDIX II:
SAMPLE COPARENTING
AGREEMENT

(Reprinted with permission, courtesy of the National Center for Lesbian Rights, 1663 Mission Street, 5th Floor, San Francisco, CA 94103.)

Note: This document is not a legally binding agreement. Its purpose is to demonstrate the intent of the parties involved. The provisions of this sample agreement may or may not be relevant to your specific circumstances. This sample is in no way intended to be a substitute for professional legal advice. Use it instead as a guide and have your lawyer review the document you create before signing.

This Agreement is made this _____ day of _____, 19___, by and between_____ (hereafter_____) and_____ (hereafter_____). We may also be referred to in this Agreement herein as the "Parties".

Now, therefore, in consideration of the promises of each other, and in acknowledgement of their mutual belief that the best interests of the *(child/children)* require stable sources of financial, academic, medical, and emotional support, the parties enter into this Agreement to guarantee that their *(child/children)* will receive the full benefit of having each and both of them as parents, including current and future financial costs and emotional support and rights to inheritance, and agree as follows:

1. Each Party acknowledges and agrees that they live together in a

primary family relationship, and have since *(date)*. The Parties further acknowledge that, during the course of their relationship, *(name of biological mother)* gave birth to *(name of child/children)* born *(date)*. The decision to have *(child/children)* was a joint decision of the Parties and was based upon the commitment of each Party to parent the *(child/children)* jointly. The Parties acknowledge that *(nonbiological mother)* has been a primary parent to *(name of child/children)* since *(her/his)* respective birth.

2. Each Party acknowledges and agrees that, while they live together as a family and if they are no longer living together, they will provide for their *(child/children)* as follows:

a) Both *(name of Party)* and *(name of Party)* will have joint custody of *(name of child/children)*.

b) The *(child/children)* will spend approximately one-half *(her/his)* time with each parent. Each parent shall share equally in the responsibility for the care of the *(child/children)* during school vacations or illness, either by caring for *(her/him)* herself or by making provisions for (her/his) care.

c) Each parent will pay one-half the normal, day to day living expenses and costs of the *(child/children)* while they live together; or, the entire cost of *(her/his)* day to day care when *(she/he)* is with each one, should they stop living together.

d) Each parent will pay one-half of the out-of-pocket costs to provide the *(child/children)* with child care, summer camp programs, clothing, religious education, medical and dental care, counseling or psychotherapy, and any medical or educational expenses necessary to promote *(her/his)* welfare.

e) Each parent shall claim the *(child/children)* as *(her/his)* dependent for tax purposes in alternate years.

f) Each parent shall maintain the *(child/children)* as a beneficiary/beneficiaries of a life insurance policy in the minimum amount of $_____ during *(her/his)* minority.

3. Both *(name of Party)* and *(name of Party)* acknowledge and agree that all major decisions regarding physical location, support, education, medical care, and religious training of *(child/children)* shall be made by them jointly.

4. Both *(name of Party)* and *(name of Party)* acknowledge and agree that they will make a good faith effort to remain in *(community/neighborhood)* until *(child/children)* has completed high school. Neither parent may change the residence of the *(child/children)* to a location outside *(community/neighborhood)* without the written consent of the other parent.

5. The Parties agree that, in the event that they separate and a significant discrepancy in their net monthly income occurs in the future, they will negotiate child support payments consistent with the schedule for child support then in effect in the County/State of _____.

6. Each Party acknowledges and agrees that in the event that either of them is no longer able to care and provide for the *(child/children)* because of death or legal disability, it would be in the best interests of the *(child/children))* to remain with the other parent. Neither parent will allow the *(child/children)* to be adopted by any other person so long as both parents are living.

7. Each Party covenants and agrees that any dispute pertaining to this Agreement which arises between them shall be resolved according to the following procedures:

a) The Parties shall participate in mediation for _____ sessions or _____ days, whichever first occurs, and, if they are unable to resolve their dispute, they shall submit it to binding arbitration according to the procedures set forth below;

b) The request for arbitration may be made by either Party and shall be in writing and delivered to the other Party;

c) Pending the outcome of arbitration, there shall be no change made in the language of this Agreement;

d) The arbitrator who will resolve any disputes regarding this Agreement shall be chosen by the Parties.

e) If an arbitrator cannot be chosen within fourteen (14) calendar days following the written arbitration request, the arbitrator shall be chosen by the Parties' attorneys.

f) Within fourteen (14) calendar days following the selection of the arbitrator, the arbitrator will hear the dispute between the Parties. The arbitration proceedings shall be held in accordance with the rules of the American Arbitration Association.

g) Within seven (7) calendar days subsequent to the hearing, the arbitrator will make a decision and communicate it in writing to each Party.

h) The decision of the arbitrator shall be binding and may be entered as a judgment by either Party.

8. Each Party acknowledges and understands that there are legal questions raised by the issues involved in this Agreement which have not been settled by statute or prior court decisions. Notwithstanding the knowledge that certain of the clauses stated herein may not be enforced in a court of law, the Parties choose to enter into this Agreement and clarify their intent to provide and nurture jointly their

(child/children), even when they are no longer living together as a family. Specifically:

a) We recognize that the current state of the law regarding financial support of children does not obligate *(name of nonbiological mother)* to support the *(child/children);* we also recognize that current law gives *(name of biological mother)* no enforceable right to collect support on behalf of the *(child/children)* from *(name of nonbiological mother).* Notwithstanding the current state of the law regarding support, *(name of nonbiological mother)* agrees to support the minor *(child/children)* and to be bound by current and future support obligations for the *(child/children)* pursuant to *(state support statute).*

The Parties intend that this agreement create an enforceable right for *(name of biological mother)* to collect support on behalf of the *(child/children)*, including the right to request that support be set pursuant to *(statute)* and that support be extended beyond minority, consistent with the child support statutes.

b) The Parties acknowledge that current state law does not clearly recognize the rights of a nonbiological parent to stand as a *de facto* parent in relation to the child. Notwithstanding, the Parties agree to do everything legally possible to create a legal relationship between *(name of nonbiological mother)* and *(child/children)*, to place the *(child/children)* in the same stead as *(name of nonbiological mother's)* biological *(child/children)* for the purposes of custody, visitation, support, and inheritance, including, but not limited to, a nomination of *(name of nonbiological mother)* as guardian of the person and estate of the *(child/children)* in *(name of biological mother's)* will, and provisions for inheritance of an appropriate portion of her estate by the *(child/children)* in the will of *(name of nonbiological mother).*

9. Each Party shall leave at least one-half of her estate to the *(child/children).* If either Party shall create a trust for the *(child/children)*, she shall name the other parent, or a person selected jointly with the other parent, as trustee. Likewise, each Party shall name the other parent, or a person mutually selected with the other parent, as guardian of the estate of the *(child/children).*

10. We intend, by this Agreement, to guide a Court, should it become involved, in determining the best interests of our *(child/children).* We agree that the Court shall have jurisdiction over any disputes arising during the *(child/children's)* minority regarding *(her/his)* custody or support.

We agree to participate in Court-ordered mediation regarding issues of custody and visitation and to be bound by court orders regarding the *(child/children).* Specifically, *(name of nonbiological mother)* agrees to be bound by any orders compelling her to pay child support to *(name of biological mother)* on behalf of the *(child/children)* or to have contact with the *(child/children)* on a set schedule. In addition, *(name of nonbiological mother)* agrees to be bound by court orders regarding a time sharing arrangement with the *(child/children)*, including custody and visitation orders.

If either Party contests the Court's jurisdiction over any dispute involving the *(child/children)*, the *(child/children's)* custody, care, or support, then that Party may be estopped from defeating the Court's jurisdiction by reason of having accepted the benefits of the mutual promises contained in this Agreement. If either Party contests the Court's jurisdiction over any issue involving the custody, care, or support of the *(child/children)* and is successful in defeating the Court's jurisdiction, then that party shall be liable for liquidated damages in the amount of $_____ for each year that this Agreement was in effect.

11. This Agreement contains the entire understanding of the Parties. There are no promises, understandings, agreements, or representations between the Parties other than those expressly stated in this Agreement.

12. Each Party acknowledges and agrees that she signed this Agreement voluntarily and freely, of her own choice, without any duress of any kind whatsoever.

13. In the negotiations of this Agreement, both Parties were represented by *(name of attorney)*, Attorney at Law. Each Party acknowledges that she had the advice of counsel prior to signing this Agreement and that she fully understands the terms of this Agreement.

IN WITNESS THEREOF, the Parties hereunto have executed this Agreement, in the County of _____, State of _____, on the day and year first above written.

DATED:_____

_____
(PARTY)

DATED:_____

_____
(PARTY)

Approved as to form:

_____
(ATTORNEY)

APPENDIX III:
DONOR SCREENING FORM

Code no. _____   Today's date _____

MEDICAL PROBLEM	YOU	MOTHER	FATHER	SIBLINGS	GRAND-PARENTS	AUNTS/UNCLES	COUSINS
1. HEART:							
stroke							
heart attack							
heart disease							
from birth							
other							
rheumatic fever							
hardening of arteries							
high blood pressure							
high cholesterol							
2. BLOOD:							
anemia							
sickle-cell anemia							
hemophilia							
leukemia							
immune deficiency							
other blood disorder							
3. RESPIRATORY (LUNGS):							
hayfever							
asthma							
emphysema							
tuberculosis							
lung cancer							
pneumonia							
other lung disease							
4. GASTRO-INTESTINAL:							
ulcer of stomach/duodenum							
gall stones							
hepatitis A (infectious)							
hepatitis B (serum)							
hepatitis C (non A-non B)							
other liver disease							
colon cancer							
ulcerative colitis							
Crohn's disease							
cystic fibrosis							
intestinal cancer							
rectal disorder							
any other cancer/problem of digestive system							

Explanation _____

Reprinted with permission, courtesy of The Sperm Bank of California.

Code no. _____   Today's date _____

MEDICAL PROBLEM	YOU	MOTHER	FATHER	SIBLINGS	GRAND-PARENTS	AUNTS/UNCLES	COUSINS
5. METABOLIC/ENDOCRINE:							
diabetes melitis							
hypoglycemia							
thyroid cancer							
thyroid disease							
goiter							
adrenal dysfunction or disorder							
hyperactivity							
hormonal dysfunction or disorder							
6. URINARY:							
polycystic kidney disease							
other kidney disease							
other disease of urinary tract							
nephritis							
7. GENITAL/REPRODUCTION:							
undescended testicle							
hypospadiasis							
prostate cancer							
uterine fibroids							
endometirosis							
ovarian cysts							
cancer of cervix, uterus or ovary							
premature menopause							
8. NEUROLOGICAL:							
migraines							
mental retardation							
senility before age 50							
multiple sclerosis							
cerebral palsy							
epilepsy							
convulsive disorders							
hydrocephalus (water on the brain)							
disorders of spinal cord							
Huntington's chorea							
Gaucher's disease							
Wilson's disease							
Alzheimer's disease							
other diseases of nervous system							

Explanation _____

Code No. _____   Today's date _____

MEDICAL PROBLEM	YOU	MOTHER	FATHER	SIBLINGS	GRAND-PARENTS	AUNTS/UNCLES	COUSINS
9. MENTAL HEALTH:							
schizophrenia							
manic depressive disorder							
other mental health disorder requiring medication/hospitalization							
10. MUSCLES/BONES/JOINTS:							
muscular dystrophy							
other chronic muscle disease							
lupus							
spine deformity (scoliosis, kyphosis)							
osteoporosis							
dwarfism							
hereditary low back disease							
arthritis							
gout							
congential dislocation of hip							
11. SIGHT/SOUND/SMELL:							
deafness before age 60							
deformity of the ear							
cataracts before age 50							
blindness							
color blindness							
glaucoma							
deviated septum							
retinoblastoma							
congenital word blindness							
other sight/sound/smell disorder							
12. SKIN:							
acne							
eczema							
skin cancer							
albinism							
other pigmentation/skin disorders							
13. SUBSTANCE ABUSE:							
alcoholism							
drug abuse or addiction							
14. BREAST CANCER:							
15. OTHER:							
other cancer not mentioned above							
other condition/disease not mentioned above							

Explanation _____

NOTES

INTRODUCTION

1. Patterson, 1992.

2. In a family created through heterosexual marriage, the lesbian or gay parent's sexual orientation often comes as new information to the family members, contradicting previously held assumptions. Sexual orientation may become the central issue in a separation. The children may have to deal with the loss of a noncustodial parent, and with feelings of having been lied to. The potential for homophobic treatment in the courts may create the need for secrecy about the parent's sexual orientation, which can be a major barrier to family relations. In addition, there is usually one heterosexual parent in these families, whose attitude toward gay men or lesbians may markedly affect the family's well-being. By contrast, when lesbians and gay men choose to create families in a gay context, there is usually openness from the beginning.

CHAPTER 1: THE BIG DECISION

1. Cheri Pies, author of *Considering Parenthood: A Workbook for Lesbians,* is an activist on behalf of lesbian and gay parenting.

2. Boarder babies are babies abandoned at birth in the hospital; they are often born addicted to drugs and/or HIV positive.

3. Patterson, 1992.

4. See Patterson, October 1992, for a review of the psychology research on the children of lesbian and gay parents. Similarly, G. Dorsey Green and Frederick Bozett review the existing body of research in "Lesbian Mothers and Gay Fathers," in Gonsiorek, John C., and Weinrich, James D., 1991. See also the early studies done by Kirkpatrick, et al, 1981, and Green, et al, 1986. More recently, studies are being done which examine the children in the planned families of lesbians. See "Children of the Lesbian Baby Boom," Patterson, in press. The children of planned gay father families have not yet been studied.

Research on the children of lesbians and gay men is far enough along that we no longer need to keep asking the question whether the children are healthy; we can now begin to investigate more about the needs of these families. Toward this end, a thirty-year longitudinal study of eighty-six lesbian families is being conducted by Drs. Nanette Gartrell and Jean Hamilton in San Francisco, with a view toward a comprehensive evaluation of the experiences in these families. As more gay men choose to become fathers, research on those families will accumulate as well.

5. Lewin, 1989.

6. For information on chemical dependence in gay men and lesbians, see *Dual Identities,* by Dana Finnegan and Emily McNally.

7. Lesser, Ronnie. "Deciding not to become a mother." In *Lesbians at Midlife,* ed. by Barbara Sang, Joyce Warshow, and Adrienne Smith, pp. 84–90.

CHAPTER 2: LESBIANS CHOOSING PREGNANCY

1. U.S. Department of Commerce, August 1988, p. 9.
2. Ibid., p. 48.
3. Ibid., pp. 48–49.
4. Noble, 1987, p. 115.
5. Ibid., p. 103.
6. U.S. Department of Commerce, August 1988, p. 59.
7. Ibid., p. 10.

CHAPTER 3: DONORS AND COPARENTS

1. Though it doesn't happen very often, a lesbian can also become a primary parent by hiring a surrogate mother to conceive with donor sperm and bear a child for her. This results in a family constellation that is basically the same as in a family formed by traditional adoption, with

the exception that the circumstances of the child's conception and birth are arranged by the lesbian mother.

2. It is advisable to wait six months and repeat the HIV antibody test before going ahead.

CHAPTER 4: GAY DADS MAKING BABIES

1. "Surrogate Mothers of Invention." *Los Angeles Herald Examiner,* May 23, 1988.

2. Lesbians have also become mothers via surrogates. In situations where a single lesbian, or both women in a lesbian couple, are either unable or averse to carrying a pregnancy, a lesbian can contribute her egg for fertilization with donor sperm, and hire a surrogate to gestate the baby. There are lesbian couples where one partner is implanted with an embryo created by her lover's ovum and donor sperm. That partner, technically a surrogate, then gets to give birth to her lover's baby.

3. United States Office of Technology Assessment, May 1988, p. 268.

4. Rothman, 1989.

5. Shalev, 1989.

6. Personal communication.

7. Personal communication.

8. Quote from Dr. Hanafin taken from Andrews, 1989, p. 84.

9. Personal communication.

CHAPTER 5: ADOPTION

1. Plumez, 1987, p. xii.

2. Ricketts and Achtenberg, 1987, p. 93.

3. "President's Column," *Adoptalk: Newsletter of the Adoptive Parents Committee,* Vol. 37, March 1992.

4. To order, send a check for $12, made payable to "The Center," with the note "for Center Kids" in the comment area. Send your mailing address and specify that you want the adoption packet. Mail to The Center, 208 West 13th Street, New York, NY 10011.

5. The higher fees for healthy white infants are a function of the fact that these children are in great demand, often by the families that can best afford to pay the agency's fees. Agencies, therefore, tend not to receive any funding which might offset the costs of these placements.

6. Sullivan, 1990.

7. To obtain, send $10 to the International Concerns Committe on Children, 911 Cypress Drive, Boulder, CO 80303.

8. Agencies which welcome openly lesbian or gay adopters do not

necessarily want to be identified, both because of possible repercussions for them, and because they want to limit their availability to parents for whom they could find a suitable child. They are therefore reluctant to invite an avalanche of inquiries from lesbian and gay applicants whom they might not be able to serve. They can be found, however, through networking and by contacting organizations listed in the Resources section.

9. The National Center for Lesbian Rights reports that a small number of joint adoptions, in which both members of a lesbian or gay couple have been considered the legal adopting parents (as opposed to second-parent adoption, where one partner later adopts a child already legally belonging to the other partner), have occurred in California and elsewhere. At present, statistics are incomplete, so it is impossible to know what the national incidence of this has been. Otherwise, lesbian or gay adopters are considered to be legally single, regardless of their partnership status.

10. For further information on opening adoption records, contact the American Adoption Congress, Suite 9, 1000 Connecticut Avenue, N.W., Washington, DC 20036.

11. A legal-risk placement is one in which the rights of the biological parents have not yet been terminated. See the section on foster-adopt programs.

12. See Plumez for the states that have such lists.

13. A guardian *ad litem* is someone appointed by the court to represent the child's interests in a legal proceeding in which a child is involved. He or she has no actual custodial guardianship of the child.

14. It is common practice to install a separate phone line for exclusive use by potential birthmothers responding to ads. It both helps to maintain the adopting parents' anonymity, and insures that when the phone rings, they will immediately prepare themselves for the nature of the ensuing conversation.

CHAPTER 6: THE LEGAL ISSUES

1. Rivera, Rhonda R. "Legal Issues in Gay and Lesbian Parenting." In Bozett, Frederick W., ed., 1987, p. 204.

2. Polikoff, 1990, p. 573.

3. Ibid., p. 483.

4. Ibid., pp. 471–472.

5. Ibid, p. 542.

6. Personal communication.

7. The National Center for Lesbian Rights.

8. *National Center for Lesbian Rights Newsletter,* Spring 1992, p. 9.
9. Gil de Lamadrid, 1991, p. 6.
10. Personal communication.
11. Gil de Lamadrid, 1991, p. 17.
12. Personal communication.
13. Arizona, Florida, Indiana, Kentucky, Louisiana, Michigan, Nebraska, North Dakota, Utah, Virginia, and Washington.
14. Arizona, Indiana, Michigan, North Dakota, and Utah.
15. Accurate national records do not yet exist, so the exact number around the country is unknown.

CHAPTER 9: BREAKING UP

1. Personal communication.
2. Kalter, 1990.

CHAPTER 10: CRISIS AND TRAGEDY

1. Mary-Helen Mautner, Susan Hester, and Jessica Hester-Mautner are their real names. The names of other people in the narrative have been changed.
2. *Washington Post,* August 26, 1989.
3. "The Mautner Project Annual Report," 1990–1991.

CHAPTER 11: OUR FAMILIES OF ORIGIN

1. Griffin et al., 1986, p. 76.
2. Ibid.

CHAPTER 12: OUT IN THE WORLD

1. Caspar, Schultz, and Wickens, 1992. The findings of this study are also being published in a book for parents, teachers, and administrators, entitled *Tentative Trust: Enhancing Communication Between Gay and Lesbian Parents in the Schools,* Bank Street College of Education, New York, 1992.

BIBLIOGRAPHY

Achtenberg, Roberta. *AIDS and Child Custody: A Guide to Advocacy.* National Center for Lesbian Rights, San Francisco, 1989.

———. "Lesbian and Gay Parenting: A Psychological and Legal Perspective." National Center for Lesbian Rights, San Francisco, 1987.

———. *Preserving and Protecting the Families of Lesbians and Gay Men.* National Center for Lesbian and Gay Rights, San Francisco, 1990.

Ambert, Anne-Marie. *The Effect of Children on Parents.* Haworth Press, New York, 1992.

Andrews, Lori B. *Between Strangers: Surrogate Mothers, Expectant Fathers, and Brave New Babies.* Harper and Row, New York, 1989.

———. *New Conceptions: A Consumer's Guide to the Newest Infertility Treatments, including in Vitro Fertilization, Artificial Insemination, and Surrogate Motherhood.* Ballantine Books, New York, 1985.

Anonymous, Sarah and Mary. *Woman Controlled Conception.* Womanshare Books, Berkeley, CA, 1979.

Arms, Suzanne. *Adoption: A Handful of Hope.* Celestial Arts, Berkeley, CA, 1990.

Barber, Virginia, and Skaggs, Merrill Maguire. *The Mother Person.* Schocken Books, New York, 1977.

Barret, Robert L., and Robinson, Bryan E. *Gay Fathers.* Lexington Books, Lexington, MA, 1990.

Barrett, Nina. *I Wish Someone Had Told Me.* Simon and Schuster, New York, 1990.

Berger, Gary S., et al. *The Couples Guide to Infertility.* Doubleday, New York, 1989.

Berzon, Betty. *Permanent Partners: Building Gay and Lesbian Relationships That Last.* E. P. Dutton, New York, 1988.

Blumstein, Philip, and Schwartz, Pepper. *American Couples.* Pocket Books, New York, 1983.

Borg, Susan, and Lasker, Judith. *When Pregnancy Fails.* Bantam, New York, 1981.

Bosche, Susanne. *Jenny Lives with Eric and Martin.* Gay Men's Press, London, 1981.

The Boston Lesbian Psychologies Collective, eds. *Lesbian Psychologies.* University of Illinois Press, Chicago, 1987.

The Boston Women's Health Book Collective. *The New Our Bodies, Ourselves.* Simon and Schuster, New York, 1984.

Bozett, Frederick W., ed. *Gay and Lesbian Parents.* Praeger, New York, 1987.

Brodzinsky, Anne Braff. *The Mulberry Bird: Story of an Adoption.* Perspectives Press, Indianapolis, 1986.

Brozan, Nadine. "Surrogate Mothers: Problems and Goals." *New York Times,* February 27, 1984.

Bull, Chris. "Presidential Group Slams Les/Gay Adoption." *Gay Community News,* Vol. 15, No. 23, 1987.

Butler, Becky, ed. *Ceremonies of the Heart: Celebrating Lesbian Unions.* Seal Press, Seattle, 1990.

Carl, Douglas. *Counseling Same-Sex Couples.* W. W. Norton, New York, 1990.

Carrieri, Joseph R. *Child Custody, Foster Care, and Adoptions.* Lexington Books, New York, 1991.

Caspar, Virginia; Schultz, Steven; and Wickens, Elaine. "Breaking the Silences: Lesbian and Gay Parents and the Schools." *Teacher's College Record,* Fall 1992.

Chesler, Phyllis. *Mothers on Trial: The Battle for Children and Custody.* Harcourt Brace Jovanovich, San Diego, 1987.

Clunis, D. Merilee, and Green, G. Dorsey. *Lesbian Couples.* Seal Press, Seattle, 1988.

Coleman, Eli, ed. *Integrated Identity for Lesbians and Gay Men: Psy-*

chotherapeutic Approaches to Emotional Well-Being. Harrington Park Press, New York, 1988.

Committee on Women in Psychology and Committee on Lesbian and Gay Concerns. "Lesbian Parents and Their Children: A Resource Paper for Psychologists." Available from the American Psychological Association, Public Interest Directorate, 1200 17th Street, N.W., Washington, DC 20036.

Corley, Rip. *The Final Closet: The Gay Parents' Guide for Coming Out to Their Children.* Editech Press, Miami, 1990.

The Council of New York Law Associates. "Adoption: A Guide for Those Who Want to Adopt." Available from the Council of New York Law Associates, 36 West 44th Street, New York, NY 10036; Tel. (212) 840-1541.

Curry, Hayden, and Clifford, Denis. *A Legal Guide for Lesbian and Gay Couples.* Nolo Press, Berkeley, CA, 1991.

D'Augelli, Anthony R., and Hart, Mary M. "Gay Women, Men, and Families in Rural Settings: Toward the Development of Helping Communities." *American Journal of Community Psychology,* Vol. 15, No. 1, 1987.

Dean, Craig R. "Gay Marriage: A Civil Right." *Sappho's Isle.* January 1992.

De Cecco, John P., ed. *Gay Relationships.* Haworth Press, New York, 1988.

DeFrain, John. *On Our Own: A Single Parent's Survival Guide.* Lexington Books, Lexington, MA, 1987.

DeFrain, John, et al. *Sudden Infant Death: Surviving the Loss.* Lexington Books, Lexington, MA, 1991.

DiLapi, E. "Lesbian Mothers and the Motherhood Hierarchy." *Journal of Homosexuality,* Vol. 18, Nos. 1–2, 1989.

Domenici, Thomas. "Young Adults Raised by Lesbians." Unpublished doctoral dissertation, University of Southern California, 1984.

Dullea, Georgia. "Gay Couples' Wish to Adopt Grows, Along With Increasing Resistance." *New York Times,* February 7, 1988.

Eckles, Erin. "Lesbians Found Project for 'Taking Care of Ourselves.'" *Washington Blade* (Washington, DC), September 8, 1989.

Editors of the Harvard Law Review. *Sexual Orientation and the Law.* Harvard University Press, Cambridge, 1989.

Ehrensaft, Diane. *Parenting Together: Men and Women Sharing the Care of Their Children.* Free Press, New York, 1987.

Eisenberg, Arlene, et al. *What to Expect When You're Expecting.* Workman Publishing, New York, 1984.

Elwin, Rosamund, and Paulse, Michele. *Asha's Mums.* Women's Press, Toronto, 1990.

Evall, Joseph. "Sexual Orientation and Adoptive Matching." *Family Law Quarterly,* Vol. XXV, No. 33, Fall 1991.

Fairchild, Betty, and Hayward, Nancy. *Now That You Know: What Every Parent Should Know About Homosexuality.* Harcourt Brace Jovanovich, San Diego, 1989.

Falco, Kristine. Psychotherapy with Lesbian Clients. Brunner/Mazel, New York, 1991.

Finnegan, Dana G., and McNally, Emily B. *Dual Identities: Counseling Chemically Dependent Gay Men and Lesbians.* Hazelden, 1987.

Folberg, Jay, ed. *Joint Custody and Shared Parenting.* Guilford Press, New York, 1991.

Fornino, Felix. "President's Column." *Adoptalk,* Vol. 37, No. 7, March 1992.

Freiberg, Peter. "Lesbian Moms Can Give Kids Empowering Models." *APA Monitor,* December 1990.

Gay Fathers of Toronto. *Gay Fathers.* Gay Fathers of Toronto, 1981.

Genevie, Louis, and Margolies, Eva. *The Motherhood Report: How Women Feel About Being Mothers.* Macmillan, New York, 1987.

Gil de Lamadrid, Maria, ed. *Lesbians Choosing Motherhood: Legal Implications of Donor Insemination and Co-Parenting.* National Center for Lesbian Rights, San Francisco, 1991.

Gonsiorek, John C., and Weinrich, James D. *Homosexuality: Research Implications for Public Policy.* Sage Publications, Newbury Park, CA, 1991.

Gracey, Lorraine. "Gay Couple's Move to Adopt Children With AIDS Stirs Debate." *New York Times,* October 15, 1989.

Green, R.; Mandel, J. B.; Hotvedt, M. E.; Gray, J.; and Smith, L. "Lesbian Mothers and Their Children: A Comparison with Solo Parent Heterosexual Mothers and Their Children." *Archives of Sexual Behavior,* Vol. 15, No. 2, 1986.

Greif, Geoffrey L. *The Daddy Track and the Single Father.* Lexington Books, Lexington, MA, 1990.

Griffin, Carolyn Welch, et al. *Beyond Acceptance: Parents of Lesbians and Gays Talk About Their Experiences.* St. Martin's Press, New York, 1986.

Grollman, Earl A. *Talking About Death: A Dialogue Between Parent and Child.* Beacon Press, Boston, 1990.

Hand, Sally I. "The Lesbian Parenting Couple." Unpublished doctoral dissertation, San Francisco Professional School of Psychology, 1991.

Hanscombe, Gillian E., and Forster, Jackie. *Rocking the Cradle.* Alyson Publications, Boston, 1981.

Harbeck, Karen M., ed. "Coming Out of the Closet: Gay and Lesbian Students, Teachers, and Curricula." *Journal of Homosexuality.* Vol. 22, Nos. 3–4, 1991.

Heron, Ann, and Meredith, Maran. *How Would You Feel If Your Dad Was Gay?* Alyson Publications, Boston, 1991.

Hoeffer, Beverly. "Children's Acquisition of Sex-Role Behavior in Lesbian Mother Families." *American Journal of Orthopsychiatry.* Vol. 51, No. 3, July 1981.

Hopson, Darlene, and Hopson, Derek. *Different and Wonderful: Raising Black Children in a Race-Conscious Society.* Simon and Schuster, New York, 1990.

Isensee, Rik. *Love Between Men: Enhancing Intimacy and Keeping Your Relationship Alive.* Prentice-Hall, New York, 1990.

Jay, Karla, and Young, Allen. *The Gay Report: Lesbians and Gay Men Speak Out About Sexual Experiences and Lifestyles.* Summit Books, New York, 1977.

Jeannechild, Penny. "When Lesbian Couples Divorce, Who Gets Custody of the Children?" *Philadelphia Enquirer.* January 24, 1992.

Johnson, Susan E. *Staying Power: Long-Term Lesbian Couples.* Naiad Press, 1990.

Jullion, Jeanne. *The Long Way Home.* Cleis Press, San Francisco, 1985.

Kalter, Neil. *Growing Up with Divorce: Helping Your Child Avoid Immediate and Later Emotional Problems.* Free Press, New York, 1990.

Kimball, Gayle. *50-50 Parenting: Sharing Family Rewards and Responsibilities.* Lexington Books, Lexington, MA, 1988.

Kirkpatrick, M.; Smith, C.; and Roy, R. "Lesbian Mothers and Their Children: A Comparative Survey." *The American Journal of Orthopsychiatry,* Vol. 51, 1981.

Kleber, David J.; Howell, Robert J.; and Tibbits-Kleber, Alta Lura. "The Impact of Parental Homosexuality in Child Custody Cases: A Review of the Literature." *Bulletin of the American Academy of Psychiatry and Law.* Vol. 14, No. 1, 1986.

Knowles, Jane Price, and Cole, Ellen, eds. *Woman Identified Motherhood.* Harrington Park Press, New York, 1990.

Krementz, Jill. *How It Feels to be Adopted.* Alfred A. Knopf, New York, 1982.

Leon, Irving G. *When a Baby Dies.* Yale University Press, New Haven, 1990.

Lewin, Elizabeth S. *Financial Fitness for New Families.* Facts on File, New York, 1989.

Lifton, Betty Jean. *Lost and Found: The Adoption Experience.* Harper and Row, New York, 1979.

Livingston, Carole. *"Why Was I Adopted?"* Carol Publishing Group, Secaucus, NJ, 1978.

Loulan, JoAnn. *Lesbian Sex.* Spinsters/Aunt Lute, San Francisco, 1984.

Love, Susan. *Dr. Susan Love's Breast Book.* Addison-Wesley, New York, 1990.

MacPike, Loralee, ed. *There's Something I've Been Meaning to Tell You.* Naiad Press, 1989.

Marcus, Eric. *The Male Couple's Guide to Living Together.* Harper and Row, New York, 1988.

Martin, April. "Bereavement Therapy with a Lesbian Widow." In Silverstein, Charles, ed. *Gays, Lesbians, and Their Therapists,* W. W. Norton, New York, 1991.

———. "The Planned Lesbian and Gay Family: Parenthood and Children." *Newsletter of the Society for the Psychological Study of Lesbian and Gay Issues,* Vol. 5, No. 3, 1989.

Martin, Cynthia. *Beating the Adoption Game.* Harcourt Brace Jovanovich, San Diego, 1988.

Martin, Del, and Lyon, Phyllis. *Lesbian/Woman.* Volcano Press, Volcano, CA, 1991.

"Mary-Helen Mautner: Lawyer and Feminist." *Washington Post,* August 26, 1989.

McKinney, Kevin. "How to Become a Gay Father." *The Advocate,* December 8, 1987.

McWhirter, David, and Mattison, Andrew. *The Male Couple: How Relationships Develop.* Prentice-Hall, Englewood Cliffs, NJ, 1984.

Melamed, Deborah K. "Internalized Homophobia and Lesbian Couple Functioning." Unpublished doctoral dissertation, City University of New York, 1992.

Melina, Lois Ruskai. *Making Sense of Adoption.* Harper and Row, New York, 1989.

Melton, Rebecca L. "Legal Rights of Unmarried Heterosexual and Homosexual Couples and Evolving Definitions of 'Family.'" *Journal of Family Law,* Vol. 29, 1990–1991.

Milex Catalogue. "Basic Infertility Procedures." Available from Milex Products, Inc., 5915 Northwest Highway, Chicago, IL 60631; Tel. (312) 631-6484; Fax (312) 631-8156.

Muller, Ann. *Parents Matter: Parents' Relationships with Lesbian Daughters and Gay Sons.* Naiad Press, Tallahassee, FL, 1987.

National Center for Lesbian Rights and National Lawyers Guild. *A Lesbian and Gay Parents' Legal Guide to Child Custody.* National Center for Lesbian Rights, San Francisco, 1989.

Newman, Leslea. *Gloria Goes to Gay Pride.* Alyson Publications, Boston, 1991.

———. *Heather Has Two Mommies.* Alyson Publications, Boston, 1989.

Noble, Elizabeth. *Having Your Baby by Donor Insemination.* Houghton Mifflin, Boston, 1987.

Osterweil, Dawn Amy. "Correlates of Relationship Satisfaction in Lesbian Couples Who Are Parenting Their First Child Together." Unpublished doctoral dissertation, California School of Professional Psychology, Berkeley, CA, 1991.

Patterson, Charlotte. "Children of the Lesbian Baby Boom." In Greene, Beverly, and Herek, Gregory, eds. *Contemporary Perspectives on Gay and Lesbian Psychology,* Sage Publications, Newbury Park, CA, in press.

———. "Children of Lesbian and Gay Parents." *Child Development,* October 1992, Vol. 63, No. 5, pp 1025–1042.

Pharr, Suzanne. *Homophobia: A Weapon of Sexism.* Chardon Press, 1988. Available from the Women's Project, 2224 Main, Little Rock, AR 72206.

Pies, Cheri. *Considering Parenthood: A Workbook for Lesbians.* Spinsters/Aunt Lute, San Francisco, 1985.

Plumez, Jacqueline Horner. *Successful Adoption.* Harmony Books, New York, 1987.

Polikoff, Nancy. "This Child Does Have Two Mothers: Redefining Parenthood to Meet the Needs of Children in Lesbian-Mother and Other Nontraditional Families." *The Georgetown Law Journal,* Vol. 78, 1990.

Pollack, Sandra, and Vaughn, Jean, eds. *Politics of the Heart: A Lesbian Parenting Anthology.* Firebrand Books, Ithaca, NY, 1987.

Rafkin, Louise, ed. *Different Daughters: A Book by Mothers of Lesbians.* Cleis Press, San Francisco, 1987.

———. *Different Mothers: Sons and Daughters of Lesbians Talk About Their Lives.* Cleis Press, San Francisco, 1990.

Register, Cheri. *"Are Those Kids Yours?"* Free Press, New York, 1991.

Rhodes, Elizabeth. "My Two Dads: Nontraditional Couple Find Adoption to Be a Love Match." *Seattle Times,* November 25, 1990.

Rich, Adrienne. *Of Woman Born.* W. W. Norton, New York, 1986.

Rickets, Wendell. *Lesbians and Gay Men as Foster Parents,* 1991. To order, send $15 to Terry Seymour, National Child Welfare Resource Center for Management and Administration, University of Southern Maine, 96 Falmouth St., Portland, ME 04103; Tel. (207) 780-4430.

————, and Achtenberg, Roberta. "The Adoptive and Foster Gay and Lesbian Parent." In Bozett, Frederick W., ed., *Gay and Lesbian Parenting*, Praeger, New York, 1987.

Riley, Claire. "The Emergence of Lesbian Kinship Patterns in the Late Twentieth Century U.S.: A Case Study in Brooklyn, N.Y." Unpublished doctoral dissertation, The City University of New York, 1992.

Rivera, Rhonda R. "Legal Issues in Gay and Lesbian Parenting." In Bozett, Frederick W., ed., *Gay and Lesbian Parenting*, Praeger, New York, 1987.

Rothblum, Esther, and Cole, Ellen, eds. *Lesbianism: Affirming Nontraditional Roles.* Haworth Press, New York, 1989.

Rothman, Barbara Katz. *Recreating Motherhood: Ideology and Technology in a Patriarchal Society.* W. W. Norton, New York, 1989.

Salzer, Linda P. *Surviving Infertility.* HarperPerennial, New York, 1991.

Sang, Barbara, et al. *Lesbians at Midlife: The Creative Transition.* Spinsters Book Company, San Francisco, 1991.

Saphira, Miriam. *Amazon Mothers.* Papers, Inc., Ponsonby, Auckland, New Zealand, 1984.

Schaffer, Judith, and Lindstrom, Christina. *How to Raise an Adopted Child.* Penguin Books, New York, 1991.

Schaffer, Patricia. *How Babies and Families Are Made: There Is More Than One Way!* Tabor Sarah Books, Berkeley, CA, 1988.

————. *Chag Sameach!* Tabor Sarah Books, Berkeley, CA, 1986.

Schulenberg, Joy. *Gay Parenting: A Complete Guide for Gay Men and Lesbians with Children.* Doubleday, New York, 1985.

Schwed, Mark. "Surrogate Mothers of Invention." *Los Angeles Herald Examiner,* May 23, 1988.

Shalev, Carmel. *Birth Power: The Case for Surrogacy.* Yale University Press, New Haven, 1989.

Shidlo, Ariel. "Homonegativity and Gay Enmeshment: An Investigation of Adjustment in Gay Males." Paper presented at the Annual Convention of the American Psychological Association, New York, 1987.

Silverstein, Charles. *A Family Matter: A Parent's Guide to Homosexuality.* McGraw-Hill, New York, 1977.

Skofield, James. *'Round and Around.* HarperCollins, New York, 1993.

Stahl, Philip Michael. *Children on Consignment: A Handbook for Parenting Foster Children and Their Special Needs.* Macmillan, New York, 1990.

Sullivan, Michael R. *Adopt the Baby You Want.* Simon and Schuster, New York, 1990.

Thomas, Marlo, and Friends. *Free to Be ... A Family.* Bantam Books, New York, 1987.

Thompson, Charlotte. *Raising a Handicapped Child.* Ballantine Books, New York, 1986.

Umans, Meg, ed. *Like Coming Home: The Coming Out Letters.* Banned Books, Austin, TX, 1988.

United States Department of Commerce, Office of Technology Assessment. *Artificial Insemination: Practice in the United States: Summary of a 1987 Survey—Background Paper.* U.S. Government Printing Office, Washington, DC, August 1988.

————. *Infertility, Medical and Social Choices.* U.S. Government Printing Office, Washington, DC, May 1988.

Van Gelder, Lindsay. "Lesbian Family Revisited." *Ms.* Vol. 1, No. 5, March/April 1991.

Weston, Kath. *Families We Choose.* Columbia University Press, New York, 1991.

Willhoite, Michael. *Daddy's Roomate.* Alyson Publications, Boston, 1990.

————. *Families: A Coloring Book.* Alyson Publications, Boston, 1991.

Winston, Robert. *What We Know About Infertility.* Free Press, New York, 1986.

INDEX

Divorce, 251
  increase in, 3
Doctors. *See* Physicians
Donor insemination. *See* Alternative
  insemination
Donor-recipient agreements, 164,
  173
  sample of, 353–55
Donors. *See* Sperm donors
Donor screening forms, sample of,
  363–66
Donors' Offspring, 338
Drug use, 2, 29–30
Dry ice, 52
Duties, family, division of, 227–29
Dwarfism, 264–67

Edel, Deborah, 4
Education of families of origin, 293
Ehrensaft, Diane, 251
El Salvador, adoption in, 149–54
Elwin, Rosamund, 191
Emotions and feelings. *See also specific
  emotions and feelings*
  consequences of involving biological
    fathers and, 83–84
  decision to have children and, 31–34
  negative, child rearing and, 26
Employers, coming out to, 311, 329–30
Ethnicity
  child rearing and, 213–15
Ettelbrick, Paula, 160, 165
Evansville GLPC, 341
Exploitation, surrogacy and, 106

Families of origin
  announcing parenthood to, 286–306
    how it works, 295–304
    parents, 286–89
  coming out and, 289–92, 296
  how to help
    communicating, 292–93, 301–2
    educating, 293
    setting limits and providing guide-
      lines, 293–94
    timing, 294–95
Family. *See also* Parents

definition of, 24, 43, 78–80
extended, 60, 304–6
  biological, 45–46
  books, 346
  breakup, 246
  lesbian and gay, 43
  nuclear, 43, 156–57
  as sperm donors, 65–66, 92–93
  support groups for, 335–36
Family life, 216–44
  adoption and, 225
  careers and money and, 234–35
  changes and stresses in, 216–21
  communications, arguments and
    negotiations and, 231–32, 247–48
  different bonds and, 225–27
  dividing roles and duties and, 227–29
  joys of, 242–44
  nonlegal parent and, 223–25
  second child and, 240–42
  sex life and, 233–34, 248–49
  single parenting and, 238–40
  social lives and, 235–37
  stepfamily and, 229–31
  triangles and, 221–23
Family planning. *See also* Decision to
    have children
  of author, 2–3
Fantasies
  of children, about adoption, 187
  of parenthood, 23
    gender considerations, 33–34
Farrell, Sharrie, 349
Fathers, 79–81
  absence of, 26–27, 82
  biological. *See* Biological fathers
  death of, 26
  definition of, 79–80
  gay. *See* Gay fathers
  use of term, 199–203
Fears
  about sperm donors, 63
  child rearing and, 25–26
  decision to have children and, 32
  of families of origin, 291–92
  of lesbian women, 3
  pregnancy and, 67

Gay Fathers of Long Beach, 340
Gay Fathers of Long Island, 343
Gay Fathers of Toronto, 345
Gay Fathers of Winnipeg, 344
Gay men. *See also* Gay fathers
  decision to have children and, 19–21
    being out and, 38
  as donors, 81
  fathers, 81
  lesbian women's conflicts with, 8–9
Gender-role behavior, children and,
  210–13
Gil de Lamadrid, Maria, 164–65
Girls. *See* Female children
Gloria Goes to Gay Pride (Newman),
  191
GLPCI Central Florida Chapter, 341
GLP/Queen City—Charlotte, 343
Go-betweens, donors found through,
  56–59
Grandparents
  announcing parenthood to, 305–6
  legal issues and, 161, 168
Grieving
  of children, 282
  coming out and, 291
  death of children and, 269–73
  decision to have children and, 36, 42
  of families of origin, 291
Griffin, Carolyn, 291
Growing Up with Divorce (Kalter), 249
Guardianship, 171–72
Guilt, 291

Hanafin, Hilary, 110–11
Handel, William, 110
*Having Your Baby by Donor Insemina-
  tion* (Noble), 82
Health insurance, 177, 330
Health issues. *See also* HIV status
  alternative insemination and, 49
  decision to have children
    children of gay and lesbian parents,
    25–27
    parents, 29–30
  donor selection and, 53–54, 56
  heterosexual sex and, 47

Heather Has Two Mommies
  (Newman), 191
Heron, Ann, 191
Hester, Susan, 273–83
Hester-Mautner family, 8
Heterosexual relationships, 209, 312
  limitations of, 2
  as source of children of gay and
    lesbian parents, 5, 17
Heterosexual sex, pregnancy and, 47
HIV status. *See also* AIDS
  adoption and, 29, 144–46
  alternative insemination and, 49, 51
  heterosexual sex and, 47
  sperm donors and, 56, 59
Home births, 70
Homophobia, 17, 20, 38–39, 42, 296,
  308, 326, 331–33
  breakup and, 246
  children and, 26–27, 204–5
  legal issues and, 156, 168
  of siblings, 304–5
Homosexuality, 3. *See also* Gay fathers;
  Gay men; Lesbian and gay parents;
  Lesbian mothers; Lesbian women
  removed from mental disease
    category, 3
Hopson, Darlene, 137
Hopson, Derek, 137
Hormones, pregnancy and, 64, 67
Hospitals, obstetrical units in
  policies, 70–71
  tours, 70
Houston Gay and Lesbian Parents
  Support, 344
*How Would You Feel If Your Dad Was
  Gay?* (Heron and Maran), 191
Human chorionic gonadotropin (hCG),
  74

Identity issues
  cultural, 38
  decision to have children and, 17–18
  of gay fathers, 9
  mothers and, 2, 18
  pregnancy and, 68
Illegitimacy, 3

statistics on, 6
vulnerability of, 32–33
Lesbian/Gay Family and Parenting Services Fenway Community Health Center, 342
Lesbian Herstory Archives, 4
Lesbian mothers, 1–9. *See also* Lesbian and gay parents
adoption and, 149–51, 153–54
black, 5–6
books for, 346
coparenting and, 95–101
gay fathers as, 9
and male children, 9, 33
nonbiological, 61, 68–70
delivery, 70–72
invisibility problem, 60, 70
support, 76–77
research on, 4–5
role models of, 4–5, 18–19
support for, 4–5
Lesbian Mothers Group of Long Beach, 340
Lesbian Mothers' National Defense Fund, 336, 351
Lesbians Choosing Children Network, 342
Lesbian/Woman (Martin and Lyon), 4
Lesbian women
decision to have children and, 18–19
being out and, 38
negative reactions, 39–40
fears of, 3
gay men's conflicts with, 8–9
Lesmos, 343
Lesser, Ronnie, 42
Life insurance, 173
Limits and guidelines for families of origin, 293–94
Liquid nitrogen, 52
Little People of America, 266
Litz, Steven, 109
Loss. *See also* Grieving
breakup and, 249, 251–52
Lyon, Phyllis, 4–5
Lyon-Martin Women's Health Clinic, 336, 340

Making Sense of Adoption (Melina), 186

Male children
alternative insemination and, 52
of lesbian mothers, 9, 33
masculinity and, 212–13
Maran, Meredith, 191
Martin, Del, 4–5
Mary-Helen Mautner Project for Lesbians with Cancer, 283
Maryland, lesbian and gay parenting groups in, 342
Masculinity, children and, 212–13
Massachusetts, lesbian and gay parenting groups in, 342
Maturity, misconceptions about, 17, 45
Mautner, Mary-Helen, 273–83
Medical professionals. *See also* Midwives; Physicians
insensitivity of, 68–69
Medical settings, coming out in, 311, 327–29
Melina, Lois, 186
Mental health
of children, 25–27
decision to have children and, 17
pregnancy and, 45
Mersky, Liz, 349
Mexican children, 214
Michigan, lesbian and gay parenting groups in, 342
Midwives, 69
delivery and, 70–72
Milex Products, Inc., 48
Miscarriage, 259–63
alternative insemination and, 48
Mom-and-dad coparenting arrangement, 80, 86, 88, 95–101
Money. *See* Financial issues
Mother-child bonding, 60
Mothers (motherhood). *See also* Birthmothers
biological. *See* Pregnancy; Surrogate mothers
books on, 347
death of, 21
decision to have children and, 40–41
identity issues and, 2, 18
lesbian. *See* Lesbian mothers
nonbiological. *See* Nonbiological mothers

Semen
  fresh, 48, 51
  frozen, 48–49, 51–52, 54, 65
  HIV testing and, 49, 51
Separatism, 9
Separatists, 39–40
Sex life, family life and, 233–34, 248–49
Sexual intercourse, pregnancy and, 47
Sexually transmitted diseases, 47, 54, 59.
    See also AIDS; HIV status
Shalev, Carmel, 107
Shame, 134–35
  child rearing and, 25–26
  decline of, 6
  families of origin and, 291, 299
Sibling rivalry, family members as bio-
    logical fathers and, 93
Siblings
  breaking the news to, 304–5
  identification problems and, 206
  nonbiological, 60–61
Single mothers (single motherhood), 3
  adoption and, 118–19
  author's considering of, 2, 18
Single parenting
  decision to have children and, 34
  family life and, 238–40
Social discomfort, "missing parent"
    and, 196–97
Social life, family life and, 235–37
Social pressures, child rearing and,
    16–17
Society, pregnancy and, 45
Sonograms, 68–69, 74
Special-needs children
  adoption of, 27, 31
Sperm
  in frozen semen, 52
  X-chromosome, 52–53
  Y-chromosome, 52–53
Sperm Bank of California, 54, 336
Sperm banks, 25, 65
  donors found through, 54–55
  frozen semen and, 48–49, 51–52
  records maintained by, 58
Sperm donors, 24
  anonymous, 54–59, 63–64, 86–87, 89,
    189

  characteristics of, 63
  definition of, 79
  donor screening form sample, 363–66
  family members as, 65–66, 92–93
  family structure and, 79–87, 89–92
    biological factors and, 82–85
  frozen semen and, 51
  gay men as, 81, 167
  health of, 53–54, 56
  HIV testing of, 49, 51
  legal issues and, 163–65
  of second child, 94–95
  sources of
    go-betweens, 56–59
    known, 89–92
    known people, 55–56, 65–66
    physicians and sperm banks, 54–55
  telling children about, 188–90
  "Yes," 54–55
Steinman, Wayne, 122
Stepfamilies, 229–31
Stern, Elizabeth, 105
Stern, William, 105
Stevens, Elizabeth, 348
Stonewall Riots (1969), 3
Strangers, coming out to, 311–17
Stresses
  alcohol and drug use and, 30
  decision to have children and,
    22–23
    being out, 38
    emotional, 32–33
    relationship, 35–37
  family life and, 216–44
  financial issues and, 28
  infertility and, 73
  pregnancy and, 68
Sudden Infant Death Syndrome
    Foundation, 271
Sudden infant death syndrome (SIDS),
    73, 268–73
Sunley, Christina, 348
Support
  child rearing and, 16
  for cultural identities, 38
  for gay fathers, 9
  infertility and, 74, 76
  for lesbian mothers, 4–5